Intelligente Glasfassaden

Intelligent Glass Façades

Andrea Compagno

Intelligente Glasfassaden

Material

Anwendung

Gestaltung

Intelligent Glass Façades

Material

Practice

Design

Birkhäuser Publishers
Basel · Boston · Berlin

Übersetzung ins Englische/Translation into
English: Ingrid Taylor, English Experts, München

A CIP catalogue record for this book is available
from the Library of Congress, Washington D. C.,
USA.

Die Deutsche Bibliothek –
CIP-Einheitsaufnahme

Compagno, Andrea:
Intelligente Glasfassaden : Material,
Anwendung, Gestaltung = Intelligent
glass façades / Andrea Compagno.
[Übers. ins Engl.: Ingrid Taylor]. - 4.,
rev. und erw. Aufl. - Basel ; Boston ;
Berlin : Birkhäuser, 1999
ISBN 3-7643-5996-X (Basel ...)
ISBN 0-8176-5996-X (Boston)

Erste Auflage 1995

4., revidierte und erweiterte Auflage 1999
4th, revised and enlarged edition 1999

© 1999 Birkhäuser – Publishers for
Architecture,
P.O. Box 133, CH-4010 Basel, Switzerland.
Printed on acid-free paper produced of
chlorine-free pulp. TCF ∞
Printed in Germany
ISBN 3-7643-5996-X
ISBN 0-8176-5996-X

9 8 7 6 5 4 3 2 1

Unterstützt von/Supported by:

Inhalt

Contents

Einleitung   # Introduction

Eine «intelligente» Glasfassade kann sich auf dynamische, gleichsam lebendige Weise durch selbstregelnde Wärme- und Sonnenschutzmaßnahmen den wechselnden Licht- und Klimaverhältnissen anpassen, um einerseits den Verbrauch an Primärenergie eines Gebäudes zu senken und andererseits für die Menschen ein angenehmes Innenraumklima zu schaffen.

Die «Intelligenz» einer Fassade zeichnet sich nicht in erster Linie durch besonders komplexe Technik aus, sondern vielmehr durch eine möglichst umweltschonende Nutzung von natürlichen, erneuerbaren Energiequellen, wie Sonnenstrahlung, Luftströmungen und Erdwärme.

Eine «intelligente» Fassade ist besonders bei großflächig verglasten, traditionellerweise vollklimatisierten, Büro- und Verwaltungsgebäuden ökologisch wie ökonomisch relevant: Einerseits können dadurch Immissionen und der damit verbundene globale Treibhauseffekt eingedämmt, andererseits die Investitions- und Betriebskosten bei der Gebäudetechnik so tief wie möglich gehalten werden.

Bei der Energiebilanz von vollverglasten Gebäuden schlagen nicht nur die Wärmeverluste zu Buche, sondern auch der Energieaufwand für Lüftung, Kühlung und Belichtung. Eine optimale Nutzung der natürlichen Luftströmungen, des Tageslichts oder der Speicherfähigkeit der Gebäudemasse kann den Energieverbrauch maßgeblich senken.

Seit den 20er Jahren sind transparente, filigrane Glasbauten ein Merkmal der modernen Architektur, nachdem zu Beginn des zwanzigsten Jahrhunderts die industrielle Produktion von Glasscheiben mit dem Ziehverfahren nach der Erfindung von Emile Fourcault (1904) und Irwin W. Colburn (1905) wesentlich erleichtert worden war und das aufwendige Gießverfahren in dieser Beziehung überholt hatte.

Bald traten allerdings die Nachteile einer Glasfassade zutage: Überhitzung und Wärmeverlust. Zu deren Beseitigung schlug Le Corbusier schon um

An "intelligent" glass façade can adapt in a dynamic, almost "living" way to changing light and weather conditions using self-regulating thermal protection and solar control measures. Thus it reduces the primary energy consumption of a building and creates a pleasant environment for the people inside.

The "intelligence" of a façade is not measured primarily by how much it is driven by technology, but how it makes use of natural, renewable energy sources, such as solar radiation, air flows and the ground heat in as environmentally compatible a way as possible.

In today's extensively glazed and traditionally fully air-conditioned office buildings an "intelligent" façade has both ecological as well as economic significance. On the one hand it helps reduce the global greenhouse effect by limiting immissions and on the other it keeps the investment and operational costs of building technology as low as possible.

In fully glazed buildings the energy budget is burdened not only by heat losses, but also by the energy consumption needed for ventilation, cooling and lighting. Optimum utilisation of natural air flows, incident daylight and the thermal storage capacity of the building mass, can bring about a considerable reduction in energy consumption levels.

Transparent, filigree glass buildings have been a feature of modern architecture since the 1920s; at that time new technology for manufacturing drawn flat sheet, based on inventions by Emile Fourcault (1904) and Irwin W. Colburn (1905), replaced the traditional, more complicated pouring process and greatly simplified the manufacture of flat glass.

However, with the increasing use of glass in façades came also a realisation of the disadvantages: overheating and heat loss. Already in about 1930 Le Corbusier suggested two measures for counteracting these problems: "la respiration

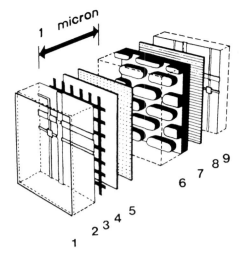

1930 zwei Gegenmaßnahmen vor: «la respiration exacte» und «le mur neutralisant», womit die mechanische Klimakontrolle ihren Anfang nahm. Das Ende der 50er Jahre von Alastair Pilkington entwickelte Floatverfahren ermöglichte die Produktion von noch größeren Mengen an Glas zu tieferen Preisen.

Etwa zur selben Zeit aber wurde die Kritik an der Energieverschwendung bei vollflächigen Glashüllen unüberhörbar. 1969 äußerte Reyner Banham in «The Architecture of the Well-Tempered Environment» seine Vorbehalte gegen den zunehmenden, von der Klimaregelung verursachten Aufwand an Energie und gegen die Loslösung der Architektur von klimatischen und regionalen Gegebenheiten. Seine Gedanken waren eben veröffentlicht und rezipiert, als die Energiekrise der Jahre 1973/74 dringender denn je nach einer Lösung rief.

Da sowohl die Nachteile als auch die Vorteile einer Glasfassade in ihrer Strahlungsdurchlässigkeit liegen, stellte der englische Architekt Mike Davies 1981 in seinem Artikel «Eine Wand für alle Jahreszeiten» die Entwicklung einer Verglasung mit veränderbaren Eigenschaften zur Diskussion, die den Energiefluß von außen nach innen und umgekehrt je nach Bedarf dynamisch steuern könnte.

Diese «polyvalente Wand» stellt die Reduktion der Außenhaut auf ein mehrschichtiges Verbundelement dar, welches durch selbstregelnde Steuerungssysteme Sonnen- und Wärmeschutz gewährleistet und zugleich den dazu notwendigen Strom erzeugt. Davies' Idee stützte sich auf bereits vorhandene Errungenschaften bei Produkten aus anderen Bereichen der Technik, wie selbstverdunkelnde Brillengläser oder Solarzellen der Weltraumkapseln, und versuchte sie auf die Glasproduktion für die Bauwirtschaft zu übertragen. Da er das sich ständig verändernde Aussehen der «polyvalenten Wand» mit der Haut eines Chamäleons verglich, führte das in der Folge zum Begriff der «intelligenten» Fassade. Verbunden mit dem Bemühen um ein ökologisches, umweltgerechtes Bauen, hat in den 80er Jahren die Entwicklung der Glasarchitektur wieder an Bedeutung gewonnen.

Der Wendepunkt lag im Erkennen des großen Energiepotentials der Sonnenstrahlung, die auf eine Fassadenfläche auftrifft, und in der Absicht, dieses Potential zu nutzen. Die Sonnenstrahlung wurde als ideale Energieform erkannt, weil sie die Umwelt nicht belastet und überall zu allen Jahreszeiten mehr oder weniger ergiebig zur

exacte" and "le mur neutralisant", thus marking the start of mechanical air conditioning systems. The float glass process developed at the end of the 1950s by Alastair Pilkington enabled the production of even larger quantities of glass at lower prices.

At about the same time, however, criticism was growing of the energy waste associated with a fully glazed building skin. In 1969, in "The Architecture of the Well-Tempered Environment" Reyner Banham spoke out against the high energy requirements of artificial air conditioning systems, and the separation of architecture from local climatic and regional conditions. Soon after the publication and general recognition of his views the 1973/74 oil crisis added a new level of urgency to the search for a solution.

As the radiation transmission properties of a glass façade can represent both an advantage and a disadvantage, the English architect, Mike Davies, in his article on "A Wall for all Seasons" published in 1981, proposed the development of multiple-performance glazing which could dynamically regulate the energy flow from outside to inside and vice versa.

This "polyvalent wall" is a reduction of the outer skin of a building to a multi-layered compound element which makes use of self-regulating control mechanisms to provide heat insulation and solar protection, while at the same time generating the necessary electrical energy needed for the operation of these systems. Davies's idea is based on principles already exploited in other areas of technology, such as automatically darkening photochromic glass used in the manufacture of spectacles, or the solar cells used in space capsules. He advocated using these ideas in the manufacture of glass for building. His comparison of the ever-changing appearance of the "polyvalent wall" with the skin of a chameleon led to the coining of the phrase "intelligent" façade.

In the 1980s, developments in glass architecture regained significance, at the same time as pressure was mounting for more ecological, environmentally-friendly building techniques.

The turning point lay in recognising the enormous energy potential of the solar radiation striking the façade of a building, and in determining to utilise this potential. Solar radiation was seen as the ideal form of energy because it does not pollute the environment and is present everywhere in more or less abundant quantities at all times of the year.

Vorschlag von Mike Davies für eine «polyvalente Wand»:

1 Silikat-Wetterhaut und Schichtenträger
2 Sensor- und Steuerungslogik außen
3 Photoelektrisches Gitter
4 Wärmestrahlende Schicht/Selektiver Absorber
5 Elektroreflektierende Schicht
6 Feinporige gasdurchströmte Schicht
7 Elektroreflektierende Schicht
8 Sensor- und Steuerungslogik innen
9 Silikat-Innenhaut und Schichtenträger.

Proposal of Mike Davies for the "polyvalent wall":

1 Silica weather skin and deposition substrate
2 Sensor and control logic layer – external
3 Photoelectric grid
4 Thermal sheet radiator/selective absorber
5 Elektro-reflective deposition
6 Micro-pore gas flow layers
7 Electro-reflective deposition
8 Sensor and control logic layer – internal
9 Silica deposition substrate and inner skin.

Verfügung steht. Im Winter und in der Übergangszeit führt sie zu Wärmeenergie- und Tageslichtgewinnen, welche zu einer Verminderung des Verbrauchs an Primärenergie führen. Im Sommer sind solche Gewinne weniger erwünscht und müssen durch wirksame Sonnenschutzmaßnahmen kontrolliert werden. Die Tageslichtnutzung ermöglicht den Bedarf an künstlicher Beleuchtung zu reduzieren, die im Sommer einen großen Teil der Kühllasten verursacht.

Die Umsetzung von Davies' Grundidee bedingt nicht nur die Entwicklung neuer Glasprodukte für eine hochwertige Gebäudehülle, sondern auch fortschrittliche Energiekonzepte, welche die Interaktion der Fassade mit der Gebäudetechnik gewährleisten. Dies führt zu einer zunehmenden Komplexität der Entwurfsaufgabe, die nur durch eine integrale oder ganzheitliche Planung bewältigt werden kann.

In diesem Buch werden die Gebäudehüllen nach der Anzahl Glasschichten beschrieben und mit Beispielen illustriert. Zu Beginn werden einzelne Scheibentypen in ihrer Zusammensetzung und der Behandlung ihrer Oberfläche vorgestellt. Es folgen der mehrschichtige Aufbau der Verbund- und Isoliergläser und die zahlreichen Möglichkeiten der Füllungen des Zwischenraums, von dünnen Folien bis zu dickeren Elementen mit wärmedämmenden oder lichtumlenkenden Eigenschaften. Schließlich werden die Einsatzmöglichkeiten im ein- und mehrschaligen Fassadenaufbau beschrieben, wobei zusätzliche Maßnahmen für den Sonnenschutz zur Anwendung kommen. Zuletzt werden die «intelligenten» Glasfassaden behandelt, die nicht nur durch einen besonderen Aufbau gekennzeichnet sind, sondern vor allem durch die Interaktion zwischen Fassade, Gebäudetechnik und Umwelt. In dieser vierten, revidierten und wesentlich erweiterten Auflage wird den «intelligenten» Fassaden ein eigenes Kapitel gewidmet. Zahlreiche neue Beispiele illustrieren die zunehmende Bedeutung dieser Fassadensysteme, die relativ einfach aufgebaut, aber auch hochkomplex organisiert sein können.

Die vorliegende Publikation will in anschaulicher Form die neuen Glasprodukte und ihre Anwendungsmöglichkeiten anhand von technischen Steckbriefen und von ausgeführten Beispielen dem Leser, der Leserin näherbringen. Dadurch soll eine gemeinsame Ausgangslage für ein fruchtbares Gespräch zwischen Architekten, Fassadenplanern und beratenden Fachingenieuren geschaffen werden.

In winter and in spring or autumn solar radiation gives rise to gains in terms of heat and light, both of which, given suitable glazing with little heat loss, lead to a reduction in energy consumption levels.

In summer such gains are less desirable and have to be controlled by appropriate solar control devices. Light-deflecting elements, on the other hand, can contribute to a reduction in the need for artificial lighting, which in summer is the cause of a large part of the cooling load.

In order to realise Davies's basic idea, not only new glass products for a high-quality building skin have to be developed, but also advanced energy concepts to guarantee the interaction of the façade with the building services. The design stages thus become increasingly complex, and can only be resolved successfully through integrated or holistic planning.

The individual chapters of this monograph divide the building skins according to the number of layers of glass in the façade, each type being illustrated with carefully chosen examples. At the beginning is a detailed description of the composition and surface treatments of the different types of glass pane. Following this is a description of the multi-layered assemblies of laminated and insulating glass, together with a look at the options available for filling the cavity, from thin films to thicker integrated units with insulating and light-deflecting properties. The following chapter deals with the various ways of using the different types of glass in single-skin and double-skin façades, in conjunction with additional solar and heat control measures.

The final chapter deals with "intelligent" glass façades which are not only characterized by a special construction, but mainly by a high degree of interaction between the façade, the building services and the environment.

In this fourth, extensively revised and extended edition, a separate chapter has now been devoted to "intelligent" façades. Many new examples illustrate the increasing significance of this kind of façade, which can be relatively simple in its construction, or highly complex.

The present work seeks to give the reader a concise summary of the new glass products and, by means of technical explanations and built examples, to illustrate possibilities for their use. As such it aims to present a joint basis for a dialogue between architects, façade planners and building engineers.

Glas ist ein anorganisches Schmelzprodukt, welches durch eine kontrollierte Kühlungstechnik ohne Kristallisation vom flüssigen in den festen Zustand übergeht. Deshalb wird es auch als erstarrte Flüssigkeit definiert. Verschiedene chemische Stoffe haben die Fähigkeit, Glas zu bilden: unter den anorganischen hauptsächlich die Oxide von Silizium (Si), Bor (B), Germanium (Ge), Phosphor (P) und Arsen (As). Da die Hauptkomponente praktisch aller Glasprodukte Siliziumdioxid ist, spricht man allgemein von Silikatgläsern

Normales Floatglas enthält Sand (SiO_2, 71 bis 75 %), Natron (Na_2O, 12 bis 16 %), Kalk (CaO, 10 bis 15 %) und einige Prozente an anderen Stoffen, die die Farbe bestimmen (z. B. Fe_2O_3). Die besonderen Eigenschaften von Glas bezüglich Lichtdurchlässigkeit, thermischen Verhaltens, Biegefestigkeit u. a. sind bedingt durch den Strukturzustand und die Zusammensetzung. Sie sind unabhängig von der Richtung, in der sie gemessen werden, weil Glas wegen des fehlenden Kristallgitters isotrop ist.

Optische Eigenschaften
Die «Transparenz» des Glases ist das wichtigste Merkmal bei seiner Verwendung im Bauwesen. Die Eigenschaften bezüglich Durchlässigkeit und damit Durchsichtigkeit sind auf den unterkühlten Zustand zurückzuführen. Da die kristalline Struktur fehlt, kommen die Lichtstrahlen durch, ohne gestreut zu werden.
Das sichtbare Licht bildet lediglich einen Teil der auf die Erde auftreffenden elektromagnetischen Sonnenstrahlung, da das menschliche Auge nur Strahlen mit Wellenlängen von 380 nm bis 780 nm wahrnehmen kann. Nicht sichtbar für uns sind die ultraviolette Strahlung (UV; mit Wellenlängen kleiner als 380 nm) und die infrarote Strahlung (IR; mit Wellenlängen größer als 780 nm).

Glass is an inorganic product of fusion which is cooled to a rigid state without crystallizing, and thus is also defined as a super-cooled liquid. Various chemical substances can form glass: among the inorganic ones are principally the oxides of silicon (Si), boron (B), germanium (Ge), phosphorus (P) and arsenic (As). Generally glass is of the soda-lime-silica type, as the main component of almost all glass products is silicon dioxide.

Normal float glass contains silica sand (SiO_2, 71 to 75 %), soda (Na_2O, 12 to 16 %), lime (CaO, 10 to 15 %) and a small percentage of other materials which have an effect on the colour (e. g. Fe_2O_3). The particular properties of glass in terms of light transmittance, thermal behaviour, strength etc. are determined by its structure and composition. These properties are independent of direction of measurement, as glass is isotropic due to its lack of a crystal lattice.

Optical Properties
The transparency of glass is its most important property for use in building. Its properties of light transmission, and thus transparence, are a result of the super-cooled state. The lack of a crystalline structure means that the light rays pass through it without being scattered. Visible light forms just one part of the solar electromagnetic radiation reaching the Earth; the human eye is only capable of detecting light in the 380 nm to 780 nm wavelength interval. We are unable to see ultraviolet radiation (UV; with wavelengths less than 380 nm) and the infrared range (IR; wavelengths longer than 780 nm). The spectral intensity of the solar radiation reaches a peak at approx. 550 nm. The human eye's sensitivity corresponds to this maximum range of solar radiation. The relative energy content of solar radiation is 3 % in the UV range,

Linke Seite: Auskragende Glasträger aus ineinander verzahnten Dreieckscheiben zeigen die Festigkeit von Glaskonstruktionen.
Yurakucho U-Bahn-Station, Tokio, Japan, 1996, Rafael Viñoly Architects mit Dewhurst Macfarlane und Partnern.
Left page: Cantilevered glass beams made up of interlocking triangular-shaped blades show the strength of glass structures.
Yurakucho underground station, Tokyo, Japan, 1996, Rafael Viñoly Architects with Dewhurst Macfarlane and Partners.

Die spektrale Verteilung der Intensität der Sonnenstrahlung ist durch ein Maximum bei etwa 550 nm gekennzeichnet. Die Empfindlichkeit des menschlichen Auges korrespondiert mit dem Maximum der solaren Strahlung. Der relative Energiegehalt der Sonnenstrahlung beträgt im UV-Bereich 3 %, im sichtbaren Bereich 53 % und im nahen IR-Bereich 44 %. Durch ein Silikatglas gelangen Strahlen mit einer Wellenlänge von 315 nm bis 3000 nm. Sie erstrecken sich vom ultravioletten Bereich von 315 – 380 nm über den sichtbaren Bereich (von 380 – 780 nm) bis zum nahen IR-Bereich von 780 – 3000 nm. Dabei werden der UV-Bereich unter 315 nm und der langwellige IR-Bereich oberhalb 3000 nm fast völlig absorbiert. Letzterer wird in der Regel nur bis 2500 nm ausgewertet, weil die Intensität der Sonnenstrahlung größerer Wellenlängen sehr klein ist. Aufgrund der Undurchlässigkeit für die langwellige Strahlung läßt sich der Treibhauseffekt einer Verglasung erklären. Die durchgelassene sichtbare und die nahe infrarote Strahlung wärmen die Gegenstände im Raum auf, aber kommen danach als längerwellige Strahlung zurück, die nicht mehr durch die Verglasung nach außen gelangen kann. Die Absorption der Strahlen im Glas produziert ebenfalls Wärme, welche vom Material an der Oberfläche durch Wärmestrahlung, Wärmeleitung und Konvektion abgegeben wird.

Thermische Eigenschaften

Beim normalen Floatglas ist der Wärmedurchgang ausschlaggebend für den Wärmeverlust und den damit verbundenen Heizaufwand. Während der Wärmewiderstand infolge Wärmeleitung nur unwesentlich mit der Scheibenstärke zu beeinflussen ist, können die Wärmestrahlung durch Beschichtungen und die Konvektion durch konstruktive Maßnahmen verändert werden. In bezug auf die Wärmedehnung des Glases hängt der spezifische Koeffizient von der chemischen Zusammensetzung des Glases ab: Bei normalem Floatglas bewirkt die Zuführung von Substanzen wie Alkalien einen Koeffizienten von $80 – 90 \cdot 10^{-7}/K$, was eine Wärmedehnung von ca. 0.5 mm/m bei Temperaturen zwischen $-20°\,C$ und $+40°\,C$ zur Folge hat. Sie nähert sich derjenigen von Stahl oder Stahlbeton und muß somit bei der Kombination mit anderen Materialien berücksichtigt werden. Allerdings weisen reinere SiO_2-Gläser, wie Kiesel- und Quarzgläser, wesentlich kleinere

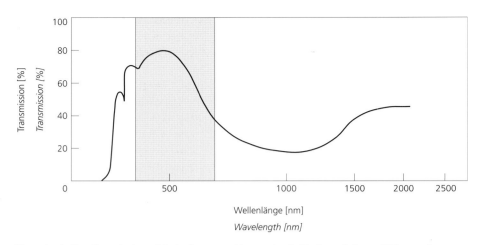

Die spektrale Verteilung der Intensität der Sonnenstrahlung weist ein Maximum bei etwa 550 nm auf.
Spectral energy transmission curve with a dominant peak at 550 nm in the visible band.

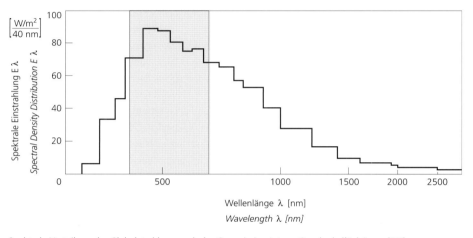

Spektrale Verteilung der Globalstrahlung nach der Commission Internationale de l'Eclairage (CIE).
Spectral energy distribution according to the Commission Internationale de l'Eclairage (CIE).

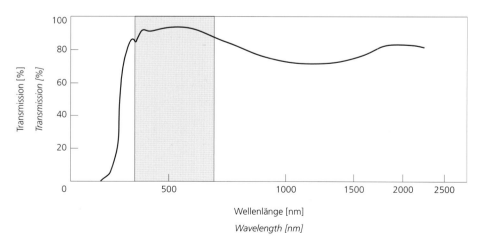

Spektrale Transmission eines üblichen Floatglases.
Spectral transmission of standard float glass.

Wärmedehnungskoeffizienten auf, die bei $5 \cdot 10^{-7}$/K liegen und sich beispielsweise für die Herstellung von Herdplatten eignen.

Technische Kenngrößen

Zahlreiche Kenngrößen stehen zur Verfügung, um die licht-, strahlungs- und wärmetechnischen Eigenschaften zu beurteilen. Mit den Begriffen der Reflexion, Absorption und Transmission beschreibt man die Strahlungsdurchlässigkeit einer oder mehrerer Glasscheiben. Sie werden als prozentualer Anteil des gesamten Strahlungseinfalls ausgedrückt. Die absorbierte Strahlung bewirkt die sekundäre Wärmeabgabe, indem sie in Wärme umgewandelt wird, welche durch Abstrahlung und Konvektion an den Scheibenoberflächen weitergegeben wird.

Die wesentlichen physikalischen Größen für die Bewertung des Lichteinfalls und der Wärmegewinne und -verluste sind die Faktoren der Tageslichttransmission τ (=«Lichtdurchlässigkeit») und der Gesamtenergietransmission g sowie der Wärmedurchgangskoeffizient k. Sie sind wie folgt definiert:

– Die Tageslichttransmission τ_L gibt den prozentualen Anteil an direkt durchgelassener, senkrecht einfallender Strahlung, bezogen auf das Helligkeitsempfinden des Auges, wieder.

– Der Gesamtenergietransmissionsgrad, g-Wert, ist die Summe aus direkt durchgelassenem Strahlungsanteil (Energietransmission τ_e) bei senkrechtem Einfall und sekundärer Wärmeabgabe q_i der Verglasung nach innen infolge Wärmestrahlung, Wärmeleitung und Konvektion.

– Der Wärmedurchgangskoeffizient k, der sogenannte k-Wert, ist der Wärmestrom, der in einer Stunde durch einen 1 m² großen Bauteil fließt bei einem Temperaturunterschied der an den Bauteil angrenzenden Luftschichten von 1 Kelvin.

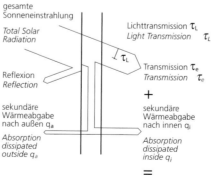

Strahlendurchgang bei einer Glasscheibe: Reflexion, Absorption, Transmission und Gesamtenergietransmission (g-Wert).

The solar radiation received by a pane of glass: reflection, absorption, transmission and total solar energy transmission (g-factor).

53 % in the visible range and 44 % in the near IR range. Radiation with wavelengths in the range from 315 nm to 3000 nm can pass through sodalime-silica glass. This range extends from ultraviolet at 315 – 380 nm across the visible range at 380 – 780 nm to the near infrared range at 780 – 3000 nm. The UV radiation with wavelengths below 315 nm and the radiation in the far infrared range above 3000 nm are almost completely absorbed. The latter is generally only recorded up to 2500 nm, because the intensity of solar radiation in the longer wavelengths is very low. The non-transmission of radiation in the longer wavelengths explains the heating-up effect behind glazing. The visible and near infrared light passing through the glass heat up the objects in the room, and are returned as longer wavelength radiation, which can no longer pass through the glass to the outside. The absorption of radiation in the glass also produces heat which is then dissipated from the surface by radiation, conduction and convection.

Thermal Properties

In normal float glass thermal transmission is a critical factor in heat loss and thus also in associated heating expenditure and requirements. While thermal resistance as a result of conduction can only marginally be affected by the thickness of the glass, radiation can be changed by applying coatings, and convection can be controlled by modifying the construction. With reference to the thermal expansion of glass, the specific coefficient is dependent on the composition of the glass: in normal float glass the addition of substances such as alkalines can produce coefficients from $80 – 90 \times 10^{-7}$/K, which in turn produces a thermal expansion of approx. 0.5 mm/m at temperatures between $-20°$ C and $+40°$ C. It approaches the values of steel and reinforced concrete, and as such must be taken into account when combining it with other materials. Purer SiO_2 glass, such as fused silica or quartz glass, has noticeably lower coefficients of thermal expansion, at around 5×10^{-7}/K; this makes it suitable for use in the manufacture of cooking surfaces.

Technical Parameters

Many parameters are available for assessing light, radiation and thermal properties. Reflection, absorption and transmission are used to describe permeability to radiation of one or

Biegefestigkeit

Der hohe Anteil an Siliziumdioxid ist für die Härte und die Biegefestigkeit maßgebend, aber auch für die unerwünschte Sprödigkeit des Glases.

Die Sprödigkeit führt bei einer minimalen Überschreitung der Grenze der elastischen Verformung zum Bruch einer Glasscheibe, weil im Bereich der Bruchdehnung praktisch keine plastischen Verformungen möglich sind.

Die theoretische Zugfestigkeit des Glases liegt bei Werten um $10^4 N/mm^2$. Die praktische Erfahrung zeigt aber, daß die effektive Zugfestigkeit maximal $30-80 N/mm^2$ erreicht, also Festigkeitswerte bis knapp 1 % der theoretischen Werte. Bei Dauerbelastungen sind sogar nur $7 N/mm^2$ bei Berechnungen zulässig. Die Verminderung ist auf die Tatsache zurückzuführen, daß Glas kein völlig gleichmäßiger Werkstoff ist, sondern Fehl- und Störstellen aufweist. Dieselbe Auswirkung haben kaum sichtbare Oberflächenrisse, die sowohl im Fertigungsprozeß als auch durch mechanische oder korrosive Beanspruchungen während der Nutzung entstehen.

Die niedrige Biegefestigkeit kann durch eine geeignete Nachbehandlung, wie thermische oder chemische Vorspannung, bis auf ca. $120 N/mm^2$ erhöht werden.

Bei der thermischen Vorspannung wird die Glasscheibe auf ca. 685° C erwärmt und dann mit kalter Luft angeblasen. Durch die rasche Abkühlung verfestigt sich die äußere Schicht zuerst und wird durch das langsame Zusammenziehen der inneren Schicht unter Druck gesetzt. Die Zugkräfte in der Kernzone und die Druckkräfte in der Oberflächenschicht bewirken einen Vorspannungszustand.

Neben der erhöhten Zugfestigkeit hat eine thermisch vorgespannte Scheibe den Vorteil, beim Zerbrechen in viele Krümel ohne scharfe Kanten zu zerfallen. Auf diese Eigenschaft weist die Bezeichnung Einscheiben-Sicherheitsglas (ESG) hin. Beim teilvorgespannten Glas (TVG) erfolgt die Kühlung langsamer, so daß der Vorspannungsgrad zwischen normaler Glasscheibe ($45 N/mm^2$) und ESG-Scheibe ($120 N/mm^2$) liegt. Es zerbricht in große Stücke wie eine normale Glasscheibe. Diese Eigenschaften spielen bei Verbundgläsern eine Rolle.

Ein ähnlicher Kräftezustand wird bei der chemischen Vorspannung durch eine Änderung in der Zusammensetzung der Glasoberfläche erreicht. Die Scheiben werden in elektrolytische Bäder eingetaucht, wo die außenliegenden Natrium-

more glass panes. These values are expressed as a fraction (in per cent) of the total incident radiation. Absorbed radiation is converted to heat (secondary heat transmission) which is then dissipated from the surfaces of the glass by radiation or convection. The main physical parameters in the evaluation of incident light and thermal gain or loss are the factors of light transmittance τ and total solar energy transmission, g-factor, as well as the thermal transmittance coefficient, the U-value. They are defined as follows:

– Light transmission, τ_L, refers to the fraction of directly transmitted light as perceived by the human eye.

– Total solar energy transmission, g-factor, is the sum of directly transmitted incident radiation (energy transmission τ_e) passing through the glass, and the secondary heat transmission q_i from the glass to the inside of the room as a result of radiation, conduction and convection.

– Thermal transmittance, the U-value, is the rate of loss of heat per hour and per square metre, for a temperature difference of one degree Kelvin between the inner and outer environments separated by glass.

Strength

The high silicon dioxide content is significant for the hardness and strength of glass, but also for its undesired brittleness. The structure of glass cannot accommodate plastic deformation so that it deforms elastically under stress up to the point where it suddenly breaks. The theoretical tensile strength of glass is $10^4 N/mm^2$. Experience shows, however, that the effective tensile strength reaches a maximum of $30-80 N/mm^2$, in other words, it values barely 1 % of the theoretical figures. When glass is subject to longer strain, values of only $7 N/mm^2$ can be expected. The reduction is due to the fact that glass is not a completely uniform material, but instead contains flaws and weak points. The same effect is produced by microcracks on the surface, which can arise during the manufacturing process or through mechanical stress or corrosion during use. Its low tensile strength can be improved up to approx. $120 N/mm^2$ by an appropriate treatment, such as thermal or chemical toughening. In the case of thermal toughening the glass pane is heated to approx. 685 °C and then exposed to a stream of cold air. This rapid cooling has the

ionen durch Kaliumionen, die einen 30 % größeren Radius aufweisen, ausgetauscht werden. Damit bildet sich eine außenliegende Druckzone. Die Vorteile der chemischen Vorspannung gegenüber der thermischen sind: keine Formänderung der Glasscheibe infolge des Aufwärmungsprozesses sowie die wesentlich weniger tiefe (ca. 0.1 mm) Oberflächenschicht, was die Härtung von dünnen Scheiben ermöglicht.

Verglasungssysteme

Für den Einsatz von Glas im Fassadenbau bietet sich heute eine Vielzahl von Systemen an, die dem Bestreben entsprechen, eine maximale Transparenz durch die Reduktion der nicht-transparenten tragenden Konstruktion zu erreichen. Die Arbeit einiger Architekten hat sich, in engem Zusammenwirken mit der Glasindustrie, intensiv mit den technischen Möglichkeiten des Werkstoffs Glas auseinandergesetzt, so daß einfachere Systeme wie Rahmen- und Pfosten-Riegel-Konstruktionen zu mehrgeschossigen hängenden Nur-Glas-Konstruktionen weiterentwickelt werden konnten.

Normale Verglasungssysteme basieren auf Glashalteleisten, die die Scheiben von innen gegen den äußeren Profilanschlag anpressen. Bei einer geschoßhohen Verglasung wird die Ansichtsbreite wegen des Glaseinstands, der Toleranzspielräume und der Breite der tragenden Profile selten weniger als 70 mm erreichen.

Verglasungssysteme mit Preßleisten ermöglichen Ansichtsbreiten von 50 mm. Da die Preßleisten aus Aluminium oder Stahl von außen angebracht werden und das Glas an die tragende Unterkonstruktion anpressen, sind hier nur Glaseinstand und Toleranzen maßgebend. Die Unterkonstruk-

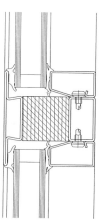

Detail einer Verglasung mit Glashalteleisten.
Detail of a glazing bead.

effect of first consolidating the outer layer, which is then subjected to compression by the contraction of the inner layer. The tensile forces in the core zone and the compressive forces in the surface layer prestress the material. In addition to increased tensile strength, a thermally toughened pane of glass has the advantage that on breakage it disintegrates into many small pieces without sharp edges, the dice. Therefore toughened or strengthened glass is indicated by the term safety glass. In the case of heat-strengthened glass cooling is slower, so that the degree of toughening achieved lies between that of normal float glass ($45 N/mm^2$) and toughened glass ($120 N/mm^2$). On failure it breaks into large pieces like normal float glass. These qualities play a role in laminated glass. A similar pattern of forces is achieved in chemical toughening by changing the composition of the surface of the glass. The panes are dipped into electrolysis baths where the external sodium ions are exchanged for potassium ions, which have a 30 % larger radius: this creates an external layer under pressure. The advantages of chemical toughening over thermal toughening are: no deformation of the glass pane as a result of the heating process, and the shallower depth of the surface layer (approx. 0.1 mm), which permits the toughening of thinner layers of glass.

Glazing Systems

Many systems are now available for the use of glass in façades, all aimed at achieving maximum transparency by reducing the non-transparent support structure. In close collaboration with the glass industry, some architects have carried out much work on the possibilities of glass for use in building, and this has led to the development of simpler systems, from frame systems and mullion and transom structures to curtain walls several floors high, made entirely of glass. Normal glazing systems are based on glazing beads which press the panes from the inside against the outer frame structure. In a curtain wall the visible face of this frame structure is seldom less than 70 mm, due to glazing rebate, the tolerances and the width of the support profiles.

Pressure glazing systems enable the visible face of the support structure to be reduced to a width of 50 mm. As the pressure caps of aluminium or steel press the glass from the outside onto the internal support structure, only the glazing bead and the tolerances are critical. The support

tion ist meistens als Pfosten-Riegel-Konstruktion ausgeführt, was zu einem gleichmäßigen filigranen Erscheinungsbild führt.

Mit dem Begriff «structural glazing» wird in der Regel ein Nur-Glas-System bezeichnet, bei dem die Glasscheiben mit hochbelastbaren Silikonen auf die tragende Konstruktion der Fassade geklebt sind. Dabei handelt es sich um eine Variation der Rahmen- oder Pfosten-Riegel-Konstruktion, welche nur das Erscheinungsbild von außen betrifft, ohne daß die tragende Struktur wesentlich verändert wird. Daher sollte eher von «geklebter Fassade» die Rede sein. Um diesen optischen Eindruck – ein Erscheinungsbild, das nur vom Glas bestimmt wird – zu erzielen, werden gefärbte oder verspiegelte Glasscheiben eingesetzt. Wenn aber das Licht von innen kommt, verliert sich das kristalline Erscheinungsbild.

Punktförmige Befestigungssysteme

Ein erster Schritt in der Entmaterialisierung der tragenden Konstruktion ist die Reduktion von linearen zu punktförmigen Befestigungssystemen mit oder ohne Glasdurchdringung.

Bei punktförmigen Befestigungen ohne Durchdringung sind die Glasscheiben durch beidseitig angebrachte Halterungen fixiert, die entweder im Fugenkreuz oder entlang der Kanten angeordnet sind.

Ein Beispiel dafür ist die Atriumsverglasung des Hotels Kempinski beim Flughafen München, welches von den Architekten Murphy/Jahn 1994 fertiggestellt wurde. Die Tragkonstruktion besteht aus kreuzweise angeordneten Seilen, die ein ebenes Seilwerk bilden. An den Kreuzungspunkten sind 1.5 × 1.5 m große, 10 mm starke

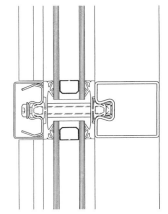

Detail einer Verglasung mit Preßleisten.
Detail of a pressure cap glazing.

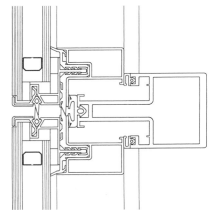

Detail eines «structural glazing»-Systems.
Detail of a structural glazing system.

frame is generally a mullion and transom frame which creates an even, filigree appearance.

The term structural glazing generally refers to an all-glass system in which the glass panels are bonded to the façade support structure using high stress silicone. Here a variation of the frame or mullion and transom structure is used, which affects only the overall appearance from the outside, without significantly altering the support structure. For this reason it would be more accurate to speak of a "bonded glazing". To heighten the optical impression that the façade is all glass, body tinted or reflecting glass panes are often used. However, when the light comes from the inside of the building, this crystalline illusion disappears.

Point Fixing Systems

A first step in the dematerialisation of the support structure is to shift from linear to point fixing systems, with or without perforation of the glass.

Verglasung mit punktförmiger Befestigung ohne Glasdurchdringung.
Kempinski Hotel, Flughafen München, 1994, Murphy/Jahn Architekten.
Point-fixed glazing without perforation.
Kempinski Hotel, Munich Airport, 1994,
Murphy/Jahn Architects.

Punktförmige Befestigung mit Glasdurchdringung und versenktem Schraubenkopf.
Renault Centre, Swindon, England, 1982, Foster und Partner.
Point fixing glazing with perforation and countersunk bolts.
Renault Centre, Swindon, England, 1982, Foster and Partners.

Zugbeanspruchte Glaskonstruktion mit Klemmhaltern.
Konstruktion von der Firma Glasbau Hahn.
Suspended glazing with clamps-fitting.
Realized by Glasbau Hahn.

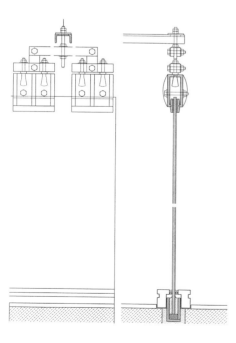

VSG-Scheiben mit eigens dafür entwickelten Klemmtellern befestigt.

Bei punktförmigen Befestigungen mit Glasdurchdringung werden die Glasscheiben mit Bohrungen versehen und mit Schrauben befestigt. Eine Variante davon sind flächenbündige Verschraubungen, bei denen der Schraubenkopf in eine Senkbohrung eingelassen wird. Der Schraubenkopf dient zugleich als Halterung und Auflager; damit konzentrieren sich Vertikal- und Horizontallasten um das Bohrungsloch.
Dank punktförmigen Befestigungssystemen kann eine Glasscheibe sowohl direkt auf der tragenden Unterkonstruktion als auch an den Knotenpunkten von gespannten Seilkonstruktionen befestigt werden.

Eines der ersten solchen Produkte war das Planar®-System «Typ 902», das Foster und Partner erstmals 1982 für die Fassade des Renault Centre in Swindon (England) einsetzten. Hier sind die 4×1.8 m großen und 10 mm starken ESG-Scheiben direkt an Edelstahlhalter geschraubt, die an den Riegeln der Fassadenkonstruktion befestigt sind.
Daraus wurde der «Typ 905» entwickelt, bei dem die Glasscheibe mit aufgeschraubten, zylindrischen Beschlägen versehen und in Konsolen aus den tragenden Pfosten der Fassadenkonstruktion eingehängt ist.
Heute sind verschiedene Produkte für Einfach- und Isolierverglasungen auf dem Markt erhältlich, die eine punktförmige Befestigung ermöglichen. Ihren Erfolg verdanken sie vor allem dem glatten Erscheinungsbild der Glasoberfläche bei der Gestaltung einer Fassade.

Glas als tragender Bauteil
Für eine weitere Entmaterialisierung der tragenden Konstruktion kann das transparente Material selbst herangezogen werden. Die Nutzung der Tragfähigkeit der Glasscheibe ist bei zug- und druckbeanspruchten Konstruktionen sogar unentbehrlich.

Die ersten zugbeanspruchten Glaskonstruktionen wurden in den 60er Jahren von der Firma Glasbau Hahn realisiert. Die Glasscheiben werden am oberen Rand mit Klemmen gehalten, die an einem Waagebalken befestigt sind. Das System hat sich weltweit rasch verbreitet. Es existieren Ausführungen mit Glasscheiben von 13 m

In point fixing systems without perforation the panes are held in place by means of fittings placed on both sides of the glass, either at the joints between the panes, or at their corners.

An example of this is the glazing in the atrium in Hotel Kempinski at Munich Airport, completed by Murphy/Jahn architects in 1994. The support structure is a cable net structure with horizontal and vertical cables. The 1.5×1.5 m, 10 mm thick laminated glass is attached to the junctions in this cable net by means of specially developed clamping plates.
In point fixing systems with perforation holes are drilled in the panes and bolts inserted. A variation on this are holes where the bolt head is countersunk to finish flush with the surface. The head of the bolt serves both as a fixing and bearing point; thus the vertical and horizontal loads are concentrated around the drill hole. Thanks to point fixing systems a glass pane can be fixed either directly onto a supporting frame or to the junctions of tensile cable constructions.

One of the first such products was the Planar® system, type 902, used by Foster and Partners for the first time in 1982 for the façade of the Renault Centre in Swindon (England). Here the 4×1.8 m, 10 mm toughened glass is bolted directly to stainless steel spring plates attached to the transoms of the façade structure.
A further development of this system was type 905, in which cylindrical bolts are fixed to the glass panes which are then suspended in pins projecting from the mullion of the façade structure. Today a number of products are available on the market which provide for point fixing of single and insulated glazing. Their main attraction is the smooth outward appearance of the glass which can be achieved in designing a façade.

Glass as a Load-Bearing Component
For further dematerialisation of the support structure, it is possible to use the transparent material itself as a load-bearing component in the structure. The load-carrying capabilities of glass are in fact indispensable in structures subject to tension and compression forces.

The first suspended glass walls were built in the 1960s by Glasbau Hahn. The glass panes were fixed at the upper edge by means of clamps attached to a horizontal balance beam. This

Höhe. Die Schwierigkeiten bei der Herstellung, dem Transport und der Montage von übergroßen Scheiben haben in der Folge zu Lösungen geführt, die mit handlicheren Formaten auskommen.

Die abgehängte Verglasung mit geschraubten Eckhalterungen, den sogenannten «patch fittings», wurde von Foster und Partnern für das Verwaltungsgebäude Willis, Faber und Dumas in Ipswich (England), 1971–75, entwickelt. Die 2 × 2.5 m großen und 12 mm starken ESG-Scheiben – die Dimension wurde damals von der Größe der Vorspannöfen begrenzt – sind mit geschraubten, 165 × 165 mm großen Eckbeschlägen aus Messing an die jeweils nächsthöhere Scheibe gehängt. Die obersten sind mit einem einzigen Bolzen von 38 mm Durchmesser am Rand der Geschoßdecke befestigt, so daß die ganze, rund 15 m hohe Fassade an der Dachgeschoßdecke abgehängt ist. Glasschwerter im Gebäudeinneren, die an den Geschoßdecken abgehängt sind, sorgen für die Windaussteifung.
Wesentlich bei dieser Glaskonstruktion ist, daß die vertikale Lastabtragung durch Anpreßdruck und Reibung der verschraubten Eckhalterungen auf der Glasoberfläche erfolgt.

Aus dem «patch fitting»-System wurden die besprochenen Systeme mit punktförmigen, geschraubten Befestigungen weiterentwickelt.

technique was rapidly adopted throughout the world, and some examples built even have glass panes 13 metres high. The difficulties of manufacturing, transporting and fitting such oversized panes led to the development of solutions which make use of more manageable sizes.

Suspended glazing with bolted corner-plate fixing points, called "patch fittings", was developed by Foster and Partners for the headquarters of Willis, Faber and Dumas in Ipswich (England), built between 1971 and 1975. The 2 × 2.5 m panes of 12 mm toughened glass – the dimensions were determined by toughening capabilities at the time – are suspended from the corners of the panes above by means of brass patch fitting plates 165 × 165 mm in size. The uppermost panes are attached by means of a single 38 mm diameter bolt to the edge of the top floor, which means that the entire 15 m high façade is thus suspended from the floor of the roof storey. Lateral restraint against wind loads is achieved by means of glass fins inside the building, suspended from the intermediate floors. A significant feature of this glass construction is that vertical in-plane forces are transferred by means of friction and pressure at the interface of the bolted patch fittings with the glass panes.
The idea of the patch fittings was taken up and developed further to produce the systems described above with point bolted fittings.

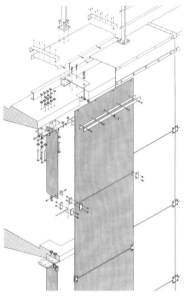

Die Verglasung mit geschraubten Eckhalterungen, «patch fittings», zeigt die Festigkeit von Glasscheiben in hängenden Konstruktionen.
Verwaltungsgebäude für Willis, Faber und Dumas, Ipswich, England, 1971–75, Foster und Partner.
The glazing system with bolted corner plates or "patch fittings", demonstrates the strength of glass in suspended constructions.
Office building for Willis, Faber und Dumas, Ipswich, England, 1971–75, Foster and Partners.

Das punktförmige Befestigungssystem RFR mit Kugelgelenk; die Unterteilung in quadratische Felder mit den Federbeschlag-Glasplatten und den darunterliegenden, wie ein Kettenhemd abgehängten Platten; Gesamtansicht.
Museum für Wissenschaft und Technik, Paris, 1986, Adrien Fainsilber in Zusammenarbeit mit RFR.
The RFR bolted fixing system with articulated point fixings; the division into square façade sections: the uppermost panes with spring connections, the remaining panes suspended below; general view.
Museum of Science and Technology, Paris, 1986, Adrien Fainsilber with RFR.

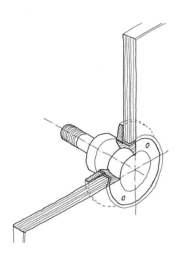

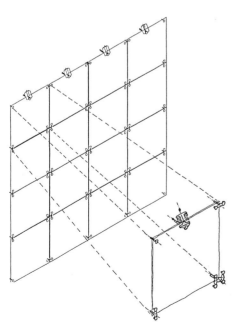

Punkthalterungen mit Kugelgelenken werden eingesetzt, um die Konzentration von hohen Biege- und Torsionskräften um das Bohrungsloch zu reduzieren.

Das erste Befestigungssystem mit gelenkiger Punkthalterung haben Adrien Fainsilber und die Spezialisten für Glaskonstruktionen Rice-Francis-Ritchie (RFR) 1986 für die Gewächshäuser des Museums für Wissenschaft und Technik in Paris entwickelt.
Die Verglasungen bestehen aus vorgespannten, 2 × 2 m großen und 12 mm starken Scheiben, die quadratische Felder von 8 m Seitenlänge bilden. Die oberen vier Platten sind jeweils mit einem Federbeschlag an den Riegeln des tragenden Gerüsts aufgehängt, während die übrigen untereinander abgehängt sind. Diese hängende Verglasung ist mit einer horizontalen Seilkonstruktion gegen die Windkräfte stabilisiert. Um große Drehmomente um das Bohrungsloch zu verhindern, sind Kugelgelenke, die in der Glasachse liegen, in die Befestigungsknoten eingebaut.

In den folgenden Jahren haben RFR mehrere Projekte mit hängenden Verglasungen realisiert,

Point fittings with articulated fixings are used to reduce the concentration of high bending and torsion forces around the drill hole.

The first fixing system with articulated point fixings was developed in 1986 by Adrien Fainsilber and the specialists for glass construction, Rice-Francis-Ritchie (RFR) for the greenhouses of the Museum of Science and Technology in Paris.
The glazing consists of 2 × 2 m, 12 mm toughened glass, grouped to form 8 m square façade sections. The four uppermost panes are each suspended by means of a spring connection to the transom of the support frame, while the remaining panes are all suspended from these, one below the other. This hanging glass wall is stabilised against wind loads by a horizontal cable construction. To avoid great torsional stress around the drill hole in the glass, spherical bearings in plane with the glass are integrated into the fixing points.

In the following years RFR designed a number of projects with suspended glazing with articulated point fixing.

bei denen Befestigungsknoten mit Kugelgelenken zum Einsatz kommen.

Ein besonderes Beispiel ist die abgerundete Eingangsverglasung des Hauptsitzes von «Channel 4» in London, 1991–94, von Richard Rogers Partnership und RFR erstellt.
Die 18 × 18 m große Glasfassade ist eine abgehängte, hinterspannte Glaskonstruktion. Ihre abgerundete Form entspricht im Grundriß einem Kreissegment von 120° und endet seitlich mit zwei rückspringenden Flanken.
Die Verglasung ist im Dachbereich mit Federbeschlägen von einer Stahlkonstruktion aus auskragenden Druckpfosten abgehängt. Sie besteht aus 12 mm starken ESG-Scheiben, die durch gelenkige Punkthalterungen miteinander verbunden sind. Die einseitig gebogenen ESG-Scheiben sind 2.1 m breit und bis zu 3 m hoch.
Die große Herausforderung bei dieser Konstruktion bestand in der Entwicklung eines Netzwerkes, das die Rundung mit ihren rückspringenden Flanken aussteift und gleichzeitig die regelmäßige Geometrie der Befestigungspunkte bildet.

One special example is the curved glazing at the entrance to the headquarters of Channel 4 in London, built between 1991 and 1994 by the Richard Rogers Partnership together with RFR.
The 18 × 18 m glass façade is a suspended glass construction, curving around a 120° segment of circle and ending at the side in two receding flanks. At the roof level the glazing is suspended by means of spring connections to a steel frame of cantilevered compression posts.
The glazing is composed of 12 mm toughened glass panes connected to each other by means of articulated point fixing. The toughened glass panes which are curved in one plane are 2.1 m wide and up to 3 m high.
The great challenge in this construction was in developing a network which would brace the curved glass and the receding flanks, as well as forming the regular geometry of the fixing points.

Another way of using glass as a load-bearing component is in using glass fins for wind bracing.

Die abgerundete Verglasung ist mit Federbeschlägen von einer Stahlkonstruktion abgehängt; die Glasscheiben sind durch gelenkige Punkthalterung miteinander verbunden.
Eingangsverglasung beim Hauptsitz von «Channel 4», London, 1991–94, Richard Rogers Partnership mit RFR.
The curved glass is suspended via spring connections to a steel frame; the individual panes are connected to each other by means of articulated point fixing. Glazing at the entrance to the headquarters of Channel 4, London, 1991–94, Richard Rogers Partnership together with RFR.

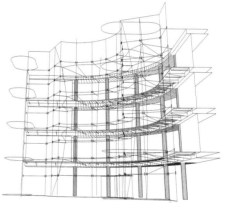

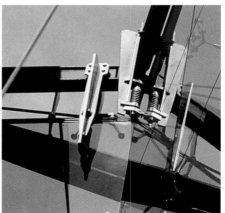

Verglasung mit Glasstreifen zur Windaussteifung.
Sainsbury Centre for Visual Arts, Norwich, England,
1974–78, Foster und Partner.
Glass wall with glass fins for wind bracing.
Sainsbury Centre for Visual Arts, Norwich, England,
1974–78, Foster and Partners.

Eine weitere Möglichkeit, Glas in tragender Funktion einzusetzten, ist die Verwendung von Glasstreifen zur Windaussteifung.

Das langgezogene Gebäude des Sainsbury Centre for Visual Arts in Norwich (England), von Foster und Partnern 1974–78 erstellt, ist an den Schmalseiten je durch eine 30×7.5 m große Verglasung abgeschlossen.
Sie besteht aus 2.4×7.5 m großen ESG-Scheiben, die mit 60 cm breiten, 25 mm starken ESG-Streifen gegen die Windkräfte ausgesteift sind.

Beim Kongreßgebäude «Congrexpo» in Lille (Frankreich), von den Architekten Rem Koolhaas/OMA in Zusammenarbeit mit R.J. van Santen 1995 fertiggestellt, sind die Laubengänge durch eine Verglasung mit geschoßhohen Glasschwertern abgeschlossen. Die 3.6 m langen und 0.3 m breiten Glasschwerter sind aus 15 mm starken ESG-Streifen gefertigt und an den Stirnen der Geschoßdecken mit Edelstahlschuhen befestigt. Sie sind mit 10 mm starken ESG-Scheiben ausgefacht, die mit Edelstahlwinkeln an die Glasschwerter geschraubt sind.

The linear-shaped Sainsbury Centre for Visual Arts in Norwich (England), built between 1974 and 1978 by Foster and Partners, has a 30 × 7.5 m glass wall on the two narrow sides. These walls consist of 2.4 × 7.5 m panes of toughened glass stiffened against wind loads with 60 cm wide, 25 mm thick fins of toughened glass.

In the Congress Building "Congrexpo" in Lille (France), completed in 1995 by architects Rem Koolhaas/OMA in cooperation with R.J. van Santen, the outside corridors are closed off by a glazing with storey-height glass fins. The 3.6 metre long and 0.3 metre wide glass fins are of 15 mm thick strips of toughened glass and fixed to the ends of the floors with stainless steel shoes.
They are infilled with panes of 10 mm toughened glass which are bolted with stainless steel angles to the glass fins. Frameless centre-pivoting windows are built into the glazing for ventilation purposes.

An example of the use of glass fins to brace a façade is presented by the Sony Center, currently

Verglasung mit Glasstreifen als Pfosten.
Kongreßgebäude «Congrexpo», Lille, Frankreich,
1994, Rem Koolhaas/OMA.
Glazing with glass fin as mullion.
"Congrexpo" congress building, Lille, France,
1994, Rem Koolhaas/OMA.

Für die Belüftung der Gänge sind rahmenlose Schwingflügel aus Glas eingebaut.

Ein Beispiel für die Verwendung von Glasstreifen zur Aussteifung einer Fassade ist das Sony Center, das die Architekten Murphy/Jahn zur Zeit am Potsdamerplatz in Berlin realisieren. Die 3.5 m langen Pfosten der geschoßhohen Fassadenelemente sind mit 22 cm breiten, 12 mm starken Glasstreifen versehen, welche als vertikale Aussteifung gegen Windkräfte dienen.

Glasstützen und -träger
Der erfolgreiche Einsatz von Glasstreifen zur Windaussteifung hat zur Idee geführt, sie auch als Stützen oder Träger zu verwenden.

Beim Wohnhaus in Almere (Niederlande), das die Architekten Benthem Crouwel 1984 fertiggestellt haben, besteht die raumhohe Verglasung des Wohnraums aus 12 mm starken ESG-Scheiben. Beim Glasstoß sind die Scheiben mit 15 mm starken ESG-Glasstreifen, die am Fußboden und am Dachrand durch Aluminiumschuhe gehalten sind, gegen Windkräfte ausgesteift. Die Glasschwerter dienen aber auch als Auflager für das in leichter Bauweise erstellte Dach. Die Stoßfugen sind mit transparentem Silikon gedichtet.

Die Architekten Benthem Crouwel haben ihre Erfahrungen beim Haus in Almere auch für den Skulpturenpavillon in Arnheim (Niederlande), 1986, genutzt. Hier sind die Glasscheiben tragend und raumabschließend eingesetzt. Die

being built by Murphy/Jahn Architects at Potsdamerplatz in Berlin.
The 3.5 m long mullions of the storey-high façade elements are stiffened with 22 cm wide, 12 mm thick glass fins which serve as vertical bracing against wind loads.

Glass Columns and Beams
Success in the use of glass fins for wind bracing has prompted the idea of using them also as columns and beams.

For the house in Almere (Netherlands) completed in 1984 by Benthem Crouwel Architects the storey-height glazing in the living room consists of 12 mm thick toughened glass which is stiffened against wind loads with 15 mm thick fins of toughened glass.
The fins are fixed at the base and at the roof edge by means of aluminium shoes. The glass fins, however, also serve as a bearing point for the roof which is of lightweight construction. The butted joints are sealed with transparent silicon.

Benthem Crouwel Architects utilised their experience with the house in Almere in building the Sculpture Pavilion in Arnheim (Netherlands), completed in 1986. Here the glass panes are used as load-bearing, and as spatial dividers. The support structure of the 24 m long and 6.2 m wide pavilion is a frame construction. The 13 frame components consist of two 15 mm thick fins of toughened glass connected to

Fassade mit Glasstreifen zur Windaussteifung.
Sony Centre, Berlin, 1992 – 99,
Murphy/Jahn Architekten.
Façade with glass fins for wind bracing.
Sony Centre, Berlin, 1992 – 99,
Murphy/Jahn Architects.

Verglasung mit Glasstreifen, die zur Windaussteifung und als Dachauflager dienen.
Wohnhaus, Almere, Niederlande, 1984,
Benthem Crouwel.
Glazing with glass fins acting as wind bracing and
support for the roof.
House, Almere, Netherlands, 1984,
Benthem Crouwel.

Glaspavillon mit aussteifenden und tragenden
Glasstützen.
Skulpturenpavillon, Arnheim, Niederlande, 1986,
Benthem Crouwel.
Glass pavilion with glass columns used for bracing
and load-bearing.
Sculptures pavilion, Arnheim, Netherlands, 1986,
Benthem Crouwel.

Tragstruktur des 24 m langen und 6.2 m breiten Pavillons ist eine Rahmenkonstruktion. Die 13 Rahmenelemente bestehen aus jeweils zwei 15 mm starken ESG-Streifen, die mit Fachwerkträgern aus Stahlprofilen verbunden sind. Als Aussteifung dienen die 16 mm starken VSG-Scheiben der Dachverglasung und die 10 mm starken ESG-Scheiben der Glaswände.
Leider stand der Pavillon nur drei Monate im Park und wurde nach der Ausstellung demontiert.

Eine spektakuläre Verwendung von Glasstützen zeigt das Glasdach des Atriums der Kommunalen Verwaltung in St-Germain-en-Laye bei Paris, von den Architekten J. Brunet und E. Saunier 1994 realisiert. Die 24 × 24 m große Dachverglasung ist von kreuzförmigen, 22 × 22 cm großen Glas-

steel trusses. The 16 mm thick laminated panes of the roof glazing and the 10 mm toughened glass panes of the walls act as bracing. Unfortunately the pavilion stood for only three months in the park and was dismantled after the exhibition.

A spectacular use of glass columns is demonstrated by the glass roof of the atrium of the Local Authority Offices in St-Germain-en-Laye near Paris, built in 1994 by the architects J. Brunet and E. Saunier. The 24 × 24 m glass roof is supported by cross-shaped, 22 × 22 cm glass columns made up of laminated glass strips with three layers of toughened glass. At the head and base of the glass columns are steel shoes which transfer the vertical loads. The cross-shaped columns are approved

Kreuzförmige Glasstützen tragen die Dachverglasung.
Kommunale Verwaltung, St-Germain-en-Laye,
Frankreich, 1994, J. Brunet und E. Saunier.
Cross-shaped glass columns carry the roof glazing.
Local Authority Office, St-Germain-en-Laye, France,
1994, J. Brunet and E. Saunier.

stützen getragen, die aus VSG-Glasstreifen mit drei ESG-Scheiben bestehen. Am Kopf- und Fußpunkt sind die Glasstützen mit Edelstahlschuhen eingefaßt, die für die Einleitung der Vertikalkräfte sorgen. Die kreuzförmigen Stützen sind für eine Belastung von 6 Tonnen zugelassen, aber für 50 Tonnen gerechnet und stellen eine Weltpremiere im Glasbau dar.

Ein Jahr früher haben die Architekten J. Brunet und E. Saunier eine Dachverglasung mit Glasträgern für die Werkstätten im Musée du Louvre, Paris, realisiert.
Die Glaskonstruktion schließt einen dreigeschossigen Lichthof ab, welcher der unterirdischen Erweiterung des Museums Tageslicht zuführt. Für die 4 × 16 m große Dachverglasung wurden VSG-Scheiben aus drei 15 mm ESG-Scheiben verwendet, die von 60 cm hohen VSG-Glasbalken aus drei 15 mm starken ESG-Scheiben getragen werden.
Das Verhalten des Materials wurde mit umfangreichen Tests untersucht. Dabei stellte sich heraus, daß die Glasunterzüge statt der zuvor geschätzten 5 Tonnen mit 12.2 bis 14 Tonnen belastet werden können.

Glaskonstruktionen

Das Experimentieren mit Glasstützen und -trägern hat verschiedene Architekten zu Projekten ermutigt, bei denen Glas alle Tragfunktionen übernimmt.

Der Eingangspavillon des Broadfield House Glass Museum in Kingswinford (England) wurde 1994

for a loading of six tons, but have been calculated to be able to withstand 50 tons. They represent a world's first in glass construction.

One year earlier the architects J. Brunet and E. Saunier created a glass roof with glass beams for the Workshops in the Musée du Louvre, Paris. The glass construction covers a three-storey lightwell which admits daylight into the underground extension to the museum. Laminated panes of three 15 mm layers of toughened glass were used for the 4 × 16 m glass roof; these panes are supported by 60 cm high laminated glass beams of three 15 mm thick strips of toughened glass.
The behaviour of the material was exhaustively tested. The tests revealed that the glass beams could take a loading of 12.2 to 14 tons, instead of the previously estimated five tons.

Glass Constructions

Experiments with glass columns and beams have encouraged a number of architects to carry out projects in which glass is used for all load-bearing functions.

The entrance pavilion to Broadfield House Glass Museum in Kingswinford (England) was built in 1994 by the architects Antenna Design, B. G. Richards and R. Dabell.
This annexe is 11 m long, 5.7 m wide and 3.5 m high. The half-frames of the support structure consist of fins of laminated glass (3 × 10 mm toughened glass). The 30 cm high glass beams

Glasbalken tragen die Dachverglasung.
Werkstätten im Musée du Louvre, Paris, 1993,
J. Brunet und E. Saunier.
Glass beams support the roof glazing.
Workshops in the Musée du Louvre, Paris, 1993,
J. Brunet and E. Saunier.

Die Tragkonstruktion des Eingangspavillons besteht aus Glasstützen und -balken.
Broadfield House Glass Museum, Kingswinford, England, 1994, Antenna Design, B. G. Richards und R. Dabell.
The support structure of the entrance pavilion is composed of glass columns and beams.
Broadfield House Glass Museum, Kingswinford, England, 1994, Antenna Design, B. G. Richards and R. Dabell.

von den Architekten Antenna Design, B. G. Richards und R. Dabell erstellt.

Der Anbau ist 11 m lang, 5.7 m breit und 3.5 m hoch. Die Halbrahmen der Tragstruktur bestehen aus VSG-Streifen (3 × 10 mm ESG). Die 30 cm hohen Glasträger sind mit 28 cm tiefen Glasstützen über eine Zapfverbindung zusammengefügt, die vor Ort mit Gießharz ausgegossen wurde. Die Halbrahmen werden von Stahlschuhen am Fußboden und an der Hausmauer gehalten. Für das flachgeneigte Glasdach wurden 1.1 × 3.7 m große Isoliergläser mit einem k-Wert von 1.7 W/m²K und einem g-Wert von 0.37 verwendet. Sie bestehen aus einem farbneutralen, 10 mm starken Sonnenschutzglas außen, einem Zwischenraum von 10 mm und einer VSG-Scheibe (2 × 6 mm ESG) innen, deren raumseitige ESG-Scheibe mit einem Streifenmuster bedruckt ist. Die Isoliergläser sind als Stufenglas gefertigt und bilden ein Vordach über der vertikalen, raumabschließenden Isolierverglasung. Alle Fugen sind mit schwarzem Silikon gedichtet.

1995 haben die Studenten des Lehrstuhls für Baukonstruktion (Tragwerkslehre) an der RWTH Aachen einen demontierbaren Ausstellungspavillon realisiert.

Der 2.5 × 6.15 m große Pavillon ist als Baukastensystem aus vorgefertigten Grundelementen konzipiert. Die 24 cm tiefen VSG-Glasstützen (3 × 12 mm ESG) sind am Fußboden zwischen zwei U-förmigen Stahlprofilen eingeklemmt und verschraubt. Die Stützenköpfe sind beidseitig mit 24 cm hohen Glasträgern aus VSG-Streifen (2 × 6 mm TVG) miteinander verschraubt. An dieser Rahmenkonstruktion sind Glaswände und

are connected to 28 cm deep glass columns via mortise and tennon joint which is moulded on site with cast resin. The half-frames are fixed in place on the ground and on the house wall via steel shoes.

For the single-pitched glass roof 1.1 × 3.7 m panes of insulated units were used with a U-value of 1.7 W/m²K and a g-factor of 0.37. They are composed of an outer 10 mm sheet of neutral-coated glass, a cavity of 10 mm and a laminated inner sheet (2 × 6 mm toughened glass). Fritted on the room-side pane of toughened glass is a stripe pattern. The insulated panes are manufactured with the inner sheet set back and form a canopy over the vertical, space-defining insulated glazing. All joints are sealed with black silicon.

In 1995 students from the Building Construction Department (static analysis) at the RWTH Aachen built a demountable exhibition pavilion. This 2.5 × 6.15 m pavilion is designed as a kit of prefabricated elements. The 24 cm deep laminated glass columns (3 × 12 mm toughened glass) are clamped at floor level between two U-shaped steel beams and bolted. The column heads are bolted to each other on both sides with 24 cm high glass beams of laminated glass strips (2 × 6 mm heat-strengthened glass). Attached to this frame construction, by means of steel angles, are glass walls and a glass roof of 12 mm thick toughened glass. They give longitudinal stiffness to the pavilion, while the columns provide stiffness in the transverse direction. To facilitate dismantling bolted connections were chosen instead of sealants.

Baukastensystem mit Stützen und Balken aus Glas. Demontierbarer Ausstellungspavillon, Aachen, 1995, Lehrstuhl für Baukonstruktion, RWTH Aachen.
Modular system with glass columns and beams. Demountable exhibition pavilion, Aachen, 1995, Department of Building Construction, RWTH Aachen.

Glasdach aus 12 mm ESG-Scheiben mit Stahlwinkeln befestigt. Sie bilden die Längsaussteifung des Pavillons, während die eingespannten Stützen in der Querrichtung aussteifen.
Für eine einfache Demontage wurden statt Klebeverbindungen Schraubenverbindungen gewählt.

Die Glasbrücke des Architekturbüros Kraijvanger und Urbis in Rotterdam (Niederlande), 1993, verbindet im 1. OG die Büroräume von zwei gegenüberliegenden Bauten. Die 3.2 m lange Brücke besteht aus VSG-Scheiben, die mit Punkthaltern aus Edelstahl miteinander verbunden sind. Die Bodenplatte ist eine 2×15 mm starke VSG-Scheibe, die auf zwei Glasträgern aus 3×10 mm starken VSG-Streifen liegt. Die Seitenwände und das Dach bestehen aus VSG-Scheiben (10 mm ESG + 6 mm TVG).

Um die wertvollen Mosaikböden aus dem 4. Jahrhundert in der Basilika von Aquileia (Italien) vor der großen Zahl der Besucher zu schützen, haben die Architekten Ottavio di Blasi Associati einen seitlichen Umgang mit einer transparenten Passerelle und einer 12 m langen gläsernen Verbindungsbrücke in der Mitte vorgeschlagen (1995–99). Die Brücke besteht aus zwei parallelen Glasträgern, die aus 1 m langen VSG-Scheiben (3×15 mm ESG) zusammengesetzt und mit zwei Edelstahlkabeln vorgespannt sind. Quer zwischen den Glasträgern sind als Sekundärkonstruktion weitere Glasscheiben vertikal angeordnet, worauf die begehbaren Glasplatten aufliegen.
Diese 12 m lange Brücke hat verschiedene Tests

The glass bridge by the architectural office of Kraijvanger and Urbis in Rotterdam (Netherlands), built in 1993, provides a first-floor link between the offices in two neighbouring buildings. The 3.2 m long bridge consists of panes of laminated glass joined to each other with point fixings of stainless steel. The floor slab is a 2×15 mm thick laminated glass slab resting on two glass beams of 3×10 mm thick laminated glass strips. The side walls and roof are of laminated glass (10 mm toughened glass + 6 mm heat-strengthened glass).

To protect the valuable 4th-century mosaic floors in the basilica of Aquileia (Italy) from the large number of visitors, architects Ottavio di Blasi Associati proposed a perimeter walkway along the sides with transparent footbridge and a 12 m long glass connecting bridge in the middle (1995–99). The bridge consists of two parallel glass beams, composed of 1 m long laminated glass panes (3×15 mm toughened glass) pre-tensioned with two stainless steel cables. Arranged at right angle between the glass beams is a

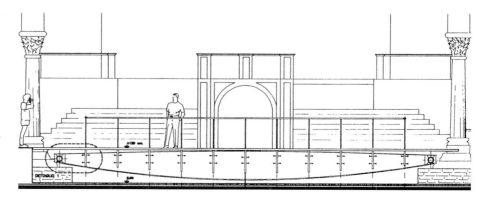

Drei auskragende Glasträger mit unterschiedlich
großen Dreieckscheiben bilden die Tragstruktur des
Vordachs.
Yurakucho U-Bahn-Station, Tokio, Japan, 1996,
Rafael Viñoly Architects mit Dewhurst Macfarlane
und Partnern.

*Three cantilevered glass beams with triangular-
shaped blades of varying sizes form the support con-
struction for the canopy.*
*Yurakucho underground railway station, Tokyo,
Japan, 1996, Rafael Viñoly Architects with
Dewhurst Macfarlane and Partners.*

hinsichtlich des Trag- und Bruchverhaltens mit
Erfolg bestanden.

1996 ist das gläserne Vordach für die Yurakucho
U-Bahn-Station in Tokio fertiggestellt worden,
von Rafael Viñoly Architects in Zusammenarbeit mit Dewhurst Macfarlane und Partnern
entworfen.
Die auskragende Glaskonstruktion ist 10.6 m
lang, 4.8 m breit und an der Spitze 4.8 m hoch.
Die Tragstruktur besteht aus drei parallelen,
auskragenden Trägern, die aus mehreren dreieckigen VSG-Scheiben (2 × 19 mm ESG) und
40 mm starken Acrylplatten – letztere wegen der
Erdbebensicherheit – zusammengesetzt sind.
Die unterschiedlich großen Dreieckscheiben
sind so ineinander verzahnt zusammenge-
schraubt, daß an der Spitze eine und beim Auflager vier davon resultieren. Hier sind sie durch
Laschen an einem Torsionsrohr befestigt.
Die Dachverglasung besteht aus 1.9 bis 2.5 m
langen und 4.8 m breiten VSG-Scheiben
(2 × 15 mm ESG), die an den Knotenpunkten
der Kragarme befestigt sind.

secondary structure of vertically placed glass
panes; bearing on these are the glass slabs on
which people walk. This 12 m long bridge has
successfully undergone a number of tests of its
load-carrying capacity and breaking behaviour.

In 1996 the glass canopy at the entrance to the Yurakucho underground railway station in Tokyo
was finished, designed by Rafael Viñoly architects
with Dewhurst Macfarlane and Partners. This cantilevered glass structure is 10.6 m long, 4.8 m wide and 4.8 m high at the apex. The support structure consists of three parallel, cantilevered beams,
composed of several triangular-shaped laminated
blades (2 × 19 mm toughened glass) and 40 mm
thick acrylic panels – the latter because of earthquake safety. The variously sized triangular blades
are bolted to interlock in with each other, with
one blade at the apex and four at the bearing point
where they are fixed by means of steel brackets to
a torsional tube. The roof glazing is made up of
1.9 to 2.5 m long and 4.8 m wide laminated sheets
(2 × 15 mm toughened glass) which are fixed at
the junctions in the cantilevered beams.

Die gespannte Konstruktion mit Glasrohren zeigt die Druckfestigkeit von Glas.
«Tensegrity»-Konstruktion, Glasstec '96, Düsseldorf, Studenten S. Gose und P. Teuffel, begleitet von J. Achenbach, Institut für Baukonstruktion und Entwerfen 2, Prof. S. Behling, und Institut für Konstruktion und Entwurf II, Prof. Dr.-Ing. Dr. h. c. J. Schlaich, Universität Stuttgart.
This tensile structure with glass tubes shows the compression strength of glass.
"Tensegrity", Glasstec '96, Düsseldorf, designed by the students S. Gose and P. Teuffel, in collaboration with J. Achenbach, Institut für Baukonstruktion und Entwerfen 2, Prof. S. Behling,
and Institut für Konstruktion und Entwurf II,
Prof. Dr.-Ing. Dr. h. c. J. Schlaich, Stuttgart University.

Weitere Experimente zielen darauf ab, die hohe Druckfestigkeit von Glas optimal einzusetzen.
Die Studenten S. Gose und P. Teuffel, begleitet von J. Achenbach, Institut für Baukonstruktion und Entwerfen 2, Prof. S. Behling, und dem Institut für Konstruktion und Entwurf II, Prof. Dr.-Ing. Dr. h. c. J. Schlaich, Universität Stuttgart, haben an der Glasstec '96 in Düsseldorf eine «tensegrity»-Konstruktion vorgestellt, bei der sie für die Druckglieder Glasrohre mit 135 mm Durchmesser und 6 mm Wandstärke verwendeten.
Der Entwurf orientiert sich am Vorbild der «tensional-tensegrity»-Konstruktion des amerikanischen Ingenieurs R. Buckminster Fuller.
Auf diesen positiven Erfahrungen aufbauend, hat der Verfasser zusammen mit J. Achenbach am genannten Lehrstuhl mit den Studenten einige Projekte über «tensegrity»-Konstruktionen weiterbearbeitet.

M. Kutterer und F. Meier vom Institut für Leichte Flächentragwerke, IL, Universität Stuttgart, haben an der Glasstec '98 in Düsseldorf den «Glasbogen 2» vorgestellt.
Die Konstruktion besteht aus vierzehn 1.64 × 4 m großen VSG-Scheiben (2 × 10 mm TVG), die im Randbereich durch drei 12 mm starke TVG-Streifen mit Stahleinlagen verstärkt sind. Für die Stabilisierung sorgt eine radiale Abspannung über die Keilknoten.

Further experiments are aimed at making optimum use of the high compression strength of glass. Students S. Gose and P. Teuffel, accompanied by J. Achenbach, Institut für Baukonstruktion und Entwerfen 2, Prof. S. Behling, and the Institut für Konstruktion und Entwurf II, Prof. Dr. Dr. h. c. J. Schlaich at Stuttgart University presented a "tensegrity" construction at Glasstec '96 in Düsseldorf. For the compression members in this construction they used glass tubes of 135 mm diameter and 6 mm wall thickness. The design was inspired by the "tensional-tensegrity" construction of the American engineer R. Buckminster Fuller.
Building upon these positive experiences, the

Eine Bogenkonstruktion zeigt die Druckfestigkeit von Glasplatten.
Glasbogen 2, Glasstec '98, Düsseldorf, M. Kutterer und F. Meier, Institut für Leichte Flächentragwerke, IL, Prof. Dr.-Ing. W. Sobek, Universität Stuttgart.
An arch structure shows the compression strength of glass panes.
"Glasbogen 2" (Glass Arch 2), Glasstec '98, Düsseldorf, M. Kutterer and F. Meier, Institut für Leichte Flächentragwerke, IL,
Prof. Dr.-Ing. W. Sobek, Stuttgart University.

Bei der Glaskuppel wird die Druckfestigkeit einer
Glasscheibe maximal genutzt.
Glaskuppel, Glasstec '98, Düsseldorf, Seele,
Gersthofen, Deutschland.
A glass dome makes maximum use of the
compression strength of a pane of glass.
Glass Dome, Glasstec '98, Düsseldorf, Seele,
Gersthofen, Germany.

Bei der Demontage der Ausstellung wurde der
Bogen mit verschiedenen Belastungen bis zur
Zerstörung ausgetestet.

Ebenfalls an der Glasstec '98 hat die Firma
Seele, Gersthofen (Deutschland), eine Glaskuppel mit 12.3 m Durchmesser und 2.5 m Stichhöhe vorgestellt, bei der dreieckige VSG-Scheiben (2 × 10 mm TVG) mit 1.1 m Kantenlänge
tragend eingesetzt sind.
Die Glasscheiben sind an den Spitzen mit runden
Klemmtellern aus Edelstahl zusammengehalten
und durch ein Netz aus Edelstahlseilen in drei
Ebenen vorgespannt.
Die Stahlseile sind an einem ringförmigen Stahlrohr verankert und verhindern das Ausbeulen
der Glaskuppel.

Alle diese Beispiele illustrieren den Trend zur
Entwicklung möglichst filigraner und transparenter Glaskonstruktionen, bei denen das
Material Glas selber herangezogen wird, um
tragende Funktionen zu übernehmen.

author, together with J. Achenbach and students
of the above-named institute, carried out further
project work on "tensegrity" constructions.

M. Kutterer and F. Meier from the Institut für
Leichte Flächentragwerke, IL, at Stuttgart University, presented "Glasbogen 2" (glass arch 2) at
Glasstec '98 in Düsseldorf. The construction
consists of fourteen 1.64 × 4 m laminated glass
panes (2 × 10 mm heat-strengthened glass)
which are strengthened at their edges by three
12 mm thick heat-strengthened glass strips with
steel inlays. Stiffening comes from radial
tensioning via the wedge-shaped joints. When
dismantling the exhibition the arch was tested
under various loads, to destruction point.

Also presented at Glasstec '98 was a glass dome
built by Seele of Gersthofen (Germany). The
dome measured 12.3 m in diameter and stood
2.5 m at the rise; triangular panes of laminated
glass (2 × 10 mm heat-strengthened glass), with
1.1 m sides, were used as a load-bearing structure. The glass panes are held together at their
corners by round clamping plates of stainless
steel and by a posttensioned network of stainless
steel cables arranged in three planes. The steel
cables are anchored to a ring-shaped steel tube
and thus prevent the glass dome bowing out.

All these examples illustrate the trend towards
developing ever more transparent structures in
glass, of ever more filigree appearance, using the
material glass itself in a load-carrying capacity.

Die Glasscheibe   The Glass Pane

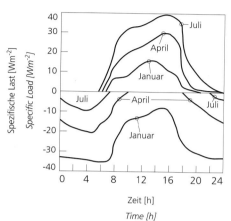

Gegenüberstellung der Wärmegewinne und -verluste verschiedener Monate des Jahres.
Comparison of heat gains and losses for different months of the year.

Linke Seite: Das «Dichroic Glass Field» ist eine lichtstreuende und reflektierende Verglasung mit senkrecht auskragenden Lamellen aus dichroitischem Glas, die das Licht je nach Einfallswinkel in wechselnde Komplementärfarben brechen.
«Dichroic Glass Field», New York, 1995,
James Carpenter Design Associates.
Left page: The "dichroic glass field" is a light-scattering, reflecting structure of vertical louvres of dichroic glass which refract the light into complementary colours according to the angle of incidence.
"Dichroic Glass Field", New York, 1995,
James Carpenter Design Associates.

Eine Glashülle bestimmt sowohl den Einfall an Licht- und Wärmestrahlung in ein Gebäude als auch deren Austritt. Die für die Heizlast maßgebenden Wärmeverluste werden bei Bürobauten allmählich unbedeutender, weil einerseits der Wärmedurchgangskoeffizient mit der fortschreitenden Glastechnologie laufend gesenkt werden konnte, andererseits die im Raum selber entstehende Abwärme durch Personen, Beleuchtung und Geräte den Wärmeverlust oft übertrifft. Hochrechnungen haben gezeigt, daß sogar im Januar, im Monat der höchsten Verluste, Gewinne durch die Sonnenstrahlung und die innere Abwärme erzielt werden können. Hinsichtlich der Kühllasten sind Licht- und Wärmegewinne unterschiedlich zu betrachten. Während eine maximale Ausnutzung der Tagesbelichtung anzustreben ist, muß gleichzeitig eine Reduktion des Wärmeeinfalls stattfinden. Damit sind die an eine Fassade gestellten Anforderungen teilweise entgegengesetzter Art und bedingen die Entwicklung anpassungsfähiger Glashüllen.
Diese Anforderungen können auf unterschiedliche Weise erfüllt werden:
– beim Einfachglas durch die Zusammensetzung der Glasmasse und/oder durch die Veränderung der Eigenschaften ihrer Oberfläche;
– bei einem mehrschichtigen Aufbau, wie bei Verbund-, Isolier- und Mehrfachisoliergläsern, durch die Addition einzelner Funktionsschichten;
– beim Aufbau einer Fassade durch die Kombination mit zusätzlichen Sonnen- und Wärmeschutzmaßnahmen.
In der Regel unterscheidet man zwischen passiven, nicht steuerbaren Maßnahmen und aktiven, steuerbaren Maßnahmen. Erstere weisen feste Eigenschaften auf (z. B. Beschichtungen) und ermöglichen somit keine Anpassung an die wechselnden Jahres- und Wetterverhältnisse. Aktiv steuerbare Maßnahmen arbeiten mit beweglichen Beschattungssystemen, sowohl mit

A glass skin determines the levels of light and heat both entering or leaving a building. Heat losses, critical for the building's heat load, are becoming less and less significant in office buildings because on the one hand the heat loss transmission coefficient has been reduced through advances in glass technology and on the other hand the heat generated by the room's occupants, lighting and equipment is often greater than the heat loss. Simulations have shown that even in January, the month with the highest heat losses, solar radiation and waste heat from within the building can produce net heat gains.
In terms of cooling loads, light and heat gains have to be considered separately. While maximum exploitation of daylight is desirable, at the same time a reduction must be achieved in solar heat gain.
The technical requirements of a façade are thus in part conflicting and determine the development of adaptable glass skins.
The requirements can be met in a number of ways:
– in the case of single-glazing, through the composition of the base glass and/or through changing the surface properties;
– in the case of multi-layered constructions, such as laminated glass, insulating glass and multiple glazed units, through the addition of various interlayers to achieve specific performances or properties;
– in façade constructions, through combining glazing with additional solar and heat insulation measures.
Generally a distinction is made between passive, non-controllable measures and active, controllable measures. The first group is characterised by fixed properties (e. g. surface coatings) and as such do not allow for adaptation to changing seasons and weather conditions.

traditionellen Produkten, wie Lamellen oder Gitterstoffstoren, als auch mit moderneren, wie integrierten Rollosystemen mit IR-reflektierenden Folien usw. Sie können manuell von den Benutzern oder automatisch von einer zentralen Gebäudeleittechnik (GLT) geregelt werden. Noch nicht ganz ausgereift sind aktiv steuerbare Systeme, die auf der Basis von physikalischen und chemischen Eigenschaftsveränderungen im mikroskopischen und molekularen Maßstab funktionieren.

Actively controllable measures work with adjustable shading systems, both with traditional products, such as louvres or screening blinds, as well as more modern products such as integrated roller blind systems with infrared-reflecting surfaces, etc. These can be operated manually by the users or automatically by a central building management system (BMS). Still undergoing technical improvement are actively controllable systems which operate on the basis of changes in physical and chemical properties at the microscopic or molecular level.

Glasmasse

Sand ist der wichtigste Rohstoff für die Glasherstellung; er enthält stets kleine Verunreinigungen, meistens Eisenoxide, die Verfärbungen bewirken. Der leichte Grünstich einer Glasscheibe ist auf einen Gehalt unter 0.1 % an Eisenoxid zurückzuführen. Der Gesamttransmissionsgrad variiert nach Glasdicke. Typische Kennwerte einer 4 mm dicken Scheibe sind τ 0.90 und g 0.87 (SGG Planilux®).

Base Glass

Sand is the most important raw material in the manufacture of glass; it always contains a small amount of impurities, mostly iron oxide, which produce colour tints. The faint green tint in a pane of glass is due to a 0.1 % content of iron oxide. Total transmittance varies according to the thickness of the glass. Typical values of a 4 mm thick pane of glass are τ 0.90 and g 0.87 (SGG Planilux®).

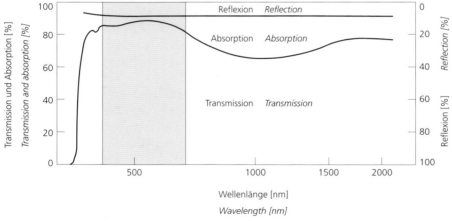

Spektrale Transmission eines üblichen Floatglases.
Spectral transmission properties of standard float glass.

Weißes Glas

Wegen der Nachfrage für die Herstellung von Solarkollektoren sind seit einiger Zeit reinere, eisenärmere Glasscheiben, das sogenannte «weiße Glas», auf dem Markt erhältlich. Die notwendige Reinheit der Zusammensetzung wird durch eine zusätzliche chemische Reinigung des Grundstoffs erreicht. Im Vergleich zu gewöhnlichem Glas verschieben sich die Kennwerte einer 4 mm dicken Scheibe auf τ 0.92 und g 0.90 (SGG-Diamant®).

Clear-White Glass

Increased demand from the manufacturers of solar collectors has led to the greater market availability of "clear-white glass" or architectural clear glass, i. e. purer panes of glass with less iron content. The required pure mix is achieved by additional chemical cleaning of the base materials. In contrast to ordinary glass panes transmittance values for a 4 mm thick pane of architectural clear glass are τ 0.92 and g 0.90 (SGG-Diamant®).

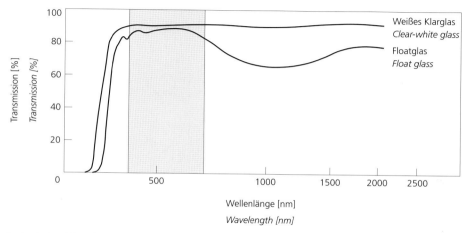

Spektrale Durchlässigkeit eines üblichen Floatglases, verglichen mit derjenigen eines weißen Glases.
Comparison of spectral transmission properties between standard float glass and clear-white glass.

Gefärbtes Glas

Der Zusatz von Metalloxiden in der Glasmasse führt zu einer stärkeren Einfärbung, die eine höhere Absorption und somit eine Aufheizung bewirkt. Da die Wärmeabgabe nach innen nur ein Drittel beträgt, erfolgt eine Reduktion des Strahlungsdurchgangs. Nachteilig wirkt sich die zum Teil starke Aufheizung der absorbierenden Gläser aus, die im Innenraum oft als unangenehm empfunden wird. Eingefärbte Scheiben werden häufig beim Fahrzeugbau verwendet, weil hier der Fahrtwind eine wirksame Kühlung gewährleistet.

Die Farbpalette der eingefärbten Gläser wird stark durch das angewandte Herstellungsverfahren eingeschränkt. Da eine Floatglas-Anlage auf die Produktion von großen Mengen ausgerichtet ist, sind die Farben heute auf Grün, Rosa, Blau, Bronze und Grau reduziert.

Body Tinted Glass

The addition of metal oxides to the base glass leads to a stronger tint which produces a higher ratio of absorption and a resulting increase in the temperature of the glass. As heat transmission to the inside of the building is only one third, there is a reduction in solar energy transmission. A disadvantage of this absorbing glass is the often noticeable increase in temperature of the glass itself which is perceived to be unpleasant. Body tinted panes are often used in car manufacture because here the airstream when the vehicle is in motion serves to produce a cooling effect.

The range of tints available is considerably restricted by the manufacturing process used. As float glass manufacturing installations are designed for the manufacture of large quantities, the only colour tints available at present are green, pink, blue, bronze and grey.

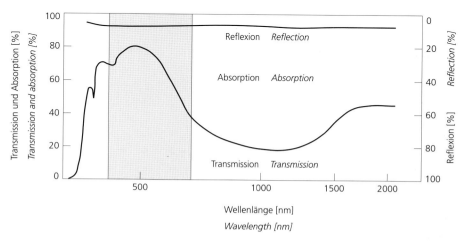

Spektrale Transmission eines grün eingefärbten Glases.
Spectral transmission properties of green body tinted glass.

33

Die grünen Gläser finden die größte Verbreitung. Sie sind für das nahe Infrarot nur wenig durchlässig, weil das Eisenoxid den Strahlungsbereich mit Wellenlängen von 700 bis 2500 nm besonders absorbiert.

Grau getönte Gläser, durch den Zusatz von Nickeloxid, und bronzefarbene Gläser, durch den Zusatz von Selen, werden zur Dämpfung der Helligkeit eingesetzt.

Heute sind aus ökologischen Gründen Fassaden aus Einfachglas für beheizte Gebäude wegen des Wärmeverlustes nicht mehr vertretbar. Sie werden aber für Überdachungen oder für unbeheizte Räume wie Ausstellungsgebäude, Wintergärten und Pufferzonen verwendet.

Die im Juli 1994 eingeweihte Waterloo International Station, Londoner Endstation der Ärmelkanal-Linie, liefert ein eindrückliches Beispiel einer einfachverglasten Halle. Die Tragstruktur des Daches wurde von Nicholas Grimshaw und Partnern mit dem Ingenieur Antony Hunt von YRM Antony Hunt Associates entwickelt. Die flache Drei-Gelenk-Konstruktion besteht aus gebogenen Dreigurtträgern mit einem seitwärts verschobenen Mittelgelenk und Spannweiten

Green-tinted glass is the most widely used. It only transmits low levels of the near infrared range because the iron oxide in the glass is a particularly good absorber of radiation in wavelengths from 700 to 2500 nm.

Grey-tinted glass, achieved by adding nickel oxide, and bronze-tinted glass, produced by adding selenium, are used to reduce glare.

Today, for ecological reasons, façades made of single glazing are no longer acceptable for use on heated buildings. However, they are still used for canopies or for unheated rooms such as exhibition halls, winter gardens and buffer zones.

An impressive example of a single-glazed hall is the London terminus of the Channel Tunnel rail link – the new Waterloo International Station, officially opened in July 1994. The support structure of the roof was developed by Nicholas Grimshaw & Partners in association with the structural engineer Anthony Hunt of YRM Anthony Hunt Associates. Essentially it is a flattened 3-pin arch construction consisting of curved trusses with the center pin displaced to one side. The roof spans decrease from 50 m to 35 m. The asymmetric structure is a response

Die asymmetrische Gestalt des Daches wird durch die Verglasung im Bereich des kürzeren Bogenabschnitts hervorgehoben.
«Waterloo International Station», London, 1994, Nicholas Grimshaw und Partner.
The asymmetrical design of the roof is underlined by the curved glass wall marking the shorter section of the arch.
Waterloo International Station, London, 1994, Nicholas Grimshaw and Partners.

Die Drei-Gelenk-Konstruktion besteht aus gebogenen Dreigurtträgern mit seitwärts verschobenem Mittelgelenk; der kürzere Dreigurtträger mit außenliegendem Zuggurt; Detail der Glasbefestigung und der Neopren-Dichtung.
«Waterloo International Station», London, 1994, Nicholas Grimshaw und Partner.

The 3-pin arch construction consists of curved trusses with the centre pin displaced to one side; the shorter truss with the tension rods on the outside; detail of the glass fixing and neoprene joint.
Waterloo International Station, London, 1994, Nicholas Grimshaw and Partners.

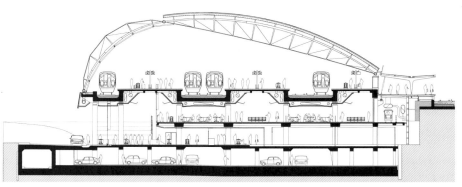

von 35 m bis 50 m. Die asymmetrische Struktur ist von der zu einem früheren Zeitpunkt geplanten außenliegenden Geleiseführung und von einer städtebaulichen Einschränkung in der Bauhöhe maßgebend geprägt worden. Ihre Gestalt ist durch die Verglasung im Bereich des kürzeren Bogenabschnitts besonders hervorgehoben. Diese Glaswand weist einen komplexen Aufbau auf, der auf die wechselnden Spannweiten der Bogenträger und den unregelmäßigen Verlauf der Geleise zurückzuführen ist. Da ein übliches System Tausende verschieden geformter und unterschiedlich großer Scheiben erfordert hätte, wurde eine schuppenartige Konstruktion mit lockeren Befestigungen entwickelt. Die 10 mm starken vorgespannten Glasscheiben sind auf der Längsseite mit Aluminiumprofilen versehen, die durch Stiftverbindungen das Einhängen an die tragenden Pfosten sichern und die Halterungsnut für eine ziehharmonikaartige Neopren-Dichtung liefern. Die Überlappung in Querrichtung ist ebenfalls durch ein

to the predetermined line of the tracks, and to specific local building regulations restricting height. The design is underlined on the curved glass wall marking the shorter section of the arch. Here the complexity is increased due to the varying span widths of the arched girders and the irregular line of the tracks.

A conventional system would have entailed using thousands of differently shaped and sized panes of glass and so, to avoid this, an imbricated structure was developed with flexible fixing points. The longer sides of the 10 mm thick toughened glass panes are mounted in aluminium profiles which are attached via pin connections to the support posts; these profiles also provide the mounting groove for the concertina-like neoprene seal. Overlapping junctions in a horizontal direction are enabled by further aluminium profiles with a sealing lip. In addition to allowing a high degree of standardisation this system also permits independent movement of all glass panes, an aspect which is essential

Aluminiumprofil mit einem lippenförmigen Dichtungsstreifen gewährleistet. Außer einem Höchstmaß an Standardisierung sichert das entwickelte System eine unabhängige Beweglichkeit aller Glasplatten, was infolge auftretender Windlasten, thermischer Ausdehnungen der Stahlkonstruktion und Torsionen der Plattform durch die einfahrenden Züge notwendig ist.

Die drei 1991 errichteten Aufzugstürme des Museums für Moderne Kunst «Reina Sofia» in Madrid sind mit einem klaren Floatglas umhüllt. Die Lösung entspricht der Vorgabe der Architekten J. L. Iñiguez und A. Vázquez an die Glasberater Ian Ritchie Architects, ein leichtes und sehr transparentes Volumen als Kontrapunkt zu der bestehenden massiven Fassade zu schaffen. Als Alternative zu klarem Glas stand auch eingefärbtes Glas zur Diskussion, aber die Computersimulationen der zu erwartenden Erwärmung infolge Absorption und sekundärer Wärmeabgabe zeigten, daß diese Lösung mehr Nachteile als Vorteile gebracht hätte. Die Glashülle besteht aus vorgespannten, 12 mm starken und 2.96 × 1.83 m großen Scheiben. Sie sind einzeln an der außenliegenden vorgespannten Edelstahlkonstruktion aufgehängt. Die punktförmige Hauptbefestigung erfolgt mit einer modifizierten Version des 905 Planar®-Systems am Kopf einer besonders gestalteten Konsole («Delphin»), die wegen der knappen Bauzeit mittels Laserschneidetechnik anstatt des Gußverfahrens gefertigt wurde. In den vier Ecken befinden sich weitere Befestigungspunkte,

under the conditions produced by wind loads, thermal expansion of the steel construction and torsions in the platform slab by trains entering and leaving.

The three lift towers built in 1991 at the "Reina Sofia" Museum of Modern Art in Madrid are enclosed in clear float glass. The design, produced by the glass specialist Ian Ritchie Architects in accordance with guidelines laid down by the architects, J. L. Iñiguez and A. Vázquez, represents the latter's wish for a light, very transparent volume as a counterpoint to the solid appearance of the existing façades. As an alternative to clear glass, tinted glass was considered, but computer modelling of the expected heating effect showed that absorption and reradiation would have resulted in more disadvantages than advantages. The glass skin consists of large toughened panes, 12 mm thick and 2.96 × 1.83 in size. They are suspended individually from the external system of prestressed stainless steel rods. Using a modified version of the 905 Planar® system, the panes are bolted to the head of a specially designed bracket, the "Dolphin", which, because of time pressure, was produced by laser-cutting and not by casting. At the four corners are further fixing points which transmit horizontal wind loads via stainless steel spacers to the concrete support structure on the interior. A 12 mm wide joint separates each pane of glass for the purposes of thermal expansion, wind loads and breakage. The hierarchy of the design concept can be seen in the choice of materials: concrete for the

Die Aufzugstürme sind mit einer Hülle aus klarem Floatglas versehen; Edelstahlteile für die Glasbefestigung: oben die tragende Konsole für die Aufhängung einer Scheibe, «Delphin», unten der Abstandhalter für die horizontalen Windlasten.
Museum für Moderne Kunst «Reina Sofia», Madrid, 1991, Ian Ritchie Architects.
The lift towers are enclosed in a clear float glass skin; stainless steel elements for the fixings: above the glass support bracket, the "Dolphin", and below the spacer transmitting the horizontal wind loads. Reina Sofia Museum of Modern Art, Madrid, 1991, Ian Ritchie Architects.

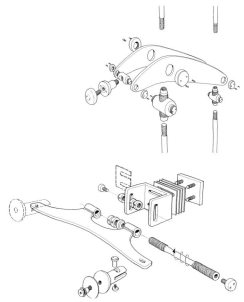

welche die horizontalen Windlasten über Abstandhalter aus Edelstahl auf die innenliegende Tragkonstruktion aus Stahlbeton übertragen. Eine 12 mm breite Fuge gewährleistet die Autonomie jeder Glasscheibe hinsichtlich thermischer Ausdehnung, Windlasten und Bruch.

Die Hierarchie des Gestaltungskonzeptes spiegelt sich in der Materialwahl: Beton für die Tragstruktur, Edelstahl für die Aufhängekonstruktion und Glas für den Raumabschluß.

Eine konkave Glaswand bildet den Raumabschluß des 1992 fertiggestellten Verwaltungs- und Druckereigebäudes der «Western Morning News» in Plymouth, England. Die von Nicholas Grimshaw und Partnern entworfene Fassade paßt sich der umliegenden hügeligen Landschaft an und weckt mit ihrem schiffartigen Aussehen Assoziationen an die Seefahrtstradition der Stadt. Gleichzeitig übernimmt sie die Funktion eines riesigen Werbeschilds. Da die Fassadenneigung die Spiegelungen reduziert und die Transparenz des Gebäudes steigert, genießen die Passanten auf der Straße auch tagsüber eine eindrückliche Sicht auf die laufenden Druckmaschinen.

Die Glashülle ist an den außenliegenden, leicht gebogenen Masten, den «Stoßzähnen», punktförmig aufgehängt. Ihre Geometrie wurde folgendermaßen festgelegt: Im Bereich des «Hecks» liegt der Glaseinteilung ein orthogonaler Raster

frame, stainless steel for the glazing support structure, and glass for the building skin.

A concave glass wall encompasses the administration building and printing works of the Western Morning News in Plymouth, England. The shape of this façade, designed by Nicholas Grimshaw & Partners, echoes the surrounding hilly landscape, and at the same time its nautical shape hints at the town's seafaring tradition. It functions, too, as an enormous advertisement for the company. As the angle of the façade has the effect of reducing reflections, it is easy to see into the building and, especially during the day, passers-by are afforded an impressive view of the printing machines in operation. The glass skin is suspended at intervals from the lightly curved masts – the building's "tusks" – positioned on the building's exterior. The geometry was defined as follows: near to the "stern" the glazing follows a 2 × 2 m orthogonal grid; near the "prow" are two segments of a circle, 70 m radius in plan and 21.5 m in section, as in a double-curved toroid. This enabled one or two simplifications in the manufacturing and erection stages, as each glass pane is identical to the ones on either side of it, and the radius of curvature can be changed into a sequence of polygons. The 12 mm thick and 2 × 2 m large, toughened glass panes are bolted at the corners to cross-shaped fixing junctions. As they are at-

Die konkave Glasfassade reduziert die Spiegelung und steigert damit die Transparenz.
«Western Morning News», Plymouth, England, 1992, Nicholas Grimshaw und Partner.
The concave glass façade reduces reflection and increases the transparency of the building skin.
Western Morning News, Plymouth, England, 1992, Nicholas Grimshaw and Partners.

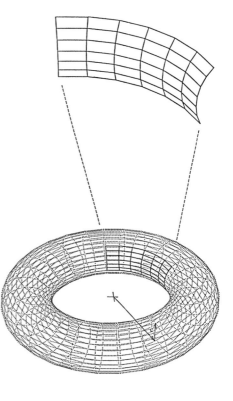

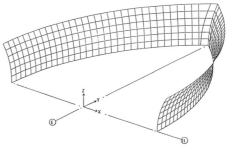

mit einer Maschenweite von 2×2 m zugrunde. Im Bereich des «Bugs» sind zwei Kreissegmente, mit einem Radius von 70 m im Grundriß und von 21.5 m im Schnitt, maßgebend, was einem Ausschnitt einer doppelgekrümmten Translationsfläche eines Torus entspricht. Das führt zu einigen Vereinfachungen hinsichtlich der Herstellung und der Montage der Fassade, da jede Glasscheibe identisch mit ihren horizontal angrenzenden Nachbarn ist und der Krümmungsradius in einen polygonalen Verlauf umgewandelt werden kann.

Die 12 mm starken und etwa 2×2 m großen vorgespannten Glasscheiben sind bei den Ecken an kreuzförmige Befestigungsknoten geschraubt. Da

tached to the top of the "tusks" via steel tie bars, vertical forces are directed upwards, while horizontal forces are transmitted to the masts via lateral cantilevers made of spheroidal graphite cast iron. The separation of support members to transfer vertical and horizontal loads is strongly reminiscent of the façade of the Financial Times printing works, built by Nicholas Grimshaw & Partners in 1988 in the London Docklands. The same distribution of forces is translated here into a distinct organic form.

The rehearsal and concert hall of the Philharmonic Chamber Orchestra of the Netherlands is housed within one fully glazed structure inside

Die Glashülle ist an den leicht nach außen gebogenen Masten, den «Stoßzähnen», abgehängt. Im Bereich des «Bugs» wurde die Einteilung der Scheiben gemäß der Geometrie eines Torus festgelegt.
«Western Morning News», Plymouth, England, 1992, Nicholas Grimshaw und Partner.
The glass skin is suspended from the slightly curved masts, the "tusks". The geometry of the glass panes near the "prow" was defined by a double-curved toroid.
Western Morning News, Plymouth, England, 1992, Nicholas Grimshaw and Partners.

sie an der Spitze der «Stoßzähne» mit Zugstangen aus Edelstahl aufgehängt sind, werden die vertikalen Kräfte nach oben abgeleitet, während die horizontalen Kräfte über seitliche Ausleger aus Kugelstahlgraphit auf die Masten übertragen werden. Die Trennung in Traglieder zur Abtragung der vertikalen und horizontalen Lasten erinnert stark an die Fassade der «Financial Times»-Druckerei, die Nicholas Grimshaw und Partner 1988 in den Londoner Docklands errichtet haben. Der gleiche Kräfteverlauf ist hier nun in eine ausgeprägt organische Form umgesetzt.

Der Probe- und Konzertsaal des Niederländischen Philharmonischen Kammerorchesters ist in einem vollverglasten Baukörper in der ehemaligen Amsterdamer Börse von Hendrik P. Berlage untergebracht. Der Entwurf der Architekten Pieter Zaanen & Associates, 1990, löst das akustische Problem der Nachbarschaft zweier Konzertsäle sehr elegant, ohne den Charakter des historischen Gebäudes durch schalldämmende Paneele an den Wänden zu verändern. Die Struktur besteht aus sechs innenliegenden kreuzförmigen Stahlstützen, mit Kreuzverbänden abgespannt, welche ein Raumfachwerk tragen. Während die gekurvte Glaswand, der «Cellobauch», an einer außenliegenden Konstruktion mit Rohrprofilen befestigt ist, hängen die drei geraden Glaswände von der Dachkonstruktion herunter. Die oberen Glas-

the former Amsterdam Stock Exchange designed by Hendrik P. Berlage. The design, drawn up in 1990 by the architects Pieter Zaanen & Associates, elegantly solves the acoustic problems created by the juxtaposition of two concert halls without the need to alter the historic character of the building by adding sound insulating panels to the walls. The structure consists of six, internally placed, cruciform steel columns, guyed with cross bracing, which support a space frame. While the "cello-shaped" curved glass wall is attached to an external tubular steel support structure, the three vertical glass walls are suspended from the top of the space frame. Each of the upper glass panes are attached via two bolted fixings. They carry the weight of the further four sheets below them, all attached to each other, like a coat of chain mail, by cross-shaped Quatro®joints (Octatube Space Structures Inc.). The toughened glass panels are grey-tinted, 8 mm thick and 180 × 180 cm in size; joints are 8–10 mm wide and stabilised with a vertical, tensile structure. An interesting effect is produced by different lighting situations: when the hall is not in use, the glass skin reflects the surrounding pale brick walls and the glass cube appears as a solid body. Yet as soon as the interior lighting is on, it appears light and transparent. The reverse is experienced from inside the cube – when the outside lights are put out, one is only aware of the space inside the glass cube.

Der vollverglaste Baukörper löst ein akustisches Problem, ohne den Charakter des historischen Gebäudes zu verändern (links); die hängenden Glaswände sind durch eine gespannte Konstruktion stabilisiert (rechts).
Probe- und Konzertsaal in der Amsterdamer Börse, 1990, Pieter Zaanen & Associates.
The fully glazed structure solves an acoustic problem without altering the character of the historic building (left); the suspended glazing is stabilized by a vertical tensile structure (right).
Rehearsal and Concert Hall in the Amsterdam Stock Exchange, 1990, Pieter Zaanen & Associates.

scheiben werden am Dachrand von zwei punktförmigen Schraubverbindungen gehalten. Sie tragen das Gewicht der weiteren vier darunterliegenden Platten, die durch die kreuzförmigen
Quatro®-Knoten (Octatube Space Structures
Inc.) wie ein Kettenhemd miteinander verbunden sind. Die Verglasung besteht aus grau getönten, 8 mm dicken und 180×180 cm großen vorgespannten Glasscheiben mit einer Fugenbreite
von 8–10 mm und wird durch eine
vertikalgestellte, gespannte Konstruktion stabilisiert.
Sehr interessant ist die Wechselwirkung, die sich
je nach Beleuchtungssituation einstellt: Wenn
der Saal nicht benutzt wird und die Glashülle die
umliegenden hellen Backsteinwände spiegelt,
wirkt der Glaskubus als fester Baukörper. Er
wirkt dagegen leicht und transparent, sobald die
Innenbeleuchtung eingeschaltet wird. Eine umgekehrte Situation erlebt man von innen, wenn
das Licht außerhalb gelöscht wird und plötzlich
nur der Raum innerhalb des Glaskubus wahr-
nehmbar ist.

Photosensitives Glas

Eine besondere Entwicklung im Bereich der
Einfärbung der Glasmasse stellen photosensitive
Gläser dar, wie Louverre®, das die Corning Glass,
New York, unter Mitwirkung des Glasspezialisten
James Carpenter 1983 auf den Markt gebracht
hat. Dieses winkelabhäng-durchsichtige Glas
besitzt sowohl die Eigenschaft der Transparenz
als auch die Sonnenschutzwirkung kleiner Jalousien. Die 1 mm dicken Lamellenstreifen haben
untereinander einen Abstand von 3 mm. Ihre
Winkeleinstellung wird bei der Herstellung bestimmt. Dazu wird die Glasplatte zuerst mit einer
gelochten Vorlage abgedeckt und mit UV-Licht im
ausgewählten Winkel bestrahlt, danach in einem
Ofen erwärmt. Dadurch entsteht eine lamellen-
förmige Struktur im Glas, die eine Lichttransmission von 0.16–0.30 und eine Gesamtdurchlässigkeit von 0.35–0.44 aufweist.
Der Architekt Norman Foster wollte die Fassade
der «Hongkong und Shanghai Bank» mit
Louverre® ausstatten. In letzter Minute entschloß
sich die Bauherrschaft – wahrscheinlich aus
Kostengründen – leider anders.

Phototropes Glas

Die Eigenschaften von gefärbten Gläsern sind
nicht veränderbar. Dagegen stellen die phototropen Gläser ein selbstregelndes System dar, da

Muster des photosensitiven Glases Louverre® von
Corning Glass werden in den Fassadenprototyp ein-
gesetzt.
«Hongkong and Shanghai Bank», Hongkong,
1979–86, Foster und Partner.
Prototypes of Louverre® photosensitive glass by
Corning Glass are installed in the façade mock-up.
Hongkong and Shanghai Bank, Hong Kong,
1979–86, Foster and Partners.

Photosensitive Glass

Photosensitive glass is a special development in
tinting base glass. One example is Louverre®, in-
troduced onto the market in 1983 by Corning
Glass, New York, in collaboration with the glass
specialist James Carpenter.
This louvred clear glass combines in a single
pane the qualities of transparence and the solar
shading effect of narrow slatted blinds. The
1 mm thick louvre strips are spaced at 3 mm
and their angle of tilt is defined at the manufacturing stage. The process consists of placing a
template of horizontal slots over the glass sheet,
then exposing the sheet to UV collimated light
at the selected angle; the glass is then heated
in a leer. This creates a louvre-shaped structure within the glass giving overall values for
light transmittance of 0.16–0.30 and a total
solar heat transmittance of 0.35–0.44.
The architect Norman Foster wanted to use Lou-
verre® to clad the façade of the Hongkong and
Shanghai Bank. Sadly the client decided against
it at the last minute – probably for reasons of
cost.

Photochromic Glass

The properties of body tinted glass are un-
changeable, whereas photochromic glass is
self-adjusting, in that the light transmission
decreases automatically in response to exposure
to ultraviolet or short-wave visible light. The
photochromic process is based on a reversible

Spektrale Transmission des phototropen Glases von Corning Glass.

Spectral transmission properties of a Corning Glass photochromic glass pane.

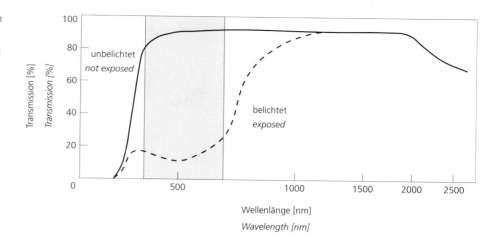

die Lichtdurchlässigkeit sich automatisch durch die Bestrahlung mit ultraviolettem oder kurzwelligem sichtbarem Licht vermindert. Die Phototropie basiert auf einer reversiblen Transformation eingelagerter silberhalogenidhaltiger Ausscheidungen. Braune oder graue phototrope Gläser werden für die Herstellung von Brillen verwendet. Sie weisen einen breiten Transmissionsbereich auf, der zum Beispiel bei den Photosolar® Superbrown-Gläsern nach 15 Minuten Belichtung von 0.91 auf 0.25 reduziert wird. Vorteile sind die lange Lebensdauer und die Beständigkeit gegen chemische Angriffe, Nachteile sind die automatische Abdunkelung sowohl im Sommer als auch im Winter und die damit verbundene Aufheizung der Scheibe.

Für eine Anwendung im Bauwesen sind die Produktionsmöglichkeiten von phototropem Glas heute bezüglich Menge und Dimensionen noch ungenügend.

Um die Preise niedrig zu halten, hat Corning Glass Prototypen mit einer Dicke von 1 mm und einer Fläche von 1 m² zum Auflaminieren entwickelt.

Beschichtungen

Die Eigenschaften des Glases bezüglich Sonnen- und Wärmeschutz hängen von der Strahlungsdurchlässigkeit ab. Sie können durch dünne Schichten aus Edelmetallen und/oder Metalloxiden wesentlich verändert werden. Solche Beschichtungen haben einen Einfluß sowohl auf den Strahlungsbereich als auch auf dessen Intensität.

Reflektierende und selektive Beschichtungen

Ein guter Sonnenschutz wird durch die Verwendung von reflektierenden Beschichtungen erzielt. Eine erhöhte Reflexion führt zu einer Verminde-

transformation taking place in the in-built silver halide crystals. Brown or grey phototropic glass is used in the manufacture of spectacles. It has a wide transmission range, as used in, for example, Photosolar® Superbrown spectacles which after 15 minutes exposure is reduced from 0.91 to 0.25.

The advantages are that the glass is very durable and resistant to chemicals; disadvantages, however, are the automatic darkening both in summer and in winter, and the associated heating up of the glass itself.

For use in building the production of this type of glass is at present still rather limited in terms of quantity and size range.

In an attempt to keep prices down, Corning Glass have developed 1 m² prototypes of 1 mm thickness, which can be used as glass laminates.

Surface Coatings

The properties of glass in terms of solar control and reduced emissivity depend on its level of radiation transmission. This can be changed considerably by the addition of thin layers of precious metals and/or metal oxides. Such coatings affect both the radiation range transmitted and also its intensity.

Reflective and Selective Coatings

Effective solar control can be achieved by the use of reflective coatings.

Increased reflection properties lead to a reduction in the level of transmission, and consequently also to a reduction in the total transmission. At present total energy transmission values g of 0.20 to 0.70, with a daylight transmittance τ of 0.10 to 0.77, are typical for insulated glaz-

41

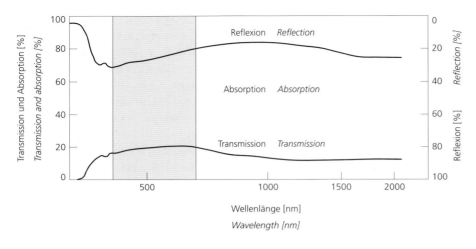

Spektrale Transmission eines reflektiv beschichteten Glases.

Spectral transmission properties of glass with a reflective coating.

rung der Transmission und damit zu einer Reduktion der Gesamtdurchlässigkeit. Zur Zeit sind bei einer Tageslichttransmission τ von 0.10 bis 0.77 Gesamtenergie-Transmissionsgrade g von 0.20 bis 0.70 für Isolierverglasungen üblich in unseren gemäßigten Breiten, da nicht nur der Sonnenschutz maßgebend ist, sondern auch Licht- und Wärmegewinne zu berücksichtigen sind.

Reflektierende Beschichtungen können sowohl auf klares als auch auf gefärbtes Glas aufgetragen werden (SGG Parsol®). Da letzteres per se eine höhere Absorption aufweist, werden tiefere g-Werte erzielt.

Ein besserer Wärmeschutz wird durch niedrigemissive Beschichtungen, die sogenannten «low-E coatings», erreicht. Sie können die Emissivität der Glasoberfläche von e ~ 0.87 bis e ~ 0.04 und damit die Abstrahlung im Infrarotbereich bis auf 20 % reduzieren, ohne die Lichtdurchlässigkeit unter 0.77 zu senken. Die heute auf dem Markt angebotenen Gläser bewegen sich im Bereich zwischen e ~ 0.04 und e ~ 0.16. Sie sind bei den Isoliergläsern besonders wichtig, da die Wärmeabstrahlung bis zu zwei Dritteln des Wärmeverlustes ausmacht. Solche Beschichtungen werden als selektiv bezeichnet, weil sie im sichtbaren Strahlungsbereich weitgehend transmittierend, im infraroten Bereich hingegen stark reflektierend sind. Zur Zeit werden Low-E-Beschichtungen für die Verglasung von Motorfahrzeugen (GM, Ford, Saint-Gobain) intensiv erforscht. Ziel ist, die sonst in den Innenraum eines Fahrzeuges einfallende Wärmestrahlung schon an den Windschutzscheiben reflektieren zu können. Die Entwicklung von hoch-lichtdurchlässigen und gleichzeitig stark IR-reflektierenden Be-

ing used in our latitudes. Not only solar shading but also light and heat gains are factors to be considered in these temperate zones.

Reflective coatings can be applied to both clear glass and tinted glass (SGG Parsol®). As the latter has higher absorption properties to start with, lower g-factors are achieved.

Better thermal insulation is achieved by low emissivity, or low-E coatings. They can reduce the emissivity of the surface of the glass from e ~ 0.87 to e ~ 0.04, thus reducing infrared radiation to 20 %, without bringing the light transmittance down below 0.77. Glass currently available on the market is generally in the area between e ~ 0.04 and e ~ 0.16. This glass is particularly important for insulating glass as heat radiation can account for up to two thirds of the heat loss. Such coatings are referred to as selective because they transmit most of the visible light, but have a high level of reflectance in the infrared range.

At present intense research is being carried out on low-E coatings for use in motor vehicles (GM, Ford, Saint-Gobain). The aim here is, at the level of the windscreen, to reflect the heat radiation normally entering the car interior.

The development of surface coatings which transmit a maximum of light and at the same time have high levels of infrared reflectivity is in tune with current demands placed on glass architecture: fully glazed building skins should ensure both maximum natural lighting and minimum heat loss.

Solar control and reduced emissivity glass is generally used in laminated glass insulating units or multiple glazing units.

schichtungen entspricht auch den Anforderungen, die heute an die Glasarchitektur gestellt werden: Bei vollverglasten Gebäudehüllen soll eine maximale natürliche Belichtung bei minimalem Wärmeverlust gewährleistet werden. Sonnenschutz- und Wärmeschutzgläser werden meistens in mehrschichtigen Konstruktionen, wie Verbund- und Isoliergläsern, verwendet.

Herstellungsverfahren

Die Beschichtungen werden entweder on-line, d. h. unmittelbar nach der Glasherstellung in der Floatanlage, oder off-line, also in einem späteren Arbeitsvorgang, aufgetragen.

On-line werden die Beschichtungen des Typs Hard-coating durch einen Pyrolyseprozeß aufgebracht. Das Ausgangsmaterial wird auf das etwa 600° C warme Floatglasband flüssig oder in Pulverform aufgetragen und eingebrannt. Damit bildet sich auf einer Seite der Glasscheibe eine harte Schicht mit einer Dicke von 100 – 400 nm, welche gegen Abnutzung und chemische Einwirkungen beständig ist. Glasscheiben mit Hard-coating können als Einfachverglasung eingesetzt werden.

Für den Sonnenschutz werden reflektierende Metalloxidschichten, vorwiegend aus Titan, Chrom, Nickel und Eisen, verwendet, die auch absorbierende Funktionen übernehmen können. Typische Kennwerte einer SGG Antelio®-Glasscheibe sind g 0.40 – 0.69 und τ 0.21 – 0.63. Als Wärmeschutzschicht wird fluordotiertes Zinnoxid mit einer Siliziumoxid-Unterschicht verwendet.

Off-line werden die Glasscheiben durch das Tauch- oder das Vakuumverfahren beschichtet.

Manufacturing Process

The surface coatings are applied either on-line, at the end of the float glass manufacturing process, or off-line, at a later point.

Hard coatings are applied on-line by pyrolysis. The base material used for the coating is poured, in liquid or powder form, onto the layer of float glass heated to 600° C and then fired. As a result of this a chemically resistant and durable hard layer, 100 – 400 nm thick, is formed on one side of the glass sheet. Glass panes with hard coatings can be used in single-glazing.

For solar shading layers of reflecting metal oxides are used, mainly titanium, chrome, nickel and iron, which also possess absorbing properties. Typical values for an SGG Antelio® glass pane are g 0.40 – 0.69 and τ 0.21 – 0.63. A layer of fluorine doped zinc oxide on a base of silicon oxide is used to reduce the radiative heat loss.

Off-line coatings are applied to glass panes by dipping them into chemical solutions or under conditions of vacuum. These methods generally, but not always, lead to softer layers, known as soft coatings. Their advantage lies in a greater flexibility in the control of light transmittance and total solar heat transmittance, by specifying composition and thickness of the layers.

In the dipping process, glass is immersed into chemical solutions, slowly extracted and then fired. The coatings, on both sides, are generally of titanium oxide and, in the near infrared range, they are more active through reflection than absorption.

In the vacuum process the coatings are applied to one side either by cathode sputtering or by evaporation in a multi-chamber high-vacuum fa-

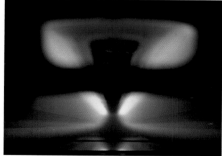

Off-line-Beschichtung in einer Hochvakuum-Anlage und Kathoden-Zerstäubung in der Prozeßkammer bei Glas Trösch, Bützberg, Schweiz.
Off-line coating in a high-vacuum facility and cathode sputtering in a chamber unit at Glas Trösch, Bützberg, Switzerland.

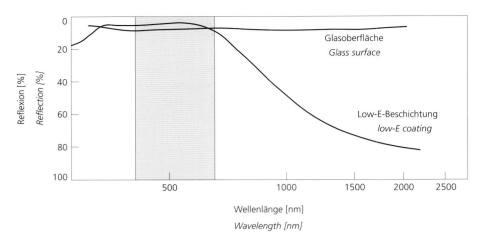

Diese Herstellungsweisen führen meistens, aber nicht immer, zu weicheren Schichten, den sogenannten Soft-coatings. Ihr Vorteil liegt in einer größeren Flexibilität bei der Einstellung der Licht- und Gesamtdurchlässigkeit durch die Wahl von Schichtenaufbau und -dicke. Beim Tauchverfahren werden die Scheiben in bestimmte Lösungen eingetaucht, langsam herausgezogen und anschließend gebrannt. Die beidseitigen Beschichtungen bestehen meistens aus Titanoxid und sind im Infrarot-Bereich hauptsächlich durch Reflexion und weniger durch Absorption aktiv.

Beim Vakuumverfahren werden die Schichten durch Kathoden-Zerstäubung (Sputtern) oder durch Verdampfung in einer Mehrkammern-Hochvakuum-Anlage einseitig auf die Glasscheiben aufgebracht. Soft-coatings bestehen aus 6 bis 9 Einzelschichten, wobei heute die Anlagen oft für 12 – 15 Schichten ausgerüstet sind. Solche Schichten können in beliebigen Dicken (6 – 12 nm) mit sehr hoher Gleichmäßigkeit aufgetragen werden, was insbesondere für eine gute Transparenz erforderlich ist. Die Soft-coatings sind weich und gegen aggressive Luftverschmutzung und mechanische Beanspruchung empfindlich, weshalb sie durch einen Schutzbelag oder durch den Einbau in Isoliergläser geschützt werden. Dennoch sind einige Produkte mit wetter- und abnutzungsbeständigen Beschichtungen erhältlich, zum Beispiel das Sonnenschutzglas SGG Cool-Lite®, welches Einstellungen von τ 0.04 – 0.52 und g 0.08 – 0.46 ermöglicht.

Für den Wärmeschutz werden Low-E-Beschichtungen aus leitfähigen Metallschichten auf der Basis von Gold, Silber, Kupfer und Aluminium verwendet. In den letzten Jahren hat sich als Basis Silber durchgesetzt, weil es eine optimale Farbneutralität bei höchster Lichttransmission bietet (SGG Planitherm®, Silverstar®).

Die Funktionsweise der Low-E-Beschichtungen basiert auf einem Interferenzvorgang, welcher durch Metall- und Metalloxidschichten und deren Reihenfolge und Dicke hervorgerufen wird. Da der mehrschichtige Aufbau einer Low-E-Beschichtung auch die optischen Eigenschaften bezüglich Reflexion und Absorption verändern kann, werden oft die Funktionen von Sonnenschutz und Wärmeschutz kombiniert (SGG Planisol®, Silverstar Combi®). Solche Soft-coatings ermöglichen somit die gleichzeitige Steuerung der Emissivität, der Reflexion, der

cility. Soft coatings consist of 6 to 9 individual layers, but many manufacturers have the capability of producing 12 to 15 layers. The layers can be applied in a range of thicknesses (6 – 12 nm) at a high degree of uniformity, which is essential for good transparence. As soft coatings are susceptible to aggressive air pollution and mechanical stress, they have an additional protective layer or are built into insulated glazing units. However, some weather and stress-resistant soft coatings are available on the market, for example SGG Cool-Lite®, a solar glass which can be manufactured with values of τ 0.04 – 0.52 and g 0.08 – 0.46.

To reduce radiative heat loss, low-E coatings of conductive metal layers basing on gold, silver, copper and aluminium are used. In recent years silver has become popular as a base because it offers optimum colour neutrality as well as high light transmittance (SGG Planitherm®, Silverstar®).

Low-E coatings work by a process of interference, brought about by the succession and various thicknesses of the layers of metals and metal oxides. As the several layers of a low-E coating can also alter the optical properties with respect to reflection and absorption, the functions of solar control and reduced radiative heat loss are often combined (SGG Planisol®, Silverstar Combi®). Such soft coatings thus enable the control of emissivity, reflection, absorption and transmission, and can even determine the colour for both transmission and reflection.

The low-E coatings are just one possibility of a number of different coatings. At present other products are also being manufactured which are based on this process of interference, e. g. cold mirror, anti-reflection and dichroic coatings.

Spektrale Reflexion eines low-E-beschichteten Glases, verglichen mit einem unbehandelten Floatglas.
Spectral reflectance properties of low-E coated glass, compared to untreated float glass.

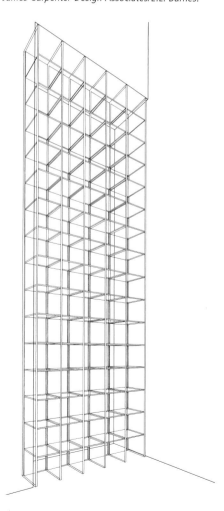

Die vertikalen Glasschwerter sind mit horizontalen dichroitischen Glasscheiben ausgesteift.
«Sweeny Chapel» im «Christian Theological Seminary», Indianapolis, USA, 1985–87, James Carpenter Design Associates/E. L. Barnes.
The vertical blades of glass are braced by horizontal bands of dichroic glass.
Sweeny Chapel in the Christian Theological Seminary, Indianapolis, USA, 1985–87, James Carpenter Design Associates/E.L. Barnes.

Absorption und der Transmission, und sie können sogar die Farbe sowohl bei der Transmission als auch bei der Reflexion bestimmen. Die Low-E-Beschichtungen bilden nur eine mögliche Variante der selektiven Beschichtungen. Zur Zeit werden auch andere Produkte hergestellt, die auf Interferenzvorgängen basieren, z. B. kaltlichtspiegelnde, entspiegelnde oder dichroitische Beschichtungen.

Kaltlichtspiegelnde Beschichtungen weisen praktisch eine umgekehrte Wirkung der Low-E-Beschichtungen auf, weil sie die sichtbaren Wellenlängen reflektieren, während der IR-Bereich durchgelassen wird. Solche Beschichtungen werden bei den Reflektoren der dichroitischen Lampen verwendet.

Entspiegelnde Beschichtungen reduzieren die Reflexion eines normalen Glases von 0.09 auf 0.02–0.03 und steigern damit die Lichttransmission. Ihre Anwendung ist nicht nur für das Ausstellen von Gegenständen hinter Glas, sondern auch bei Mehrfach-Isolierverglasungen von Vorteil, da sie die natürliche Reflexion an den zahlreichen Glasoberflächen verringern.

Dichroitische Beschichtungen werden normalerweise für Spezialfilter in der Meß- und Labortechnik eingesetzt. Durch Interferenzvorgänge zerlegen sie das Licht in die Spektralfarben, die je nach Einfallswinkel durchgelassen oder reflektiert werden. Damit ergeben sich unterschiedliche Farben in Reflexion und Transmission. Bei der Herstellung im Tauchverfahren oder durch Kathoden-Zerstäubung werden 10 bis 40 Schichten auf 1×1 m große Scheiben aufgetragen. Der Vorgang wird mehrmals wiederholt, bis die optische Spezifikation erreicht ist.

Dichroitische Gläser wurden von James Carpenter Design Associates mehrmals für Kunst am Bau eingesetzt. 1985–87 hat er zwei Fenster für die «Sweeny Chapel» im «Christian Theological Seminary» in Indianapolis, Indiana, USA (Architekt: E. L. Barnes), realisiert. Sie zeigen, wie ein einfacher, weißer, rechteckiger Raum durch ein Spiel von Licht und Farbe vollständig verändert werden kann. Das größere Fenster, 9.35 m hoch und 3.06 m breit, ist durch aussteifende Glasschwerter in fünf Felder unterteilt und mit waagerecht liegenden Scheiben ausgefacht. Da in der Vertikalen normales Floatglas und in der

Cold Mirror Coatings
The effect of cold mirror coatings is the opposite of that of low-E coatings, because they reflect visible light wavelengths, while admitting the infrared range.
Such coatings are used in the reflectors of dichroic lamps.

Anti-Reflection Coatings reduce the reflection of normal glass from 0.09 to 0.02–0.03 and thus increase light transmission.
The use of this type of glass is not just restricted to use in displaying objects behind glass, but is also advantageous in multiple glazed units where it brings about a reduction of the reflection from the various glass surfaces.

Dichroic Coatings are normally used for special filters in measuring and laboratory instruments. The interference effect of these coatings divides the light into spectral colours, such that, depending on angle of incidence, one range of wavelengths is transmitted and the remainder reflected. This gives rise to different colours in reflection and transmission.
10 to 40 layers of dichroic coatings can be applied to 1×1 m panes of glass by means of a vacuum deposition process. The process is repeated until the optical specification is reached.

Dichroic glass was used for several art works for buildings by James Carpenter Design Associates. Between 1985 and 1987 they designed two windows for the Sweeny Chapel in the Christian Theological Seminary in Indianapolis, Indiana (Architect: E. L. Barnes).
They show how a simple, square, white room can be completely transformed by the play of light and colour. The largest window, 9.35 m high and 3.06 m wide, is divided into five sections by vertical clear glass blades, which are stabilized with horizontal stiffeners of dichroic glass.
As the vertical glass sections are of ordinary float glass, but the horizontal ones are dichroic glass, light falls through these glass strips in a coloured interplay of transmitted and reflected rays along the wall.
Interesting changes take place according to the time of day or year, due to the changing position of the sun and angle of incidence of the sun's rays.

Die transmittierten und reflektierten Lichtstrahlen lassen ein farbiges Lichtspiel entlang der Wand entstehen, das sich je nach Tages- und Jahreszeit ständig verändert.
«Sweeny Chapel» im «Christian Theological Seminary», Indianapolis, USA, 1985–87, James Carpenter Design Associates/E. L. Barnes.
The transmitted and reflected light creates a colourful play of light along the wall which constantly changes in accordance with time of day and season. Sweeny Chapel in the Christian Theological Seminary, Indianapolis, USA, 1985–87, James Carpenter Design Associates/E. L. Barnes.

Horizontalen dichroitische Gläser verwendet wurden, zeichnet sich ein farbiges Lichtspiel der transmittierten und reflektierten Strahlen entlang der Wand ab. Interessant ist, wie sich der Licht-Farbe-Effekt je nach Tages- und Jahreszeit verändert, weil der Winkel der einfallenden Sonnenstrahlen mit dem Sonnenstand immer wieder wechselt.

Auf dem Papier geblieben ist der Entwurf für die Gestaltung des Eingangsbereiches des Bürogebäudes Chiswick Park, London, 1989–91, von Foster und Partnern. James Carpenter Design Associates entwarfen dafür die «Dichroic Glass Spine», eine 21.5 m hohe, gespannte Struktur, die vor der Schrägverglasung des Atriums schwe-

One design which did not get past the drawing board stage was intended for the entrance area of the Chiswick Park office building in London, 1989–91, designed by Foster and Partners.
For this project James Carpenter Design Associates designed the "dichroic glass spine", a 21.5 m high tensile structure which was to be suspended in front of the inclined glazing of the atrium. The filigree construction of stainless steel rods was to have been filled in with panels of dichroic glass. This arrangement of variously angled, red-reflecting and blue-transmitting, diamond-shaped panes would have produced a graduated play of coloured light in the atrium.

Gespannte Konstruktion mit dichroitischen Glasscheiben.
Entwurf von James Carpenter Design Associates für den Haupteingang des Bürogebäudes «Chiswick Park», London, 1989–91, Foster und Partner.
Tensile structure of dichroic glass panes.
Designed by James Carpenter Design Associates for the main entrance of the Chiswick Park office building, London, 1989–91, Foster and Partners.

Die Fassadenverkleidung besteht aus einer lichtstreuenden und reflektierenden Verglasung und dichroitisch beschichteten Glaslamellen.
«Dichroic Glass Field», New York, 1995, James Carpenter Design Associates.
The façade cladding consists of light-scattering reflecting glass and dichroically-coated glass blades.
"Dichroic Glass Field", New York, 1995, James Carpenter Design Associates.

ben sollte. Die filigranartige Konstruktion aus Edelstahl-Zugstangen sollte mit dichroitischen Gläsern ausgefacht werden.
Die rhombusförmigen, rot reflektierenden, blau transmittierenden und aufgrund der raffinierten Geometrie in verschiedenen Neigungswinkeln stehenden Scheiben hätten dem Betrachter im Atrium ein abgestuftes farbiges Lichtspiel geboten.

Um die monotone Backstein-Rückwand des Millennium Building in Manhattan, New York, optisch zu beleben, haben James Carpenter Design Associates 1995 das «Dichroic Glass Field» entworfen.
Ihre Idee bestand darin, das einfallende Licht zu modulieren und den Eindruck von Tiefe zu erwecken. Die 50 m lange und 14 m hohe Grundfläche ist eine hochreflektierende Verglasung aus 12 mm starken VSG-Scheiben mit einer lichtstreuenden Oberfläche außen und einer reflektierenden innen.
Sie ist mit einer Unterkonstruktion aus Stahlprofilen an der Backsteinwand befestigt. Senkrecht dazu kragen 216 dichroitisch beschichtete Glaslamellen aus 15 mm starken VSG-Streifen aus, die 62 cm lang und 15 cm breit sind. Sie brechen das Licht je nach Einfallswinkel immer wieder in andere Komplementärfarben und schaffen damit ein ständig wechselndes Erscheinungsbild.

In 1995 James Carpenter Design Associates designed a "dichroic glass field" to visually enliven the somewhat monotonous brick wall at the back of the Millennium Building in Manhattan, New York.
Their idea was to modulate the incident light to produce an illusion of depth.
The 50 m long and 14 m high basic surface is highly reflective glazing, composed of 12 mm laminated glass panes with an outer light-scattering surface and an inner reflecting surface.
It is fixed to the brick wall by a frame of steel profiles. Cantilevered perpendicular to this are 216 dichroic coated blades of 15 mm laminated glass strips, 62 cm long and 15 cm wide.
Depending on the angle of incidence, they continuously refract the light into different complementary colours, thus creating an ever-changing picture.

Still under construction is the project for the glazing of the atrium for the extension to the German Foreign Office in Berlin, 1996–2000. The architects, Thomas Müller and Ivan Reimann, have commissioned James Carpenter Design Associates and the engineers Schlaich Bergermann and Partners, to design the glazing for the entrance area and for the roof.
The basic idea is to develop a kind of "light

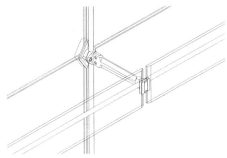

Noch im Bau befindet sich das Projekt für die
Atriumsverglasung der Erweiterung des Auswär-
tigen Amtes in Berlin, 1996 – 2000. Die
Architekten Thomas Müller und Ivan Reimann
haben James Carpenter Design Associates und
die Ingenieure Schlaich Bergermann und
Partner beigezogen, um die Verglasung des Eingangsbereichs und des Daches zu gestalten.
Der Leitgedanke ist, eine «Lichtmaschine» zu
entwickeln, welche das Licht umlenkt und die
nordgerichtete Eingangshalle beleuchtet.
Bei der Dachverglasung sind die hohen Stahlträger mit einer lichtstreuenden Verkleidung
versehen, um das einfallende Tageslicht zu
reflektieren.
Bei der Eingangsverglasung werden Glasscheiben mit veschiedenen Beschichtungen verwendet, die das Tageslicht moduliert reflektieren.
Die Tragkonstruktion ist ein vorgespanntes Seil-
netz. Die vertikalen Seile sind zwischen Dach-
randträger und Boden gespannt. Daran sind
maschinengefertigte Kragarme montiert, welche
die horizontalen Seile im Abstand von 50 cm
halten. Außen an den Köpfen der Kragarme sind
die 2.7×1.8 m großen, 25 mm starken VSG-
Scheiben aus extra-weißem Glas befestigt.
Um der Verglasung einen schwebenden Charakter zu verleihen, sind sie mit einer 30 % reflektierenden Beschichtung versehen, der Randbereich hingegen nicht. An den innenliegenden
Köpfen der Kragarme sind 2.7×0.3 große VSG-
Streifen aus dichroitischen Gläsern montiert,
welche ein Lichtspiel von komplementären
Farben bewirken.

machine", which will redirect the light and
illuminate the north-facing entrance hall.
To enhance this effect, the high steel beams of
the roof glazing have been encased in light-scattering cladding which reflects the daylight entering the space.
For the entrance glazing glass panes with various
coatings are used which reflect the light in a
modulated fashion.
The support structure is a tensile cable net. The
vertical cables are tensioned between the floor
and the perimeter beams of the roof. To these
are attached machine-made cantilever arms
which hold the horizontal cables at 50 cm spacing. Bolted to the outside, on the ends of the
cantilevers are the 2.7×1.8 m, 25 mm thick
panes of laminated, extra-white glass. To give the
glazing the impression of floating, the panes
have a 30 % reflective coating, except on the
perimetral zone. Attached to inside ends of the
cantilevers are 2.7×0.3 m strips of laminated,
dichroic glass which create a play of light in
complementary colours.

Ceramic-Enamel Coatings

Frit-coated glass has a 100 – 150 nm thick ceramic-enamel layer which is both weather resistant and durable. The hard layer is produced by
applying an enamel frit, composed of finely
ground glass powder with various additives and
colour pigments, onto a sheet of glass, and firing
at approx. 650° C, the temperature at which
glass softens sufficiently to fuse the frit to the
glass surface. The glass is then cooled in air to

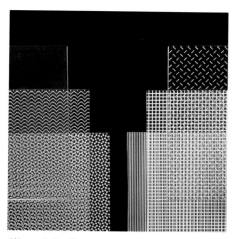

Gläser mit Emailmustern.
Glass panes with fritted patterns.

Emailbeschichtung

Ein emailliertes Glas weist eine 100–150 nm dicke keramische Beschichtung auf, die abnutzungs- und witterungsbeständig ist. Die harte Schicht entsteht, wenn eine Emailfritte, bestehend aus feingemahlenem Glas mit Zusatzmitteln und Farbpigmenten, auf die bereits fertiggestellte Glasscheibe aufgetragen wird und nochmals bei ca. 650° C, etwa der Erweichungstemperatur des Glases, eingebrannt und mit der Scheibe unlösbar verschmolzen wird. Anschließend werden die emaillierten Scheiben mit Luft gekühlt, um eine Vorspannung zu bewirken. Diese Behandlung wäre ohnehin erforderlich, weil die Farbschichten die Absorption des Glases steigern und damit zu einer erhöhten thermischen Beanspruchung führen. Für die Emailschichten steht eine große Anzahl von opaken bis transparenten Farben zur Verfügung. Ganzflächige opake Scheiben werden in blinden Brüstungs- und Deckenbereichen als hinterlüftete Verkleidung eingesetzt (Emalit®, Litex®). In den letzten Jahren sind vermehrt emaillierte Glasscheiben mit Punkt-, Linien- und Strichmustern mit gleichmäßigem oder verlaufendem Bedruckungsgrad zur Anwendung gekommen. Die Muster werden entweder durch Walzendruck oder durch Siebdruck aufgetragen.

Die Verwendung von emaillierten Glasscheiben führt zu interessanten Tag- und Nacht-Effekten, wie beim Glasdach auf dem Quai de Londres entlang der Meuse in Verdun, Frankreich, 1988 von RFR entworfen. Die Tragstruktur des Glasdaches besteht aus leicht schräggestellten Masten im Abstand von 5 m, und jedes dritte Feld ist durch

toughen it, a process which would in any case be necessary because the coloured layers increase the absorption of the glass and lead to increased thermal stress. A wide range of ceramic-enamel coatings are available, from opaque to transparent colours. Opaque glass is used as ventilated cladding in spandrels and parapets (Emalit®, Litex®). In recent years more fritted glass panes are becoming available which have various patterns and extents of dots, lines or meshes. The patterns are either applied in a rolling process or by screen printing.

The use of fritted glass panels can produce interesting effects by day and night, as for example the glass roof at the Quai de Londres along the Meuse river in Verdun, France, designed by RFR, in 1988. During the day the white dashed frit pattern on the glass roof makes it appear like a cloud floating between the masts, but at night it becomes a light-scattering surface when lit by indirect light. The support structure of the glass roof consists of slightly inclined masts, 5 m apart; every third span being stabilised by a tubular steel support. Two Vierendeel girders form the roof construction. They are fixed by means of a pin-joint connection to the masts and supported in their inclined position via tie rods attached to the head and foot of the masts. The 1.3 × 1.5 m large glass panels are suspended under the roof construction at intervals via articulated fixings RFR and spring spacers.

In the Commercial Building on the Avenue de Montaigne 50 in Paris, completed in 1993, the architects Epstein, Glaimann and Vidal, in coop-

Dank dem weiß gestrichelten Emailmuster scheint das Glasdach zwischen der filigranen Stahlstruktur zu schweben.
«Quai de Londres», Verdun, Frankreich, 1988, Rice-Francis-Ritchie, RFR.
The fritted white dashed pattern gives the impression of the glass roof floating in the filigree steel structure.
Quai de Londres, Verdun, France, 1988, Rice-Francis-Ritchie, RFR.

ein Stahlrohr stabilisiert. Zwei Vierendeel-Träger bilden die Dachkonstruktion. Sie sind gelenkig an den Masten befestigt und in ihrer leicht geneigten Lage mit Zugstangen vom Mastenkopf und -fuß abgespannt. Die 1.3×1.5 m großen Glasscheiben sind mit dem punktförmigen Befestigungssystem mit Kugelgelenk RFR und mit Stahlfedern von unten an der Dachkonstruktion aufgehängt.

Beim Geschäftshaus an der Avenue de Montaigne 50 in Paris, 1993, haben die Architekten Epstein, Glaimann und Vidal in Zusammenarbeit mit RFR das Atrium durch eine gebäudehohe Verglasung gegen den benachbarten Innenhof abgeschlossen. Die 16×24 m große, abgehängte Verglasung besteht aus 1.3×3 m großen Glasscheiben, die untereinander durch kreuzförmige Verbindungsteile mit gelenkiger Punkthalterung abgehängt sind. Die obere Reihe der 15 mm starken ESG-Scheiben ist mit Federbeschlägen an einem unterspannten Stahlträger befestigt. Bei jedem Geschoß sind die kreuzförmigen Halterungen durch eine horizontale Seilkonstruktion gegen Winddruck und -sog gesichert. Da die Verglasung nach Süden gerichtet ist, sind die Glasscheiben für den Sonnenschutz mit einer weiß emaillierten Bedruckung versehen.

Die Erweiterung des Flughafens Charles de Gaulle in Paris-Roissy, von Paul Andreu mit ADP Architekten und RFR, Peter Rice, 1994 fertiggestellt, umfaßt auch einen neuen Bahnhof, der quer zur Symmetrieachse des Terminals liegt. Der Bahnhof dient als Knotenpunkt verschiedener Verkehrsmittel, unter anderem für die Hochgeschwindigkeitszüge TGV. Bahngleise und Perrons sind unterirdisch angelegt und mit vier 159×149 m großen, leicht geneigten Glasflächen von RFR überdacht. Um die Transparenz der Dachverglasung nicht zu beeinträchtigen, wurden schmale, sichelförmige Dreigurtträger aus Stahlrohren entwickelt, welche einen Trägerrost mit Maschenweite 159×149 cm aus Dreigurtträgern und Walzprofilen tragen. Die Verglasung besteht aus 8 mm starken ESG-Scheiben, die jeweils mit acht runden Punkthaltern an der Unterkonstruktion befestigt sind. Eine solche ESG-Überkopfverglasung ist in Frankreich zulässig, wenn sie die erforderlichen Tests für Druck- und Soglasten bestanden hat. In Deutschland hingegen müssen Überkopfverglasungen aus VSG-Scheiben bestehen.
Um blendfreies und gleichmäßiges Tageslicht zu

eration with RFR, closed off the atrium to the neighbouring inner courtyard by means of a glass wall the height of the building. The 16×24 m high, suspended glazing consists of 1.3×3 m glass panes, suspended one below the other by means of cross-shaped spiders with articulated point fixing. The upper row of 15 mm thick toughened glass is attached to a steel truss by means of spring connections. At each floor the cross-shaped spiders are secured against wind pressure and suction via horizontal cables. As the glass wall faces south, the glass panes are printed with a white frit for solar control.

The extension of Charles de Gaulle Airport in Paris-Roissy, completed in 1994 by Paul Andreu in cooperation with ADP Architects and RFR, Peter Rice, also incorporates a new railway station, situated at an angle to the axis of symmetry of the terminal. The station is an interchange for various means of transport, including the high-speed TGV trains. The tracks and platforms are located below ground level and are roofed over by RFR with four 159×149 m, low-pitched glass surfaces. In order not to impair the transparence of the roof glazing, narrow, sickle-shaped tubular steel trusses were developed which support a structural grid, with a mesh of 159×149 cm, of trusses and roll-formed steel beams. The glazing consists of panes of 8 mm toughened glass each restrained with eight round point fittings to the frame. Such overhead glazing of toughened glass is permitted in France if it has passed the requisite tests for pressure and suction loads.

Die Atriumsverglasung besteht aus weiß bedruckten Glasscheiben, die durch kreuzförmige Verbindungsteile mit gelenkiger Punkthalterung untereinander abgehängt sind.
Geschäftshaus an der Avenue de Montaigne, Paris, 1993, Epstein, Glaimann und Vidal Architekten mit RFR.
The atrium glazing consists of white fritted glass panes which are suspended one below the other by means of cross-shaped spiders with articulated point fixing.
Commercial building on the Avenue de Montaigne, Paris, 1993, Epstein, Glaimann and Vidal Architects in cooperation with RFR.

Um die Transparenz der Dachverglasung nicht zu beeinträchtigen, wurde eine filigrane Stahlkonstruktion entwickelt. Die Verglasung ist mit einem hellblauen Streifenmuster von unterschiedlicher Dichte bedruckt.
Erweiterung des Flughafens Charles de Gaulle, Paris-Roissy, 1994, Paul Andreu mit ADP Architekten und mit RFR, Peter Rice.
In order to preserve maximum transparency in the roof glazing a filigree steel construction was developed. The glazing is printed with a pale blue stripe pattern of varying thickness.
Extension to Charles de Gaulle Airport, Paris-Roissy, 1994, Paul Andreu with ADP Architects and in cooperation with RFR, Peter Rice.

gewähren, sind die Glasscheiben mit einem hellblauen Streifenmuster bedruckt. Der Bedeckungsgrad variiert von 20, 40, 60 bis 80 %, entsprechend den lichttechnischen Anforderungen.

Winkelabhängige selektive Beschichtungen
Eine Variante stellen winkelabhängige selektive Beschichtungen dar, welche die Sonnen- und Lichtstrahlen nur bei bestimmten Einfallswinkeln durchlassen. Erfolgversprechend sind Entwicklungen, die die Erzeugung einer lamellenförmigen metallischen Mikrostruktur direkt auf der Glasoberfläche durch magnetischen Niederschlag vorsehen. Da der Durchblick nach außen meistens einen anderen Winkel als der Strahlungseinfall aufweist, hindert die mikroskopische Struktur die Sicht nach außen kaum. Durch die Wahl der Schichtdicken, der Zwischenabstände und der Neigungswinkel kann die Sonnenschutzwirkung beliebig eingestellt werden.

Einen weiteren Schritt in der Beschichtungstechnologie stellt die Entwicklung von veränderbaren Schichten mit thermotropen oder -chromen Materialien sowie mit elektrochromen Substanzen oder Flüssigkristallen dar. Obwohl zur Zeit die Entwicklung von Schichten zum Auflaminieren noch viele Probleme stellt, hat der Gedanke großes Zukunftspotential. Mike Davies meint, daß eine ausgereifte industrielle Herstellung von solchen Beschichtungen enorme ökonomische Konsequenzen im Bauwesen haben wird. Sie würde die Rückkehr zur schlichten Bearbeitungstechnologie der Einfachverglasung bedeuten und so zu einer Verminderung der Verglasungskosten führen, da die zweite Glasscheibe, der Randverbund und die Versiegelung überflüssig würden.

In Germany, however, overhead glazing can only be of laminated glass. To give glare-free and evenly distributed daylight the glass panes are printed with a pale blue stripe pattern. Coverage ranges from 20, 40, 60 to 80 %, according to the particular requirements of lighting at the various points.

Angular Selective Coatings
Angular selective coatings control the solar and visible transmission according to the selected directions. A promising new development is the creation of a microscopic metallic slatted structure directly on the glass surface, using a process of magnetic deposition. This structure has minimal effect on the ability to see through the glass from inside the building, as the angle at which radiation strikes the glass is different from the angle at which we look out. By regulating the thicknesses of the strips, the spacing between them, and their angle of tilt, the level of solar control required can be determined.

A further step in coatings technology is the development of controllable devices involving thermotropic or thermochromic materials and electrochromic or liquid crystal layers.
Although at present the development of coatings which can be laminated onto the glass is still unsatisfactory, the idea has great potential for the future. Mike Davies believes that the developed industrial manufacture of such coatings will have enormous economic consequences in building. It would mean the return to the simple manufacturing processes used for single glass pane and as such would lead to a reduction in glazing costs, as the second glass pane, the edge bond and sealing would be superfluous.

Das Verbundglas   Laminated Glass

Ein mehrschichtiger Aufbau ermöglicht die weitgehend unbeschränkte Kombination von Glasscheiben mit oder ohne Beschichtungen und die Schaffung von unterschiedlich breiten Scheibenzwischenräumen mit verschiedenen Möglichkeiten für die Integration von Wärme- und Sonnenschutzmaßnahmen.

Verbundgläser (VSG) bestehen aus zwei oder mehreren Scheiben, die durch eine zäh-elastische Kunststofffolie, z. B. aus Polyvinyl-Butyral (PVB), verbunden sind. Sie werden hauptsächlich als Sicherheitsgläser verwendet, weil die PVB-Folie bei einem Bruch das Ablösen der Splitter verhindert.

Bei Verbundgläsern werden oft vorgespannte oder teilvorgespannte Glasscheiben verwendet, die eine höhere Festigkeit als normales Floatglas aufweisen. Teilvorgespannte Glasscheiben (TVG) haben gegenüber vorgespannten Glasscheiben (ESG) den Vorteil, daß sich beim Zerbrechen größere Stücke ergeben, die eine bessere Resttragfähigkeit aufweisen.

Die Sicherheit bei Durchbruch, Beschuß und Explosion läßt sich durch unterschiedliche Glas- und Foliendicken optimieren.

Als Zwischenschicht können verschiedene Arten von Folien eingelegt werden: durchsichtige, gefärbte und gemusterte; wärmedämmende, UV-absorbierende und reflektierende Folien; Folien mit Drahteinlagen für Sicherheits-, Alarm- oder Heizzwecke. Einen Sonderfall stellt der Gießharzverbund dar, welcher für dickere Einlagen, z. B. bei Photovoltaik-Modulen und Schallschutzgläsern, verwendet wird.

Verbundgläser werden praktisch immer bei Schräg- und Dachverglasungen verwendet, um das Verletzungsrisiko bei Personen auf ein Minimum zu reduzieren.

Ein Beispiel dafür ist die Überdachung des Bahnhofs und der Postautostation in Chur, 1985–92 von den Architekten Brosi, Obrist und Partnern

The use of bonded panes of glass enables an almost limitless combination of glass panes with or without coatings; spacings between the panes can be of various widths, and various measures for solar and thermal protection can be integrated in the cavities between the panes.

Laminated glass consists of two or more panes of glass which are bonded together with a plastic material, e. g. polyvinyl butyral (PVB). This type of glass is generally used as safety glass because the PVB layer prevents the glass splinters from scattering in case of breakage.

Often toughened or heat-strengthened laminated glass is used where a higher strength than that of normal float glass is required. Heat-strengthened glass has the advantage over toughened glass that it breaks into larger pieces thus giving a better residual load-bearing capacity.

By combining different types and thicknesses of glass and bonding materials, specific performances can be achieved in terms of increased resistance to breakage, bullets or explosions.

A number of different materials can be used as an interlayer: transparent, coloured or patterned film; thermally insulating, ultraviolet-absorbing or reflecting film; or wired interlayers to meet safety, security or heating requirements.

A special type of laminated glass is bonding with resin, which is used for thicker interlayers, such as those incorporating photovoltaic modules, or for acoustic glass.

Laminated glass is almost always used for glass roofing and sloping glazing, so as to reduce the risk of injury from flying glass in case of breakage.

An example of this is the roof of the railway and bus station in Chur (Switzerland), 1985–92, designed by the architects Brosi, Obrist and Partners, in cooperation with RFR. The large curved glass roof gives passengers protection

Linke Seite: Das «Main Terminal Building» des Flughafens «Kansai» ist seitlich durch zwei Verglasungen mit einer filigranen Stahlkonstruktion und getönten VSG-Scheiben abgeschlossen.
Flughafen «Kansai», Osaka, Japan, 1989–94, Renzo Piano Building Workshop.
Left page: The side walls of the main terminal building of Kansai Airport are of body tinted laminated glass on a filigree steel frame.
Kansai Airport, Osaka, Japan, 1989–94, Renzo Piano Building Workshop.

in Zusammenarbeit mit RFR entworfen. Das
große, gewölbte Glasdach bietet den Benutzern
der öffentlichen Verkehrsmittel Schutz vor der
Witterung und stellt gleichzeitig eine architektonisch gelungene Nahtstelle zwischen Alt- und
Neustadt dar.

Das 50 m weit gespannte Dachtragwerk wird
über den Geleisen und der Postautoplattform
von Doppelstützen getragen. Es besteht aus
12 Paaren von Stahlrohrbögen, die an beiden
Seiten gelenkig aufgelagert sind. Zum Scheitel
der Tonne hin laufen sie, gleichsam wie «Zitro-
nenschnitze», auseinander. Bei der Dachhaut
wurden Verbundgläser mit dem Achsmaß
2.02 × 0.95 m aus zwei 8 mm dicken Floatglas-
Scheiben verwendet. Die vom Scheitel bis zur
Wasserrinne verlaufende Fuge ist mit einem Neo-
prenprofil und Aluminium-Preßleisten gedichtet,
während in der Querrichtung eine Silikonfuge
die Wasserdichtheit sicherstellt.

Verbundgläser mit weißen Scheiben wurden
1988 für die Glaspyramide des Louvre in Paris
verwendet. Diese signalisiert den neuen Haupteingang des Museums und überdacht das unter
dem Bodenniveau liegende Informationszentrum
für die Besucher. Da sie in der Mitte der Cour
Napoléon steht, umgeben von historischen
Fassaden, haben die Architekten I. M. Pei und
Partner ein abstraktes, kristallines Volumen
vorgeschlagen, das den Kontrast mit der alten
Bausubstanz auf ein spannungsvolles Minimum
reduzieren sollte. Die Vorstellung der Architekten, die Pyramide als möglichst unsichtbaren

from the weather, and at the same time it forms
an architectural link between the old part of the
town and the new.

Supported on paired tubular columns, the
roof structure spans 50 m across the tracks and
the platforms. The roof consists of 12 pairs of
tubular steel arcs, bearing at both ends on the
paired columns by means of an articulated
connection. Towards the apex of the roof the
arcs diverge, defining the outer rim of a "lemon
slice".

The laminated glass units used in the roof skin
each consist of two 8 mm thick float glass panes,
2.02 × 0.95 m in size.

The panel-to-panel junctions running from the
apex to the gutter are sealed with neoprene profiles and aluminium compression caps while the
horizontal joints are silicon-sealed.

Laminated glass with clear white panes were
used for the glass pyramid built in 1988 at the
Louvre in Paris.

The pyramid marks the new main entrance to
the museum and acts as the roof over the
visitors' information centre which is situated
underground directly below this point.

As the entrance is located in the middle of the
Cour Napoléon, surrounded by historic façades,
the architects, I. M. Pei and Partners, proposed
an abstract crystalline volume which would
provide an exciting, but not intrusive contrast to
the existing buildings.

The architects' idea of making the pyramid
appear as invisible and immaterial as possible

Verbundgläser aus «weißen» Scheiben wurden eingesetzt, um den Kontrast mit der historischen Bausubstanz auf ein Minimum zu reduzieren; Detail der unterspannten Konstruktion mit Druckstäben und Zugstangen aus Edelstahl.
Glaspyramide des Louvre, Paris, 1988, I. M. Pei und Partner in Zusammenarbeit mit PCF und RFR.
Laminated panes of clear white glass have been selected to reduce the contrast with the historic building to a minimum; detail of the tensile structure with compression studs and tension rods in stainless steel.
Grande pyramid at the Louvre, Paris, 1988, I. M. Pei and Partners in cooperation with PCF and RFR.

und immateriellen Baukörper erscheinen zu lassen, hat sowohl die Bauingenieure PCF und RFR als auch die Glashersteller vor große Herausforderungen gestellt. Die Tragstruktur sollte so leicht wie möglich sein und die Verglasung ein Maximum an Transparenz bei einem Minimum an Verspiegelung gewährleisten. Insbesondere die Transparenz stellte herstellungstechnische Probleme. Es mußten aus Sicherheitsgründen Verbundscheiben verwendet werden. Als Folge davon hätten aber die beiden um 45° geneigten Seitenflächen der Pyramide bei horizontalem Durchblick durch eine Gesamtdicke der Verglasung von 60 mm einen starken Grünstich aufgewiesen, so daß die Architekten extra-weißes Glas verlangten. Da aber damals die industrielle Fertigung für solche Dimensionen noch nicht ausgereift war, mußten die Scheiben handwerklich gegossen, geschliffen und poliert werden.
Die konstruktive Antwort auf all diese Anforderungen ist eine räumlich unterspannte Tragstruktur mit Edelstahldruckstäben von 50 mm und -zugstangen von 10–15 mm Durchmesser. Die filigranartige Konstruktion trägt die Profile der sekundären Konstruktion, wo die 3 × 1.9 m großen rhombusförmigen Verglasungselemente befestigt werden. Letztere sind Verbundgläser mit zwei 10 mm starken extra-weißen Scheiben, die durch Silikon-Verklebung mit einem Aluminiumrahmen verbunden sind, um sie auf der sekundären Konstruktion zu befestigen. Die nur 2 mm breiten Fugen sind mit einem silberfarbenen Silikon-Spezialkitt ausgefüllt.

was a great challenge to both construction engineers (PCF and RFR) and glass manufacturers alike.
The support structure was to appear as light as possible, and the glazing should reduce reflection to a minimum while guaranteeing maximum transparence.
The transparence presented the greatest difficulties for the manufacturers. Safety considerations dictated the use of laminated glass, but as a result of the 45° angle of the sides, the pyramid would have appeared distinctly green when viewed horizontally through a total thickness of 60 mm. For this reason the architects specified the use of extra-clear white glass. At the time the pyramid was built, however, industrial manufacturing processes were not capable of producing this specification to such a size, and the panes had to be poured, ground and polished by hand.
The structural answer to all these requirements was a tensile structure supporting the glass from underneath with 50 mm diameter stainless steel compression struts and 10–15 mm diameter tension rods.
This filigree construction carries the profiles of the secondary construction to which are attached the 3 × 1.9 m sized rhombus-shaped glazing units. The units are composed of 10 mm thick, clear white glass which is silicon bonded to an aluminium frame for attachment to the secondary construction.
The narrow, 2 mm joints are finished with a special silver-coloured silicon seal.

Ein Beispiel für die Verwendung von getönten Verbundgläsern ist der Flughafen Kansai in Osaka, Japan, von Renzo Piano Building Workshop 1994 fertiggestellt. Das 1700 m lange Terminalgebäude setzt sich zusammen aus einer Zentralhalle mit allen Passagierfunktionen, dem Main Terminal Building, und aus zwei seitlichen Flügelbereichen mit Wartezonen, den Wings, wo die Flugzeuge andocken. Das geschwungene Dach über der Zentralhalle besteht aus wellenförmig gekrümmten Dreigurtbindern, die auf Gabelstützen liegen und 83 m überspannen. Die 135 m lange und bis zu 12 m hohe Seitenverglasung der Halle ist eine Pfosten-Riegel-Konstruktion mit 35 mm breiten Profilen aus geschweißtem Flachstahl. Die Pfosten sind durch eine doppelte Hinterspannung außen und innen gegen Windkräfte ausgesteift und halten selbst den Kräften eines Taifuns oder Erdbebens stand. Für die Verglasung sind 3.6 × 1.16 m große Verbundgläser aus 8 mm starken ESG-Scheiben außen und 6 mm starken, graugetönten Scheiben innen eingesetzt, die – wie Autoverglasungen – mit umlaufenden Neoprenprofilen befestigt sind. Die Tragstruktur der Flügel besteht aus diagonal verstrebten, gebogenen Stahlrohren, die eine ausgefachte Schale bilden. Zu den außenliegenden Enden hin ist ihre Form leicht abfallend, um

An example of the use of body tinted laminated glass is Kansai Airport in Osaka, Japan, completed in 1994 by the Renzo Piano Building Workshop. The 1700 m long terminal building is composed of the main terminal building and two "wings", with waiting areas. The air-craft dock at these wings. The curved roof over the central hall consists of undulating roof trusses spanning 83 metres and resting on forked columns. The 135 m long and up to 12 m high glass walls of the hall are fixed to a post and frame construction with 35 mm wide profiles of welded flat steel. The posts are doubly braced inside and out against wind loads and can even withstand the loads occurring in a typhoon or earthquake. The glazing itself is of 3.6 × 1.16 m laminated glass panes composed of 8 mm toughened glass on the outside and 6 mm grey-tinted panes on the inside, the latter being fixed around their perimeters with neoprene profiles, like car windscreens. The support frame for the wings consists of a trussed shell made of curved tubular steel with diagonal bracing struts. Towards the far ends the shape flattens out so as not to block the view between the control tower and the runway. The glass used for the airside of these curved wings is 3.6 × 1 m, 12 mm grey-tinted toughened glass, which also has a sound-insulating function.

die Sichtverbindung zwischen Kontrollturm und Flugpiste nicht zu behindern. Für die gekrümmte Verglasung der Flügelbereiche zum Flugfeld hin sind 3.6 × 1 m große, 12 mm starke graugetönte ESG-Scheiben eingesetzt, die auch Schallschutzfunktion übernehmen.

Funktionsschichten

Vielversprechend ist zur Zeit die Entwicklung von Funktionsschichten, die für Licht- und Wärmeschutz eingesetzt werden können: winkelabhängig-selektive oder lichtumlenkende Schichten sowie aktiv veränderbare Schichten, die mit thermotropen oder thermochromen Substanzen sowie mit Flüssigkristallen oder elektrochromen Materialien funktionieren.

Winkelabhängig-selektive Schichten
Winkelabhängig-selektive Schichten sind licht-

Functional Layers

A promising new development are functional layers, which can be used to achieve specific performances in terms of light transmittance and thermal insulation; these layers consist either of films which are angle-selective or light-bending, or layers which have actively variable transmission characteristics, based on thermotropic and thermochromic materials, or liquid crystals or electrochromic materials.

Angle-Selective Films
Angle-selective layers are light-transmitting films which only scatter incident light from a particular angle and thus become non-transparent. In principle they are composed of a microscopic louvred grid structure created on a 0.28 mm thick polymer film by a process of photopolymerisation, mostly by ultraviolet light. During the

2000 mm Distanz   *2000 mm distance*

1000 mm Distanz   *1000 mm distance*

300 mm Distanz   *300 mm distance*

C-Typ   A-Typ   B-Typ

Winkelabhängig-selektive Schichten weisen eine mikroskopische Struktur wie ein Lamellenraster auf, welche die Lichtstrahlen bei einem bestimmten Winkeleinfall zerstreut und die Durchsicht verhindert.
Angle-selective films are composed of a microscopic louvred grid structure which is light-scattering from a particular angle and thus become non-transparent.

durchlässige Folien, welche die Lichtstrahlen nur bei einem bestimmten Winkeleinfall zerstreuen und damit undurchsichtig werden. Im Prinzip bestehen sie aus einer mikroskopischen Lamellenstruktur, die in einer 0.28 mm dicken Polymerfolie durch Photopolymerisation, meistens UV-Bestrahlung, hervorgerufen wird. Beim Belichtungsvorgang während der Herstellung können verschiedene Winkel eingestellt oder Teilbelichtungen ausgeführt werden. Auf dem Markt sind Produkte mit drei Winkeleinstellungen (in der maximalen Größe von 2.40 × 1.80 m) erhältlich, die beim Sichtschutz zum Einsatz kommen (Angle 21®).

Schichten mit holographisch-optischen Elementen

Eine weitere Maßnahme zur Kontrolle der einfallenden Sonnenstrahlung bieten holographisch-optische Elemente (HOE). Durch den physikalischen Effekt der Beugung ermöglichen sie verschiedene Varianten der Lichtlenkung, vergleichbar derjenigen von Spiegeln, Linsen, Prismen und anderen optischen Elementen. Die HOE sind Aufzeichnungen von Interferenzmustern, die durch Laserlicht auf einem hochauflösenden photographischen Film erzeugt werden, welcher dann in ein Verbundglas eingebettet wird. Das Beugungsgitter bewirkt die Lichtumlenkung, welche nur für den eingestellten Einfallswinkel erfolgt, was bedeutet, daß die Hologramme dem Lichteinfall nachgeführt werden müssen.

Aus herstellungstechnischen Gründen werden derzeit die einzelnen kleinformatigen, 10 × 10 cm großen Hologramme zuerst im Taktverfahren auf einen 1 × 2 m großen Film belichtet, welcher danach entwickelt wird. Der Einsatz von HOE in der Fassade wurde bisher durch die unzureichende UV-Stabilität verhindert. Durch ein neues Produktionsverfahren ist dieses Problem nun gelöst. Hinsichtlich einer vollautomatischen Serienproduktion sind einige Fortschritte zu verzeichnen, insbesondere was die Herstellung von großformatigen Masterhologrammen betrifft.

Sofern die lichtempfindliche Schicht nicht direkt auf Glas aufgebracht wurde, ist das Endprodukt eine Folie, die zum Schutz vor Feuchtigkeit und Verschmutzung zwischen zwei Glasscheiben eingebettet werden muß.

In der Architektur können holographisch-optische Elemente für Lichtumlenkung,

exposure at the manufacturing stage, a particular angle can be set, or only part of the film exposed. The range available at present consists of three different fixed angle settings (maximum pane size of 2.40 × 1.80 m), for use where visual screening is required (Angle 21®).

Holographic Diffractive Films

A further method of controlling solar radiation is presented by holographic diffractive structures (HDS). Various possibilities for light deflection result from the physical effect of diffraction, similar to the effects created by mirrors, lenses, prisms and other optical elements. The HDS are three-dimensional recordings of laser light pat-

Verschiedene Arten von holographisch-optischen Elementen (HOE).
Different kinds of holographic diffractive structures (HDS).

Art	Aufsicht	Vertikalschnitt	Horizontalschnitt
Kind	*Top view*	*Vertical section*	*Horizontal section*
Gitter (parallele Linien mit gleichen Abständen) *Grating (equidistant parallel lines)*		Umlenkung und Dispersion in einer Richtung *Changing the direction of light and dispersion without focusing*	
Zylinderzonenplatte (parallele Linien mit unterschiedlichen Abständen) *Cylindrical zone plate (parallel lines with different distances)*		Umlenkung und Fokussierung in Brennlinien, die aufgrund der Dispersion für die einzelnen Spektralfarben an verschiedenen Orten liegen *Changing the direction of light and focusing in focal lines, separate for each wavelength*	
Seitenbandzonenplatte (konzentrische Ellipsen mit unterschiedlichen Abständen) *Off-axis zone plate (concentrical elliptical lines with different distances)*		Umlenkung und Fokussierung in Brennpunkten, die aufgrund der Dispersion für die einzelnen Spektralfarben an verschiedenen Orten liegen *Changing the direction of light and focusing in focal points, separate for each wavelength*	
Infrarot *Infrared*	Rot *Red*	Blau *Blue*	

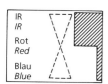

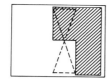

IR	
IR	
Rot	
Red	
Blau	
Blue	
100% Transmission	IR-Ausblendung
100% transmission	*IR-cutting out*

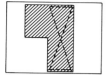

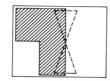

100% Ausblendung   50% Ausblendung
100% cutting out   *50% cutting out*

Eine Seitenbandzonenplatte fokussiert die einzelnen Spektralfarben auf unterschiedliche Brennpunkte, so daß der Strahlungsdurchgang mit einer beweglichen Blende nach Spektralbereichen geregelt werden kann.

An off-axis zone plate concentrates the individual spectral colours on different focal points; this makes it possible to use a movable stop to regulate transmission of the various spectral wavelengths.

Kombination von passiven und aktiven Maßnahmen zur Nutzung der Sonnenstrahlung.
Reihenhäuser an der IGA '93, Stuttgart,
HHS Planer + Architekten.
Combination of passive and active measures to exploit solar radiation.
Terrace housing at the IGA '93, Stuttgart,
HHS Planners + Architects.

Verschattung und Ausblendung sowie für Displayholographie eingesetzt werden.
Ein Beugungsgitter mit parallelen Linien mit gleichen Abständen lenkt das Sonnenlicht an die Decke wie ein Spiegel und steigert die Tageslichtbeleuchtung in der Raumtiefe.
Eine Struktur mit parallelen Linien mit unterschiedlichen Abständen, die Zylinderzonenplatte, fokussiert dagegen das Licht auf eine Brennlinie wie eine Linse, was den Wirkungsgrad von Streifen mit Photovoltaikzellen für die Gewinnung von Solarenergie steigern kann.
Eine Auslegung mit konzentrischen Ellipsen mit unterschiedlichen Abständen, die sogenannte Seitenbandzonenplatte, zerlegt das einfallende Licht in einzelne Spektralfarben und fokussiert sie auf Brennpunkte, welche an verschiedenen Orten liegen. Damit besteht die Möglichkeit, eine bewegliche Blende einzusetzen, um den Strahlungsdurchgang nach Spektralbereichen zu regeln und sogar eine totale Ausblendung unerwünschter Wellenlängen, z. B. IR-Strahlung, zu bewirken.
Displayhologramme sind von den Kreditkarten her bekannt. Sie können auch eine Fassade in einen Informationsträger verwandeln, da sie Schriften oder Signete durch Reflexion des Lichteinfalles visualisieren können.

Eine erste Anwendung von HOE-Schichten zeigen die experimentellen Reihenhäuser an der Internationalen Gartenbauausstellung in Stuttgart 1993 (IGA '93) des Architekturbüros HHS Planer + Architekten in Zusammenarbeit mit dem Institut für Licht- und Bautechnik der Fachhochschule Köln (ILB).
Das Grundkonzept des Entwurfs kombiniert aktive und passive Maßnahmen: einerseits die Nutzung der Sonnenstrahlung für die Tagesbe-

terns created on high-resolution photographic film which is then laminated between two panes of glass. The diffraction grating deflects light only from a predetermined angle of incidence, which means that the holograms are electronically controlled to track the sun, or changing angle of light across the sky. Current manufacture is limited to a process of scanning exposure of small, 10×10 cm format holograms, aligned next to each other across a 1×2 m large sheet of film which is then developed. A former problem concerned with the stability of the film on exposure to ultraviolet light has now been solved by a new manufacturing process.
Some progress has been made in moving towards fully-automated series production, particularly in the manufacture of large-format master holograms. When the light-sensitive layer is not applied directly to the glass, then the final product is a film which has to be laminated between two sheets of glass for protection against damp and dirt.
In architecture holographic diffractive structures can be used for light direction, shading and visual screening, as well as for display holography. A diffraction grating with equally spaced parallel lines redirects the sunlight onto the ceiling like a mirror and increases daylight levels further back in the room.
On the other hand a structure with parallel lines and varying spacing, known as a cylindrical zone plate, concentrates light on focal lines, in the same way as a lens; this effect can be used to increase the performance of strips with photovoltaic cells for exploiting solar energy.
An arrangement of concentrical elliptical lines with varying spacing, known as the off-axis zone plate, divides incident light into the individual spectral colours and concentrates them on focal

nicht bewegliche Solarzellen
fixed solar cells

drehbare holographisch-photovoltaische Glaslamellen
movable holographic-photovoltaic louvres

holographische Displays
holographic displays

leuchtung und für die Erzeugung von Wärme-energie und elektrischem Strom, andererseits ihre Regelung durch ein geeignetes Sonnen-schutzsystem, welches das ganze Jahr über eine optimale Anpassung an die Wetter- und Licht-verhältnisse ermöglicht. Zu diesem Zweck sind drehbare Lamellen mit holographisch-optischen Elementen entwickelt worden, die dem Sonnen-azimut computergesteuert nachgefahren werden und die nach Süden geneigte Verglasung der Wintergärten verschatten.

Die einfallende direkte Sonnenstrahlung wird von konzentrierenden Hologrammen, die im außenliegenden Verbundglas der Lamellen ein-gebettet sind, auf einer 11 mm dahinterliegen-den, mit Siebdruckstreifen versehenen Glas-scheibe gebündelt und dort reflektiert. Da die undurchlässigen Streifen nur 50 % der Fläche belegen, kann das diffuse Tageslicht ungehindert durchkommen und die Wohnräume belichten. Um die konzentrierte direkte Strahlung aktiv zu nutzen, wurden die Siebdruckstreifen im mittle-ren Haus mit Solarzellen belegt.

Elektrischer Strom wird auch im oberen Teil des Glasdachs durch 0.9 × 2.7 m große Photovoltaik-Module gewonnen, die mit 10 × 10 cm messen-den polykristallinen Silizium-Solarzellen aus-gestattet sind. Sie bieten zugleich einen Sonnen-schutz: Da zwischen den einzelnen Modulen nur 35 % der Strahlung durchkommt, wird bei der steilen sommerlichen Sonnenstrahlung eine Ver-schattung der Wohnräume erzielt.

points at different places. This makes it possible to use a movable stop to regulate the transmis-sion of the various spectral wavelengths; thus a particular wavelength, such as infrared, can be blocked out totally.

Display holograms are already known from their use on credit cards. They can also transform a façade into an information carrier, in that they can present lettering or symbols by reflecting the incident light.

One of the first examples of HDS layers in build-ing is in the experimental terrace housing at the International Garden Show in Stuttgart in 1993 (IGA '93) by the architects HHS Planners + Architects in collaboration with the Institute for Light and Building Technology of the Polytechnic of Cologne. The basic design idea combines pas-sive and active methods in a system with a two-fold purpose: firstly to provide a solar protection system which is effective throughout the whole year and adaptable to light and weather con-ditions; and secondly to exploit solar energy for daylighting in the building and for heat energy and electricity. To achieve this aim, movable lou-vres were designed with integrated holographic diffractive structures which shade the south-facing glazing in the winter gardens. In addition these structures are computer-controlled to track the azimuth of the sun. Direct sunlight falling on the glass is concentrated in focal lines by cylin-drical holograms laminated in the exterior glass

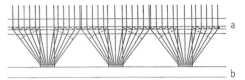

Direkte Sonnenstrahlung
Direct sunlight

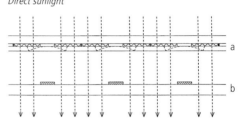

Diffuse Sonnenstrahlung
Diffuse sunlight

Die nach Süden geneigte Verglasung der Winter-gärten (links) und die drehbaren Lamellen mit holographisch-voltaischen Schichten (rechts); Schnitt durch die Lamellen: Verbundglas mit fokussierenden Hologrammen (a) und Scheibe mit Solarzellen (b). Reihenhäuser an der IGA '93, Stuttgart, HHS Planer + Architekten.

The south-facing angled glazing of the winter gardens (left) and the tracking louvres with holo-graphic-photovoltaic layers (right); section through the louvres: laminated glass with concentrating holograms (a) and glass with photovoltaic strips (b). Terrace housing at the IGA '93, Stuttgart, HHS Planners + Architects.

Außerhalb der gedeckten Wintergärten sind weitere Verbundgläser mit holographischen Schichten in die Schrägverglasung eingesetzt. Hier zerlegen die HOE das Licht in einen abstrakten Regenbogen. Durch die Möglichkeit, die aufgebrachten Strukturen mit Schriftzügen oder Logos zu versehen, kann die Fassade zu einem Kommunikationsträger für die Betrachter werden.

Ein neueres Beispiel für die Anwendung von Hologrammen als Informationsträger ist die Verkleidung der dreieckförmigen Ablufthauben des Umspannwerks der GEW im Mediapark Köln, 1996.
Die holographischen Displays zeigen stilisierte Glühbirnen, die in quadratische Bildpunkte von 2.5 × 5 cm aufgelöst sind, von denen jeder einem einfarbigen holographischen Gitter entspricht.
Die Lichtzerlegung läßt Spektralfarben von ungewöhlicher Leuchtkraft entstehen, die sich bei unterschiedlichem Einfallswinkel und wechselnder Intensität der Beleuchtung ständig verändern.

Die holographischen Glaslamellen der IGA '93 wurden zu drehbaren Sonnenschutzelementen weiterentwickelt, welche die Verwendung von Solarzellen in der Standardgröße von 13 × 13 cm ermöglichen. Die Prototypen bestehen aus einem V-förmigen Metallgestell, das mit zwei 15 cm breiten VSG-Glasstreifen mit Hologrammen und einem mittig tieferliegenden, ebenfalls 15 cm breiten VSG-Glasstreifen mit PV-Zellen ausgestattet ist. Durch den Konzen-

of the louvres, and directed onto a pane of glass placed 11 mm behind; this glass is patterned with fritted strips from which the direct sunlight is then reflected. As the non-transmitting strips cover only 50 % of the surface area, diffuse daylight can pass through to illuminate the interior. To make use of the concentrated direct light, the fritted strips in the middle house were fitted with photovoltaics. On the upper part of the glass roof, too, photovoltaic modules convert solar energy into electricity; here the modules are 0.9 × 2.7 m in size and fitted with 10 × 10 cm polycrystalline silicon solar cells. The modules also offer a degree of shading from the steeply angled radiation in the summer, because only 35 % of the radiation penetrates the spaces between the modules through to the living areas below.
Beside the covered winter gardens are further laminated glass areas with holographic layers incorporated in the sloping sections. Here the HDS break the light up into an abstract rainbow. The possibility of altering fixed structures by adding wording or logos can transform the façade into an information carrier displaying messages or advertising to those passing by outside.

A more recent example for the use of holograms as an information carrier is the cladding on the triangular-shaped roof over the ventilation shafts of the electricity substation of the GEW in the Mediapark Cologne, completed in 1996. The holographic displays show stylised electricity bulbs, depicted in 2.5 × 5 cm sized square pixels. Each pixel corresponds to a single-colour holographic grid. The light refracted in this display gives rise to spectral colours of extraordinary luminance,

Holographische Displays mit stilisierten Glühbirnen werden als Verkleidung der dreieckigen Ablufthauben verwendet.
Umspannwerk der GEW im Mediapark, Köln, 1996, Krämer, Sieverts und Partner mit Sandro von Einsiedeln.
Holographic displays with stylised electric bulbs are used as cladding in triangular-shaped ventilation hoods.
Electricity substation of the GEW in the Mediapark, Cologne, 1996, Krämer, Sieverts and Partners in cooperation with Sandro von Einsiedeln.

trationsgrad der einfallenden Sonnenstrahlung ermöglicht diese Konstruktion einen anderthalbfachen Stromgewinn gegenüber konventionellen PV-Systemen. Diese gläsernen Sonnenschutzelemente werden durch Drehung um ihre Achse dem Lauf der Sonne nachgeführt.

Schichten mit Photovoltaik-Modulen

Innerhalb des Kapitels Verbundgläser stellen Photovoltaik-Module (PV) ein Sonderthema dar. Sie ermöglichen die aktive Nutzung der Sonnenstrahlung durch Umwandlung in elektrischen Strom; daneben können sie eine passive Sonnenschutzmaßnahme darstellen.

Die bekanntesten PV-Produkte sind Silizium-Solarzellen, wobei zwischen mono- und polykristallinen sowie amorphen, also nicht-kristallinen Solarzellen unterschieden wird.

Die monokristallinen Solarzellen sind opak, blau oder dunkelgrau bis schwarz und weisen einen hohen Wirkungsgrad (14–16 %) auf. Sie sind teuer, weil sie in einem aufwendigen Verfahren aus Silizium-Kristall hergestellt werden müssen.

Die polykristallinen Solarzellen sind meistens blau und opak. Sie sind günstiger, weil sie aus gegossenen Silizium-Blöcken gewonnen werden, weisen aber einen etwas niedrigeren Wirkungsgrad (14 %) auf.

Kristalline Solarzellen werden als 0.4 mm dicke Scheiben mit den Maßen von 10×10 cm bis 15×15 cm hergestellt. Danach werden sie zu Modulen zusammengebaut und in den Zwischenraum des Verbundglases mit Gießharz eingebettet. Je nach Aufbau sind durchsichtige, transluzide und undurchsichtige Module verfügbar. Bei transparenten und transluziden Modulen kann die Lichttransmission je nach Wahl der Abstände zueinander zwischen 4 % und 30 % eingestellt werden.

Polykristalline Silizium-Zellen sind für die Sanierung der Glasfassade des Verwaltungsgebäudes Stawag, Stadtwerke Aachen, 1991, vom Architekten Georg Feinhals verwendet worden. Um die Werbewirkung mit licht- und wärmetechnischen Anforderungen in Einklang zu bringen, wurden spezielle lichtstreuende und isolierende Glaselemente entwickelt. Im außenliegenden Verbundglas sind die PV-Zellen mit einem Abstand von 5 mm miteinander vergossen (SGG Optisol®-Fassade). Innenliegend wurde ein Verbundglas mit einer milchigen Zwischenschicht verwendet.

creating a picture which constantly changes as the angle of incidence and light intensity changes.

The holographic glass louvres at the IGA '93 were further developed to produce rotating solar shading elements which enable the use of standard-sized solar cells of 13×13 cm. The prototypes consist of a V-shaped metal frame fitted with two 15 cm wide strips of laminated glass with holograms and, placed lower down, in the middle, another 15 cm wide strip of laminated glass with photovoltaic cells. The degree of concentration of the incident solar radiation enables these glass louvres to produce one and half times more energy than conventional photovoltaic systems. These glass solar shading elements rotate on their axis to track the sun.

Layers with Photovoltaic Modules

Within this chapter on laminated glass, photovoltaic modules (PVs) are a special topic. They enable the active use of solar radiation by turning it into electrical energy; in addition they can also represent a form of passive solar protection. The most well known PV products are silicon solar cells, available in three types: monocrystalline, poly- or multicrystalline, and amorphous, i. e. non-crystalline solar cells. The monocrystalline solar cells are opaque, blue or dark grey to black, and they have a high efficiency (14–16 %). They are expensive because they are made from silicon crystals in a complicated manufacturing process. The polycrystalline solar cells are mostly blue or opaque. These are cheaper because they are made from poured silicon blocks, but they have a lower efficiency (14 %). Crystalline solar cells are produced as 0.4 mm thick discs in sizes from 10×10 cm to 15×15 cm. These discs are then put together to form modules and embedded with resin in the cavity in a laminated glass unit. According to composition, the result can be either a transparent, translucent or non-transparent module. Light transmission through transparent and translucent modules can be set from 4 % to 30 % according to the choice of spacing. Polycrystalline silicon cells were used in 1991 in Aachen by the architect Georg Feinhals for the renovation of the glass façade of the Stawag administration building. Special light-scattering and insulating glass elements were developed in order to meet both the needs in terms of lighting

Drehbare, V-förmige Sonnenschutzelemente mit Hologrammen ermöglichen den Einbau von Solarzellen in Standardgrößen.
GLB-Köln.

Pivoting, V-shaped solar shading elements with holograms enable standard-sized solar cells to be built in.
GLB-Köln.

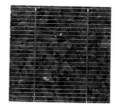

Verschiedene Photovoltaik-Module: oben eine
monokristalline Solarzelle, in der Mitte polykristalline
Solarzellen, unten eine semitransparente amorphe
Solarzelle.

*Different photovoltaic modules: a monocrystalline
solar cell (top), two polycrystalline solar cells
(middle), and a semi-transparent amorphous solar
cell (bottom).*

Die Verglasung läßt ca. 0.08 des einfallenden
Lichts durchkommen und beleuchtet den Innenraum gleichmäßig.

Wegen ihrer potentiell geringeren Kosten erwecken amorphe Solarzellen derzeit großes
Interesse. Dank der Dünnschichttechnologie erfordert ihre Herstellung weniger Material und
niedrigere Temperaturen. Damit können die
Schichten auf verschiedene Träger wie Glas,
Stahl- oder Kunststoffolien aufgetragen werden.
Leider ist der Wirkungsgrad mit 5−7 % noch
recht tief. Vollflächige amorphe Siliziumzellen
sind meistens rotbraun oder rötlich durch-
scheinend.

Auf dem Markt sind auch semitransparente
amorphe Solarzellen erhältlich. Dafür werden
Teilflächen der auf Glas aufgebrachten dünnen
Schichten mittels Lasertrenntechniken abge-
tragen, so daß transparente Stege zwischen den
aktiven Flächen resultieren, welche bis 12 % des
Lichtes durchlassen und einen Blick wie durch
eine halbgeschlossene Jalousie gewähren
(Asi-Glas®).

Als Alternative zu den amorphen Silizium-Solarzellen wecken auch andere Materialien vermehrt
Interesse, wie CdTe und CuInSe$_2$, die sich mittels
bewährten Dünnfilm- und Tauchverfahren her-
stellen lassen. Für kleine Flächen sind im Labor
bis 16 % Wirkungsgrad erreicht worden. Pro-
duktionswerte liegen aber heute noch bei 8 %.
Durch die Kombination von mehreren Dünn-
film-Solarzellen mit unterschiedlicher Spektral-
charakteristik läßt sich die Nutzung der einfallenden Strahlung optimieren. Sogenannte
«Tandemzellen» haben im Labor bis 12 %
Wirkungsgrad erreicht; eine weitere Steigerung
scheint möglich. Vielversprechender sieht es
mit «Tripelzellen» mit einer dreifachen Schicht-
abfolge aus. Hier scheinen 10 % Wirkungsgrad
auch für größere Produktionsmengen reali-
stisch.

Obwohl die PV-Zellen wirtschaftlich gesehen
noch nicht mit anderen Stromerzeugungsarten
konkurrieren können, sorgen wachsendes
Umweltbewußtsein, unterstützende Vorschriften
sowie Finanzierungshilfe durch öffentliche
Kreditgelder schon jetzt für ihre Verbreitung.

Temperaturabhängige Schichten
Es handelt sich dabei um Schichten, die bei
Temperaturwechsel den Strahlungsdurchgang
durch reversible physikalische Veränderungen
automatisch steuern können.

and insulation, as well as the desire to maintain
and exploit the corporate image as projected
through the façade. In the exterior laminated
glass the PV cells have a gap of 5 mm between
them (SGG Optisol®Façade). On the inside a
laminated glass with an opaque interlayer was
used. The glazing lets through approx. 0.08 of
the incident light and provides an even illumination of the interior space.

Amorphous solar cells are attracting great interest at present, because of their potentially lower
costs. Thanks to thin-film technology they can be
manufactured using less material and at lower
temperatures. The films can be applied to various carriers such as glass, plastics or steelfoils.
Unfortunately the efficiency is still relatively low,
values of 5−7 % are typical. Large areas of
amorphous silicon cells are mostly red-brown-
ish, or, when transparent, slightly reddish.

Also available are semi-transparent amorphous
solar cells. They are produced by removing par-
tial areas of the thin film by means of a laser
separation process, in order to create narrow
transparent strips between the opaque surfaces,
which allow up to 12 % of the incident light to
pass through. The impression gained is that of
looking through a half-open louvre blind
(Asi-Glass®).

As alternatives to amorphous silicon solar
cells other materials are attracting increasing
interest – materials such as CdTe and CuInSe$_2$.
These cells can be built using established thin
film technologies or even by a dipping process.
In smaller areas up to 16 % efficiency has
been reached under laboratory conditions.
Production values, however, do not exceed 8 %
so far.

Optimised exploitation of solar energy can be
achieved by combining several thin film layers
with different spectral responses. So-called tan-
dem cells have reached up to 12 % efficiency
under laboratory conditions, slightly higher
values seem possible. Further possibilities are
offered by triple cells which consist of a succession of three thin film layers. Efficiencies of
10 % in production quantities are becoming
realistic.

Although PV cells cannot yet compete economi-
cally with other ways of generating energy,
they are gaining ground due to a generally
increasing concern for the environment, sup-
portive regulations and financial help from
public funding.

Thermotrope Schichten

Thermotrope Schichten wirken über den gesamten solaren Spektralbereich und gehen bei steigender Temperatur vom klaren und lichtdurchlässigen zum opaken und lichtstreuenden Zustand über.

Das Grundmaterial besteht aus zwei Komponenten mit unterschiedlichem Brechungsindex, zum Beispiel aus Wasser und einem Kunststoff (Hydrogel) oder aus zwei verschiedenen Kunststoffen (Polymerblend). Bei niedrigen Temperaturen ist die Mischung homogen und durchsichtig.

Bei höheren Temperaturen ändern die Polymere ihre Konfiguration – von gestreckten Ketten hin zu zusammengeklumpten Kügelchen, die eine Lichtstreuung verursachen. Die Veränderung vom transmittierenden zum streuenden Zustand ist reversibel. Typische Werte im sichtbaren Bereich bewegen sich zwischen 0.80–0.90 und 0.10–0.50 und die Gesamttransmissionen zwischen 0.80–0.90 und 0.05–0.40.

In den vergangenen Jahren sind zwei Produkte entwickelt worden: Cloud Gel® und TALD®.

Cloud Gel® von Suntek Co. ist ein Hydrogel, das mit einer Schichtdicke von beispielsweise 1 mm zwischen zwei Glasscheiben bei Temperaturvariation eine Reduktion der solaren Transmission von 0.82 auf 0.05 bewirkt, die zwischen 25° C und 30° C sehr stark und bis 50° C gleichmäßig abnimmt.

TALD® (temperaturabhängige Lichtdurchlässigkeit) ist ebenfalls ein Hydrogel. Eine Schicht mit einer Dicke von 1 mm, eingebettet zwischen zwei Glasscheiben, weist solare Transmissionswerte zwischen 0.47 und 0.84 auf. Die Eintrübungstemperatur kann durch die Zusammenstellung der Mischung beliebig zwischen 5° C und 60° C eingestellt werden.

Das Hauptproblem der Hydrogele liegt in ihrem Wasseranteil, welcher eine gute Dichtigkeit und Maßnahmen bei Erreichung des Gefrierpunkts verlangt.

Thermotrope Schichten aus Kunststoffen (Polymerblends) hingegen haben bessere Erfolgsaussichten, weil sie diese Probleme umgehen. Die Eintrübung ist gleichmäßiger abgestuft, und der Beginn des Prozesses kann durch das Verhältnis bei der Mischung zwischen 25° C und 120° C eingestellt werden.

Wegen der höheren Schalttemperatur kommen die Polymerblends auch als Überhitzungsschutz für Sonnenkollektoren in Frage.

Temperature-Dependent Layers

Temperature-dependent layers can automatically control light transmission by reversible physical changes which are activated by a change in temperature.

Thermotropic Layers

Thermotropic layers operate mainly over the entire solar spectrum, changing state with increasing temperature from clear and light-transmitting to opaque and light-scattering. The basic material consists of two components with differing refractive indices, for example water and a polymer (hydrogel) or two different polymers (polymer blend). At lower temperatures the mixture is homogeneous and has a high transparency. At higher temperatures, however, the configuration of the polymers alters – from stretched chains to clumps which scatter light.

This change from a transmitting to a scattering state is reversible. Typical visible transmission values lie between 0.80–0.90 and 0.10–0.50 and solar energy transmission values lie between 0.80–0.90 and 0.05–0.40.

In recent years two products have been developed: Cloud Gel® and TALD®.

Cloud Gel®, by Suntek Co., is a hydrogel which, as a 1 mm thick layer sandwiched between two glass panes and subjected to temperature changes, displays a reduction in solar energy transmission from 0.82 to 0.05; between 25° C and 30° C the drop is most marked, and a more even transition takes place up to 50° C.

TALD® is also a hydrogel. A 1 mm thick layer of TALD® sandwiched between two panes of glass has solar energy transmission values of between 0.47 and 0.84. The temperature at which cloud-

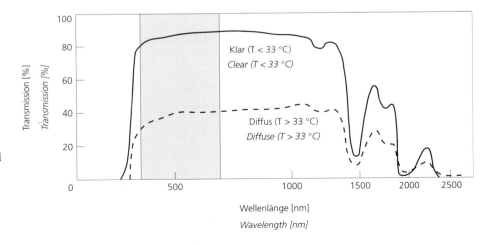

Thermotrope Schicht

Klarer Zustand (tiefe Temperatur)   Geschalteter Zustand (hohe Temperatur)

☐ homogene Mischung   ● Streumaterial
■ Deckschicht/Träger   ☐ Matrixmaterial

Aufbau von thermotropen Schichten: bei steigenden Temperaturen gehen sie vom klaren, lichtdurchlässigen zum opaken, lichtstreuenden Zustand über.
Thermotropic layers: when the temperature rises they change from a clear, light-transmitting to an opaque, light-scattering state.

Spektrale Transmission einer 1 mm dicken thermotropen Schicht von TALD®.
Spectral transmission of a 1 mm thick thermotropic layer of TALD®.

Transmission [%] / *Transmission [%]*

Klar (T < 33 °C)
Clear (T < 33 °C)

Diffus (T > 33 °C)
Diffuse (T > 33 °C)

Wellenlänge [nm]
Wavelength [nm]

Am Fraunhofer Institut für Solare Energie-systeme, Fraunhofer-ISE, Freiburg im Breisgau, sind seit einigen Jahren Experimente im Gange mit thermotropen Prototypen von Verglasungen in Verbundsystemen mit transparenter Wärme-dämmung und Sonnenkollektoren.

Thermochrome Schichten
Beim Erwärmen verändern thermochrome Schichten die Strahlungstransmission hauptsäch-lich im nahen IR-Bereich, so daß sie im metal-lischen Zustand als niedrig-emissive Schichten eingesetzt werden können, um die langwellige Sonnenstrahlung oder die Wärmeverluste durch Emissivität zu dämmen. Dafür eignen sich Über-gangmetalloxide, zum Beispiel Vanadiumoxid (VO$_2$). Unterhalb einer bestimmten Temperatur ist das Material halbleitend oder dielektrisch mit geringer Absorption im IR-Bereich, darüber tritt das metallische, IR-reflektierende Ver-halten ein.
Einige Forschungen laufen in diese Richtung, und Experimente mit dünnen Vanadiumoxid-Schichten sind bereits durchgeführt worden.

Elektrooptische Schichten
Im Hinblick auf eine «intelligente Glasfassade» scheinen Entwicklungen von Schichten mit Flüs-sigkristallen oder mit elektrochromen Materia-lien die meisten Aussichten auf Erfolg zu haben. Sie ermöglichen eine aktive Steuerung der Strah-lungsdurchlässigkeit durch das Anlegen einer elektrischen Spannung und können über eine zentrale Gebäudeleittechnik (GLT) oder über integrierte Mikrochips die Glashülle an die ver-änderlichen Licht- und Wetterverhältnisse an-passen.

Schichten mit Flüssigkristallen
Schichten mit Flüssigkristallen (liquid crystals, LC) sind von Uhren und PC-Displays her be-kannt. Diese LC-Systeme arbeiten nach dem Prinzip, daß sich die kettenförmigen Moleküle der Flüssigkristalle elektrisch ausrichten lassen und damit der Durchgang von polarisiertem Licht gesteuert werden kann. Im normalen, spannungslosen Zustand sind die Moleküle zufällig gerichtet, so daß sie das einfallende Licht zerstreuen. Beim Anlegen einer Spannung richten sie sich entlang der Linien des elek-trischen Feldes aus. Das System wird dann licht-durchlässig und bleibt es, solange das Span-nungsfeld aufrechterhalten wird. Daß sie ohne

ing occurs can be predetermined by controlling the chemical composition at the manufacturing stage – the range lies between 5° C and 60° C. The main problem of hydrogels is their water content which requires a good seal and special measures when temperatures reach the freezing point.
Thermotropic layers of plastics (polymer blends), however, have better prospects of suc-cess, as they avoid these problems. The clouding is more evenly graduated and the start of the process can be set to between 25°C and 120°C according to the proportions of the mix. The higher switching temperature means the polymer blends can also be considered as protection against overheating in solar collectors.
At the Fraunhofer Institute for Solar Energy Sys-tems, the Fraunhofer-ISE in Freiburg im Breis-gau, experiments have now been underway for a number of years into thermotropic prototypes of glazing with laminated systems with transparent thermal insulation and solar collectors.

Thermochromic Layers
On being heated, thermochromic layers undergo a change in their transmission properties, mainly in the near infrared range; this makes them suit-able for use in their metallic state as low-emissi-vity coatings to reduce long-wave solar radiation or heat loss by emission. Particularly suited here are transition metal oxides, such as vanadium dioxide (VO$_2$). Below a certain temperature the material assumes a semiconductor or dielectric state with low absorption in the infrared range; as the temperature increases, it proceeds to a metallic state causing infrared reflectivity. Re-search is being carried out in this direction at present, and experiments using thin-film vana-dium dioxide have already been performed.

Electro-Optic Layers
With respect to an "intelligent glass façade", developments in the field of liquid crystal layers or layers of electrochromic material seem to hold the most promise. By applying a voltage, the light and/or solar transmission of these layers can be actively controlled in accordance with the prevailing light or weather conditions, either via a central building management system (BMS) or via microchips integrated into the glass skin.

Liquid Crystal Layers
We are already familiar with liquid crystal layers

Stromzufuhr undurchsichtig sind, ist denn auch der große Nachteil von LC-Schichten.

Das Einstellen von verschiedenen Stufen erfolgt durch aufwendige und daher teure Steuerungssysteme, welche den Lichtdurchgang dimmen.

Für die Verwendung als Verglasung bereiten insbesondere die großen Flächen und die Aufwärmung der Scheibe Probleme, was Funktionsstörungen hervorrufen kann. Darum kommen Systeme mit Flüssigkristallen zur Zeit vor allem im Innenbereich zur Anwendung.

In Kombination mit Sonnenschutzgläsern besteht aber die Möglichkeit, sie auch im Fassadenbau zu verwenden. Künftig sollte die Stabilität der Moleküle bei UV-Strahlung verbessert werden.

Eine weitere Möglichkeit sind die sogenannten «Guest-Host»-Typen. Hier sind dichroitische Farbmoleküle mit den Flüssigkristallen gemischt, um eine stärkere Absorption zu bewirken. Im cholesterinischen Zustand sind die Moleküle in parallelen Ebenen geschichtet, wobei die Flüssigkristalle aber eine unterschiedliche Ausrichtung aufweisen. Vorteil der «Guest-Host»-Systeme ist eine Funktionstüchtigkeit bis 100° C. Sie wurden für Brillengläser und Autorückspiegel entwickelt. Prototypen von Rückspiegeln haben eine Reflexion von 0.12 und 0.48 im sichtbaren Bereich erreicht.

Die aussichtsreichste Lösung stellt die Mikroverkapselung («polymer dispersed liquid cristal», PDLC; «nematic curvilinear aligned phase», NCAP) dar. Bei der Mikroverkapselung (PDLC/NCAP) sind die kettenförmigen Moleküle in Kügelchen von $1-10 \cdot 10^3$ nm Durchmesser eingeschlossen und in einer Kunststoffschicht zwischen zwei elektrisch leitfähigen ITO-beschichteten Kunststofffilmen eingebettet.

Unter elektrischer Spannung werden die Moleküle ausgerichtet, und die Folie wirkt fast transparent. Die verbleibende leichte Eintrübung ist auf die restliche Reflexion der Kügelchen zurückzuführen und bildet einen Nachteil der Mikroverkapselung. Ohne elektrisches Feld wird das Licht gestreut, und das System erscheint milchig-trüb beziehungsweise opak. Unbefriedigend ist auch die geringe Beständigkeit gegenüber der UV-Strahlung.

Prototypen mit einer Lichttransmission von 0.48 bis 0.76 sind schon hergestellt worden.

Im Handel sind Produkte wie Priva-Lite® und Transopac®, die eine Lichtdurchlässigkeit von 0.70 im opaken und 0.73 im durchsichtigen

(or LCs) in watches and PC screens. These LC systems work on the principle that liquid crystal molecule chains can be influenced electrically to permit the transmission of polarized light. Without an applied voltage, the molecules are randomly orientated and the incident light is scattered. When a voltage is applied, the molecules align themselves along the lines of the electrical field; in this state the system is then able to transmit light, as long as the electrical field is maintained. The main disadvantage, however, of LC layers is the fact that they are non-transparent when no voltage is applied across them.

The setting of various levels is achieved by complicated – and therefore also expensive – control systems to adjust light transmission.

For use in glazing, problems occur when large surfaces of glass are used and as a consequence of the temperature increase in the glass itself, which can lead to malfunctioning of the light control. For this reason liquid crystal systems are primarily used for inside applications at present. However, in combination with solar control glazings there is also a possibility of using them in façades. Development work is going on to improve the ultraviolet stability of the molecules.

A further possibility is presented by the so-called "guest-host types". Here dichroic dye molecules mixed with liquid crystals are used with the aim of achieving higher absorption. In the cholesteric-nematic structure the direction of the long axis of the molecules is slightly displaced with the liquid crystals displaying a different alignment. The advantage of the "guest-host" systems is their functionality up to 100° C. They were developed for use in spectacles and rear view mirrors for cars. Prototypes for rear view mirrors have achieved reflectances of 0.12 to 0.48 in the visible range.

The most promising solution is presented by micro-encapsulation ("polymer dispersed liquid crystal", PDLC; and "nematic curvilinear aligned phase", NCAP). This material (PDLC/NCAP) contains encapsulated chains of molecules as balls of $1-10 \cdot 10^3$ nm radius within a polymer matrix sandwiched between two electrodes, which are usually ITO-coated polyester films.

When subject to an electrical charge, the molecule chains straighten and the film appears almost transparent. Any remaining slight clouding is due to the reflection from the balls and as such is one of the disadvantages of micro-encapsulation. When no electrical charge is present,

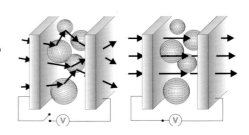

Mikroverkapselte Flüssigkristalle: im spannungslosen Zustand sind die Moleküle zufällig gerichtet, so daß sie das Licht zerstreuen; beim Anlegen einer Spannung richten sie sich entlang der Linien des elektrischen Feldes aus, und das System wird lichtdurchlässig.

Beispiel einer Glastrennwand mit Flüssigkristallen im opaken und im durchsichtigen Zustand: Priva-Lite®.

Micro-encapsulated liquid crystals: without an applied voltage the molecules are randomly orientated and the system scatters light. When a voltage is applied, the molecules align themselves with the electrical field and the system transmits light.

Example of a glass partition with liquid crystals in opaque and transparent states: Priva-Lite®.

Zustand aufweisen Die Folien sind ca. 0.3 mm stark und maximal 1×2.80 m groß. Je nach Einbau im Verbundglas sind verschiedene Gesamtdicken und neutrale, bronzefarbene, graue und grüne Farbtöne erhältlich.

Zur Zeit können LC-Folien bei Temperaturen von $-40°$ C bis $+40°$ C einwandfrei eingesetzt werden, was zwar den problemlosen Einbau in Innenräumen, jedoch die Verwendung im Fassadenbau nur in Kombination mit zusätzlichen Sonnenschutzmaßnahmen gestattet. Bei höheren Temperaturen bilden sich Flecken mit unterschiedlicher Opazität, und ab $+100°$ C sind die Folien vollständig transparent.

Elektrochrome Schichten

Elektrochrome Schichten nutzen die Eigenschaft einiger Materialien, Ionen aufzunehmen oder abzugeben und damit ihre Transmission im sichtbaren und solaren Strahlungsbereich zu ändern. Im Prinzip funktionieren sie wie ein Akkumulator: ein Ionenspeicher, ein Ionenleiter und ein elektrochromes Material sind zwischen zwei Trägermaterialien – Glas oder Kunststoff – mit transparenten Elektroden gestellt. Die chemische Reaktion findet statt, wenn bei Anlegen einer elektrischen Spannung Ionen hin- und herverschoben werden. Da die Schichten einige Zeit aufgeladen bleiben, ist die Stromzufuhr nur während des Ionenaustauschs notwendig.

Dieser Aufbau läßt sich aber verschiedentlich variieren. Zum Beispiel können gewisse Elektrolyten auch als Ionenspeicher wirken. Oder es können zwei elektrochrome Materialien, das eine gefärbt im reduzierten Zustand und das andere im oxidierten Zustand, kombiniert werden, was zu einer verstärkten Wirkung beitragen kann. Oder es können mehrere Schichten verwendet werden, da der Effekt additiv ist.

Wolframoxid (WO_3) ist die elektrochrome Substanz, mit der am häufigsten experimentiert wird, weil sie im sichtbaren Bereich die größte Intensitätsvariation zwischen transparent und dunkelblau aufweist. Es können aber auch bronzefarbene (NiO) oder schwarze (IrO_2) Tönungen, oder sogar Farbwechsel – wie Rot zu Blau (CoO_x) und Gelb zu Grün (Rh_2O_3) – erzielt werden.

Die Schichten können mit der Dünnschichttechnologie, durch Sputtern oder Aufdämpfen, sowie mit chemischen Verfahren hergestellt werden. Elektrochrome Systeme, die, über Abstufungen, zwischen einem transparenten und einem absor-

light is scattered and the system appears milky white or opaque. One further problem is the low stability against ultraviolet radiation.

Prototypes with light transmission factors from 0.48 to 0.76 have already been produced. Available on the market are products such as Priva-Lite® and Transopac®, which have a light transmission factor of 0.70 in the opaque state, and 0.73 in the transparent state. The film is approx. 0.3 mm thick and a maximum of 1×2.80 m in size. Depending on the particular laminated glass construction different overall thicknesses can be obtained, and a range of colour tints in neutral, bronze, grey and green.

At present LC-films can be used without problems in the temperature range from $-40°$ C to $+40°$ C, which makes them perfectly adequate for interior use, but restricts their use in façades to combinations with other solar shading devices. At higher temperatures patches of differing opacities develop, and above $100°$ C the films are completely transparent.

Electrochromic Layers

Electrochromic layers exploit the ability of some materials to accept or shed ions, thus influencing the transmission properties in the visible and invisible radiation range. In principle they function in the same way as an accumulator: an ion storage layer, an ion conductor and an electrochromic material are placed between two substrates – glass or plastic – with transparent conductors. The chemical reaction takes place when the ions are shuttled forwards and backwards through the application of a voltage. As the layers remain charged for some time, the voltage need only be applied during the ion exchange process.

This system can be varied somewhat. For example certain electrolytes can act as an ion storage layer. Or two electrochromic materials can be combined to increase the desired light regulating effect; one of them is coloured in the reduced state and the other in the oxidized state, which increases the desired effect. Or several layers can be used to create an additive effect.

Tungsten oxide (WO_3) is a chromogenic material which is subject to most testing at present, because it has the greatest variation of intensity in the visible range between transparent and dark blue. However, other colours can also be produced, from bronze (NiO) or black (IrO_2) to

Aufbau von elektrochromen Schichten:
1 Glasscheibe;
2 transparente Elektrode;
3 Ionenspeicher;
4 Ionenleiter;
5 elektrochromes Material;
6 transparente Elektrode;
7 Glasscheibe.
– Die chemische Reaktion findet statt, wenn beim Anlegen einer elektrischen Spannung Ionen hin- und herverschoben werden.

Basic design of electrochromic layers:
1 glass;
2 transparent conductor;
3 ion storage film;
4 ion conductor (electrolyte);
5 electrochromic film;
6 transparent conductor;
7 glass.
– The chemical reaction takes place when the ions are shuttled forwards and backwards through the application of an electrical field.

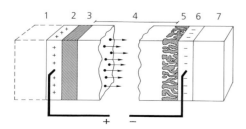

bierenden Zustand eingestellt werden können, eignen sich als Sonnen- und Blendschutz hervorragend sowohl für Gebäudeverglasungen als auch für die Scheiben von Flugzeugen, Straßen- und Bahnfahrzeugen. Daß daran ein großes Interesse besteht, zeigt die hohe Anzahl an Patentgesuchen, die in den letzten Jahren in Japan und den USA eingereicht wurden.

Zur Zeit wird die Entwicklung von elektrochromen Gläsern für die Anwendung bei Automobilen und Flugzeugen intensiv betrieben. Die Beanspruchung durch hohe Temperaturen von 90° C bis 120° C und die kleinen Dimensionen der Scheiben wirken sich in diesem Bereich – anders als bei einer Anwendung im Bauwesen – auch wegen der relativen Kurzlebigkeit der Objekte weniger nachteilig aus. Auf dem Markt finden sich bereits aktiv steuerbare Autorückspiegel von Donnelly und Gentex, aber auch Prototypen von Glasschiebedächern für Autos (Nissan Motors, Donnelly, Daimler-Benz-Dornier).

Für die Verwendung im Bauwesen sind Verbundgläser mit elektrochromen Schichten als Prototypen mit maximal 0.5 m² Fläche produziert worden. Probleme bereiten die hohen Kosten für die transparenten Elektroden und deren relativ geringe Leitfähigkeit, die die Schaltgeschwindigkeit der elektrochromen Elemente mit zunehmender Fläche stark herabsetzt.

Als Idealwerte für solche Verglasungen definiert Dr. Carl Lampert, Lawrence Berkeley Laboratory, California, eine Steuerung der Transmission wie folgt: im nahen infraroten Bereich zwischen 0.10 und 0.70; im sichtbaren Bereich zwischen 0.10 und 0.20 im farbigen, abgedunkelten Zustand, und 0.60–0.80 im klaren, transparenten Zustand; eine Schaltgeschwindigkeit von 1 bis 50 Sekunden bei einer Schaltspannung von 1–5 V sowie ein «Gedächtnis» von 1 bis 24 Stunden.

Beim Museum «Seto Bridge», Kojima, Japan, 1988, wurden von der Asahi Glass versuchsweise 196 elektrochrome Scheiben von 40×40 cm installiert. Sie ermöglichen die Betrachtung des Unterwasserpanoramas, während sich ihre Farbe im Takt der Musik von Hell- zu Dunkelblau verändert. Weitere 45×40 cm große Prototypen sind 1988 für die Verglasung im Haus Daiwa, Mita-City, Japan, eingesetzt worden.

An der Glasstec '98 in Düsseldorf sind Prototypen von Isoliergläsern mit EC-Scheiben

changing colours, such as red to blue (CoO_x) and yellow to green (Rh_2O_3).

The layers can be applied either by thin film technology, as sputtering or chemical vapour deposition, or by sol-gel technology.

Electrochromic systems which can be switched back and forth between transparent and absorbing states, are an ideal device of protection against sun and glare both in buildings as well as for glazing in aircraft, road vehicles or trains. The great interest in this area is witnessed by the large number of patent applications which have been registered in Japan and the USA in recent years.

At present intense research is being carried out in the development of electrochromic glass for use in cars and airplanes. In contrast to use in building, the stress from high temperatures from 90° C to 120° C and the small dimensions of the panes are not so critical, not least because of the relative short operational lifespan. Already available on the market, produced by Donnelly and Gentex, are actively controllable rear view mirrors for cars; prototypes for glass sunroofs for cars (Nissan Motors, Donnelly, Daimler-Benz-Dornier) have also been developed.

For use in buildings, so far the only developments in laminated glass with electrochromic layers are limited to prototypes with a maximum size of 0.5 m². Problems arise due to the high costs of the transparent conductors and the drop in the electrical field with increasing surface area, which greatly reduces the switching speed of the electrochromic elements.

According to Dr Carl Lampert, of the Lawrence Berkeley Laboratory in California, the ideal ranges for control of transmission in glazing are as follows: between 0.10 and 0.70 in the near infrared range; in the visible range between 0.10 and 0.20 in the coloured, darkened state and 0.60–0.80 in the clear, transparent state; a switching speed of 1 to 50 seconds at a switching voltage of 1–5 V and a "memory" of 1 to 24 hours.

In 1988 at the Seto Bridge Museum in Kojima, Japan, Asahi Glass installed as an experiment 196 electrochromic panes, 40×40 cm in size. They allow the visitor to view the underwater panorama, while, in time to the music, the colours change from pale to dark blue. More prototypes, in a size of 45×40 cm have been installed as part of the glazing in Daiwa House, built in 1988 in Mita-City, Japan.

Prototyp einer Verbundscheibe mit elektrochromen Schichten aus Wolframoxid im klaren und im verdunkelten Zustand.
Dornier Aerospace, Friedrichshafen, Deutschland.
Prototype of a laminated glass with electrochromic layers of tungsten oxide in clear and coloured states. Dornier Aerospace, Friedrichshafen, Germany.

Installation mit 196 elektrochromen Scheiben von
40 x 40 cm, die ihre Farbe im Takt der Musik von
Hell- zu Dunkelblau verändern.
Museum «Seto Bridge», Kojima, Japan, 1988, Asahi
Glass.
Installation with 196 electrochromic panes
40 x 40 cm in size; the panes change colour from
pale to dark blue in time to the music.
Seto Bridge Museum, Kojima, Japan, 1988, Asahi
Glass.

(E-Control®) vorgestellt worden, die eine Lichttransmission von 0.50 im klaren und von 0.15
im abgedunkelten Zustand erreichen. Damit
kann der Gesamtenergiedurchlaßgrad zwischen
0.40 und 0.15 eingestellt werden. Trotzdem
bereiten EC-Schichtensysteme immer noch
Schwierigkeiten, vor allem was ihre Beständigkeit und die großflächige Produktion betrifft.

Gasochrome Systeme
Ausgehend von den thermochromen Schichten
wurden gasochrome Systeme entwickelt, bei
denen die Farbveränderung durch eine Gasmischung stattfindet. An der Glasstec '98 wurden
Prototypen von gasochromen Isoliergläsern vorgestellt, wo die mit Ni_2 stark verdünnten H_2- oder
O_2-Gasmischungen diese Veränderung her-
beiführen. Die Glasscheiben sind mit einer
Schicht Wolframoxid (WO_3) und einem Kata-
lysator versehen. Sie sind so zusammengebaut,
daß ein Zwischenraum entsteht, der mit einer
Gasmischung durchströmt wird. Durch Zu-
fügen von wenigen H_2-Anteilen färbt sich die
WO_3-Schicht ein, während sie sich durch kleine
O_2-Konzentrationen entfärbt. Neben dem blau
färbenden WO_3 werden auch farbneutrale
Mischungen aus Metalloxiden von Wolfram,
Titan und Molybdän untersucht. Durch die
Variation der Schichtdicke und der Gaskonzen-
tration lassen sich beinahe beliebige Trans-
missionsgrade einstellen.
Die gasochromen Systeme sind einfach in der
Herstellung des Schichtenaufbaus und weisen
eine hohe Transmission im entfärbten Zustand
auf. Zur Zeit sind Forschungen im Gange, um
das System der Gaszufuhr zu verbessern sowie
die Bildung von Wasser beim Zuführen von
Wasserstoffatomen zu verhindern.

Presented at Glasstec'98 in Düsseldorf were prototypes of insulating glass with electrochromic
panes (E-control®), which achieve light transmission of 0.50 in a clear state and 0.15 in a
darkened state. This enables the degree of energy transmitted to be set at between 0.40 and
0.15. Nevertheless electrochromic layer systems
still present considerable difficulties, above all
as regards their resilience and suitability for
production of large panes.

Gasochromic Systems
Thermochromic systems gave rise to the idea for
gasochromic systems, in which colour change
takes place by means of a gas mixture. At
Glasstec'98 prototypes of gasochromic insulating
glass were presented, using H_2 or O_2 gas mixtures heavily diluted with Ni_2 to produce the
colour change. The glass is coated with a layer
of tungsten oxide (WO_3) and a catalyser. They
are constructed in such a way to create a space
through which a gas mixture is passed. By
adding a little H_2 the WO_3 layer colours, but by
adding small quantities of O_2 concentrations the
colour disappears. In addition to the blue-
colouring layer of WO_3, colour-neutral mixtures
of the metal oxides of tungsten, titanium and
molybdenum are also being investigated. By
varying the thickness of the layer and the concentration of the gas, virtually any degree of
transmission can be achieved.
The layers in gasochromic systems are simple to
manufacture and these systems have high transmission levels in the colour-neutral state. At
present research is underway to improve the gas
injection system and to avoid the build-up of
water when adding hydrogen atoms.

Das Isolierglas   Insulating Glass

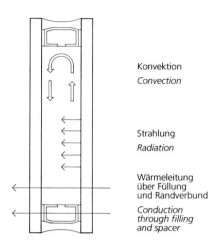

Konvektion
Convection

Strahlung
Radiation

Wärmeleitung
über Füllung
und Randverbund

*Conduction
through filling
and spacer*

Beim Isolierglas erfolgt der Wärmetransport über vier Wege: Konvektion, Strahlungsaustausch zwischen den Glasoberflächen und Wärmeleitung über die Füllung oder über den Randverbund.
The heat transport through an insulating glass unit takes place in four different ways: convection, radiation exchange between the glass surfaces and conduction through the filling or the edge seal.

Linke Seite: Durch den spiegelnden Schleiereffekt silberfarbig bedruckter Isoliergläser wirkt die Glasfassade wie ein pointillistisches Bild.
Neues Verwaltungsgebäude des «Palais des Beaux-Arts», Lille, Frankreich, 1992–97, J. M. Ibos und M. Vitart Architekten.
Left page: The reflecting veil-like effect of silver-printed insulating glass gives a Pointilliste effect to the glass façade.
New administration building of the Palais des Beaux-Arts, Lille, France, 1992–97, J. M. Ibos and M. Vitart Architects.

Die Wärmeverluste einer einfachen Verglasung können mit dem Einsatz von Isoliergläsern mindestens halbiert werden.

Ein Isolierglas ist eine Verbundkonstruktion aus zwei oder mehreren Glasscheiben, die am äußeren Rand durch ein oder mehrere Abstandprofile schubfest und gasdicht verbunden sind. Damit entsteht ein Scheibenzwischenraum von 8–20 mm Tiefe, der mit einer Füllung aus trockener Luft oder Edelgas als Wärmepuffer wirkt.

Der Wärmetransport von der Warmseite zur Kaltseite erfolgt über vier Wege: durch Strahlungsaustausch zwischen den gegenüberliegenden Glasoberflächen, durch Konvektion im Scheibenzwischenraum, durch Wärmeleitung über die Füllung oder über den Randverbund.

Die Wärmeleitung über den üblichen Abstandhalter läßt sich nur begrenzt beeinflussen, weil dort Druck-, Zug- und Schubkräfte aufgenommen werden müssen. Eine Reduktion der Wärmeverluste kann durch die Veränderung der anderen drei Parameter erzielt werden.

Die Abstrahlung der Glasoberfläche kann mit einer niedrig-emissiven (Low-E) Beschichtung von etwa 0.85 bis auf 0.10 oder sogar darunter gesenkt werden. Während ein normales Isolierglas mit unbeschichteter Oberfläche und einem 12 mm breiten, mit Luft gefüllten Zwischenraum einen k-Wert von 3 W/m²K aufweist, führt die Low-E-Beschichtung zu einem k-Wert unter 2 W/m²K.

Füllungen mit Gas

Die Wärmeleitfähigkeit einer Füllung mit trockener Luft ist niedrig. Durch Edelgase wie Argon, Krypton oder Xenon können die Werte aber noch weiter gesenkt werden, weil sie eine niedrigere Wärmeleitung und eine geringere Konvektionsneigung aufweisen. Bei der Wahl sind ökonomische Überlegungen ausschlaggebend. Das Argon kann kostengünstig aus der Luft gewonnen werden, weil es 1 % der Luftanteile ausmacht; dagegen sind Krypton zu 0.0001 % und

Heat losses associated with standard single glazing can be reduced by at least 50 % by using insulating glass units.

Insulating glass consists in two or more panes separated along the edges by one or more spacers, which seal the cavity and are shear resistant. The resulting 8–20 mm cavity between the panes acts as a thermal buffer and can be filled with dehydrated air or inert gas.

Heat transport from the warm side to the cold side takes place in four different ways: by convection in the cavity, by radiation exchange between the opposite glass surfaces, and by conduction through the filling and the edge seal. Conduction levels through the standard spacers can only be slightly reduced, because here compression, tension and shear forces have to be taken up. A reduction in heat losses can be achieved by altering the other three parameters. The radiative heat losses from the surface of the glass can be reduced from approximately 0.85 to 0.10 or even lower by the application of a low-emissivity (low-E) coating. While normal insulating glass with an uncoated surface and 12 mm cavity filled with air has a U-value of 3 W/m²K, a low-E coating produces a U-value of below 2 W/m²K.

Gas Fillings

The thermal conductivity of a filling with dehydrated air is low. By using inert gases such as argon, krypton or xenon the values can be further reduced, because these gases have lower thermal conductivity and convection properties than normal air. The choice of which gas to use depends on economic factors. Argon is cheap to obtain, because it makes up 1 % of normal air; krypton on the other hand makes up only 0.0001 % and xenon 0.000009 %, and therefore are correspondingly more expensive. The U-values of a double pane insulating glass with a low-E coating and a 15 mm cavity filled with

Xenon gar nur zu 0.000009 % in der Luft enthalten und daher wesentlich teurer. Die k-Werte eines Zweifach-Isolierglases mit einer Low-E-Beschichtung, einem 15 mm breiten Zwischenraum und einer Füllung mit Argon liegen bei 1.1 W/m²K, mit Krypton bei 0.8 W/m²K.

Zur Zeit sind die Amortisationskosten von Krypton und ähnlichen Gasen noch sehr hoch, aber eine größere Nachfrage könnte eine Preissenkung mit sich bringen.

Eine Senkung des k-Werts deutlich unter 1 W/m²K kann durch das Anbringen einer dritten Scheibe, durch das Einspannen mehrerer low-E-beschichteter Folien oder durch Evakuierung des Scheibenzwischenraumes erfolgen.

Ein Dreifach-Isolierglas wird mit zwei low-E-beschichteten Scheiben und unterschiedlichen Gasfüllungen hergestellt: mit Argon wird ein k-Wert von 0.7 W/m²K im Silverstar® (g = 0.42, τ = 0.64), mit Krypton ein k-Wert von 0.7 W/m²K im SGG Climatop® (g = 0.45, τ = 0.66) und ein k-Wert von 0.5 W/m²K im Silverstar Selekt® (g = 0.35, τ = 0.60) erreicht.

Eine andere Möglichkeit besteht im Einspannen von Folien mit Low-E-Beschichtungen. Damit wird das Gewicht und die Dicke der dritten Glasscheibe vermieden. Das HIT® mit zwei low-E-beschichteten Folien in einem Zwischenraum von 60 mm erreicht einen k-Wert von 0.6 W/m²K (z. B. g = 0.40 und τ = 0.55), und das Superglass®, ebenfalls mit zwei low-E-beschichteten Folien, aber mit einem schmaleren Zwischenraum von 17 mm bis 33 mm, weist einen k-Wert von 0.7 W/m²K (g = 0.34, τ = 0.62) auf.

Die Variante der Evakuierung des Scheibenzwischenraumes schaltet den Kostenfaktor der Edelgase aus, läßt aber andere Probleme auftreten. Der Randverbund eines Vakuumglases muß eine sehr hohe Dichtigkeit garantieren und die unterschiedlichen thermischen Ausdehnungen der beiden Glasscheiben schubfest aufnehmen. Dafür scheint ein Glasverbund (Glaslote) sehr geeignet, aber dieser erhöht die Wärmeleitung und damit die Verluste im Randbereich. Wegen des Vakuums sind Abstandhalter im Zwischenraum notwendig. Dimensionierung und Abstand der beiden ESG-Scheiben voneinander müssen hinsichtlich punktueller Spannungen auf der Glasoberfläche, Wärmeleitung bei den Kontaktstellen und klarer Durchsicht optimiert werden. Am US Solar Energy Research Institute (SERI, Golden, Colorado, USA) sind Prototypen mit sehr kleinen Glaskugeln von 0.5 mm Durchmesser im

argon are about 1.1 W/m²K; a krypton filling gives a U-value of 0.8 W/m²K.

The amortization costs of krypton and similar gases are at present still very high, but increased demand could lead to a drop in price.

The U-value can clearly be lowered below 1 W/m²K by introducing a third pane of glass or through the use of several low-E coatings or by evacuating the air space.

Triple-pane insulated glazing presents two low-E coated panes and various gas fillings: argon produces a U-value of 0.7 W/m²K in Silverstar® (g = 0.42, τ = 0.64); krypton achieves a U-value of 0.7 W/m²K in SGG Climatop® (g = 0.45, τ = 0.66) and of 0.5 W/m²K in Silverstar Selekt®glass (g = 0.35, τ = 0.60).

A further possibility is presented by inserting various suspended low-E coated films between the insulating glass panes; this saves the weight and thickness of a third pane of glass. HIT®glass with two low-E coated films in a 60 mm cavity achieves a U-value of 0.6 W/m²K (e. g. g = 0.40 and τ = 0.55), and Superglass®, also with two low-E coated films, but with a smaller cavity of 17 mm to 33 mm, achieves a U-value of 0.7 W/m²K (g = 0.34, τ = 0.62). The option of creating a vacuum in the cavity avoids the costs involved with using inert gases, but gives rise to other problems. The edge seal of vacuum glass must be extremely tight and able to withstand the stress from thermal expansion and shear forces between the glass panes. A glass edge seal (soldered glass) would seem to be suitable for such situations, but is associated with higher heat losses in the edge zone through conduction. Vacuum cavities also require spacers, or pillars, in the cavity itself. Spacing and dimensions of the toughened glass must be carefully balanced to fit in with the stress pattern across the surface of the glass, conduction at the contact points and the need for unobstructed visibility. At the US Solar Energy Research Institute (SERI, Golden, Colorado, USA) prototypes have been developed using very small

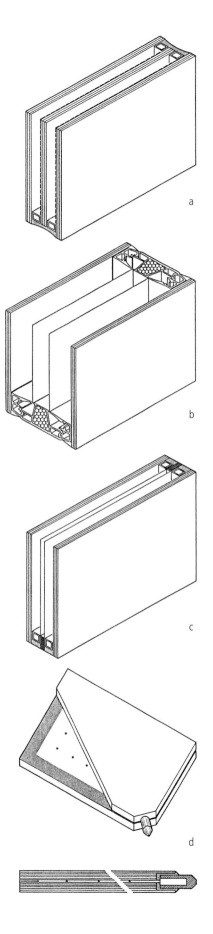

a

b

c

d

Verschiedene Typen von Isoliergläsern:
a) Dreifach-Isolierglas: Silverstar®; b) Isoliergläser mit Folien: HIT®; c) Superglass®; d) Vakuumgläser mit Abstandhalter und Randverbund aus einer Glaslote.

Different types of insulating glass units:
a) Triple glazing: Silverstar®; b) Insulating glass with films: HIT®; c) Superglass®; d) Vacuum glazing with spacer and soldered glass edge seal.

Abstand von 50 mm untersucht worden. Aufgrund der Ergebnisse könnte ein Vakuumglas, bestehend aus zwei Scheiben mit einer Low-E-Beschichtung, einen k-Wert von 0.6 W/m²K erreichen, doch wird die Entwicklung bis zur industriellen Reife noch einige Jahre in Anspruch nehmen.

Bei den Isoliergläsern finden alle bis jetzt beschriebenen Glasscheiben ihren Einsatz. Das Niederländische Architekturinstitut (NAI) in Rotterdam, vom Architekten Jo Coenen 1988–93 erbaut, kann als typisches Beispiel für die neuen Ganzglasfassaden mit Wärme- und Sonnenschutzfunktion angesehen werden.
Die Anlage befindet sich zwischen der stark befahrenen Rochussenstraat und dem Museumspark. Entlang der Straße erstreckt sich das Archivgebäude, welches die Besucher zum Eingang des Hauptgebäudes lenkt. Der viergeschossige, vollverglaste Baukörper wirkt wie in die monumentale Pergola eingehängt. Er beherbergt die Bibliothek und die Verwaltung, darunter liegen das Foyer und die Cafeteria. Seitlich ist die große Aula mit Galerien für Ausstellungen angeschlossen. Die Glasfassade ist eine Pfosten-Riegel-Konstruktion mit einem Achsabstand von 3.12 m und einer regelmäßigen Unterteilung von 1.12 m in der Höhe. Die Isoliergläser bestehen aus einem innenliegenden Verbundglas (4 + 4 mm) mit einer Low-E-Beschichtung, einem Zwischenraum von 16 mm mit Gasfüllung und einer außenliegenden 8 mm starken

glass balls of 0.5 mm diameter, spaced at 50 mm. Tests indicate that these prototypes, used with a vacuum cavity between two panes of glass with a low-E coating, could achieve a U-value of 0.6 W/m²K, but several years of work lie ahead before this type of glass can go into industrial production.

All the various types of glass so far described can be used in insulating glass units. A typical example of the new all-glass façades which provide thermal protection and solar shading is the Netherlands Architectural Institute (NAI) designed and built by the architect Jo Coenen between 1988 and 1993. The building complex is located between the busy Rochussenstraat and the Museum Park. Following the line of the road is the archives building which leads the visitors to the entrance of the main building, a four-storey, fully glazed structure which appears to be suspended in a monumental pergola. Inside are the library and the administration areas with a foyer and cafeteria below. At the side there is access to the main auditorium with exhibition galleries. The glass façade is a mullion and transom frame construction with horizontal spacing of 3.12 m and a regular 1.12 m vertical spacing. The insulating glazing consists of an interior laminated glass unit (4 + 4 mm) with a low-E coating, a 16 mm cavity filled with gas, and an external 8 mm thick pane. The units are attached to the façade structure by means of an encircling EPDM gasket fixing system.

Klare Isoliergläser steigern die Transparenz und die Leichtigkeit eines Gebäudes.
Niederländisches Architekturinstitut, Rotterdam, 1988–93, Jo Coenen.
Clear insulating glass enhances the transparency and the lightness of a building.
Netherlands Architectural Institute, Rotterdam, 1988–93, Jo Coenen.

Scheibe. Sie sind mit einem umlaufenden Kunststoffprofil (EPDM) an der Fassadenkonstruktion befestigt.

Ein weiteres Beispiel einer vollverglasten Hülle ist der neue Flughafen von London, «Stansted», 1991 von Foster und Partnern fertiggestellt. Ziel des Entwurfskonzepts war ein transparenter Terminal, welcher eine einfache Orientierung der Passagiere durch Sichtverbindung zu den Flugzeugen ermöglicht. Die eingeschossige Abfertigungshalle befindet sich zwischen dem geschlossenen Sockelgeschoß, das alle Serviceeinrichtungen beherbergt, und der filigranartigen Dachkonstruktion mit Gitterwerkkuppeln und Lichtöffnungen. Sie ist an allen vier Seiten durch eine 11.5 m hohe Glasfassade in Pfosten-Riegel-Bauweise abgeschlossen. Die Unterkonstruktion ist in Felder mit einem Achsabstand von 3.60 m und einer Höhe von 1.83 m unterteilt, auf welchen die Glaselemente durch Anpreßleisten von außen befestigt sind. Da die Glasfassade bei der Vorfahrt und der Flugpiste mit einem breiten Vordach weitgehend vor den Sonnenstrahlen geschützt ist, wurden hier nur transparente Isoliergläser eingesetzt. Dagegen sind die seitlichen, der Sonne ausgesetzten Ost- und Westfassaden im oberen Teil mit transluzenten Isoliergläsern ausgestattet. Um den wärmetechnischen Anforderungen zu genügen, wurden die Isoliergläser SGG Climaplus® N verwendet. Der Aufbau der 3.6 × 1.83 m großen Glaselemente besteht aus einer außenliegenden vorgespannten, 8 mm starken Scheibe, einem

A further example of a fully glazed skin is the new London airport, Stansted, designed and completed in 1991 by the architects Foster and Partners. The aim of the design was a transparent terminal which would facilitate passenger orientation by enabling visual contact with the aeroplanes. The one-storey departures and arrivals hall is topped by a filigree roof construction with grid domes and light openings; below the hall is an enclosed basement containing all the services.
The hall is enclosed on all four sides by an 11.5 m high framed façade in glass. The subframe grid is divided into rectangular sections, spaced 3.60 m horizontally and 1.83 m vertically. The glazing units are attached to this frame from the outside by means of a pressure caps system. As the glass façades facing the apron and at the passenger approach side are protected from the sun by a wide canopy, only standard transparent insulating glass was used here. However, the east and west façades, both subject to strong solar radiation, have translucent insulating glass in the upper parts. The type of glass used to meet the thermal insulation requirements was SGG Climaplus®N. The 3.6 × 1.83 m glazing units consist of an exterior, 8 mm thick pane of toughened glass, a 16 mm wide cavity filled with inert gas and an interior, 6 mm thick pane of toughened glass with a low-E coating.
The junction between roof edge and façade shows an interesting detail: as the movements between roof and façade can be as much as 20 cm in any of three directions, a scissors-like

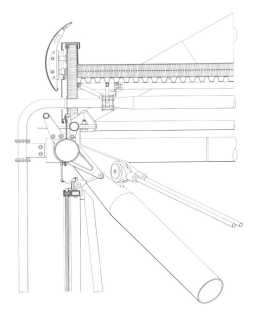

16 mm breiten Zwischenraum mit Edelgasfüllung und einer innenliegenden vorgespannten, 6 mm dicken low-E-beschichteten Scheibe.

Interessant ist das Anschlußdetail zwischen Dachrand und Fassade. Da die Bewegungen zwischen Dach und Fassade in den drei Richtungen bis zu 20 cm ausmachen, wurde ein Verbindungselement entwickelt, welches nur die horizontalen und nicht die vertikalen Lasten überträgt. Die verbleibende horizontale Fuge ist durch einen transparenten, 12 mm dicken Glasstreifen und eine Kunststoffmembrane luftdicht abgeschlossen.

Einen interessanten Lösungsansatz bietet die Verwendung von Sonnenschutzgläsern mit verschiedenen Reflexionseinstellungen im selben Objekt. Die Verglasung der ersten U-Bahn-Station in Genua, vom Renzo Piano Building Workshop 1990 erbaut, besteht aus Gläsern mit unterschiedlich blauem Reflexionsgrad. Ihre Lage ist in bezug auf die Neigungswinkel und die entsprechende Sonneneinstrahlung gewählt, wobei die Unterschiede mit bloßem Auge kaum feststellbar sind. Die Verglasung besteht aus Isoliergläsern von etwa 60×240 cm Größe. Außenliegend wurden blaue Reflexionsgläser mit einer Lichtdurchlässigkeit τ von 0.18, 0.27 und 0.36 (SolarSiv®) gewählt, innenliegend ein Verbundglas wegen der Bruchgefahr durch den erhöhten Luftdruck beim Einfahren der U-Bahn-Züge. Die Scheiben sind mit Silikon auf horizontallaufende Profile aus Aluminium verklebt und mit Sicherungsklammern gegen das Ablösen versehen. Die Unterkonstruktion

connection was developed which would transfer only the horizontal and not the vertical loads. The remaining horizontal gap is an airtight joint consisting of a transparent, 12 mm thick glass strip and a plastic membrane.

Seldom insulating glass with different reflective properties is used in the same building. An example is Renzo Piano Building Workshop's underground station in Genoa, built in 1990, which uses insulating glass with varying blue reflection properties according to their position on the building's skin and their angle in relation to the sun. The differences are hardly perceptible to the human eye. The glazing units are of insulating glass and approximately 60×240 cm in size. On the outer layer blue reflecting glass is used, with a light transmittance τ of 0.18, 0.27 and 0.36 (SolarSiv®). The inner layer is a laminated glass to meet the safety requirements in view of increased air pressure caused by incoming trains. The panes are silicon-bonded onto horizontal aluminium profiles, and secured with safety clamps to guard against loosening. The glazing support frame is fixed directly to the steel arch structure by means of cast aluminium elements. The whole structure of the underground station is basically a barrel vault composed of 36 two-pin curved steel girders divided into five sections which are cross-braced in a longitudinal direction.

Die Isoliergläser mit unterschiedlich blauen Reflexionsscheiben wurden in bezug auf die Neigungswinkel und die entsprechende Sonneneinstrahlung gewählt.
U-Bahn-Station, Genua, Italien, 1990,
Renzo Piano Building Workshop.
Insulating glass with varying blue reflection properties according to the position of the individual panes in relation to the sky.
Underground station, Genoa, Italy, 1990,
Renzo Piano Building Workshop.

ist durch Gußteile aus Aluminium direkt auf der Tragstruktur aus gebogenen Stahlträgern befestigt. Im Prinzip bildet die Konstruktion ein Tonnengewölbe aus 36 zweigelenkigen Bogenträgern, die in fünf Abschnitte unterteilt und mit Kreuzverbänden in der Längsrichtung ausgesteift sind.

Ungewöhnlich ist auch der Einsatz von geprägtem Gußglas. Das Glasdesign für den Hauptsitz der Lloyd's Versicherungsgesellschaft in London, von Richard Rogers Partnership 1986 fertiggestellt, hat eine fast zweijährige Entwicklungsarbeit beansprucht. Zunächst waren hohe Anforderungen an die lichttechnischen Eigenschaften gestellt: Einerseits sollte eine gute Streuung des Tageslichts erreicht werden, um den Innenraum weitgehend auszuleuchten, andererseits eine diffuse Reflexion des Kunstlichts im Raum selbst, so daß abends keine Vorhänge nötig sind. Auch die Herstellung bereitete einige Probleme, so die Einhaltung des strengen geometrischen Noppenmusters, die Notwendigkeit der Vorspannung sowie die Realisierung einer geeigneten Oberfläche für eine gute Haftung des Randverbundes. Bei der Ausführung wurden beide Glasoberflächen geprägt, die eine mit einem engen, kontinuierlichen Raster, die andere mit einem breiteren, linsenförmigen Design, das von der Abwicklung des Walzendurchmessers und der Unterteilung der Fassade bestimmt wurde.

Die Verwendung emailbeschichteter Gläser in der Isolierverglasung stellt ein Sonderthema dar. Seit längerer Zeit sind in der Fassadengestaltung vollflächige, undurchsichtige Glasscheiben im Brüstungs- und Deckenbereich bekannt. Dagegen ist der Einsatz von Scheiben mit bedruckten Mustern relativ neu. In der Automobilindustrie werden emailbeschichtete Scheiben sowohl aus funktionellen als auch aus ästhetischen Gründen verwendet. Die schwarzen, emaillierten Randstreifen der Front- und Heckscheiben schützen die Klebefläche zwischen Glas und Karosserie vor der negativen Auswirkung der UV-Strahlung. Inzwischen sind solche Streifen aus dekorativen Gründen immer breiter und mit verlaufendem Bedruckungsgrad gestaltet worden. Bei der Gestaltung von Glasfassaden ist eine ähnliche Entwicklung festzustellen. In den 70er Jahren waren emaillierte Randstreifen beim rahmenlosen «Structural glazing» notwendig, um die Klebeflächen des Randverbundes gegen die UV-Strahlung zu schützen. Dann kam aus mehr ästhetischen als funktionel-

Rolled glass is a type of glass seldom used. The patterned glass used by the Richard Rogers Partnership for the headquarters of Lloyd's Insurance in London in 1986 took almost two years to develop. High technical optical specifications were required of the glass: on the one hand it should achieve an optimum scattering of daylight, to bring light into the back of the offices, and on the other it should be capable of diffusely reflecting the artificial light in the interior, so as to obviate the need for screening the windows from the inside in the evening. Manufacturing problems were encountered, e. g. in producing an even geometric sparkle pattern, in toughening the glass panes and in producing a suitable surface for a good seal at the edges. In fact both sides of the glass were rolled, one side being pressed with a narrow continuous grid pattern, the other with a wider lens-shaped design determined by the diametre of the metal roller and the division of the façade.

The use of fritted glass in insulated glazing units is a special topic. Large expanses of nontransparent glass panels have long been used for parapets and spandrels in façade design, but the use of patterned glass is relatively new. In the automobile industry fritted glass panes are used for both functional and aesthetic reasons. The black fritted edge strip on the front and rear windscreens protects the seal between the glass and the bodywork from the negative effects of ultraviolet radiation. These strips have gradually become wider and more decorative, sometimes printed with a decreasing pattern. In the design of glass façades a similar de-

Isoliergläser mit geprägtem Gußglas sind ungewöhnlich. Das in fast zweijähriger Arbeit entwickelte «Lloyd's»-Design soll eine gute Streuung des Tageslichts und eine diffuse Reflexion der künstlichen Beleuchtung im Innenraum erreichen.
Lloyd's Hauptsitz, London, 1978–86,
Richard Rogers Partnership.
Insulating glass units with rolled glass are seldom used: Developed over a two year period, this special "Lloyd's" glass is reputed to both scatter daylight well and to give diffuse reflection of the artificial lighting inside.
Lloyd's Headquarters, London, 1978–86,
Richard Rogers Partnership.

len Gründen die Idee auf, auch die restliche Fläche mit Mustern zu versehen. Das Musterdesign und der Bedruckungsgrad können auch als Sonnenschutzmaßnahme eingesetzt werden, weil der Durchlaßfaktor g genau nach den Anforderungen eingestellt werden kann. Dagegen hat eine Emailbeschichtung keine Auswirkung auf den k-Wert eines Isolierglases. Bedruckungsmuster können interessante Tiefenwirkungen erzielen, da sie aus großer Entfernung wie ein Schleier wirken, der sich, aus der Nähe betrachtet, auflöst. Der Vorhangeffekt kann sich aber als Nachteil herausstellen, besonders wenn emailbeschichtete Gläser im Durchsichtsbereich eingesetzt werden.

Emailbeschichtete Gläser wurden für die Fassade des 1989 fertiggestellten Bürogebäudes «B3», heute British Petroleum, Stockley Park, London, von Foster und Partnern, verwendet. Im Bereich der Deckenkonstruktion sind vollflächig weiß emaillierte Scheiben eingesetzt worden, im Durchsichtsbereich der Büros ein Klarglas mit

velopment can be observed. In the 1970s a fritted edge strip for use in "structural glazing" was necessary to protect the edge seal against ultraviolet radiation. The idea was then developed, more for aesthetic reasons than functional ones, of extending the pattern to cover the whole of the glass surface. The pattern and the extent of cover can also be used for solar shading, because the total solar energy transmission coefficient, g-value, can be set exactly to the required specifications. On the other hand a fritted surface has no effect on the U-value of insulating glass. Fritted glass can achieve interesting veiling effects, because the further you are away from the glass, the more difficult it is to see through it. This "curtain" effect can be a disadvantage, particularly when fritted glass is used for glazing at view out level.

Fritted glazing was used by Foster and Partners in the façade of the B3 office building, now British Petroleum offices, at Stockley Park, completed in 1989. White fritted glass was used at

Isoliergläser mit Emailrastern können eine Schleierwirkung hervorrufen. Im Durchsichtsbereich wurden Scheiben mit einem weißen Rand und punktförmigen Verlaufrastern eingesetzt.
Gebäude «B3», heute British Petroleum, Stockley Park, London, 1989, Foster und Partner.
Fritted glazing can achieve veiling effects. A fritted glass with a white edge and decreasing dot pattern was used for the window sections.
"B3" building, today British Petroleum, Stockley Park, London, 1989, Foster and Partners.

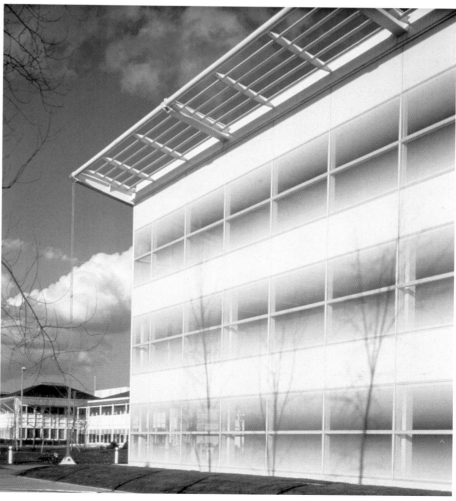

einem weißen Rand und punktförmigen Verlaufrastern mit einem Bedruckungsgrad von 5 % bis 95 %. Das Isolierglas besteht aus zwei vorgespannten, 6 mm dicken Scheiben mit einer Low-E-Beschichtung; der k-Wert beträgt 1.6 W/m²K, der g-Wert 0.48 und der τ-Wert 0.60. Die Glaselemente wurden bei der Herstellung mit einem umlaufenden Rahmen versehen, welcher einerseits der Einhängung in die Pfosten-Riegel-Konstruktion dient, andererseits als mechanische Halterung der Glasscheibe. Die 15 mm breiten Fugen zwischen den Glaselementen sind mit grauem Silikon versiegelt.

Die Schleierwirkung kann auch ein wesentliches Merkmal eines Gestaltungskonzeptes bilden, wie bei der Glasfassade des Verwaltungsgebäudes für «Cartier» in Fribourg, Schweiz, 1990, der Architekten Jean Nouvel, Emmanuel Cattani et Associés. Die Glaswand dient als Werbeträger der Firma und ist einfach und direkt mit dem Schriftzug «Cartier» versehen. Da die Lage in Sichtweite der Autobahn eine gewisse Dynamik mit sich bringt und eine banale Wiederholung monoton wäre, wurde der Kontrast Schrift zu Hintergrund, positiv zu negativ, allmählich umgekehrt und aufgelöst. Der Effekt entsteht durch die Kombination von Punktmustern mit zwei unterschiedlichen Bedruckungsgraden. Dafür wurde auf der innenliegenden Seite des Isolierglases eine silberfarbige Beschichtung kalt aufgetragen, welche den Unterschied zwischen bedruckten und unbedruckten Flächen durch die Spiegelung des umliegenden Panoramas zusätzlich steigert.

the level of the floor slabs. For the transparent view out sections clear glass with a white edge and a decreasing dot pattern covering between 5 % and 95 % was used. The insulating glass consists of two panes of 6 mm toughened glass with a low-E coating; the U-value is 1.6 W/m²K, the g-value is 0.48 and the τ-value is 0.60. At the manufacturing stage the glass elements were fitted with an edge frame which would both hold the glass in position and serve as the fixing attachment to the façade support frame. The 15 mm wide joints between the glazing units are sealed with a grey silicon seal.

The veiling effects which can be achieved on glass can be used as a major component of the design concept of a building, as, for example, the glass façade of the "Cartier" administration building in Fribourg, Switzerland, built by Jean Nouvel, Emmanuel Cattani and Associates in 1990. The glass wall serves as an advertising carrier for the company with the wording "Cartier" appearing simply and directly on the façade itself. As the building's location within sight of the motorway lends a certain dynamism to the situation, the monotony which would result from simple repetition of the wording has been avoided through a gradually reversed contrast between wording and background across the length of the façade – from positive to negative. This effect is achieved by using two dot patterns with varying coverage; on the inside of the insulating glass a silvery coating was cold applied, which further increases the difference between printed and unprinted sections by reflecting the surrounding panorama.

Mit Schriftzügen bedruckte Gläser können als Werbeträger dienen. Das Logo «Cartier» wird hier durch die Wechselwirkung zwischen Buchstaben und Hintergrund hervorgehoben.
«Cartier»-Gebäude, Fribourg, Schweiz, 1990, Jean Nouvel, Emmanuel Cattani et Associés.
Glazing printed with wording serves as an advertising carrier: the logo "Cartier" is emphasized through a gradually reversed contrast between lettering and background
Cartier building, Fribourg, Switzerland, 1990, Jean Nouvel, Emmanuel Cattani and Associates.

Die Isoliergläser der Hoffassade sind mit einem
silberfarbenen, an Strichcodes erinnernden Muster
beschichtet.
Neues Verwaltungsgebäude des «Palais des
Beaux-Arts», Lille, Frankreich, 1992–97,
J. M. Ibos und M. Vitart Architekten.
The insulating glass of the courtyard façade is
coated with a silver-coloured pattern reminiscent of
bar codes.
New administration building for the Palais des
Beaux-Arts, Lille, France, 1992–97,
J. M. Ibos and M. Vitart Architects.

Als spiegelnder Schleier wirkt auch die Glasfassade des neuen Verwaltungsgebäudes des
«Palais des Beaux-Arts» in Lille, von den Architekten J. M. Ibos und M. Vitart 1992–97 erbaut.
Der Entwurf umfaßt die Sanierung des bestehenden Gebäudes und die Erweiterung durch einen
schmalen, sechsgeschossigen Verwaltungstrakt;
dazwischen liegen unterirdische, von oben
beleuchtete Ausstellungsräume.
Die 70 m lange Hoffassade des Verwaltungstrak-
tes ist eine punktgehaltene Verglasung mit 2.67
bis 2.84 m breiten und 1.10 m hohen Isoliergläsern. Sie bestehen außen aus einer 12 mm starken ESG-Scheibe, die mit einem silberfarbenen,
an Strichcodes erinnernden Muster beschichtet
ist, einem Zwischenraum von 15 mm und innen
aus einer 12 mm starken VSG-Scheibe. Die
Gläser sind mit einer gelenkigen Punkthalterung
an Gußarmen aus Edelstahl befestigt, die ihrer-
seits mit den tragenden Pfosten aus hochglanz-
polierten, elliptischen Edelstahlprofilen verschraubt sind. Die 16 mm breiten Fugen sind
mit schwarzem Silikon gedichtet.
Die unterirdischen Ausstellungsräume sind
durch eine 19×38 m große, nur 1 % geneigte
Dachverglasung belichtet, die auf Bodenniveau
des Hofes liegt und wie eine Wasserfläche wirkt.
Die Tragstruktur besteht aus sechs mit Aluminiumblech verkleideten Stahlträgern, welche
die Belüftungs- und Beleuchtungstechnik be-
herbergen. Oberhalb der Träger befindet sich
ein Rost aus U-förmigen Stahlprofilen mit auskragenden Konsolen, woran die 5.45×1.90 m
großen Isoliergläser mit gelenkiger Punkthalterung befestigt sind.
Die Isoliergläser sind aus einer 15 mm starken
ESG-Scheibe außen, einem Zwischenraum von

The glass façade of the new administration
building for the Palais des Beaux-Arts, in Lille,
built 1992–97 by the architects J. M. Ibos and
M. Vitart has the appearance of a reflective veil.
The task was to refurbish the existing building
and to add an extension – a narrow, six-floor office wing. Between the old and the new sections
are underground exhibition rooms illuminated
from above.
The 70 m long courtyard façade of the new office
wing is a wall of point-fixed glazing composed of
panels of insulating glass 2.67 to 2.84 m wide
and 1.10 m high. Each panel consists of an outer
sheet of 12 mm toughened glass coated with a
silver-coloured pattern reminiscent of bar
codes, a 15 mm cavity and an inner sheet of
12 mm laminated glass. The panes are fixed by
means of articulated point fixing to cast steel
members bolted to the load-bearing mullions
of high-gloss, elliptical stainless steel profiles.
The 16 mm wide joints are sealed with black
silicon.
The underground exhibition rooms are lit via a
19×38 m, 1 % sloping glass roof at ground level
in the courtyard, where it has the appearance of
a water surface. The support structure consists of
six steel beams clad with aluminium sheet. Ducts
for ventilation and cabling for lighting are fed
through these beams. Above the beams is a grid
of U-shaped steel profiles with cantilevered
brackets to which the 5.45×1.90 m insulated
glazing is attached with articulated point fixing.
The insulating glass is composed of an outer
sheet of 15 mm toughened glass, a cavity of
15 mm and an inner sheet of 20 mm laminated
glass. The 16 mm wide joints are also sealed
with silicon.

15 mm und einer 20 mm starken VSG-Scheibe innen aufgebaut. Die 16 mm breiten Fugen sind ebenfalls mit Silikon gedichtet.

Füllungen mit wärmedämmenden Eigenschaften

Transparente Wärmedämmungen (TWD) sind weitere Maßnahmen zur Senkung der Wärmeverluste. Ihr Vorteil gegenüber den üblichen Wärmedämmungen ist ihre hohe Durchlässigkeit für die eintreffende Licht- und Wärmestrahlung, was die zusätzliche Nutzung der Sonnenenergie ermöglicht.

Da die transparenten Wärmedämmungen meistens lichtstreuend sind, wird die diffuse Transmission τ_{diff} maßgebend.

Zur Anwendung kommen transparente und transluzente Materialien wie Glas, Acrylglas (PMMA), Polycarbonat (PC) und Quarzschaum in verschiedener Schichtdicke und Strukturierung. Da sie einen Schutz vor Witterung und mechanischer Beschädigung benötigen, werden sie zwischen zwei Scheiben eingebaut.

Eine Aufteilung nach vier unterschiedlichen geometrischen Anordnungen der Struktur vereinfacht die Übersicht.

Eine erste Gruppe bilden mehrere, parallel zur Außenfläche hintereinander angeordnete Ebenen, die getrennte Luftschichten bilden. Dieses Anordnungsprinzip bringt höhere Reflexionsverluste mit sich, die zum Teil mit antireflektierenden Beschichtungen zu mildern sind. Es bietet aber dafür die Möglichkeit, mehrere Low-E-Be-

Fillings with Insulating Properties

Transparent insulation materials (TIM) are a further device used to reduce heat losses. The advantage of TIM over traditional insulation lies in their high transmission of incident light and near infrared radiation which leaves the possibility open for exploiting the solar energy.

As most transparent insulation materials scatter light, light transmission is given in terms of diffuse transmission, or τ_{diff}.

Various transparent and translucent materials can be used for transparent insulation, such as glass, acrylic glass (PMMA), polycarbonate (PC) and quartz foam, in varying thicknesses and structures. To protect them from the effects of weather and mechanical stress, these layers are sandwiched between two panes of glass.

A division into generic types of geometric media of the structure simplifies their classification.

The first group consists of a build-up of several layers, arranged behind one another parallel to the glass surfaces and enclosing separate air spaces. This arrangement entails higher reflection losses, an effect which can be partly reduced by the use of anti-reflection coatings. However this type offers the possibility of using several low-E coatings to reduce heat loss through reradiation. Examples in this first category are glazing systems comprising multiple panes of glass, such as double or triple glazings, or plastic films.

A second group are the structures arranged perpendicular to the exterior surface, such as lou-

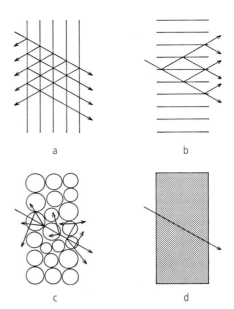

a   b

c   d

Transparente Wärmedämmungen können nach vier geometrischen Ordnungsprinzipien eingeteilt werden:
a) Strukturen parallel zur äußeren Glasebene;
b) Strukturen senkrecht zur äußeren Glasebene;
c) Kammerstrukturen;
d) quasi-homogene Strukturen.

Transparent insulation materials can be classified into four geometric structure types:
a) structures parallel to the exterior surface;
b) structures perpendicular to the exterior surface;
c) cavity structures;
d) quasi-homogeneous structures.

Verschiedene transparente Wärmedämmungen: TWD®-Wabenstrukturen, Oka-Lux®-Kapillarstrukturen und Basogel®-Aerogelkügelchen.
Different transparent insulation materials: TWD®-honeycomb structures, Oka-Lux® capillary structures and granular aerogel Basogel®.

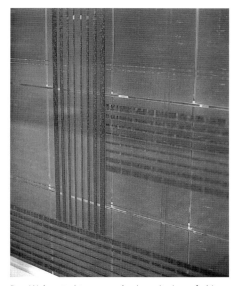

Den Wabenstrukturen wurde eine mit einem farbigen Bandmuster bedruckte Außenscheibe vorgelagert. Technorama-Gebäude, Düsseldorf, 1990, Gottfried Böhm.

An outer pane printed with a coloured stripe pattern is placed in front of the honeycomb structures. Technorama building, Düsseldorf, 1990, Gottfried Böhm.

Isolierglas mit eingelegten Kapillarstrukturen: Oka-Lux®.

Insulating glass unit with integrated capillary structures: Oka-Lux®.

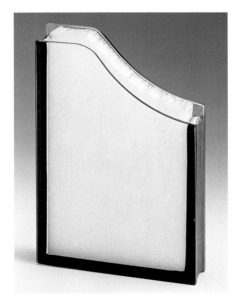

schichtungen einzusetzen, welche die Wärmeverluste durch Abstrahlung reduzieren. Zu dieser Gruppe gehören Mehrfachverglasungen, wie Zweifach- und Dreifachisoliergläser, sowie Mehrfachfoliensysteme.

Eine zweite Gruppe stellen senkrecht zur Außenfläche gerichtete Strukturen dar, wie Lamellen, Waben oder Kapillaren, die den Scheibenzwischenraum in kleine Luftzellen unterteilen. Diese Anordnung weist den Vorteil geringerer Reflexionverluste auf, da die einfallende Sonnenstrahlung durch Mehrfachreflexion an den parallelen Wänden weitergeleitet wird, was zusätzlich für die Tiefenausleuchtung von Räumen mit Tageslicht genutzt werden kann. Ein anderer Vorteil ist die weitgehende Ausschaltung der Konvektion, die durch das Verhältnis der Zellendurchmesser zur Tiefe bestimmt wird. Wabenstrukturen bestehen aus transparentem Polycarbonat (PC) mit UV-stabilisierenden Zusätzen. Sie werden als endlose Multistegplatte mit quadratischen Zellenquerschnitten von 4 mm Seitenlänge in einer Breite von 700 mm und einer Höhe von 15 mm extrudiert (AREL®, TWD® Kaiser). Danach werden sie in der gewünschten Länge mittels Heizdrahttechnik geschnitten und die Seiten auf diese Weise automatisch miteinander verschweißt. Eine Färbung des Kunststoffes ist möglich, was allerdings eine höhere Absorption bewirkt. Die Wabenstrukturen werden bei der üblichen Einbaudicke von 50 mm bis 100 mm lose in eine Doppelverglasung eingeschlossen. Der k-Wert einer 100 mm dicken Wabenstruktur (PC) liegt zwischen 0.80 und 0.90 W/m²K, der τ_{diff}-Wert bei 0.57 und der g_{diff}-Wert bei 0.64.

Ein Beispiel für die Anwendung transparenter Wärmedämmung bietet das Technorama-Gebäude in Düsseldorf, vom Architekten Gottfried Böhm 1990 in Zusammenarbeit mit dem Ingenieurbüro Kaiser Bautechnik erstellt. Hier wird eine mit einem farbigen Bandmuster bedruckte Außenscheibe dem regelmäßigen Lochbild der Wabenstruktur spielerisch vorgelagert, was der Fassade eine Tiefenwirkung verleiht. Kapillarstrukturen sind aus vielen Röhrchen aus Kunststoff oder Glas zusammengesetzt. Die Kunststoffröhrchen aus Acryl (PMMA) oder Polycarbonat (PC) haben einen Durchmesser von 1 – 4 mm, je nachdem, ob vorwiegend lichtstreuende Eigenschaften oder eine hohe Strahlungstransmission gefragt sind. Sie werden aufeinandergeschichtet und mittels Heizdrahttechnik in der benötigten Dicke geschnitten und

vres, honeycombs and capillaries, which divide the cavity into small air cells. This type has the advantage of lower optical losses, as the incoming beam is reflected several times from the parallel surfaces and transmitted in a forward direction. This opens up the possibility of increasing levels of natural daylight at the back of deep rooms. A further advantage is that convection currents are suppressed, an effect resulting from the relationship between the diameter and the depth of the air spaces.

Honeycomb structures consist of transparent polycarbonate (PC) with ultraviolet-stabilising additives. They are extruded as continuous honeycomb structures, 700 mm wide and 15 mm high (AREL®, TWD® Kaiser); the rectangular honeycomb cells have 4 mm side lengths. These structures are then cut to the required length using resistance wire technology, and the sides are automatically welded together. The material can be colour-tinted, but this leads to higher absorption. Generally these honeycomb structures are used in thicknesses of between 50 mm and 100 mm, and they are sandwiched loosely in a double glazed unit. The U-value of a 100 mm thick honeycomb structure (PC) is between 0.80 and 0.90 W/m²K, the τ_{diff} value is approximately 0.57 and the g_{diff} is 0.64.

An example of the use of transparent insulation material is in the Technorama building in Düsseldorf, designed in 1990 by Gottfried Böhm, in collaboration with Kaiser Bautechnik. Here a playful effect is created by placing a pane of glass with a coloured stripe pattern in front of the regular cell spacing of the TIM honeycomb structure. This has the effect of adding depth to the façade.

Capillary structures are made up of many small plastic or glass tubes. The plastic tubes, of acrylic (PMMA) or polycarbonate (PC), have a diameter of 1 – 4 mm, depending on whether light-scattering properties or higher radiation transmission are desired. The tubes are built up in layers and cut to the desired thickness by means of resistance wire technology and automatically bonded together at the edges. A 100 mm thick capillary sheet made from acrylic tubes, 3 mm in diameter, will achieve a U-value of 0.89 W/m²K and a τ_{diff} of 0.69 (Oka-Lux®). Capillary structures made of glass have great resistance to high temperatures and are more durable than plastic, but require an extremely careful choice of diameter and thickness, as

damit automatisch am Rand zusammengeklebt. Eine 100 mm dicke Kapillarplatte aus Polycarbonatröhrchen von 3 mm Durchmesser erreicht einen k-Wert von 0.89 W/m²K und einen τ_{diff} von 0.69 (Oka-Lux®).

Kapillarstrukturen aus Glas weisen eine große Beständigkeit gegenüber hohen Temperaturen und eine längere Lebensdauer als Kunststoff auf, verlangen aber eine äußerst sorgfältige Optimierung bei der Wahl von Durchmesser und Wandstärke, da Glas eine siebenfach höhere Wärmeleitung als Kunststoff aufweist. Prototypen mit Röhrchen von 1–8 mm Durchmesser, einer Wandstärke von 0.1 mm und 100 mm Länge haben k-Werte um 1 W/m²K erzielt.

Ein drittes Prinzip stellen Kammerstrukturen dar, die aus der Kombination von parallelen und senkrechten Anordnungen resultieren. Dazu gehören Materialien mit Strukturen in der Größenordnung von einigen Millimetern, wie Acrylschaum. Obwohl sich damit Wärmeverluste durch Konvektion weitgehend ausschalten lassen, sind die Verluste durch Reflexion, wie bei den parallelen Strukturen, und durch die Wärmetransporte mittels Wärmeleitung maßgebend.

Der vierten Gruppe werden quasi-homogene Strukturen zugeordnet, wie Aerogele und Xerogele, die mikroskopische Kammerstrukturen aufweisen. Ein Aerogel ist ein hochporöses filigranes Skelett aus 2–5 % Silikat und 95–98 % Luftfüllung, das eine hohe Strahlungsdurchlässigkeit und Wärmedämmfähigkeit aufweist.

Beide Eigenschaften sind auf seine Struktur zurückzuführen. Da die Skelettpartikel kleinere Dimensionen als der größte Teil der sichtbaren Wellenlängen aufweisen, bewirken sie eine minimale Lichtstreuung, und das Auge nimmt das Aerogel als homogenes Material wahr. Hingegen ist die milchige oder leicht bläuliche Färbung auf die Absorption von kleinen Inhomogenitäten in der Struktur zurückzuführen. Hinsichtlich der Wärmedämmeigenschaften sind die Dimensionen der Luftzellen ausschlaggebend. Da sie weniger als 20 nm groß sind, werden die Luftmoleküle in ihrer Bewegung gehindert, was die Konvektion reduziert. Der Wärmetransport dagegen wird durch kontinuierliche Absorptions- und Emissionsprozesse im Material selbst stark gedämpft. Damit kann ein Isolierglas mit einer Füllung aus einer 20 mm dicken Aerogelplatte einen theoretischen k-Wert von 0.7 W/m²K und

glass has a seven times higher heat conductivity than plastic. 100 mm thick prototypes with tubes of 1–8 mm diametre and of 0.1 mm wall thickness have achieved U-values of around 1 W/m²K.

A third variety is the cavity type, which combines parallel and vertical structures. Here materials with bubble structures in the order of a few millimeters are used, such as acrylic foam. Although these largely suppress heat losses through convection, the losses through reflection, as with the parallel structures, and through heat conduction are a limiting factor.

The fourth group consists in the quasi-homogeneous structures, such as aerogels and xerogels which have microscopic cavity structures. An aerogel is a highly porous filigree structure of 2–5 % silicate and 95–98 % air interspace. It has high radiation transmission and thermal insulation properties. Both properties are a result of its structure. Since most of the particles in the structure are smaller than the wavelengths of visible light, they are not strongly scattering, and the eye perceives the aerogel as a homogeneous material. The milky or slightly blue tinge, however, is due to the absorption of small non-uniformities in the structure. With regard to the thermal insulation properties the dimensions of the air microcells are critical. As they are smaller than 20 nm, the movement of the air molecules is restricted and convection is reduced. Heat transport on the other hand is strongly suppressed by the continuous absorption and reradiation processes in the material itself. Thus insulating glass with a filling of 20 mm thick aerogel can have a theoretical U-value of 0.7 W/m²K and a transmission of τ_{diff} 0.69. The thermal insulation properties can be additionally increased by creating a vacuum in the cavity, and at a pressure of 50–100 mbar the U-value could be reduced to 0.37 W/m²K. As the monolithic filling also acts as a spacer between the two panes of glass, it simplifies the manufacturing process for vacuum insulating glass.

Development work is being carried out on these areas at present, with the aim of bringing onto the market a product with a U-value below 0.4 W/m²K, which would mean 0.5 W/m²K for a 1 × 1 m unit.

Apart from improvements in light transmission, transparence and thermal insulating properties there are further problems encountered with the

eine Strahlungstransmission von 0.69 τ_{diff} erreichen. Die Wärmedämmeigenschaften lassen sich durch Evakuierung des Zwischenraumes zusätzlich verbessern, und der k-Wert könnte mit einem Druck von 50–100 mbar bis auf 0.37 W/m²K gesenkt werden. Da die monolithische Füllung gleichzeitig als Abstandhalter für die beiden Scheiben dient, wird die Herstellung eines Vakuumisolierglases vereinfacht. Aufgrund solcher Voraussetzungen sind Forschungsarbeiten im Gange, um ein Produkt mit einem k-Wert unter 0.4 W/m²K, was 0.5 W/m²K für ein 1 × 1 m großes Element mit Randverbund bedeutet, zur Marktreife zu entwickeln.

Neben der Verbesserung bezüglich Lichtdurchlässigkeit, Transparenz und Wärmedämmeigenschaften sind aber bei den Aerogelen noch weitere Probleme zu lösen. Der Randverbund soll eine niedrige Wärmeleitfähigkeit aufweisen und vollständig dicht bleiben, weil Aerogele aufgrund der Kapillarkräfte hochgradig wasserempfindlich sind.

Zur Zeit ist die Herstellung von Aerogelplatten auf eine Größe von bis zu 60 × 60 × 3 cm beschränkt, weil sie sehr aufwendig und damit teuer ist (Airglass AB, Schweden). Einerseits ist ein spezielles Trocknungsverfahren mit hohem Druck und hoher Temperatur notwendig, andererseits muß die Platte selbst planparallel und ohne Oberflächenfehler sein, um die optischen Qualitäten von Glas zu erreichen.

Eine kostengünstigere Alternative bietet die Herstellung von Aerogelkügelchen von 1–6 mm Durchmesser, die lose in den Scheibenzwischen-

aerogels. The edge seal should have low heat conductivity and remain completely tight, because aerogels are very susceptible to water penetration due to their capillary structure.

At present the manufacture of monolithic aerogels is limited to a panel size of 60 × 60 × 3 cm, because their production is very complicated and expensive (Airglass AB, Sweden). On the one hand a special high-pressure, high-temperature drying process is needed, on the other the panel faces must be absolutely parallel and have no surface flaws, so as to achieve the required optical specification of the glass.

A less expensive alternative is the manufacture of granular aerogel which consists of 1–6 mm diameter pellets loosely filled in the cavity between the panes. However, this granular form of aerogel has poorer optical and thermal properties. Reflection is increased due to the many surfaces of the spheres, which reduces transmission. In addition this type of filling scatters light and is less transparent. The spaces between the pellets also lead to a reduction in thermal insulation properties; thus a 16 mm thick granular aerogel filling achieves a U-value of under 0.8 W/m²K, a τ_{diff} of 0.41 and a g_{diff} of 0.52.

Xerogel is very similar to aerogel, but cheaper because it needs no special drying process during manufacture. As its structure is less homogeneous and the air spaces are larger, xerogel has better radiation transmission but worse thermal insulation properties than aerogel.

A comparison of the four groups of transparent

Kügelchen aus Aerogel: Basogel®.
Granular form of aerogel: Basogel®.

raum eingefüllt werden. Das Granulat weist allerdings etwas schlechtere optische und thermische Eigenschaften auf. Die Reflexion wird wegen der vielen Kugeloberflächen erhöht, was die Transmission vermindert. Die Füllung wirkt zudem lichtstreuend und weniger durchsichtig. Wegen der Kugelzwischenräume werden auch die Wärmedämmeigenschaften schlechter; so weist eine 16 mm dicke Granulatfüllung einen k-Wert unter 0.8 W/m²K, ein τ_{diff} von 0.41 und ein g_{diff} von 0.52 auf.

Das Xerogel ist dem Aerogel sehr ähnlich, aber kostengünstiger, weil es ohne spezielles Trocknungsverfahren hergestellt wird. Da seine Struktur weniger homogen ist und die Luftzellen größer sind, weist das Xerogel eine bessere Strahlungstransmission, aber schlechtere Wärmedämmeigenschaften als das Aerogel auf. Bei einem Vergleich der vier Gruppen transparenter Wärmedämmungen sind nicht nur bauphysikalische Eigenschaften maßgebend, sondern auch Überlegungen hinsichtlich Nutzung und Konstruktion zu berücksichtigen.

Heute sind Mehrfachglas- und Mehrfachfoliensysteme bezüglich der Transparenz führend und damit für eine Verwendung im Durchsichtsbereich geeignet. Zudem erreichen sie k-Werte zwischen 0.5 W/m²K und 1 W/m²K. Dagegen sind die anderen Strukturen mehr oder weniger lichtstreuend und opak, was für Oberlichter und Brüstungsbereiche sowie für die passive Nutzung der Sonnenenergie durch Sonnenkollektoren und wärmespeichernde Wände geeigneter ist. Zur Zeit weisen Waben- und Kapillarstrukturen eine bessere Strahlungstransmission als Aerogelkügelchen auf, obwohl ihre Einbaudicke 100 mm gegenüber den 16 mm eines Aerogelgranulats beträgt.

Eine Weiterentwicklung der monolithischen Aerogele, besonders hinsichtlich der Transparenz, ist vielversprechend. In einer Studie der Technical University of Denmark wurde geschätzt, daß die Verwendung von Aerogel-Isolierglas im Wohnungsbau eine Reduktion der Heizkosten um 20 % bewirken würde.

Transparente Wärmedämmungen sind Maßnahmen mit festen Eigenschaften. Die im Winter vorteilhaften Strahlungsdurchlässigkeits- und Wärmedämmeigenschaften entpuppen sich daher im Sommer als nachteilig.

Zur Steuerung des Strahlungseinfalls im Sommer müssen Verschattungssysteme in Form von reflektierenden Geweberollos, Lamellenstoren

insulating materials makes it clear that not only the physical properties of the material have to be taken into consideration, but also the type of use to which the material will be put and the way in which it is incorporated into the glazing units. Today glazing systems comprising multiple panes of glass or plastic films lead the field in terms of transparence and thus are most suited for use where transparent glazing is needed. Moreover they reach U-values of between 0.5 W/m²K and 1 W/m²K. The other structures are more or less light-scattering and opaque, thus more suited for use in rooflights or parapets, as well as in passive solar energy measures such as solar collectors or thermal store walls. At present honeycomb and capillary structures have better radiation transmission properties than granular aerogels, although at 100 mm they are considerably thicker than the 16 mm of the granular aerogel.

The development of monolithic aerogels, particularly with regard to transparence, would seem to be very promising. In a study by the Technical University of Denmark it was estimated that the use of aerogel insulating glass in housing would lead to a 20 % reduction in heating costs.

Transparent insulation materials have fixed properties. Thus their radiation transmission and thermal insulation properties, which are so advantageous in winter, become a disadvantage in summer. To control incident solar radiation in summer, various shading systems are necessary in the form of reflecting fabric blinds or louvres. In future it could be possible to use systems with adjustable optical qualities, such as thermochromic or electrochromic systems.

Little research has so far been carried out on thermally insulating fillings with adjustable properties. For this purpose blinds with infrared-reflecting films and louvre systems with infrared-reflecting surfaces are used.

In the 1970s a system using polystyrene pellets was patented by Zomeworks, Albuquerque, USA. The antistatic granulate can, as required, either be blasted into or sucked out of an approximately 60 mm cavity between two panes of glass. As a result of the thickness of the layers a U-value of 0.6 W/m²K can be achieved. The disadvantage of this system lies in the extra space needed for the fan and the storage of the polystyrene pellets.

oder Jalousien vorgesehen werden. In Zukunft könnten Systeme mit veränderbaren optischen Eigenschaften eingesetzt werden, wie thermochrome und elektrochrome Systeme. Wenig erforscht sind bisher Wärmedämmfüllungen mit veränderbaren Eigenschaften. Dafür werden Rollos mit IR-reflektierenden Folien sowie Lamellensysteme mit IR-reflektierenden Oberflächen verwendet.

In der 70er Jahren wurde ein System mit Styroporkügelchen von Zomeworks, Albuquerque, USA, patentiert. Das antistatisch behandelte Granulat wird je nach Bedarf in den etwa 60 mm breiten Scheibenzwischenraum einer Doppelverglasung eingeblasen oder abgesaugt. Aufgrund der Schichtdicke ergibt sich ein k-Wert von 0.6 W/m²K. Nachteilig ist der Platzbedarf für das Gebläse und den Kugelspeicher.

Füllungen mit sonnenschützenden Eigenschaften

Im Scheibenzwischenraum lassen sich auch Vorrichtungen zum Sonnenschutz unterbringen. Sie sollen im Sommer die direkte Strahlung und die Blendung abwehren, ohne die Raumbeleuchtung zu beeinträchtigen und ohne im Winter die Energiegewinne zu vermindern. Sonnenschutzmaßnahmen mit festen Eigenschaften sind eingespannte Folien sowie Lamellen oder ähnliche Strukturen, welche entsprechend dem unterschiedlichen Sonnenstand ausgelegt sind. Solche Füllungen sollen keine Aufheizung des Scheibenzwischenraums verursachen, da sonst durch den wechselnden inneren Druck der Randverbund beschädigt würde.

Bei der Entwicklung von steuerbaren Sonnenschutzmaßnahmen, welche sich in den Scheibenzwischenraum einschließen lassen, versucht man, die Vorteile einer Anpassungsfähigkeit an die variablen Licht- und Wetterverhältnisse mit der Möglichkeit eines Schutzes gegen Luftverschmutzung und Witterungseinflüsse sowie einer Reduktion des Reinigungs- und Wartungsaufwands zu verbinden.

Elektrisch regelbare Verschattungssysteme, wie Rollos oder Lamellen, können samt den Elektromotoren in den Scheibenzwischenraum eingeschlossen werden. Da eine Betriebsstörung das Ersetzen der ganzen Scheibe zur Folge haben kann, wurden Produkte entwickelt, bei denen der Motor von der Seite oder von vorne entfernt werden kann.

Fillings with Solar Shading Properties

Solar shading devices can be incorporated into the cavity between the glass panes. In summer they are intended to block direct sunlight and to prevent glare, without reducing the levels of light in the room or the energy gains in winter. Solar shading devices with fixed properties are films, louvres or similar structures positioned according to a particular angle of solar radiation. These fillings should not cause a rise in temperature in the space between the panes as this would produce varying pressures which would eventually damage the edge seal. Developments in controllable solar shading devices to be placed between panes have a three-fold aim: to exploit the advantages of systems which can adapt to variable light and weather conditions; to create the possibility of protection against pollution and weather influences; and to reduce the time and effort needed in cleaning and maintaining the devices. Electrically controlled shading systems such as blinds or louvres, together with their control mechanisms, can be incorporated in the cavity between the panes. As repairs to the mechanism would entail replacing a whole pane, products have been developed in which the motor can be removed from the side or the front.

Roller blinds can be fitted with solar shading fabric layers or films. Coloured polyester blinds can have an aluminium coating on the outside to reflect radiation and to reduce thermal reradiation and glare (Trisolux®). Solar shading films are available in a variety of different reflection levels. They consist of two polyester films, each with a metal coating, which are laminated to-

Isolierglas mit im Scheibenzwischenraum integrierten Sonnenschutzrollos: Trisolux®.

Insulating glass with solar shading roller blinds integrated in the cavity between the panes: Trisolux®.

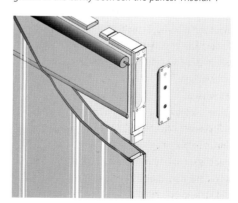

Rollos werden mit Sonnenschutzgeweben oder -folien ausgestattet. Farbige Polyestergewebe sind an der Außenseite mit einer Aluminiumbeschichtung versehen, welche die Sonnenstrahlung reflektiert, die Wärmeabstrahlung und die Blendung vermindert (Trisolux®). Sonnenschutzfolien sind mit verschiedenen Reflexionsgraden erhältlich. Sie bestehen aus zwei Polyesterfolien, die mit einer Metallbeschichtung versehen und gegeneinander laminiert sind. Da sie glatt hochgradig spiegeln würden, werden sie mit einer Prägestruktur versehen (Agero®).

Systeme mit Lamellen sind eine weitere Möglichkeit. Zusätzlich zu den obenerwähnten, vollkommen integrierten Systemen sind Produkte auf dem Markt, die mit einem elektromagnetischen Schieber von der Außenseite der Isolierscheibe verstellt werden können. Je nach Farbe, Beschichtung und Einstellungswinkel können g-Werte von 0.11 bis 0.77 erreicht werden (Luxaclair®, Velthec®).

Eine andere Möglichkeit, Sonnenschutzfunktion und Isolierglas zu verbinden, liegt in der Verwendung von emailbeschichteten Gläsern. Zwei parallel angeordnete Muster können so aufeinander abgestimmt werden, daß sie sich bei einem bestimmten Einfallswinkel ergänzen und eine totale Ausblendung der direkten Sonnenstrahlung bewirken, wie z. B. das Produkt Bi-Therm®: Im Isolierglas ist die eine Scheibe beidseitig mit horizontalen Linienmustern bedruckt, so daß horizontale Lichtstrahlen durchkommen, während steilere ausgeblendet werden.

Für eine dynamische Anpassung an den wechselnden Sonnenstand wurde das System «Zebra®» entwickelt. Es adaptiert laufend die Position der zwei bedruckten Muster zueinander. Eine der beiden bedruckten Scheiben ist beweglich in den Zwischenraum des Isolierglases eingebaut und wird mechanisch hin und her verschoben. Als Muster können Streifen oder Punktraster verwendet werden, die durch geringe Verschiebung eine Ausblendung bewirken. In Kombination mit einer Low-E-Beschichtung können eine Lichttransmission zwischen 0.17 und 0.35 und g-Werte zwischen 0.20 und 0.35 eingestellt werden.

gether. As the smooth surfaces would tend to act as a mirror, they have a textured surfacing (Agero®). Louvre systems are a further possibility. In addition to the above-mentioned, fully integrated systems, products are available which can be adjusted by means of a magnetic control operated from the outside of the insulating glass unit. Depending on colour, coating and angle, g-values of 0.11 to 0.77 can be achieved (Luxaclair®, Velthec®).

Another method of combining solar control functions and insulating glass lies in the use of fritted glass. Two patterns, aligned in parallel to each other, can thus be positioned that at a given angle of incidence the two patterns work together to block out all direct solar radiation. One such product is Bi-Therm® insulating glass, which has one sheet printed on both sides with a pattern of horizontal lines. This arrangement admits light entering horizontally, but blocks light falling from steeper angles of incidence.

The "Zebra®" system was developed to give dynamic adjustment to the changing angle of the sun. It constantly shifts the position of the two patterns in relation to one another. One of the two printed panels is built into the cavity in the insulating glass as a movable component which

Isolierglas mit im Scheibenzwischenraum integrierten verstellbaren Lamellen: Luxaclair®.
Insulating glass with integrated adjustable louvres for solar control: Luxaclair®.

Isolierglas mit zwei bedruckten Emailmustern, deren Position laufend adaptiert wird. Eine im Zwischenraum der Isolierscheibe eingebaute, bedruckte Glasscheibe wird mechanisch hin und her verschoben: Zebra®.
Insulating glass with two printed frit patterns whose position is adapted continuously. A printed glass pane built into the cavity of the insulating glass can be moved backwards and forwards mechanically: Zebra®.

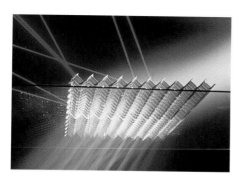

Das Sonnenschutzraster reflektiert die direkte Strahlung, läßt aber das diffuse Tageslicht durchkommen.
The light-grid system reflects direct sunlight, but allows diffuse light to penetrate.

Füllungen mit lichtumlenkenden Eigenschaften

Einen ganz anderen Lösungsansatz für den Sonnenschutz bieten Systeme zur Lichtumlenkung. Sie nutzen optische Gesetzmäßigkeiten wie Reflexion, Transmission oder Brechung, um einerseits das direkte Sonnenlicht auszublenden, andererseits das diffuse Tageslicht in den Innenraum durchzulassen oder sogar in die Raumtiefe zu lenken.

Das Sonnenschutzraster wurde von der Lichtplanung Christian Bartenbach und der Siemens AG entwickelt. Es besteht aus speziell geformten, mit Reinaluminium hochglänzend beschichteten Kunststofflamellen in Längs- und Querrichtung, die eine Struktur von eng aneinandergereihten kleinen Lichtschächten bilden. Aufgrund der Geometrie der Lamellenform und der Ausrichtung der Öffnungen nach Norden gelangt das diffuse Tageslicht ungehindert in den Innenraum, während die von Süden auftreffende direkte Sonnenstrahlung reflektiert wird. Die Sonnenschutzraster finden hauptsächlich bei horizontalen Verglasungen Anwendung. Da die Orientierung genau der einfallenden Lichtstrahlung entsprechen muß, wird der Zuschnitt des Rasters nach Lage und Himmelsrichtung des Gebäudes durch Computerprogramme ermittelt. Der Einbau des Sonnenschutzrasters verändert den k-Wert einer Isolierverglasung kaum, und je nach Glasaufbau sind g-Werte um 0.2 erzielbar.

Ein solches Sonnenschutzraster wurde für die Glasüberdachung des Kongreß- und Ausstellungsgebäudes in Linz, geplant von Herzog und Partnern, 1993, verwendet. Die Tragstruktur des flachen Tonnengewölbes besteht aus speziell gefertigten, bogenförmigen Kastenträgern, die

can be shifted backwards and forwards mechanically. The patterns used are either stripes or dot grids, and the shading effect can be achieved with only a slight adjustment of position. In combination with low-E coatings a light transmittance factor of between 0.17 and 0.35 can be achieved and g-factors of between 0.20 and 0.35.

Fillings with Light Redirecting Properties

A completely different type of solar protection is offered by systems for light deflection. These exploit optical principles such as reflection, transmission or refraction in order to block direct sunlight on the one hand, and on the other to admit diffuse light into the interior or to deflect it into the back of the room.

The light-grid system has been developed by Lichtplanung Christian Bartenbach and Siemens AG. This device consists of specially shaped plastic louvres coated with highly reflective pure aluminium; the louvres are arranged in a regular grid pattern to create light shafts set next to each other in tight rows. The special shape of the louvres and the alignment of the openings towards the north create a situation whereby diffuse light can easily penetrate into the room while direct radiation from the south is reflected. The light-grid systems are mainly used in horizontal glazing. As the orientation must exactly correspond to the angle of the direct sunlight striking the glass panels, the grids are cut to suit the building's specific location and orientation to the sun. Light-grid systems built into insulated glazing units have little effect on the U-value, and depending on the type of unit construction g-values of around 0.2 can be achieved.

A light-grid system for solar protection was used for the congress and exhibition hall in Linz,

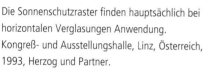

Die Sonnenschutzraster finden hauptsächlich bei horizontalen Verglasungen Anwendung.
Kongreß- und Ausstellungshalle, Linz, Österreich, 1993, Herzog und Partner.
The light-grid systems are mainly used in horizontal glazing.
Congress and Exhibition Hall, Linz, Austria, 1993, Herzog and Partners.

eine Halle von 74 m Spannweite und 204 m Länge mit einer Scheitelhöhe von 12 m stützenfrei überdachen. Die Glaswölbung ist in der Längsrichtung in Streifenfelder unterteilt, die mit 2.70 × 0.80 m großen Isoliergläsern ausgefacht sind. Der Aufbau der Scheibe besteht aus einem innenliegenden Verbundglas (2 × 6 mm), einem Zwischenraum von 25 mm mit 16 mm hohen Spiegelrastern und einer außenliegenden, 8 mm dicken low-E-beschichteten Glasscheibe. Für die Zuschnittgeometrie der einzelnen Spiegelraster mußten nicht nur der Sonnenstand und die Orientierung des Gebäudes, sondern auch ihre Lage auf dem Gewölbe berücksichtigt werden.

Eine zweite Möglichkeit stellen die Tageslichtsysteme mit Prismenplatten aus Acrylglas (PMMA) dar, wie sie von der Lichtplanung Christian Bartenbach für die Siemens AG entwickelt wurden. Die Wirkungsweise der Sonnenschutzprismen beruht auf der Totalreflexion der direkten Lichtstrahlen, die an der Grenzfläche zwischen einem dichten und einem weniger dichten Material bis zu einem bestimmten Einfallswinkel reflektiert werden. Da der Spielbereich für die Totalreflexion sehr klein ist, muß die Prismenplatte dem Sonnenstand konstant nachgeführt werden. Dieser Winkelbereich läßt sich durch das Beschichten einer Prismenflanke mit Reinaluminium deutlich vergrößern. Damit können die Sonnenschutzprismen auch in vertikale, nicht nachführbare Verglasungen eingebaut werden, um die steil auftreffenden, direkten Lichtstrahlen zu reflektieren.
Für eine Umlenkung der diffusen Lichtstrahlung kommen Lichtlenkprismen zum Einsatz. Sie werden hinter der Sonnenschutz-Prismenplatte angeordnet und lenken das diffuse Tageslicht an die Decke des Raumes, wo eine gleichmäßige Lichtverteilung durch die geeignete Gestaltung der Deckenuntersicht erzielt werden kann. Die Ausrichtung der Prismenplatten muß der Fassadenorientierung und der geographischen Lage des Gebäudes entsprechen und wird vom Computer errechnet.
Da Kunststoffe eine geringere Wärmeleitung als Luft aufweisen, sinkt der k-Wert eines normalen Isolierglases mit einer eingebauten Prismenlage auf 2.15 W/m²K, mit zwei Prismenlagen auf 1.65 W/m²K. Ein einlagiges Sonnenschutzsystem erreicht einen g-Wert von 0.13 − 0.15 und für eine Kombination von Sonnenschutz- und Umlenkprismen einen g-Wert von 0.15 − 0.17.

planned by Herzog and Partners in 1993. The support structure of the flat 204 m long barrel vault consists of specially welded box plate arched girders free-spanning 74 m across the hall and reaching an apex at 12 m. In its longitudinal direction the glass vault is divided into strips of 2.70 × 0.80 m panes of insulating glass. Each pane consists of an interior layer of laminated glass (2 × 6 mm), a 25 mm cavity with 16 mm high reflecting grids and an exterior 8 mm thick coated low-E glass pane. In calculating the exact geometry of the individual reflecting grids not only the angle of the sun and the orientation of the building had to be taken into account, but also the angle of slope of each pane on the vaulted roof.

A second possibility for daylight control is presented by prismatic systems made of acrylic panes (PMMA); one such system was developed for Siemens AG by Lichtplanung Christian Bartenbach.
The way these daylight prismatic systems work is through total reflection of the direct sunlight falling up to a certain angle of incidence on the border between a thicker and a thinner material. As this angle of operation has very limited tolerances, the prismatic panel has to constantly track the position of the sun.
To increase the angle range available one of the prism edges can be coated with pure aluminium. This enables the solar shading prisms to be built into vertical, non-trackable glazing units, with the aim of reflecting the direct light falling from a steep angle.
The deflection of diffuse light can be achieved through light-control prismatic panels. They are placed behind the solar shading prismatic panel and deflect diffuse daylight onto the ceiling of the room which, given a suitable ceiling design, can ensure an even distribution of light across the room. The positioning of the prismatic panels must be suited to the orientation of the façades and the geographical location of the building; calculations are worked out by computer.
As plastics have a lower thermal conductivity than air, the U-value of a normal pane of insulating glass with built-in prismatic panel can be lowered to 2.15 W/m²K; if two prismatic panels are fitted, this value reaches 1.65 W/m²K. A single-layer solar protection achieves a g-value of 0.13 − 0.15 and in cases where solar protec-

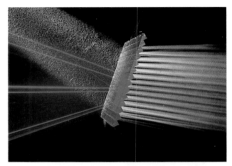

a

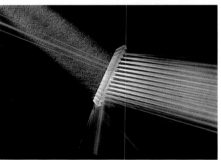

b

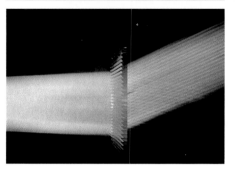

c

Prismenplatten aus Acrylglas reflektieren die direkte Sonnenstrahlung durch Totalreflexion an der Prismenflanke. Sie werden entweder dem Sonnenstand nachgeführt (a) oder mit einer verspiegelten Flanke fest eingebaut (b). Lichtlenkprismen können dagegen die diffuse Strahlung in die Raumtiefe umlenken (c).
Prismatic acrylic panes reflect all direct sunlight on the edge of the prism. They can either be set to track the sun's angle (a) or fitted with a fixed, reflective prism edge (b). Light control prismatic panels allow the deflection of diffuse light (c).

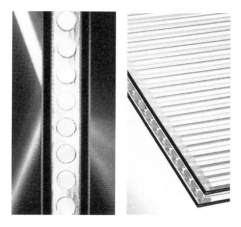

Im Isolierglas eingebaute, runde Acryl-Profile zerstreuen das direkte Tageslicht; dreieckige Acryl-Profile blenden die direkte Lichtstrahlung bei einem bestimmten Einfallswinkel aus: Ekoss®.
Acrylic profiles built into the insulating glass scatter the direct incident daylight; triangular acrylic profiles protect from direct light radiation falling from a certain angle of incidence: Ekoss®.

Im Isolierglas eingebaute, leicht gebogene Acryl-Profile lenken das einfallende Tageslicht um: SGG-Lumitop®.
Lightly curved acrylic profiles built into the insulating glass deflect the incident daylight: SGG-Lumitop®.

Die Möglichkeiten der Lichtumlenkung wurden in den USA schon Ende des 19. Jahrhunderts genutzt: Mit horizontal gerippten Gläsern konnte ein Teil des einfallenden Tageslichts in die Tiefe der Räume umgelenkt werden, z. B. beim Carson-Pirie-Scott-Kaufhaus, vom Architekten Louis Sullivan 1906 vollendet. Durch das Aufkommen des elektrischen Lichts geriet diese Idee aber in Vergessenheit, bis Christian Bartenbach sie in den 80er Jahren wieder aufgriff und erstmals einsetzte beim Geschäftshaus Vaucher, Niederwangen bei Bern, vom Atelier 5 1980–83 fertiggestellt.

Ebenfalls mit runden oder dreieckigen Kunststoffprofilen aus Acrylglas (PMMA) funktionieren die Ekoss®-Produkte des japanischen Glasherstellers Figla.
Die runden Acryl-Profile zerstreuen das direkte Tageslicht bei jedem Einfallswinkel, sowohl im Winter als auch im Sommer. Damit eignen sie sich für eine diffuse Beleuchtung von Kunstgalerien oder Museen.
Die dreieckigen Acryl-Profile können in verschiedenen Ausrichtungen eingebaut werden, so daß der Einfallswinkel für die Totalreflexion der direkten Lichtstrahlen der Einbausituation angepaßt werden kann. Mit den genannten Ekoss®-Produkten können g-Werte zwischen 0.38 und 0.52 bzw. zwischen 0.30 und 0.48 erzielt werden.

Ein weiteres Lichtumlenksystem mit Acryl-Profilen ist das SGG-Lumitop®, das zum ersten Mal als Prototyp beim Bürohaus Geyssel in Köln, von Prof. E. Schneider Wessling 1994 entworfen, eingesetzt wurde. Bei diesem System werden leicht gebogene Acrylprofile in den Scheibenzwischenraum eingebaut. Die abgerundete Form ermöglicht die Totalreflexion der eintreffenden Lichtstrahlen für ein großes Spektrum sowohl horizontal als auch vertikal.

tion and deflection prisms are used, this can reach 0.15–0.17.

The possibilities of light deflection were already being used in the US at the end of the 19th century.
Horizontal ribbing on glass could deflect a portion of the incident light into the back of the room, e. g. as used at the Carson-Pirie-Scott department store, completed in 1906 by the architect Louis Sullivan.
With the advent of electric light, however, this idea was forgotten until Christian Bartenbach took it up again in the 1980s and reintroduced it again, in the Vaucher commercial building in Niederwangen near Berne, built by Atelier 5 in 1980–83.

Another product also using round or triangular profiles of acrylic glass (PMMA) is the Ekoss® range by the Japanese glass manufacturer Figla.
The round acrylic profiles scatter direct daylight from all angles of incidence, both in winter and summer. Thus it is suitable for diffuse lighting in art galleries or museums.
The triangular acrylic profiles can be variously angled, as required, to completely block out direct radiation. Ekoss® products can achieve g-factors of between 0.38 and 0.52 and between 0.30 and 0.48.

Another light deflection system using acrylic profiles is SGG-Lumitop®, used for the first time as a prototype for the Geyssel office building in Cologne, designed by Professor E. Schneider Wessling in 1994.
In this system slightly curved acrylic profiles are built into the cavity between the panes. The rounded form enables total reflection of incident light across a wide angle, both in the horizontal and vertical planes.

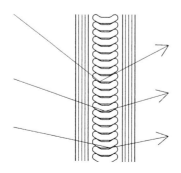
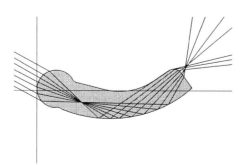
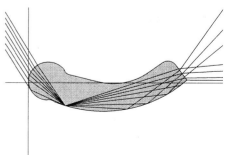

Die fest eingebauten Spiegelprofile Oka-Solar® übernehmen die Funktion des Sonnenschutzes oder der Lichtumlenkung je nach Sonnenhöhe. Das System besteht aus speziell geformten Spiegellamellen, deren Profil nach den verschiedenen Einfallswinkeln der Sonnenstrahlung ausgelegt ist. Damit wird die steileinfallende direkte Lichtstrahlung im Sommer nach außen reflektiert, während die tiefliegende Strahlung im Winter durchgelassen und in die Raumtiefe umgelenkt wird. Da der Stahlungsdurchgang von der Winkeleinstellung abhängig ist, geschieht dies aber zu bestimmten Tageszeiten auch im Sommer. Das System ist sowohl für vertikale als auch für geneigte Verglasungen geeignet. Die Lamellen werden in einer für die spezielle Anwendung optimalen Winkeleinstellung in einen 16 bzw. 18 mm breiten Scheibenzwischenraum eingebaut. Sie beeinflussen den k-Wert wenig; hingegen variiert der g-Wert je nach Sonnenhöhe von 0.22 bis zu 0.51, und τ von 0.03 bis 0.51, wobei der tiefste Wert τ_{diff} von 0.33 von Bedeutung ist (Oka-Solar® Typ 55/15).

Obwohl das System mit fest eingebauten Spiegelprofilen keine Verstellung ermöglicht, zeigt es trotzdem einen differenzierten Umgang mit der Sonnenstrahlung: Bei einer hohen Sonnenlage setzt es die Kühllasten und die Blendung herab, bei tiefliegender Einstrahlung ermöglicht es die Nutzung des Tageslichts durch die Umlenkung in die Raumtiefe.

Der Architekt Jo Coenen hat Oka-Solar® Spiegelprofile 1992 für die Fassade des Geschäftshauses Haans in Tilburg, Niederlande, verwendet. Wie beim Niederländischen Architekturinstitut in Rotterdam ist das Thema «Glaspavillon» durch einen Wasserteich, hohe freistehende Stützen und ein weit auskragendes Dach verwirklicht. Die Glasfassade ist eine Pfosten-Riegel-Konstruktion aus Aluminiumprofilen mit einem Raster von 2.4 m in der Breite und 1.05 m in der Höhe. Damit ist die geschoßhohe Verglasung bei den Großraumbüros in drei Bänder unterteilt. Im Brüstungsbereich sorgen die Spiegelprofile für eine weitgehende Ausblendung der direkten Sonnenstrahlen. Dagegen lenken sie im Deckenbereich ein Maximum an Licht in die Raumtiefe. Die Lamellen sind in Isolierscheiben mit Low-E-Beschichtung und Argonfüllung eingebaut (k-Wert 1.6 W/m²K). Im Durchsichtsbereich wurden dieselben Isolierscheiben ohne Lamellen

Oka-Solar® built-in mirror profiles take on either the function of solar shading or of light deflection depending on the angle of the sun. The system consists of specially formed mirror louvres whose profile is angled to match the various incident angles of sunlight. This means that the steeply angled daylight in summer is reflected back outside, while the lower angled light in winter can penetrate into the building's interior and is deflected into the back of the room. As the level of light admitted is dependent on the angle of the mirror louvres, this occurs also in summer, depending on the time of day. The system is suited to both horizontal and vertical glazing. The louvres are built into a 16 to 18 mm cavity between two panes and set at the optimum angle suited to the particular use and situation. The louvres have little influence on the U-value, but the g-value can vary between 0.22 and 0.51 depending on the height of the sun, and the τ-value varies between 0.03 and 0.51, whereby the lowest τ_{diff} value of 0.33 is significant (Oka-Solar® Type 55/15).

Although the system with fixed, built-in mirror profiles cannot be adjusted, it reacts in an intelligent way to differing solar radiation conditions; when the sun is high it reduces cooling loads and glare, and when the sun is low, it permits the use of daylight for deflection into the depths of the room.

The architect Jo Coenen used Oka-Solar® mirror profiles for the façade of the Haans office building in Tilburg, Netherlands, built in 1992. As with the Architectural Institute of the Netherlands in Rotterdam, the theme in this office building is also that of a glass pavilion, with pond, high free-standing support pillars and a wide cantilevered roof. The glass façade is a mullion and transom frame of aluminium profiles, spaced horizontally at 2.4 m and vertically at 1.05 m. At the office levels this gives a triple banded effect across the glazed façade. At the parapet levels the mirror profiles practically block all direct sunlight. However, at ceiling levels maximum levels of light are admitted to the back of the room.

The louvres are built into insulated glazing units with a low-E coating and argon filling (U-value 1.6 W/m²K). In the transparent section the same insulating panes, but without louvres, were used either as tilting windows or fixed glazing. On the south side the 12 m high glass façade is posi-

Speziell geformte Spiegellamellen ermöglichen die Reflexion der steileinfallenden direkten Sonnenstrahlung, lenken aber die tiefliegende Strahlung in die Raumtiefe um: Oka-Solar®.

Specially shaped mirror louvres reflect steeply angled direct sunlight, but allow low-angled light to pass into the room: Oka-Solar®.

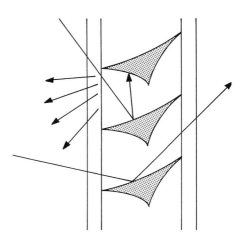

Die gebäudehohe Glasfassade ist mit Oka-Solar® Spiegelprofilen ausgestattet, und dennoch ist der Ausblick in die Umgebung weitgehend möglich. Geschäftshaus «Haans», Tilburg, Niederlande, 1992, Jo Coenen.

The fully glazed façade is fitted with Oka-Solar® mirror louvres which still permit a view of the surroundings.
Haans office building, Tilburg, Netherlands, 1992, Jo Coenen.

alternierend als Kippfenster und als feste Verglasung eingesetzt. Auf der Südseite ist die 12 m hohe Glasfassade den Arbeitsflächen vorgelagert, so daß ein viergeschossiger offener Raum mit gestaffelten Büroetagen geschaffen wird. Die schmalen vertikalen Pfosten sind von innen gegen horizontale Lasteneinwirkung mit Stahlfachwerken verstärkt, die gegen seitliches Auskippen durch Laufstege für die Fensterreinigung stabilisiert sind.

Vorteile der festen Lichtumlenksysteme sind der Schutz vor direkter Sonnenstrahlung und die Erhöhung der Lichtverteilung in der Raumtiefe, was Kühllasten und Brennstunden der Beleuchtung reduziert.
Nachteile sind die schlechte Anpassung an die wechselnden Licht- und Wetterverhältnisse und eventuell eine gewisse Behinderung des freien Durchblicks nach außen.
Die energetischen Einsparungen decken, ökonomisch betrachtet, die hohen Investitionskosten noch nicht, aber dafür erübrigen sich die Anschaffung und der Unterhalt einer außenliegenden Sonnenschutzanlage.

tioned in front of the working levels with a four-floor high open space between them. The narrow vertical posts are braced from the inside against horizontal forces by steel framing; these steel frames are in turn stabilised against lateral shift by gantries for window cleaning and maintenance.

The advantages of the light-deflecting systems are the protection they give against direct sunlight and the increase in distribution of light into the depth of the room, which reduces both cooling loads and lighting hours.
The disadvantages are the poor adaptation to changing light and weather conditions and a certain obstruction to a clear view out of the windows.
From an economic point of view the savings in energy do not yet cover the high initial investment costs, but the costs and the cleaning of an exterior sun shade device are saved.

Die Fassade   Façades

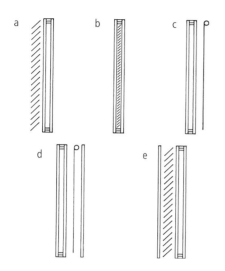

Die Vielzahl an Glasfassaden läßt sich in wenige typische Varianten einteilen: Einschalige Fassaden weisen außenliegenden (a), integrierten (b) oder innenliegenden (c) Sonnenschutz auf; bei mehrschaligen Fassaden, z. B. Abluftfassaden (d) oder zweischaligen Fassaden (e), ist der Sonnenschutz dazwischen angeordnet.
The many different types of glass façades can be broadly grouped into a few categories: single-skin façades with exterior (a), integrated (b) or interior (c) shading devices; in the case of multiple-skin façades, e. g. ventilated cavity (d) or double-skin (e) façades, the solar shading is placed between the skins.

Linke Seite: Die zweischalige Fassade dient aufgrund der verkehrsreichen Lage hauptsächlich als Lärmschutz.
Ensemble der Victoria Lebensversicherung, Köln, 1990–96, T. van den Valentyn und A. Tillmann
Left page: The double-skin façade serves mainly as noise protection against the heavy traffic.
Victoria Life Insurance buildings, Cologne, 1990–96, T. van den Valentyn and A. Tillmann.

Die Planung einer Glasfassade umfaßt den Einsatz von verschiedenen Maßnahmen, um einerseits die Wärmeverluste niedrig zu halten, andererseits die unerwünschten Wärmegewinne durch sommerliche Sonnenstrahlung zu vermeiden. Die Vielzahl der möglichen Kombinationen von Maßnahmen läßt sich in wenige typische Fassadenvarianten einteilen. Ein erstes Kriterium ist die Anzahl Verglasungsebenen, daher die Bezeichnung einschalige oder mehrschalige Fassaden.

Das zweite Kriterium ist die Positionierung der Sonnenschutzmaßnahme. Es gibt einschalige Fassaden mit außenliegendem, innenliegendem oder im Luftzwischenraum der Verglasung integriertem Sonnenschutz. Bei den mehrschaligen Fassaden, z. B. Abluft- oder «Zweite Haut»-Fassaden, ist der Sonnenschutz meistens zwischen den Verglasungsebenen angeordnet.

Einschalige Fassaden

Eine Glasfassade erhält einen gewissen Sonnenschutz durch IR-reflektierende oder auch im sichtbaren Bereich absorbierende und reflektierende Beschichtungen. Da deren Eigenschaften nicht veränderbar sind, werden sowohl die Energiegewinne in kälteren Jahreszeiten verhindert als auch der Tageslichteinfall herabgesetzt. Darum ist das Anbringen von zusätzlichen, variablen Sonnenschutzmaßnahmen bei Gebäuden mit großflächiger Verglasung und hohen Klimaanforderungen unerläßlich.

Außenliegender Sonnenschutz

Diese Maßnahme weist den Vorteil eines erhöhten Wirkungsgrades auf, weil die durch direkte Sonneneinstrahlung auf dem Sonnenschutz entstehende sekundäre Wärmeabgabe außerhalb der Gebäudehülle bleibt. Ein typischer g-Wert liegt heute bei etwa 0.10. Nachteilig ist, daß der außenliegende Sonnenschutz – als Stoffstoren oder Lamellen – den Witterungseinflüssen aus-

In designing glass façades a variety of different devices are implemented to, on the one hand, keep heat losses low, and, on the other, to avoid undesired heat gains through solar radiation in summer. The range of possibilities and combinations of measures can be broadly grouped into a few typical categories. The first main criterion is the number of glazing skins incorporated in the design – here the terms used are single-skin façades and multiple-skin façades.

The second criterion is the positioning of the solar control devices. There are single-skin façades with exterior or interior shading, or with integrated shading devices incorporated in the cavity between the panes. In the case of multiple-skin façades, e. g. ventilated cavity or double-skin façades, the solar control devices are generally placed between the glazing skins.

Single-Skin Façades

To achieve a certain level of solar control in a single-skin façade, coatings can be applied to the glass, such as infrared-reflecting coatings and/or coatings to absorb and reflect wavelengths in the visible range. As their properties are fixed, they also restrict solar gain in the colder months and reduce daylighting levels. For this reason it is necessary to provide additional adjustable solar control measures in buildings with large surface areas of façade glazing and in buildings where air conditioning requirements are strictly regulated.

Exterior Solar Control Devices

The advantage of exterior solar control devices is that the heat, resulting from reradiation from the device itself, remains on the outside of the building. A typical g-value nowadays for a façade with exterior devices is around 0.10.

A disadvantage is the fact that the devices, in the form of fabric blinds or louvres, are exposed to the effects of weather, which can give rise to

gesetzt ist, was periodische Reinigungsarbeiten bedingt und hohe Wartungskosten verursachen kann.

Man unterscheidet zwischen starren und beweglichen Maßnahmen. Erstere sind in Form von Dachvorsprüngen und auskragenden Bauteilen, Sonnensegeln, «brise-soleils» und Lamellen allgemein bekannt.

Zur zweiten Gruppe gehören ebenfalls übliche Produkte wie Gewebe- und Gitterstoffstoren sowie Jalousien, Rafflamellen und großformatige Lamellen. Seltener sind Lösungen mit verschiebbaren Fassadenelementen, wie Paneele, Gitterroste oder Lichtumlenkungs-Elemente.

Ein weit auskragendes Dach charakterisiert die südliche Ansicht der neuen Bibliothek der Technischen Hochschule in Cranfield, Bedfordshire, Großbritannien, 1989–92 von Foster und Partnern erstellt. Als seitliche Verschattungsmaßnahme wurden gebäudehohe Module mit starren horizontalen Lamellen aus anodisiertem Aluminium verwendet.

Ein Beispiel für starre Lamellensysteme ist die Fassade der «Hongkong und Shanghai Bank» in Hongkong, 1979–86 ebenfalls von Foster und Partnern erbaut.
Die schräggestellten Lamellen sind zwischen Aluminiumkonsolen eingespannt und bieten einen wirksamen Sonnenschutz, ohne den Blick nach unten zu behindern.

Für die Regionalverwaltung des Royal Automobile Club (RAC) in Bristol, 1992–94, haben die

high costs for regular cleaning and maintenance. Exterior devices can either be fixed or movable. Familar types of construction which fall into the first category are projecting roofs or building sections, awnings, brise-soleils and fixed-angle louvre shading.
In the second category are such products as fabric blinds or screens, Venetian blinds or large louvres.
A less common type are sliding façade units such as panels, screening grids and light-deflecting elements.

An example of the use of a wide projecting roof is the library building of Cranfield Institute of Technology in Bedfordshire, England, built between 1989 and 1992 by Foster and Partners. To shade the sides of the building, full-height modules were used with fixed horizontal louvres made of anodised aluminium.

For the Hongkong and Shanghai Bank in Hong Kong, built 1979–86, also by Foster and Partners, a solar shading device was developed with louvres fixed at an angle to the façade plane, and held between aluminium brackets. The design of this system offers effective protection without obstructing the downward view for people inside the building.

For the Regional Headquarters of the Royal Automobile Club (RAC) in Bristol, 1992–94, the architects Nicholas Grimshaw and Partners used cantilevered "brise-soleils" and dark glazing for solar protection. The building is situated

Auskragende «brise soleils» und eine grau getönte
Verglasung dienen als Sonnenschutz.
Regionalverwaltung des Royal Automobile Club,
Bristol, 1992 – 94, Nicholas Grimshaw und Partner.
Projecting "brise-soleils" and grey-tinted glass are
used as solar shading.
Regional Control Centre of the Royal Automobile
Club, Bristol, 1992 – 94, Nicholas Grimshaw and
Partners.

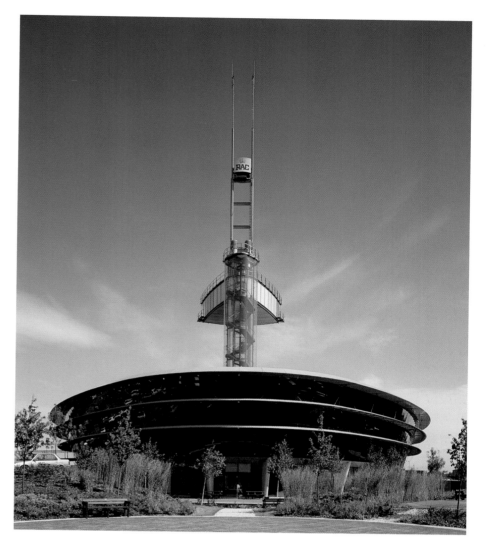

Architekten Nicholas Grimshaw und Partner für
den Sonnenschutz auskragende «brise-soleils»
und eine dunkle Verglasung verwendet.
Das Gebäude liegt unmittelbar an der Kreuzung
zweier Autobahnen und hat einen leicht abgerundeten, dreieckigen Grundriß. Die nach
außen geneigte Glasfassade kann als Weiterentwicklung der Verglasung bei der Druckerei «Western Morning News», Plymouth, 1992, betrachtet werden.
Die innenliegende Tragkonstruktion besteht aus
runden Stahlpfosten mit 250 mm Durchmesser,
die sich zum Ende hin verjüngen und durch
horizontale Stahlrohre von 115 mm Durchmesser miteinander verbunden sind. Die 1.8 × 2.5 m
großen Isoliergläser sind an den Ecken mit
gelenkigen Punkthalterungen an den horizontalen Stahlrohren befestigt. Sie bestehen aus
einer grau getönten, 6 mm starken ESG-Scheibe
mit einer Low-E-Beschichtung außen, einem

at the intersection of two motorways and has a
slightly rounded, triangular ground plan. The
outward tilt of the glass façade can be regarded
as a further development of the glazing used for
the offices of the Western Morning News in Plymouth, completed in 1992.
The inner support structure is of 250 mm diameter tubular steel posts, tapering towards one
end, and connected to each other via 115 mm diameter horizontal tubular steel.
The 1.8 × 2.5 m insulated glass panes are fixed at
the corners to the horizontal steel members by
means of articulated point fixings. They consist
of an outer sheet of grey-tinted 6 mm toughened
glass with a low-E coating, a cavity of 12 mm and
an inner sheet of 12 mm toughened glass; this
produces a U-value of 1.9 W/m^2K. The 15 mm
wide joints are sealed with black silicone.
The outward-tilting glass façade is topped with a
projecting roof which protects against the sun

Zwischenraum von 12 mm und einer 12 mm starken ESG-Scheibe innen; sie ergeben einen k-Wert von 1.9 W/m²K.

Die 15 mm breiten Fugen sind mit schwarzem Silikon gedichtet. Die nach außen geneigte Glasfassade ist mit einem weit auskragenden Vordach bekrönt, das als Sonnen- und Wetterschutz dient. Als weitere Sonnenschutzmaßnahme dienen zwei ausladende Gitterrost-Laufstege, die mit Zugseilen vom Vordach abgehängt sind. Für den Blendschutz sind innenliegende Stoffrollos eingebaut.

Ein Vordach aus perforierten Aluminiumlamellen und ein emailliertes, weißes Streifenmuster schützen das Bürogebäude «B8» im Stockley Park, London, vor der Sonne. Ian Ritchie Architects haben den Bau nach dem Prinzip «Kern und Hülle» in nur 36 Wochen 1990 fertiggestellt. Aus Zeitgründen ist die Glasfassade mit kleinen Änderungen aus dem standardisierten Planar®-System entwickelt worden.

Die 3×1.385 m großen Isoliergläser sind in den vier Ecken mit der punktförmigen Befestigung Planar® 905 versehen und durch Edelstahlkonsolen in die tragenden Pfosten eingehängt. Ihr Aufbau besteht aus einer 6 mm starken ESG-Scheibe mit einer Low-E-Beschichtung innen, einem Zwischenraum von 16 mm mit Argonfüllung und einer 12 mm starken ESG-Scheibe außen, die im Decken- und Brüstungsbereich ein weiß emailliertes Streifenmuster mit einem Bedruckungsgrad von 70 % aufweist. Die un-

and the weather. Other solar control measures include two widely projecting metal gantries suspended by ties from the roof canopy. Inside the building roller blinds made of material are used for protection against glare.

A canopy of perforated aluminium louvres and an enamelled white stripe pattern give solar control in office building B8 in Stockley Park, London.

Ian Ritchie Architects constructed the building on the "shell and core" principle in just 36 weeks in 1990. For reasons of time the glass used for the façade was a slightly modified version of the standardised Planar® system.

The 3×1.385 m sized insulating glass units are fitted at the four corners with Planar® 905 point fixings and suspended in the support mullions by means of stainless steel pins. The inner sheet of each unit is 6 mm toughened glass with low-E coating separated by a 16 mm cavity filled with argon gas from an outer sheet of 12 mm toughened glass. On the outside at the level of the parapets and floor slabs, the glazing has a white fritted stripe pattern with 70 % cover.

The unusual thickness of the outer panes is necessary to give acoustic protection from a nearby heliport. This thickness also gives rise to the characteristic green tint of the glass façade.

The 12 mm joints are sealed with black silicon.

Another approach to solar control is to combine an angled façade with louvred sunshades can-

Isoliergläser mit einem Streifenmuster wurden für die Abgrenzung des Durchsichtsbereichs eingesetzt. Die ungewöhnlich dicke Außenscheibe verleiht der Fassade einen Grünstich. Die Scheiben sind durch Bolzen an den vier Ecken befestigt.
Gebäude «B8», Stockley Park, London, 1990, Ian Ritchie Architects.

Insulating glazing with fritted stripe pattern was used to define the view out. The unusual thickness of the outer pane gives the façade a green tint. The glass units are fixed at the four corners with bolts.
B8 building, Stockley Park, London, 1990, Ian Ritchie Architects.

gewöhnliche Dicke der Außenscheibe ist aus akustischen Gründen wegen des naheliegenden Heliports notwendig und verleiht der Fassade den typischen Grünstich der Glasmasse. Die 12 mm breiten Fugen sind mit schwarzem Silikon abgedichtet.

Als Sonnenschutzmaßnahme kann auch eine schräggestellte Fassade mit auskragenden Lamellenvordächern dienen, wie beim neuen Koordinationszentrum der British Airways, London-Heathrow, das von Nicholas Grimshaw und Partnern 1994 fertiggestellt wurde. Die nach vorne geneigte, schräge Stellung der Fassade ist eine Maßnahme zur Vermeidung der Reflexion von Radarwellen vom nahe gelegenen Flughafen. Ihre Konstruktion besteht aus Pfosten in 3 m Achsabstand und aus Riegeln, die entsprechend der geneigten Geometrie jedes Geschoß in drei etwa 1.40 m hohe Felder unterteilen. Im Brüstungsbereich sind undurchsichtige, wärmedämmende Paneele eingesetzt, welchen emailbeschichtete Gläser mit einem hellblauen Punktraster vorgelagert sind. Im Durchsichtsbereich sind schalldämmende, transparente Isoliergläser eingesetzt, die aus einer 5 mm dicken äußeren Scheibe, einem 10 mm dicken innenliegenden Verbundglas und einem 17.5 mm breiten Zwischenraum bestehen. Die Lamellen werden von Konsolen aus gegossenem Aluminium getragen, die an der Spitze mit einem extrudierten Aluminiumprofil miteinander verbunden sind. Glasstreifen, die ebenfalls mit einem hellblauen Punktraster

tilevered out beyond the façade plane. Such a design was used by Nicholas Grimshaw & Partners in 1994 for the Combined Operations Centre for British Airways at Heathrow in London.
The forward tilt of the façade is a measure intended to avoid the reflection of radar waves from the nearby airport.
The structure of the façade consists of 3 m spaced vertical mullions with a tripartite banding of each floor by means of transoms spaced at roughly 1.40 m, varying a little depending on the angled façade geometry at individual points.
At parapet level the architects used thermally insulating panels, and in front of them a fritted glass with a pale blue dot pattern.
At seated and standing eye levels the transparent glazing has both thermal and acoustic insulating properties. The insulating glass units consist of a 5 mm thick sheet outside, a 10 mm thick laminated glass inside and a 17.5 mm air space between the two.
The louvred sunshade is supported by cast aluminium brackets joined together at the ends by extruded aluminium profiles. The 12 mm thick louvres are made of glass strips, also with a pale blue dot pattern.

Movable solar shading devices in the form of fabric blinds or screens are now quite common. Examples include the glass façade of the extension to the IRCAM building in Paris built 1988/89 by the Renzo Piano Building Workshop, or the

Sonnenschutz durch eine nach vorne geneigte Fassade und Glaslamellen mit einem hellblauen, emaillierten Punktraster.
Koordinationszentrum der British Airways, London-Heathrow, 1994, Nicholas Grimshaw und Partner.
Solar protection is given by an angled façade and glass louvres with a pale blue fritted dot pattern. Combined Operations Centre for British Airways, Heathrow, London, 1994, Nicholas Grimshaw and Partners.

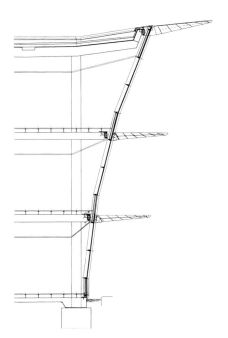

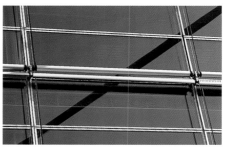

Außenliegende Gitterstoffstoren weisen den Vorteil eines erhöhten Wirkungsgrades auf, da die sekundäre Abwärme außerhalb des Gebäudes bleibt. «Fondation Cartier», Paris, 1994, Architectures Jean Nouvel.
Exterior movable fabric blinds offer effective solar protection, as the heat reradiation remains on the outside of the building.
Fondation Cartier, Paris, 1994, Architectures Jean Nouvel.

versehen sind, bilden die schräggestellten, 12 mm starken Lamellen.

Bewegliche Sonnenschutzmaßnahmen in Form von Gewebe- oder Gitterstoffstoren sind allgemein bekannt. Als Beispiele können die Glasfassade des Erweiterungsgebäudes für die IRCAM in Paris, 1988–89 vom Renzo Piano Building Workshop gebaut, oder die «Fondation Cartier», ebenfalls in Paris, von Architectures Jean Nouvel 1994 fertiggestellt, angeführt werden.

Eine spezielle Lösung für den Sonnenschutz zeigt die «Banque Populaire de l'Ouest et de l'Armorique» in Rennes, 1989 von den Architekten Odile

"Fondation Cartier", Paris, completed in 1994, by Architectures Jean Nouvel.

An unusual design for solar shading was realized in the "Banque Populaire de l'Ouest et de l'Armorique" in Rennes, built in 1989 by the architects Odile Decq and Benoît Cornette in collaboration with RFR, Peter Rice. Two metres in front of the glazed wall is a filigree steel framework which gives both horizontal stability to the façade in terms of restraining wind pressure and suction and serves as an attachment for the external roller blinds.
The 8 m high masts are spaced at 12 m and are

Das filigrane Stahlgerüst dient gleichzeitig zur horizontalen Aussteifung der Glasfassade und zur Befestigung des Sonnenschutzes.
«Banque Populaire de l'Ouest et de l'Armorique», Rennes, Frankreich, 1989, Odile Decq und Benoît Cornette, mit RFR, Peter Rice.
The filigree steel framework gives both horizontal stability to the glass façade and serves as an attachment for the external roller blinds.
Banque Populaire de l'Ouest et de l'Armorique, Rennes, France, 1989, Odile Decq and Benoît Cornette, with RFR, Peter Rice.

Bei der hängenden Glasfassade sind die oberen Scheiben in der Mitte durch einen gefederten Beschlag am Dachrand befestigt, und die nächsten Scheiben sind durch kreuzförmige Verbindungsknoten miteinander verhängt (rechts). Im Eingangsbereich wurden vorgespannte Einfachscheiben verwendet (links oben), im Bürotrakt dagegen Isolierscheiben (links unten).

«Banque Populaire de l'Ouest et de l'Armorique», Rennes, Frankreich, 1989, Odile Decq und Benoît Cornette, mit RFR, Peter Rice.

In the suspended glass façade the upper row of panes is attached to the roof edge via spring assemblies at the centre. The next rows are suspended below them via cross-shaped bolted fixings (right). The glazing in the entrance area consists of toughened single panes (top left). Insulating glass units are used in the office section (bottom left).

Banque Populaire de l'Ouest et de l'Armorique, Rennes, France, 1989, Odile Decq and Benoît Cornette, with RFR, Peter Rice.

Decq und Benoît Cornette in Zusammenarbeit mit RFR, Peter Rice, erbaut. Vor der Verglasung ist in einem Abstand von 2 m ein filigranes Stahlgerüst errichtet, welches gleichzeitig zur Stabilisierung der Fassade gegen Winddruck und -sog sowie zur Befestigung der Sonnenschutzrollos dient. Die 8 m hohen Masten stehen in einem Achsabstand von 12 m und werden durch horizontale Verbindungsrohre und einen darüberliegenden Fachwerkträger ausgesteift. Die Verglasung des Eingangsbereichs besteht aus 2 × 2 m großen, vorgespannten Einfachscheiben. Die obere Reihe ist in der Mitte durch einen gefederten Beschlag am Dachrand befestigt, und die nächsten Scheiben sind mittels kreuzförmigen Verbindungsknoten miteinander abgehängt. Letztere sind durch runde Edelstahlstäbe mit dem außenliegenden Traggerüst verbunden, um die horizontalen Windlasten zu übertragen. Beim Bürotrakt sind nach demselben konstruktiven Prinzip Isolierscheiben eingesetzt worden, wahrscheinlich die erste Ausführung in dieser Art überhaupt. Außen- und Innenscheibe bestehen aus 12 mm starkem ESG und sind durch einen runden Abstandhalter von 15 mm Durchmesser verbunden, so daß eine punktförmige Befestigung an den kreuzförmigen Verbindungsknoten erfolgen kann.

Diese Konstruktion kann als Weiterentwicklung

guyed and braced with horizontal steel tubes and a lattice girder on top.

The glazing in the entrance area consists of 2 × 2 m sheets of toughened single glass. The upper row is attached at the centre via spring assemblies to the roof edge, and the next rows are suspended below them via cross-shaped bolted fixings. These fixings are connected to the external support frame by means of stainless steel rods, which restrain wind loads.

The same type of construction is used in the office section, with insulating glass replacing the single panes.

Probably this is the first suspended glazing with double insulating glass units. Outer and inner sheet consist of 12 mm thick toughened glass and are separated by round, 15 mm diameter spacers which enable the glass unit to be bolted to the cross-shaped fixings.

This construction can be seen as a further development of the "greenhouse" type glazing to the Museum of Science and Technology in Paris built in 1986 by Rice-Francis-Ritchie (RFR) for the architect Adrien Fainsilber.

Movable solar control devices in the shape of Venetian blinds or metal louvres are also widespread. Products with an adjustable angle of tilt have the advantage that they can be angled to

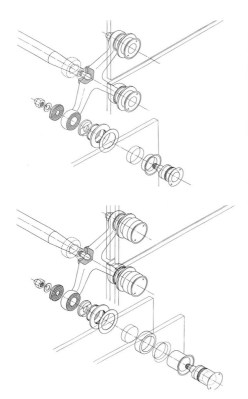

Rafflamellen ermöglichen die Anpassung an die wechselnden Sonnenstellungen und Witterungsverhältnisse.
Büro- und Produktionsgebäude der Firma Seele, Gersthofen, Deutschland, 1992, Kauffmann und Theilig.
Louvre blinds can be adjusted to the changing angles of the sun and weather conditions.
Office and factory building Seele, Gersthofen, Germany, 1992, Kauffmann and Theilig.

der Gewächshaus-Verglasung des Museums für Wissenschaft und Technik in Paris betrachtet werden, welche Rice-Francis-Ritchie (RFR) für den Architekten Adrien Fainsilber 1986 ausgearbeitet haben.

Bewegliche Sonnenschutzmaßnahmen in Form von Raffstoren oder Metallamellen sind ebenfalls weit verbreitet. Produkte mit verstellbarem Neigungswinkel haben den Vorteil, daß sie sich nach allen Licht- und Wetterbedingungen ausrichten lassen. Der Nachteil von kleinen Rafflamellen ist ihre geringe Windsteifigkeit. Beispiele für die Verwendung von Rafflamellen sind das Büro- und Produktionsgebäude der Firma Seele in Gersthofen, Deutschland, von den Architekten Kauffmann und Theilig 1992 fertiggestellt, und das Bürogebäude der Werbeagentur Thompson in Frankfurt am Main, 1992–95 von den Architekten Schneider + Schumacher realisiert (Siehe S. 158/159).

Drehbare Großlamellen hingegen bieten einen wirksamen Sonnenschutz und gleichzeitig eine gute Windsteifigkeit. Meistens bestehen sie aus extrudierten Aluminiumprofilen oder abgekanteten Blechen; seit ein paar Jahren sind auch großformatige Glaslamellen beliebt.
Ein Beispiel für Aluminiumlamellen ist das Bürogebäude «TAD», Milano-Lainate, 1989 von den Architekten Ottavio di Blasi Associati erbaut.

Beim Konstruktionsbüro der Firma Gartner & Co., Gundelfingen, Deutschland, von Prof. K.

suit all light and weather conditions. The disadvantage of small louvres is that they have little resistance to wind pressure. Examples of the use of metal louvres can be seen in the office and production building of Seele in Gersthofen, Germany, completed in 1992 by the architects Kauffmann and Theilig, and the offices of Thompson Advertising Agency in Frankfurt am Main, built between 1992–95 by the architects Schneider + Schumacher (see p. 158/159).

Large, rotating louvres, however, offer effective solar protection and have good wind stability. They consist mostly of extruded aluminium profiles or bent metal sheet; recently large-sized glass louvres have also become popular.
One example of the use of aluminium louvres is

Drehbare Großlamellen bieten einen wirksamen Sonnenschutz und eine gute Windsteifigkeit.
Bürogebäude «TAD», Milano-Lainate, 1989, Ottavio di Blasi Associati.
Large, pivoting louvres give effective solar shading and are wind-resistant.
TAD office building, Milan-Lainate, 1989, Ottavio di Blasi Associati.

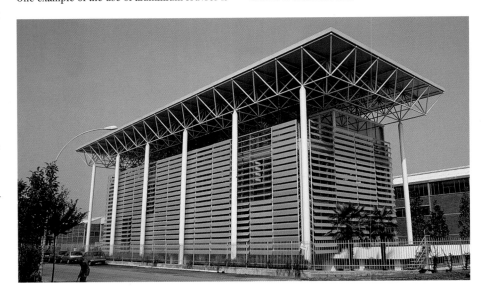

Drehbare Großlamellen aus speziellen Reflexions-
gläsern ermöglichen die freie Sicht nach außen.
Konstruktionsbüro der Firma Gartner & Co,
Gundelfingen, Deutschland, 1992, Prof. K. Acker-
mann und J. Feit als Partner.
Large, pivoting louvres of special reflecting glass give
an unrestricted view outside.
Design offices of Gartner & Co., Gundelfingen,
Germany, 1992, Prof. K. Ackermann with J. Feit as
partner.

Ackermann mit J. Feit als Partner 1992 vollendet, wurden drehbare Glaslamellen aus speziellen Reflexionsgläsern verwendet. Durch die
geeignete Winkeleinstellung bewirken sie ein
streifenfreies Ausblenden der direkten Sonnenstrahlung, ohne die Sicht nach außen zu behindern. Bei diffusen Lichtverhältnissen können
sie nach innen geschwenkt werden, um das
Tageslicht in den Innenraum zu lenken.

Glaslamellen mit Hologrammen sind eine
weitere Möglichkeit für einen transparenten
Sonnenschutz. Sie wurden 1997 beim Umbau
der REWE-Hauptverwaltung in Köln vom
Architekten H. Heidrich in Zusammenarbeit mit
Prof. H. Müller, GLB-Köln, auf dem Glasdach

the TAD office building in Milan-Lainate, built in
1989 by the architects Ottavio di Blasi Associati.

For the construction offices of Gartner & Co.,
Gundelfingen, Germany, completed in 1992 by
Prof. K. Ackermann with J. Feit as partner, rotating
glass louvres made of special reflecting glass were
used. They can be angled to cut out direct radiation completely, but without blocking the view outside. In diffuse light conditions they can be tilted
inwards, to direct daylight into the interior.

Glass louvres with holograms are a further possibility for transparent solar protection. They were
installed on the glass roof of an atrium in 1997 in
the conversion of the headquarters of REWE in

Glaslamellen mit Hologrammen blenden das direkte
Licht aus, lassen aber das diffuse Licht durch.
Umbau der REWE-Hauptverwaltung, Köln, 1997,
H. Heidrich zusammen mit Prof. H. Müller, GLB-Köln.
Glass louvres with holograms screen out the direct
light, but allow diffuse light to enter.
Renovation of REWE headquarters, Cologne, 1996,
H. Heidrich in cooperation with Prof. H. Müller,
GLB-Köln.

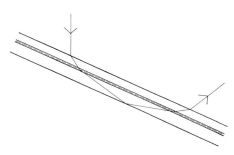

des Atriums installiert. Die Hologramme sind in einem 4 + 10 mm starken Verbundglas eingebettet. Sie lenken die eintreffende direkte Sonnenstrahlung so weit um, daß das Licht auf der Rückseite der unteren Glasscheibe total reflektiert wird. Das diffuse Licht kommt hingegen ungehindert durch. Die Lamellen werden mit einem computergesteuerten hydraulischen System dem Sonnenlauf nachgeführt.

Drehbare Glaslamellen mit integrierten Photovoltaik-Zellen hat der Architekt Theo Hotz beim Betriebsgebäude im Gaswerkareal der Städtischen Werke in Winterthur eingesetzt (1990–96). Die 114 m lange Südostfassade ist mit 14 Reihen übereinander montierter Glaslamellen ausgestattet, die mechanisch dem Sonnenstand nachgeführt werden. Ihre Fläche ist ungefähr zur Hälfte mit PV-Zellen belegt.

Eine ungewöhnliche Lösung zeigt das System mit Rohrgitterrosten beim Flughafen München von Hans-Busso von Busse, 1993. Die Konstruktion besteht aus drei übereinander liegenden Rosten aus weiß beschichteten Aluminiumrohren von 50 mm Durchmesser. Sie sind mit einem Schwenkhebel verbunden, so daß der obere und der untere Rost gegeneinander verstellt werden können, während der mittlere Rost festbleibt. Je nach Stellung wird die direkte Sonnenstrahlung entweder durchgelassen oder in verschiedene Richtungen reflektiert, während das Eintreffen des diffusen Lichts und der Ausblick weitgehend erhalten bleiben. Die Verschiebungen erfolgen

Cologne, by the architect H. Heidrich in co-operation with Prof. H. Müller, GLB-Köln. The holograms are embedded in a 4 + 10 mm layer of laminated glass. They deflect the direct solar radiation to such an extent that it is totally reflected on the rear side of the lower glass pane. Diffuse light, however, can enter unimpeded. The louvres are adjusted to track the sun by means of a computer-controlled hydraulic system.

Rotating glass louvres with integrated photovoltaic cells were used by the architect Theo Hotz in a building on the site of the municipal gasworks in Winterthur (1990–96). The 114 m long south-east façade is fitted with 14 rows of glass louvres arranged one above the other. They can be moved mechanically to track the sun. Half of the surface area of these louvres is fitted with photovoltaic cells.

An unusual system of tubular lattice grids was developed for the new Munich airport by Professor Hans-Busso von Busse in 1993. The device is made up of three levels of grids one on top of the other; each grid is made of 50 mm diameter, white-coated aluminium tubes. The three levels are connected to each other by a swivel lever which enables the upper and lower grids to be adjusted in relation to each other, independent of the middle layer, which remains fixed. Depending on how this lever is set, the direct solar radiation can either be admitted, or reflected in a number of different directions, while the admission of diffuse light remains unaffected, as does to a large extent the view to the

Drehbare Glaslamellen mit integrierten PV-Zellen, die dem Sonnenstand nachgeführt werden. Betriebsgebäude im Gaswerkareal der Städtischen Werke, Winterthur, Schweiz, 1990–96, T. Hotz. *Large, pivoting glass louvres with integrated photovoltaic cells which can track the sun. Building at the town gas works, Winterthur, Switzerland, 1990–96, T. Hotz.*

Verstellbare Rohrgitterroste ermöglichen die Ausblendung der direkten Sonnenstrahlung. Flughafen München, 1976–93, Hans-Busso von Busse. *A system of movable tubular grids enables the control of daylight transmission. Munich airport, 1976–93, Hans-Busso von Busse.*

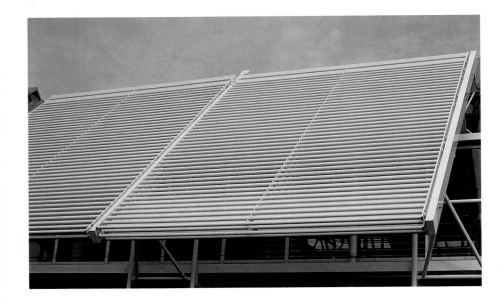

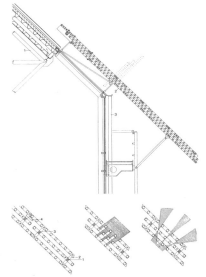

durch Stellmotoren, die von einem Leitrechner zentral gesteuert werden.

Einen Sonnenschutz mittels eines verschiebbaren Fassadenteils weist der Pavillon der Siemens AG für die Expo '92 in Sevilla (1992) auf, welcher zum Büro- und Schulungszentrum umgebaut werden soll. Der von der Siemens-Architekturabteilung mit Gunter Standke u. a. realisierte Pavillon ist mit einem gebäudehohen, in die Dachkonstruktion eingehängten gebogenen Sonnenschutzschild versehen. Der 17 m hohe und 28 m breite Bauteil wird, dem Lauf der Sonne folgend, um den runden Pavillon herumgefahren. Auf dem Schild sind bewegliche horizontale Lamellen mit Prismenplatten von etwa 25 × 250 cm auf Edelstahlrahmen befestigt, welche die direkte Sonnenstrahlung reflektieren, das diffuse Licht hingegen durchlassen. Die Nachführung des Sonnenschutzschildes und die Einstellung der Neigungswinkel der Lamellen

outside. The grids are adjusted by actuators controlled from a central computer control unit.

Solar control using sliding façade elements can be seen in the example of the Siemens Pavilion at Expo '92 in Seville. The building will be converted into a training and office centre. Designed by Gunter Standke and others from the Siemens architecture department, the building is fitted with a full height, curved solar shield suspended from the roof construction. The 17 m high and 28 m wide shield moves around the circular pavilion tracking the position of the sun. Mounted on the shield are movable horizontal louvres made up of 25 × 250 cm prismatic acrylic panels attached to a stainless steel frame; these panels reflect direct daylight while admitting diffuse light. A central electronic control system governs the tracking of the shield around the building, and automatically adjusts the angle of the prismatic louvres. The energy required to

Der gebäudehohe Sonnenschutzschild wird, dem Lauf der Sonne folgend, um den runden Pavillon herumgefahren. Die beweglichen horizontalen Lamellen aus Prismenplatten werden durch Computersteuerung nach dem jeweiligen Sonnenstand ausgerichtet.
Pavillon der Siemens AG an der Expo' 92, Sevilla, Spanien, 1992, Siemens Architekturabteilung mit G.R. Standke u. a.
The full-height curved solar shield moves around the circular pavilion tracking the position of the sun. The movable horizontal louvres are made up of prismatic acrylic panels, and are automatically adjusted in accordance with the position of the sun. Siemens pavilion at Expo' 92, Seville, Spain, 1992, Siemens Architecture Department, G.R. Standke et al.

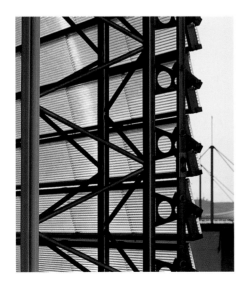

entsprechen dem Sonnenstand und werden durch einen Steuerungsrechner festgelegt. Die notwendige elektrische Energie liefern Solarzellen auf dem Dach. Die kontinuierliche Umstellung der Prismenlamellen verleiht dem Pavillon ein immer wieder neues Erscheinungsbild.

Integrierter Sonnenschutz

Diese Maßnahme ist zur Zeit weniger verbreitet. Während die Reinigung besonders unproblematisch ist, kann die Wartung teuer ausfallen, wenn die Elektromotoren in den Scheibenzwischenraum eingeschlossen sind. Eine Alternative dazu sind Produkte mit magnetischem Schieber außerhalb des Isolierglases.

Die Architekten Benthem Crouwel haben eine solche Maßnahme bei der Verglasung des Gebäudes «Mors» in Opmeer, Niederlande, 1988 eingesetzt. Die Tragkonstruktion besteht aus zehn Portalrahmen mit einer Spannweite von 21.6 m und einer Höhe von 7.6 m, welche im Achsabstand von 5.4 m angeordnet sind. Auf der Nordwestseite befinden sich die Ausstellungs- und Bürobereiche. Die doppelgeschossige Verglasung ist eine Pfosten-Riegel-Konstruktion mit einem quadratischen Raster von 1.8 m Seitenlänge. Die Isolierscheiben sind insgesamt 36 mm stark, mit je einer 6 mm dicken Scheibe außen und innen sowie einem 24 mm breiten Zwischenraum für die magnetisch verstellbaren, 16 mm breiten Lamellen.

Ein integriertes festes Lamellensystem wurde von den Architekten Jerôme Brunet und Eric Saunier für die Fassade des Hauptgebäudes der Internationalen Schule in Saint-Germain-en-Laye,

operate this system comes from solar cells mounted on the roof. The ever-changing position of the shield and the angle of the louvres give the pavilion continuously a new appearance.

Integrated Solar Control Devices

Solar control devices integrated into a glazing unit are less common at present. Costs associated with cleaning are much lower, but maintenance may be more expensive, especially in cases where the electric motors are also incorporated in the cavity between the panes. An alternative is presented by systems which make use of a magnetic control placed outside the insulating glass.

The architects Benthem Crouwel used such an integrated solar device in the glazing of the "Mors" building in Opmeer, Netherlands, built in 1988. The support structure consists of 10 portal frames with a span of 21.6 m, a height of 7.6 m and an axial spacing of 5.4 m. The offices and exhibition areas are located on the northwest side of the building. The double-height glazing is a mullion and transom frame construction based on a 1.8 m square grid. The insulated glazing units have a depth of 36 mm, composed of a 6 mm thick pane on the outside and inside, separated by a 24 mm cavity which incorporates the 16 mm wide, magnetically adjustable louvres.

A system with integrated, non-adjustable louvres was chosen for the façade of the main building of the International School in Saint-Germain-en-Laye, France, built between 1989 and 1992

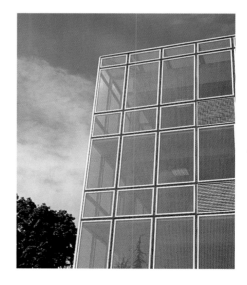

Frankreich (1989–92), verwendet. In den 50 mm breiten Zwischenraum der Isolierverglasung sind perforierte Aluminiumprofile eingebaut, die als Sonnenschutzgitter nur ein gedämpftes Licht durchlassen.

Ein weiteres Beispiel mit fest eingebauten Maßnahmen ist das Geschäftshaus «Haans» in Tilburg, Niederlande, 1992, vom Architekten Jo Coenen, in dem lichtumlenkende Spiegelprofile Oka-Solar® zum Einsatz kommen (siehe Seite 90–91).

Innenliegender Sonnenschutz
Diese Maßnahme ist insofern etwas weniger wirkungsvoll, als die entstehende Wärme im Raum gefangen bleibt, was durch ein Absaugen der warmen Luft oberhalb des Sonnenschutzes zum Teil vermieden werden kann. Ein typischer g-Wert liegt bei etwa 0.30. Dafür sind Reinigung und Wartung des Sonnenschutzes wesentlich einfacher. Handelsübliche Produkte bestehen aus textilen Materialien, wie vertikale Lamellenstoren, Rollos oder Gitterstoffstoren.

Beim 1990 fertiggestellten Gewerbe- und Bürogebäude «Hôtel industriel Jean-Baptiste Berlier» in Paris, vom Architekten Dominique Perrault, erfährt die übliche Monotonie einer geschoßhohen Verglasung durch die innenliegenden, horizontal laufenden Sonnenschutzlamellen eine diskrete, aber sehr elegante Unterteilung. Die Fassade besteht aus 1.8 × 3.3 m großen, vorfabrizierten Glaselementen, die jeweils an der oberen Geschoßdecke abgehängt sind. Bei der Herstellung wurden die Isolierscheiben mit Silikon auf die tragende Rahmenkonstruktion verklebt und mit mechani-

by the architects Jerôme Brunet and Eric Saunier. Sandwiched in the 50 mm space in the double glazing are perforated aluminium profiles arranged in a grid pattern; they only admit subdued light.

A further example of fixed integrated devices is the "Haans" building in Tilburg, The Netherlands, built in 1992 by the architect Jo Coenen. Here he makes use of Oka-Solar® light-deflecting mirror profiles (see page p. 90–91).

Interior Solar Control Devices
This type of solar control is less effective in so far as the heat produced by the solar reradiation remains in the room; however, this can to some extent be counteracted by drawing off the warm air above these devices. A typical g-value is about 0.30. Cleaning and maintenance of interior solar control devices are considerably simpler than with the other two types mentioned above. Products generally available on the market are made of textile materials in the form of vertical blinds, roller blinds or fabric screens.

An elegant example of the use of interior solar control is found in the Hôtel industriel Jean-Baptiste Berlier, a building for small industrial activities and offices in Paris built 1986–90 by the architect Dominique Perrault; the usual monotony associated with an all-glass façade is broken up by discretely placing horizontal louvres on the inside.
The façade consists of 1.8 × 3.3 m large prefabricated glass units each suspended from the floor above. During manufacture the insulating glass

Innenliegenden Sonnenschutz können horizontal laufende Lamellen, offene Elektrokanäle und Lüftungsrohre bieten.
«Hôtel industriel Jean-Baptiste Berlier», Paris, 1986–90, Dominique Perrault.
Interior solar shading can be achieved with horizontal louvres, cable tray and air conditioning ducts. Hôtel industriel Jean-Baptiste Berlier, Paris, 1986–90, Dominique Perrault.

schen Sicherheitsklammern an den Ecken versehen. Der Glasaufbau weist eine 6 mm dicke Außen-, eine 10 mm dicke Innenscheibe und einen Zwischenraum von 12 mm mit einer Argonfüllung auf, was einen k-Wert von 1.76, einen g-Wert von 0.52 und einen τ-Wert von 0.72 ergibt. Der innenliegende Sonnenschutz besteht aus mehreren horizontallaufenden Lamellen aus Aluminium, die wie Tablare aus Streckmetall aussehen, sowie aus dem offenen Elektrokanal und den Lüftungsrohren.

Die «Bibliothèque Nationale de France» in Paris, ebenfalls von Dominique Perrault (1989–95), ist von vier L-förmigen, 20geschossigen Glastürmen gekennzeichnet, die an den Ecken eines mehrgeschossigen, teilweise im Boden versenkten Sockels mit Innenhof plaziert sind. Im unteren Bereich der Türme befinden sich sieben Bürogeschosse, darüber elf Geschosse für Bücherlager sowie zwei für die technische Zentrale. Die ungewöhnliche Konstruktion der Glasfassade wird von den Planern als «pressurisé» bezeichnet. Die geschoßhohen Fassadenelemente haben einen breiten Scheibenzwischenraum von 90 mm, der an ein Druckluftsystem angeschlossen ist. Die Druckluft wird über Ventile im unteren Rahmenprofil zugeführt und oben bei den vertikalen Profilen abgeführt. Je nach Bedarf ist die filtrierte Luft vorgewärmt oder -gekühlt, um die Temperaturunterschiede zwischen außen und innen auszugleichen. Damit wird Kondensat raumseitig der Innenverglasung verhindert, das sich in den Lagergeschossen infolge der Feuchtigkeit, die für die Konservierung von Büchern notwendig ist, bilden würde. Die 1.8 × 3.6 m großen Fassadenelemente bestehen aus zwei getrennten Rahmen-

units were fixed with silicon to their support frames and mechanical safety clamps were attached to the corners. The insulating glass unit itself consists of a 6 mm thick outer sheet, a 10 mm thick inner sheet and a 12 mm cavity filled with argon gas; this combination produces a U-value of 1.76, a g-value of 0.52 and a τ-value of 0.72. The interior solar control device is mainly a horizontal, aluminium louvre made of expanded mesh grid; cable trays and air ventilation ducts are also used as solar control devices.

The Bibliothèque Nationale de France in Paris, also by Dominique Perrault (1989–95) has four distinctive L-shaped, 20-storey-high glass towers, positioned at the corners of a multi-storey base, partly sunk into the ground, with inner courtyard. In the lower part of the towers are seven office floors, and above these eleven storeys for book storage and two for building services. The unusual construction of the glass façade is described by the planners as "pressurisé". The storey-height façade units have a wide cavity of 90 mm, which is connected to a pressurised air system. The pressurised air is fed through valves in the lower frame profile and led out at the top near the vertical profiles. Depending on requirements the filtered air can be pre-heated, or cooled, to balance the temperature difference between outside and inside. This prevents condensation forming on the room side of the inner pane which would otherwise be present in the storage floors, due to the humidity levels necessary for conserving the books. The 1.8 × 3.6 m façade elements consist of two separate frame profiles fitted together as one unit and suspended from the head of the floor slabs. The ex-

Die vier L-förmigen Glastürme sind an den Ecken eines teilweise im Boden versenkten Sockels mit Innenhof aufgestellt.
«Bibliothèque Nationale de France», Paris, 1989–95, Dominique Perrault.
The four L-shaped glass towers are placed at the corners of a base with central courtyard. The courtyard is partly recessed into the ground.
Bibliothèque Nationale de France, Paris, 1989–95, Dominique Perrault.

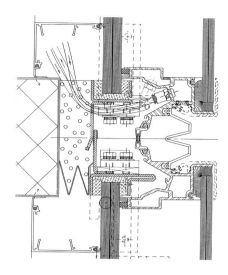

Im unteren Bereich der Türme befinden sich sieben Bürogeschosse, darüber elf Geschosse für Bücherlager und zwei für die technische Zentrale.
Die Konstruktion der Fassade wird von den Planern als «pressurisé» bezeichnet, weil der Zwischenraum an ein Druckluftsystem angeschlossen ist.
«Bibliothèque Nationale de France», Paris, 1989–95, Dominique Perrault.

In the lower part of the towers are seven office floors, with eleven floors above for book storage and two for technical services.
The façade construction is described by the designers as "pressurisé", because the cavity is connected to a pressurised air system.
Bibliothèque Nationale de France, Paris, 1989–95, Dominique Perrault.

profilen, die als Einheit zusammenmontiert und von den Deckenstirnen abgehängt sind. Die Außenverglasung ist ein Verbundglas, je nach Höhe aus zwei 6 mm oder 8 mm starken Scheiben, das mit Silikon an den außenliegenden Hauptrahmen aus Aluminiumprofilen geklebt ist. Innen liegt eine Brandschutzverglasung F60 Sekuriflam® aus 2 × 10 mm starken Scheiben. Sie ist in einer eigenständigen Rahmenkonstruktion aus Edelstahl montiert und am Hauptrahmen befestigt. Es wurden extra-weiße Scheiben verwendet. Als Schutz gegen die Sonnenstrahlung sind ca. 90 cm hinter der Glasfassade drehbare Holzpaneele angeordnet.

terior glazing is laminated glass, either of two 6 mm or 8 mm thick panes, depending on the height; these panes are bonded to the exterior frames of aluminium profiles with silicon. The inner pane is of 2 × 10 mm F60 Sekuriflam® fire-resistant glass. This is fitted in a separate frame construction of stainless steel and attached to the main frame. Extra-white glass was used. As protection against solar radiation, pivoting wooden panels are fitted about 90 cm behind the glass façade.
Originally Perrault wanted to use phototropic or electrochromic glass. But for reasons of time and cost this idea was not pursued.

Ursprünglich wollte Perrault phototrope oder elektrochrome Scheiben für die Verglasung verwenden. Aus zeitlichen und ökonomischen Gründen konnte diese Idee aber nicht weiterverfolgt werden.

Die realisierte Glaskonstruktion erinnert an den «fluidized glazing»-Prototyp von F. McKee, der 1994 anläßlich des internationalen Workshops «Architectural Visions for Europe» in Düsseldorf vorgestellt wurde. Diesem Fassadensystem liegt die Idee zugrunde, ein Medium, z. B. Wasser, mit einem Vor- und Rücklaufsystem zwischen zwei Glasscheiben fließen zu lassen. Diese Flüssigkeit soll durch die Veränderung der Farbe einen variablen Sonnenschutz bilden und gleichzeitig als Wärme- oder Kälteträger dienen. Im Winter könnte die Konstruktion als transparenter Heizkörper funktionieren, ohne die Transmission der Sonnenstrahlung zu vermindern, im Sommer würde die Flüssigkeit für Kühlung und Sonnenschutz sorgen.

Ein letztes Beispiel für innenliegenden Sonnenschutz ist die «Bolla» (Blase) auf dem Dach des Fiat-Werks «Lingotto» in Turin, von Renzo Piano Building Workshop 1996 realisiert. Die Blase ist ein gewölbter, verglaster Raum, der als Konferenzsaal für besondere Anlässe dienen soll. Im Grundriß mißt der Durchmesser 13 m, die Scheitelhöhe beträgt 7 m. Die innenliegende Tragkonstruktion ist eine filigrane Gitterschale aus Stahlrohren, die mit dünnen Zugstangen aus Edelstahl diagonal ausgesteift ist. Die Meri-

The glass construction which was built is reminiscent of the "fluidized glazing" prototype by F. McKee which was presented in 1994 at the international workshop on "Architectural Visions for Europe" in Düsseldorf.
This façade system is based on the idea of circulating a fluid, e. g. water, between two panes. This liquid changes colour and thus provides variable solar protection as well as serving as a carrier of cold or heat.
During winter it would act as a transparent heat radiator without reducing the transmission of solar radiation, in summer the liquid would act as a cooler wall and protect from the solar radiation.

A final example for interior solar protection is the "Bolla" (bubble) on the roof of the Fiat "Lingotto" factory in Turin, built by the Renzo Piano Building Workshop in 1996. The bubble is a vaulted, glazed room which can be used as a conference hall for special occasions.
In plan it has a diameter of 13 m and is 7 m high at the rise. The interior frame is a filigree grid structure of tubular steel braced diagonally with thin stainless steel rods. The meridians have a diameter of 38 mm, the parallels of 60 mm. The special feature of the glass skin is that it consists of insulating glass curved in two planes. The largest panes are 1.4 m wide and 0.9 m high, the smallest measure 0.5 × 0.9 m. On the outside 6 mm toughened glass was used printed with a black frit along the edges

Die transparente Schale besteht aus einer filigranen Gitterschale mit einer außenliegenden Verglasung aus doppelt gekrümmten Isoliergläsern.
«Bolla» (Blase) beim Fiat-Werk «Lingotto», Turin, 1996, Renzo Piano Building Workshop.
The transparent shell consists of a filigree grid structure with an outer layer of glazing made of insulating glass curved in two planes.
The "Bolla" (bubble) at the Fiat Lingotto factory, Turin, 1996, Renzo Piano Building Workshop.

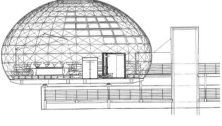

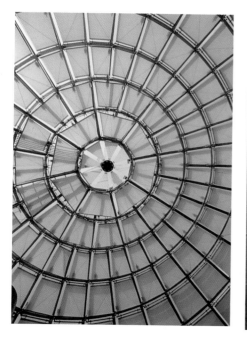

Der vollklimatisierte Raum dient als Konferenzsaal für besondere Anlässe.
Die innenliegenden Gitterstoffstoren sorgen für den Sonnen- und Blendschutz.
«Bolla» (Blase) beim Fiat-Werk «Lingotto», Turin, 1996, Renzo Piano Building Workshop.
The fully air-conditioned space is used as a conference hall for special occasions.
Interior screens give solar control and glare protection.
The "Bolla" (bubble) at the Fiat Lingotto factory, Turin, 1996, Renzo Piano Building Workshop.

diane haben einen Durchmesser von 38 mm, die Parallelen einen Durchmesser von 60 mm. Das Besondere an der außenliegenden Verglasung sind die doppelt gekrümmten Isoliergläser. Die größten Scheiben sind 1.4 m breit und 0.9 m hoch, die kleinsten messen 0.5 × 0.9 m. Außen wurden 6 mm starke ESG-Scheiben verwendet, die mit schwarzen emailbeschichteten Randstreifen für die Verklebung der Abstandhalter versehen sind. Innen wurden Verbundgläser aus zwei 4 mm starken Scheiben mit einer low-E-Beschichtung eingesetzt. Der Zwischenraum von 10 mm ist mit Luft gefüllt. Dieser Aufbau ergibt einen k-Wert von $2 \ W/m^2K$, einen g-Wert von 0.28 und einen τ-Wert von 0.58. Um der Verglasung Transparenz und Leichtigkeit zu verleihen, wurden die Scheiben mit einem aufgeklebten Winkelprofil versehen und mit einem Gußteil aus Aluminium an der Stahlkonstruktion befestigt. Um den hohen Anforderungen an den Komfort zu genügen, ist die «Bolla» vollklimatisiert. Warm- oder Kaltluft werden am Fuß der Glasschale in den Raum eingeblasen und gelangen im Scheitel durch eine runde Öffnung, die mit einem Elektroantrieb bedient wird, ins Freie. Für den Sonnen- und Blendschutz sind innenliegende, helle Gitterstoffstoren mit Elektroantrieb eingebaut. Die Steuerung erfolgt automatisch durch einen Leitrechner, der neben der Helligkeit auch den Sonnenstand erfaßt, so daß der Konferenztisch immer im Schatten bleibt. Die Stoffstoren sind an

for adhesive fixing of the spacers. Inside laminated glass was used, composed of two 4 mm panes with a low-E coating. The 10 mm cavity is filled with air. This construction produces a U-value of $2 \ W/m^2K$, a g-factor of 0.28 and a τ-value of 0.58. To give an appearance of transparence and lightness to the glazing, an angle profile was bonded to the sheets and bolted with a cast aluminium fitting on the steel structure. To meet the high comfort requirements the bubble is fully air-conditioned. Warm or cold air is blown in at the foot of the glass bowl and escapes through a circular opening at the apex. This opening is electrically operated. For solar control and protection from glare electrically operated light-coloured screens have been added on the inside. These are controlled by a central computer which monitors brightness and the position of the sun and makes the necessary adjustments to ensure the conference table is always in the shade. The screens are affixed to 40 cm round steel bars which are bolted at the intersections of meridians and parallels. These "spiedini" (spits) are also used as a fixing point for the angled 6 mm glass sheets which reduce the noise caused by the hard surface of the glass and the double-curved bubble shape.

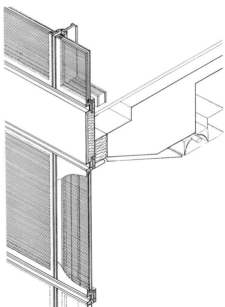

40 cm langen Rundstäben aus Edelstahl befestigt, die an den Knotenpunkten von Meridianen und Parallelen angeordnet sind. Diese sogenannten «Spiedini» (Spieße) dienen auch zur Befestigung von schräggestellten, 6 mm starken Glasscheiben, welche die Schallreflexion wegen der harten Glasoberfläche und der doppelt gekrümmten Schalenform brechen.

Mehrschalige Fassaden
Die Anordnung des Sonnenschutzes hinter einer Deckscheibe bietet die Möglichkeit, Unterhaltskosten, Reinigungs- und Wartungsarbeiten zu reduzieren.

Beim Bürokomplex «Les Collines» in Paris-La Défense, 1990 fertiggestellt, gelang dem Architekten Jean-Pierre Buffi die Realisierung einer Fassade mit geschoßhohen Verglasungen trotz der baurechtlichen Einschränkung durch einen zulässigen g-Wert von maximal 0.17. Dafür wurde ein starrer, gewebeartiger Sonnenschutz aus Mikrolamellen gewählt, die aus nur 1.27 mm breiten weißbeschichteten Bronzeprofilen bestehen, welche durch ein Drahtgeflecht in der Neigung von 17° gehalten werden. Sie bieten Sonnenschutz, ohne den Ausblick zu behindern. Die Pfosten-Riegel-Fassade weist einen Achsabstand von 1.35 m und eine gesamte Geschoßhöhe von 3.15 m auf, die in drei 90 cm hohe Glaselemente und ein 45 cm hohes Paneel aus Aluminium bei der Deckenstirn unterteilt ist. Die Mikrolamellen sind in die Brüstungs- und die

Multiple-Skin Façades
The possibility of incorporating solar control devices behind a cover pane reduces cleaning and maintenance costs.

For the "Les Collines" office complex in Paris-La Défense, built in 1990 by Jean-Pierre Buffi, the architect managed to realise his aim of a fully glazed façade despite building regulations stating a maximum permissible g-value of 0.17. To fit in with these strict requirements, a stiff, textile-like layer of 1.27 mm wide, white-coated bronze profile microlouvres, held at an angle of 17° to a wire mesh support, were placed in front of the façade to give protection from the sun, but without obstructing the view outside. The mullion and transom façade has an axial spacing of 1.35 m and a total floor height of 3.15 m, divided into three 90 cm high glass units and a 45 cm high aluminium panel at the slab level. The microlouvres are integrated into the parapet and into the ceiling glass units. As these louvres give off heat to the surrounding air, they are placed between the interior insulating glass unit (6 mm outer pane, 12 mm cavity, 4 mm inner pane) and the exterior, black-tinted glass sheet (SGG Cool-Lite®AS 120). To compensate for the change in air pressure resulting from reradiation in the additional cavity, four air vents were provided.

A similar approach towards finding a solution was used by Jean Nouvel with Pierre Soria and

Ein starrer, gewebeartiger Sonnenschutz aus Mikrolamellen wird vor der Witterung geschützt, indem er zwischen der innenliegenden Isolierverglasung und einer außenliegenden schwarzen Einfachverglasung eingebaut wird.
Bürokomplex «Les Collines», Paris-La Défense, 1986–1990, Jean-Pierre Buffi.

Stiff, textile-like sunshading microlouvres are protected from the weather by placing them between the interior insulating glass and an exterior black-tinted single glass pane.
Les Collines office complex, La Défense, Paris, 1986–1990, Jean-Pierre Buffi.

Deckenelemente integriert. Da sie eine hohe Aufheizung der Luft hervorrufen, sind sie zwischen die innenliegende Isolierverglasung (äußere Scheibe 6 mm, Zwischenraum 12 mm und innere Schreibe 4 mm) und eine außenliegende, schwarz eingefärbte Glasscheibe (SGG Cool-Lite® AS 120) eingebaut. Zum Ausgleich des wegen der Aufwärmung im Scheibenzwischenraum entstehenden Drucks wurden vier Ventile eingebaut.

Einen ähnlichen Lösungsansatz hat Jean Nouvel mit Pierre Soria und Gilbert Lézénès beim «Institut du Monde Arabe» in Paris (1981–87) verfolgt: Für die Südfassade des Kulturinstituts wurde ein regulierbarer Sonnenschutz entwickelt, der sich an die traditionellen, mit Ornamenten versehenen arabischen Fenstergitter (Maschabijja) anlehnt. In die 62.4 × 26 m große Fassade wurden 27000 Blendmechanismen aus Aluminium eingebaut, die sich elektropneumatisch, dem Einfall des Sonnenlichts entsprechend, öffnen oder schließen lassen und damit die Tageslichttransmission von 0.10 bis 0.30 regulieren. Sie sind mit photoelektrischen Zellen versehen,

Gilbert Lézénès for the "Institut du Monde Arabe" in Paris (1981–87). For the south façade of this cultural institute a special, adjustable solar control device was developed, along the lines of the ornate window gratings (Maschabijja) traditionally found in the Arab world. Built into the 62.4 × 26 m façade are 27,000 aluminium shutter elements, which open and close by means of an electro-pneumatic mechanism, regulating daylight transmission between 0.10 and 0.30. They are fitted with photoelectric cells and controlled by computer. In order to protect the sensitive mechanisms the 240 square glazed areas, 1.80 × 1.80 m in size, and the 0.40 m wide framing friezes are built up according to the principle of the "cavity façade", i. e. on the outside a fixed pane of insulating glass, and on the inside an opening sheet of toughened glass, with the shutter mechanism between the two.
Despite high construction costs and certain problems with the functional efficiency of the mechanism, this façade design by Jean Nouvel represents a modern, technological interpreta-

Für die große Südfassade wurde ein regulierbarer Sonnenschutz aus 27 000 Blendmechanismen entwickelt. Die Blenden öffnen und schließen sich elektropneumatisch dem Einfall des Sonnenlichts entsprechend. Sie sind zwischen der außenliegenden Isolierverglasung und einer innenliegenden Einfachverglasung eingebaut.
«Institut du Monde Arabe», Paris, 1981–87, Jean Nouvel, Pierre Soria und Gilbert Lézénès.
For the south façade an adjustable solar control device consisting of 27,000 shutter mechanisms was developed. The shutters open and close by means of an electro-pneumatic mechanism which regulates daylight transmission. The shutters are placed between the exterior insulating glass and an interior single glass pane.
Institut du Monde Arabe, Paris, 1981–87, Jean Nouvel, Pierre Soria and Gilbert Lézénès.

und die Steuerung erfolgt durch einen Computer. Um die empfindlichen Mechanismen zu schützen, sind die 240 quadratischen, 1.80×1.80 m großen Felder und die 0.40 m breiten umrahmenden Friese nach dem Prinzip eines Kastenfensters aufgebaut: außen ein festeingebautes Isolierglas, innen ein Flügel zum Öffnen aus ESG-Scheiben und dazwischen die Blendmechanismen.

Trotz hohen Baukosten und gewissen Problemen mit der Funktionstüchtigkeit der Mechanismen ist es die ästhetische Anlehnung an die arabische Kultur und ihre Umsetzung in modernste Technologie, die diese Fassadenlösung Nouvels auszeichnet.

Beide oben aufgeführten Beispiele zeigen die Unterbringung der Sonnenschutzmaßnahmen in einem schmalen Zwischenraum, der vor oder hinter der eigentlich wärmeschützenden Isolierscheibe liegt, aber keine mechanisch belüftete Raumschicht bildet.

Abluftfassaden

Eine Abluftfassade ist durch einen breiten Luftzwischenraum gekennzeichnet, welcher durch die Anordnung einer einfachen Scheibe raumseitig einer mit innenliegendem Sonnenschutz versehenen Fassade entsteht. Ein Teil der Raumabluft wird durch Unterdruck in diesen Zwischenraum eingesaugt, wo er den größten Teil der im Sonnenschutz entstehenden Wärme aufnimmt und anschließend durch eine mechanische Entlüftung abgeführt wird. Die Luftführung erfolgt meistens geschoßweise, entweder steigend oder fallend. Aus der Abluft können über einen Wärmetauscher Wärmerückgewinne erzielt werden. Für den Sonnen-

tion of a traditional Arab device, and sets up an aesthetic link with Arab culture.

Both examples detailed above show how solar control devices can be incorporated in a narrow cavity, without mechanical ventilation, either in front of or behind the actual thermally insulating glass skin.

Mechanically Ventilated Cavity Façades

Characteristic of this kind of façade is an air cavity, which is created by adding a single glass sheet behind a façade with interior solar control device. Lower pressure in the cavity draws part of the exhaust air from the room into this space; here the air warms up, taking most of the heat from the solar control devices, and is then drawn off by means of mechanical ventilation. The air is extracted on each floor separately, either flowing upwards or downwards in the cavity. A heat exchanger may be used to reclaim energy from the exhaust air stream. The types of solar control devices which can be used in the cavity are textile blinds or vertical louvre blinds. For reasons of optimum air flow, horizontal blinds are not suitable. The blinds, the cavity and the internal glass surfaces can be cleaned by opening up the internal single sheets of glass. The g-value is approximately 0.15, which is considerably lower than if the additional, internal sheet had not been used. The advantages of ventilated cavity façades lie in the minimising of the temperature differences between the air in the room and the surface of the glass. This improves the thermal comfort conditions in the

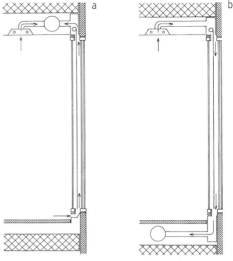

Schematische Darstellung von Abluftfassaden mit steigender (a) bzw. fallender Luftführung (b).
Diagram of a mechanically ventilated cavity façade, either with upward (a) or downward air flow (b).

Abluftfenster mit steigender Luftführung. Museum für Kunsthandwerk, Frankfurt a. M., 1979–84, Richard Meier.
Mechanically ventilated cavity façade with upward air flow.
Museum of Arts and Crafts, Frankfurt a. M., 1979–84, Richard Meier.

schutz kommen Gitterstoffstoren oder Vertikallamellen in Frage, horizontale Lamellen hingegen sind strömungstechnisch ungünstig. Die Reinigung von Zwischenraum, angrenzender Glasoberfläche und Sonnenschutzmaßnahmen erfolgt durch das Öffnen der innenliegenden Glasflügel. Der g-Wert beträgt etwa 0.15, liegt also deutlich unter einer Ausführung ohne zusätzliche Scheibe. Die Vorteile einer Abluftfassade liegen in der Minimierung der Temperaturunterschiede zwischen Raumluft und Fensteroberfläche, was zu einem erhöhten Komfort in Fensternähe führt, und in der Senkung des Energieverbrauchs für Heizung und Kühlung.

Das Museum für Kunsthandwerk in Frankfurt am Main, 1979–84 von Richard Meier erbaut, ist mit einer Abluftfassade ausgestattet. Die Raumluft wird durch einen Schlitz unter dem innenliegenden Fensterrahmen abgesaugt, an der inneren Fläche der äußeren Isolierverglasung durch die besondere Ausbildung der Quersprossen nach oben geleitet und dort abgeführt.

Ein weiteres Beispiel ist der Hauptsitz der Lloyd's Versicherungsgesellschaft in London, 1978–86, von Richard Rogers Partnership. Hier ist die Fassade der Bürogeschosse mit Abluftfenstern versehen. Die erwärmte Raumluft wird über die Beleuchtungskörper angesaugt, womit sie deren Wärme aufnimmt, und mit einem speziell geformten Anschlußstück beim oberen Fensterriegel in den schmalen Zwischenraum der geschoßhohen Abluftfenster weitergeleitet. Dort erwärmt sich die Abluft durch die sekundäre Wärmeabgabe zusätzlich und wird schließlich im untersten Fensterbereich angesaugt und zur Klimaanlage abgeführt. Die Luftführung über die Leuchten und dann von

office space nearer to the window and reduces energy costs for heating and cooling.

The Museum of Arts and Crafts in Frankfurt am Main, built 1979–84 by Richard Meier, has a mechanically ventilated cavity façade. The air in the room is drawn out through a slit below the inner frame of the window and then directed upwards along the inside of the outer window to be extracted at the top. This air flow is facilitated by the special design of the transverse glazing bars.

A further example is the headquarters of the Lloyd's Insurance Company in London, built 1978–86 by the Richard Rogers Partnership. The façade of the office levels has mechanically ventilated windows. The warm air in the room is extracted above the lighting units, so that the air also takes up their additional heat. Then this air is fed via specially shaped ducts at the level of the topmost transoms into the narrow cavity of the storey-height ventilated windows. Here the air is warmed further by taking up heat from reradiation of the glass, it is then taken out at the bottom of the window and drawn forward to the air conditioning system of the building. The aim in extracting the air via the lighting and then down from the top to the bottom of the cavity, is to utilise the internal heating loads as much as possible in achieving higher temperatures on the surface of the window during colder periods; this improves the thermal comfort in the office space near the windows. The façade itself is constructed of 1.80 × 3.35 m prefabricated units. On the outside is an insulating glass unit, on the inside is a side-hinged single glazed casement and

Abluftfenster mit fallender Luftführung. Die Abluft wird mit einem speziell geformten Anschlußstück beim oberen Fensterriegel eingespeist und unten abgeführt.
Hauptsitz der Lloyd's Versicherungsgesellschaft, London, 1978–86, Richard Rogers Partnership.
Mechanically ventilated cavity façade with downward air flow. The exhaust air is fed via a specially shaped duct at the level of the topmost transom into the cavity and extracted at the bottom.
Headquarters of the Lloyd's Insurance Company, London, 1978–86, Richard Rogers Partnership.

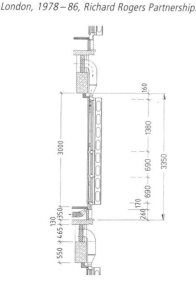

oben nach unten in den Fassadenzwischenraum soll die Nutzung eines Großteils der internen Wärmelasten ermöglichen, um in kälteren Jahreszeiten höhere Temperaturen an der Fensteroberfläche und damit einen erhöhten Komfort in Fensternähe zu erzielen. Die Fassade selbst wurde aus 1.80×3.35 m großen, vorfabrizierten Elementen konstruiert. Sie sind mit einem Isolierglas außen, einem einfach verglasten Drehflügel innen und einem 40 mm breiten Luftspalt dazwischen aufgebaut. Die Isolierverglasung besteht aus einem 6 mm starken SGG Gußglas Lloyd's®, einem 12 mm breiten Scheibenzwischenraum und einer 6 mm low-E-beschichteten Scheibe. Der Drehflügel besteht aus einem 6 mm starken außenliegenden SGG Gußglas Lloyd's®. Im Sichtbereich ist eine transparente Verglasung mit einem Isolierglas außen (6 mm SGG Cool-Lite® SC20, 12 mm Scheibenzwischenraum, 6 mm SGG Planilux®) und einer 6 mm starken SGG Planilux®-Scheibe innen eingesetzt, die jeweils alternierend fest oder beweglich als Kippflügel ausgeführt ist.

Die geplante Abluftfassade für das neue «Parliamentary Building» in Westminster, London, 1989 begonnen, wird von Michael Hopkins und Partnern entwickelt und nutzt die Forschungsergebnisse des «Solar House»-Programms der

between the two a 40 mm air cavity. The insulating glass comprises a 6 mm layer of SGG Lloyd's® design rolled glass outside, a 12 mm wide intermediate cavity and a 6 mm low-E coated sheet of SGG Cool-Lite® SC20 inside. The side-hinged casement is a 6 mm pane of SGG Lloyd's® rolled glass. At seated eye level the glazing is transparent, with an external layer of insulating glass (6 mm SGG Cool-Lite® SC20, 12 mm cavity, 6 mm SGG Planilux®) and internally a 6 mm thick sheet of SGG Planilux®; this band is designed alternately as fixed glazings or bottom hung windows.

The design for a ventilated cavity façade for the new Parliamentary Building in Westminster, London, was begun in 1989 by Michael Hopkins and Partners and utilizes results of research carried out in the "Solar House Programme" of the European Union.
The aim of the project was to investigate the thermal behaviour and energy requirements of a mechanically ventilated cavity façade, using computer simulations and prototypes, in order to test the effects for low-energy buildings.
In the project, the street façade is composed of loadbearing sandstone piers and glazed bay windows. As these windows are not intended to be opened, for reasons of safety and acoustic insu-

Städtebaulicher Kontext des neuen Gebäudes und ein detailliertes Studienmodell der Abluftfassade. «New Parliamentary Building», Westminster, London, 1989 – 2001, Michael Hopkins und Partner.
City context of the new building and detailed study model of the cavity façade.
New Parliamentary Building, Westminster, London, 1989 – 2001, Michael Hopkins and Partners.

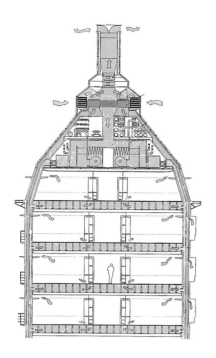

Schnitt mit Führung der Frisch- und der Abluft im Gebäude (oben); detaillierter Schnitt durch den verglasten Erker (unten links); Luftführung und Lichtumlenkung bei einem typischen Büroraum (unten rechts). «New Parliamentary Building», Westminster, London, 1989–2001, Michael Hopkins und Partner.
Section through building showing fresh air and exhaust air path (top); detailed section through glazed bay window (bottom left); system of air flow and light redirection in a typical office unit (bottom right).
New Parliamentary Building, Westminster, London, 1989–2001, Michael Hopkins and Partners.

Europäischen Union. Dabei sollen Erkenntnisse über das thermische Verhalten und den Energiebedarf einer Abluftfassade anhand von Computersimulationen und Prototypen gewonnen werden, um die Ergebnisse für energiesparende Gebäude umzusetzen.

Im Projekt sind die zur Straßenseite orientierten Fassaden durch Pilaster aus Sandstein und verglaste Erker charakterisiert. Da Fenster zum Öffnen aus Schallschutz- und Sicherheitsgründen nicht möglich sind, wurde eine Abluftfassade vorgeschlagen. Ihre Konstruktion besteht aus einem außenliegenden Isolierglas – außen ein weißes Verbundglas, eine Argonfüllung im Zwischenraum, innen ein Floatglas mit einer Low-E-Beschichtung – und innenliegend einem Flügel zum Öffnen aus einer vorgespannten Glasscheibe. Für den Sonnenschutz sind in den 75 mm breiten Luftzwischenraum integrierte, verstellbare Lamellen sowie ein Lichtumlenkschwert oberhalb des Erkers vorgesehen, das den nahen Fensterbereich verschattet und das direkt einfallende Tageslicht in die Raumtiefe umlenkt.

Die in der Klimaanlage aufbereitete Luft fließt von Bodenauslässen im hinteren Teil des Raumes ein und wird über Öffnungen unterhalb der Erkerverglasung sowie bei der Leuchte oberhalb des Lichtumlenkschwerts abgesaugt. Damit wird sowohl eine energiesparende Durchlüftung des Raums als auch die Beseitigung der Abwärme der Leuchte erreicht. Die Abluft wird seitlich im oberen Fensterbereich abgesaugt und entlang der Pilaster bis ins Dachgeschoß abgeführt, wo Anlagen für die Wärmerückgewinnung installiert sind.

lation, a ventilated cavity façade was proposed. The window construction is composed of an external insulating unit (an external clear laminated glass, an argon gas filling in the cavity, and an internal float glass with a low-E coating), and internally an opening sheet of toughened glass.

Solar shading is taken care of by adjustable louvre blinds integrated in the 75 mm wide cavity between the outer and inner skins, and by light shelves positioned above the bays; these shelves shade the area immediately next to the window and they are designed to reflect daylight into the back of the room.

The air from the air handling plant is supplied as displacement ventilation through air vents in the floor at the back of the room and drawn off again through openings situated at the bottom of the bay windows and at the level of the lighting above the light shelf. This ensures sufficient cross ventilation in the room and it reduces the warming up caused by the lighting. In the upper window area the exhaust air is drawn off through the exhaust ducts on either side of the windows and drawn along the piers up to the roof where heat exchangers reclaim the energy from the exhaust air stream.

The combined effects of the various measures have been tested on a two-floor prototype set up at the Conphoebus test centre building near Catania in Italy in summer and winter 1994. The target is to reduce energy consumption from the general level of $270–360$ kWh/m²a to $90–110$ kWh/m²a.

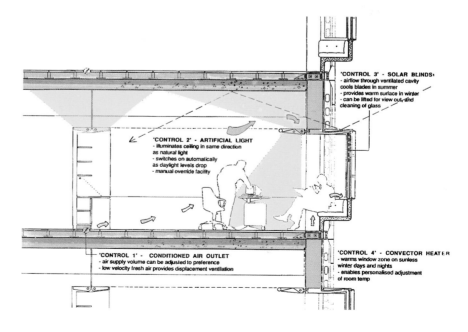

Das Zusammenwirken der verschiedenen Maßnahmen wurde anhand eines zweigeschossigen
Prototyps, erstellt im Forschungszentrum Conphoebus in der Nähe von Catania, Italien, im
Sommer und Winter 1994 überprüft. Ziel ist eine
Senkung des Energieverbrauchs von üblichen
270 – 360 kWh/m^{2}a auf 90 – 110 kWh/m^{2}a.

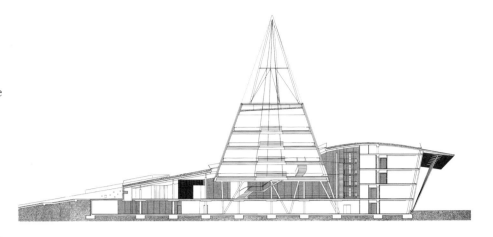

Ein aktuelles Beispiel für die Anwendung einer
geschoßhohen Abluftfassade ist die neue Bibliothek der Technischen Hochschule in Delft, welche von den Architekten Mecanoo 1992 – 98 erstellt wurde.
Um eine architektonische Konfrontation mit dem
benachbarten berühmten Hörsaalgebäude von
Van der Broek und Bakema (1959 – 66) zu vermeiden, haben die Architekten das Gebäude
nach Westen hin im Boden versenkt. Das leicht
ansteigende Dach ist als grasbewachsene «Landschaft» gestaltet. Die Rasenfläche wird durch
den eingeschnittenen Zentraleingang und einen
aus der Mitte herausragenden, kegelförmigen
Baukörper durchbrochen. Nach Süden, Osten
und Norden ist das Gebäude mit einer schräg
nach außen geneigten Abluftfassade in einer Pfosten-Riegel-Konstruktion abgeschlossen. Die
außenliegende Verglasung besteht aus Isolierglas
mit einem k-Wert von 1.5 W/m^{2}K, das außen aus
einer 8 mm starken Glasscheibe und innen aus
einer 6 mm starken Glasscheibe mit Low-E-Beschichtung aufgebaut ist, mit einem Zwischenraum von 15 mm. Das Isolierglas ist am
oberen und unteren Rand durch Deckleisten,
seitlich durch eine Silikon-Verklebung an der
Unterkonstruktion aus Aluminiumprofilen befe-

A current example of the use of a storey-high
ventilated façade is the new library at the University of Technology of Delft, which was built by
the architects Mecanoo in 1992 – 98.
In order to avoid an architectural confrontation
with the neighbouring building, the famous Lec-
ture Hall built by Van der Broek and Bakema
(1959 – 66), the architects lowered the library
into the ground towards the west. The gently
sloping roof is designed as a "landscape"
planted with grass. The lawn is dissected by the
central entrance and a cone-shaped structure
rising out of the middle. To the south, east and
north the building is finished with a ventilated
façade on a mullion and transom frame tilted
outwards. The external glazing is of insulated
glass with a U-value of 1.5 W/m^{2}K, made up of an
8 mm outer sheet and a 6 mm inner sheet with
low-E coating. The cavity is 15 mm.
The insulating glass is fixed to the frame of aluminium profiles by means of pressure caps at

Nach Westen ist das Gebäude im Boden versenkt
und das leicht ansteigende Dach als grasbewachsene
«Landschaft» gestaltet. Die Rasenfläche ist durch
den eingeschnittenen Zentraleingang und einen aus
der Mitte herausragenden, kegelförmigen Baukörper
durchbrochen.
Bibliothek der Technischen Hochschule, Delft,
1992 – 98, Mecanoo Architekten.
*Towards the west the building is lowered into the
ground and the roof designed as a grassy "landscape". The lawn surface is broken by a centrally
placed entranceway and a conical building volume
rising up out of the centre.*
*Library of the University of Technology of Delft,
1992 – 98, Mecanoo Architects.*

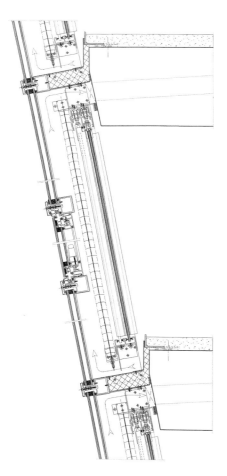

Die schräg nach außen geneigte Abluftfassade ist eine Pfosten-Riegel-Konstruktion. Das Isolierglas ist horizontal durch Deckleisten, vertikal duch eine Silikon-Verklebung an der Unterkonstruktion befestigt. Die innenliegende Verglasung besteht aus Schiebeflügeln.
Bibliothek der Technischen Hochschule, Delft, 1992–98, Mecanoo Architekten.
The ventilated façade tilted slightly outwards is a transom and mullion construction. The insulating glass is fixed horizontally by pressure caps, and silicon-bonded vertically to the frame. The inner glazing is of sliding panes.
Library of the University of Technology of Delft, 1992–98, Mecanoo Architects.

stigt. Die innenliegende Verglasung besteht aus einer 8 mm starken ESG-Scheibe, die als Schiebeflügel gestaltet ist und den Zugang zum Zwischenraum für Reinigungsarbeiten sicherstellt. Die Raumluft strömt in den 14 cm breiten Zwischenraum durch einen Schlitz unter dem verglasten Schiebeflügel. Aufgrund der Erwärmung steigt sie und wird im Bereich der Geschoßdecken von der mechanischen Lüftung abgesaugt. Der Zwischenraum bildet so eine temperierte Pufferzone, die im Winter die Wärmeverluste und die Kälteabstrahlung, im Sommer die Wärmeabstrahlung reduziert. Damit können Arbeitsplätze in der Nähe der Verglasung ganzjährig genutzt werden. Für den Sonnen- und Blendschutz sind Aluminium-Lamellen im Zwischenraum eingebaut.

the upper and lower edges and at the side by means of a silicon seal.
The inner glazing consists of an 8 mm sheet of toughened glass which is designed as a sliding door and gives access to the cavity for cleaning purposes. The air from the room enters the 14 cm wide cavity through a slit underneath the sliding door. As it warms, it rises at the level of the floors and is drawn off by a mechanical ventilation system. The cavity thus forms a kind of buffer zone which reduces heat loss and cold radiation in winter and heat radiation in summer. This means that workplaces situated close to the glass can be fully used all the year round. For solar and glare control aluminium louvres are built into the cavity.

«Zweite Haut»- oder zweischalige Fassaden

Der Begriff «Zweite Haut»- oder zweischalige Fassade bezeichnet eine Fassade und eine Verglasung, die außen vor dem eigentlichen Raumabschluß angeordnet ist. Im Zwischenraum werden meistens die Sonnen- und Blendschutzmaßnahmen untergebracht, die so vor Witterungseinflüssen und Luftverschmutzung geschützt sind, was besonders bei hohen oder an stark befahrenen Straßen liegenden Gebäuden von Bedeutung ist. Ein weiterer Vorteil der zweischaligen Fassade liegt in der sommerlichen Sonnenschutzwirkung. Da die infolge der absorbierten Sonnenstrahlung entstehende Sekundärstrahlung an die Luft im Zwischenraum abgegeben wird, entsteht thermischer Auftrieb. Rechnerische und praktische Untersuchungen haben gezeigt, daß durch natürliche Luftzirkulation bis zu 25 % der im Zwischenraum in Wärme umgesetzten Sonnenstrahlung abgeführt werden können. In der Regel werden, mit entsprechend ausgewählten Scheiben und Sonnenschutzmaßnahmen, g-Werte um 0.10 erreicht.

Aufgrund der mit steigender Höhe zunehmenden Lufttemperatur sind aber durchgehend geöffnete Zwischenräume meistens auf wenige Geschosse einzuschränken. Hinzu kommen noch technische Anforderungen an Schall- und Feuerschutz. Durch die Verminderung des Winddrucks mit der zusätzlichen Scheibe können die Fenster auch in hochgelegenen Stockwerken geöffnet und die angrenzenden Räume natürlich belüftet werden.

Diese Konzepte werden im nächsten Kapitel eingehend behandelt.

Eine zweischalige Fassade reduziert auch die Wärmeverluste, weil die geringere Luftgeschwindigkeit und die erhöhte Temperatur im Zwischenraum den Wärmeübergang auf der Glasoberfläche vermindern. Damit ergeben sich höhere Oberflächentemperaturen raumseitig der inneren Verglasung, was sich auf den Komfort im Fensterbereich positiv auswirkt. Ferner besteht die Möglichkeit, über Wärmetauscher eine Energierückgewinnung aus der Abluft zu erzielen. In konstruktiver Hinsicht kann die äußere Schale als Einfach- oder als Isolierverglasung ausgeführt werden. Für die Reinigung muß der Zwischenraum begehbar oder durch die Fenster erreichbar sein.

Zweischalige Fassadensysteme sind zwar nicht neu; vereinzelte Beispiele wurden schon in den

Double-Skin Façades

The term "double-skin façade" refers to an arrangement with a glass skin in front of the actual building façade. Solar control devices are placed in the cavity between these two skins, which protects them from the influences of weather and air pollution, a factor of particular importance in high-rise buildings or ones situated in the vicinity of busy roads.

A further advantage of the double-skin façade is the solar shading it affords in the summer. As reradiation from absorbed solar radiation is emitted into the intermediate cavity, a natural stack effect results, which causes the air to rise, taking with it additional heat.

Computer simulations and tests have shown that natural air circulation can remove up to 25 % of the heat resulting from solar radiation in the cavity. Generally, given appropriate panes of glass and solar control devices, g-values of approximately 0.10 can be achieved. As the temperature of the air increases as it rises upwards, it is usual to restrict the height of the continuous opening to just a few floors. Technical considerations concerned with fire protection and acoustic insulation also play a role.

The reduction of wind pressure by the addition of the extra pane of glass means that the windows can be opened even in the uppermost floors of a high-rise building to ventilate the neighbouring rooms.

These concepts will be dealt with at length in the next chapter.

A double-skin façade also reduces heat losses because the reduced speed of the air flow and the increased temperature of the air in the cavity lowers the rate of heat transfer on the surface of the glass. This has the effect of maintaining higher surface temperatures on the inside of the glass, which in turn means that the space close to the window can be better utilised as a result of increased thermal comfort conditions. An additional possibility with double-skin façades is to reclaim energy from the exhaust air stream using a heat exchanger.

The outer skin can either be made up of single glazing or an insulating glass unit. The intermediate cavity must be accessible for cleaning, either directly, or by opening windows.

Double-skin façade systems are not new; examples were already built in the 1960s, such as the

Die «Zweite-Haut»-Fassaden wurden schon in den 60er Jahren realisiert.
Geschichtswissenschaftliche Fakultät der Universität Cambridge, Cambridge, 1964–67, J. Stirling.
Double-skin façades were already built in the 1960's.
Library of the History Faculty at Cambridge University, Cambridge, 1964–67, J. Stirling.

60er Jahren realisiert, wie die Bibliothek der Geschichtswissenschaftlichen Fakultät der Universität Cambridge, England, 1964–68, von James Stirling.

Bis Anfang der 80er Jahre wurden Zweite-Haut-Fassaden aber nur vereinzelt gebaut. Seit Mitte der 80er Jahre liegen sie zunehmend im Trend und werden bei zahlreichen Bauten in Europa realisiert.

Ein frühes Beispiel ist das Bürogebäude Leslie und Godwin in Farnborough, England, auch «Briarcliff House» genannt, 1984 von Arup Associates fertiggestellt. Es ist mit einer zweischaligen Fassade mit Wärmerückgewinnung ausgestattet. Die vorgelagerte Verglasung erfüllt zwei Aufgaben: Einerseits dient sie als Lärmschutz gegen Fahrzeug- und Flugverkehr, andererseits als Sonnenschutz für die Büroräume, die mit Computern und anderen wärmeerzeugenden Geräten ausgestattet sind.

Die Außenhaut besteht aus einer 10 mm starken, wärmeabsorbierenden Verglasung und ist der inneren Fassade 120 cm vorgelagert, welche aus geschlossenen Blechpaneelen, festen Isolierglasfenstern und sensorgesteuerten Lamellen besteht. Der breite Zwischenraum dient der Reinigung und der Führung der vertikalen Lüftungsrohre. Im Winter nimmt die steigende Außenluft die entstehende Wärme auf und führt sie zur Wärmerückgewinnungsanlage im Dachgeschoß. Im Sommer wird sie nicht weiter genutzt und durch offenstehende Lüftungsklappen direkt ins Freie geleitet.

library of the History Faculty at Cambridge University, England, built 1964–68 by James Stirling.

Up until the 1980s, however, double-skin façades were not very common. Since the mid 1980s they have become increasingly popular and are now being used in many buildings all around Europe.

An early example is the office building of Leslie and Godwin in Farnborough, England, also called "Briarcliff House", completed in 1984 by Arup Associates.

The building has a double-skin façade fitted with a heat recovery system. The double skin serves two purposes: on the one hand it protects against noise from traffic and aircraft, on the other it gives solar control in the offices which contain computers and other heat-producing equipment.

The outer skin is a 10 mm thick heat-absorbing glass pane, placed 120 cm in front of the actual building skin. This inner façade consists of metal panels, fixed insulating glass windows and sensor-controlled louvre blinds. The wide intermediate cavity aids cleaning and houses the vertical ventilation ducts.

In winter the upward air flow absorbs the heat and draws it up to the roof where the heat energy gets reclaimed by a heat exchanger system. In summer this is not necessary, and the air is directed freely via ventilation louvres to the outside.

Zweischalige Fassade mit einem breiten Luftzwischenraum: Die steigende Außenluft nimmt die entstehende Wärme auf und führt sie bis ins Dachgeschoß; die äußere Glashaut besteht aus einem bronzegefärbten, vorgespannten Einfachglas. Bürogebäude Leslie und Godwin, Farnborough, England, 1984, Arup Associates.

Double-skin façade with wide air space: the upward air flow absorbs the heat and draws it up to the roof; the outer skin consists of bronze-tinted toughened single glazing. Leslie und Godwin office building, Farnborough, England, 1984, Arup Associates.

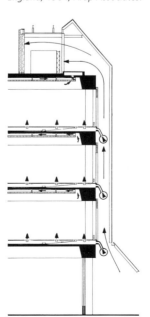

Das Haus der Wirtschaftsförderung und das Technologiezentrum in Duisburg, von Foster und Partnern in Zusammenarbeit mit Kaiser Bautechnik 1993 fertiggestellt, bilden den ersten realisierten Teil des Mikroelektronik-Parks.

Die gekrümmte zweischalige Fassade des linsenförmigen Kopfbaus besteht aus einer klaren Einfachverglasung, die ca. 20 cm vor der geschoßhohen Isolierverglasung angeordnet ist. Ihre 1.50 × 3.30 m vorgespannten, 12 mm starken Scheiben sind mit Planar®-Bolzen in vertikale Aluminiumprofile eingehängt. Letztere sind vom Dachrand abgehängt und mit den Geschoßdecken zur Übertragung der horizontalen Lasten verbunden.

Die innenliegende Fassadenschale besteht aus geschoßhohen Drehflügelfenstern mit thermisch

The Business Promotion Centre and the Technology Centre in Duisburg, built in 1993 by Foster and Partners in cooperation with Kaiser Bautechnik is the first completed section of the Microelectronic Park.

The curved, double-skin façade of the lens-shaped building at the edge of the complex consists of clear single glazing situated 20 cm in front of the full-height insulating glass façade. The single glazing consists of 1.50 × 3.30 m toughened, 12 mm thick panes suspended in vertical aluminium mullions by means of Planar® bolts. The mullions are suspended from the edge of the roof and attached to the intermediate floors for transfer of horizontal loading.

The inner façade skin consists of storey-high side-hung windows with thermally broken aluminium profiles and insulating glass units; outside is a

Die zweischalige Fassade des linsenförmigen Gebäudes besteht aus einer klaren Einfachverglasung, die der innenliegenden Isolierverglasung vorgehängt ist.
Haus der Wirtschaftsförderung, Duisburg, 1988–93, Foster und Partner.
The double-skin façade of the lens-shaped building consists of a clear single glazing suspended in front of the insulating glass façade.
Business Promotion Centre, Duisburg, Germany, 1988–93, Foster and Partners.

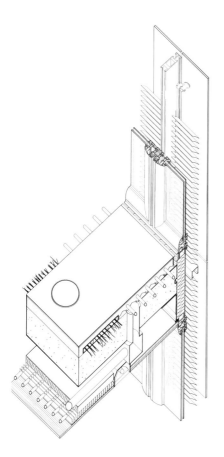

Detail des Fassadenaufbaus und Anschluß an die Geschoßdecke (links).
Die Büroräume sind mit Quellüftung, Kühldecken und Fußbodenheizung ausgestattet (Mitte); Sonnen- und Blendschutz erfolgen durch perforierte Lamellen (rechts).
Haus der Wirtschaftsförderung, Duisburg, 1988–93, Foster und Partner.
Detail of the façade construction and the connection with the floor slab (left).
The offices are supplied with displacement ventilation, chilled ceilings and underfloor heating (centre); sun and glare protection is achieved through perforated blinds (right).
Business Promotion Centre, Duisburg, Germany, 1988–93, Foster and Partners.

getrennten Aluminiumprofilen und einer Isolierverglasung, außen 6 mm Floatglas, innen 8 mm Verbundglas mit Low-E-Beschichtung und einer Argonfüllung im Zwischenraum.

Der k-Wert der gesamten Konstruktion liegt im Bereich von 1.4 W/m²K. Perforierte, computergesteuerte Aluminiumlamellen sind in den Zwischenraum eingebaut.

Die Luft wird mit einem leichten Überdruck in den unteren Bereich des Zwischenraums eingeblasen. Beim Durchströmen nimmt sie die an den Lamellenstoren entstehende Abwärme auf, um schließlich dank des Auftriebs zu steigen und durch kleine Öffnungen am Dachrand ins Freie auszutreten.

Da das Gebäude direkt an einer stark befahrenen Straße liegt, wurde eine Vollklimatisation der Räume anderen Lösungen mit natürlicher Belüftung vorgezogen.

Im Gegensatz zu Nur-Luftklimaanlagen, wo die Temperatur durch Zufuhr von Kalt- und Warmluft reguliert wird, ist hier eine Quellüftung eingebaut, die nur den Frischluftanteil zuführt, während für die Heizung und die Kühlung getrennte Wasserkreisläufe benutzt werden.

Die Frischluft fließt durch schmale Schlitze entlang der Fensterfront ein und breitet sich, gleichsam als Frischluftsee, am Boden aus. Sie wird durch Wärmequellen – Personen oder Geräte – erwärmt und steigt zur Decke, wo sie durch Schattenfugen bei den Beleuchtungskörpern abgesaugt wird.

Für die Kühlung der Büros sind wasserdurchströmte Kühldecken eingesetzt, für die Heizung sorgt entlang der Fassade ein 60 cm breiter Streifen mit Fußbodenheizung.

Seit der Inbetriebnahme des Gebäudes sind Überhitzungsprobleme bei den oberen Geschossen gemeldet worden.

Diese Probleme entstehen, weil die Luft im Zwischenraum sehr heiß werden kann und

6 mm float glass, inside is an 8 mm laminated glass with low-E coating and the cavity between is filled with argon gas.

The U-value of the whole double-skin façade is around 1.4 W/m²K.

Perforated, computer-controlled aluminium louvres are incorporated into the cavity between the two skins.

Air is injected at slightly higher than ambient pressure into the lower part of this cavity and through the effects of warming a natural stack effect results. This air rises and removes heat from the louvre blinds and continues upwards to be expelled into the open air through small openings by the roof edge.

As the building is situated next to a very busy road the option of full air conditioning was preferred to other solutions with natural air ventilation.

In contrast to air-only conditioning systems, in this case a displacement ventilation system is used which supplies only the required fresh air, while for heating and cooling separate water return systems are provided.

The fresh air flows in through narrow slits along the window front and spreads out along the floor forming a "fresh air pool". This air is then naturally heated by various heat sources, such as people, or equipment, and rises to the ceiling where it is extracted through vents above the lighting.

To cool the offices, chilled ceilings are used, and heating is taken care of by means of a 60 cm strip of underfloor heating along the façade.

Since the building went into operation overheating problems have been reported in the top floors.

These problems occur because the air in the cavity can become very hot and on rising it collects at the top; this can be avoided by

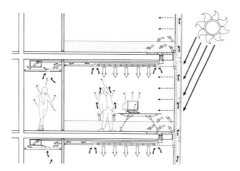

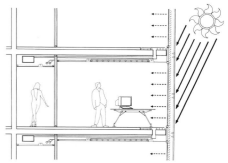

sich beim Aufsteigen staut; sie können aber mit der akkuraten Dimensionierung des Zwischenraums und einer entsprechenden Gestaltung der Lüftungsöffnungen im Dachbereich vermieden werden.

Bei der zweischaligen Fassadenkonstruktion für das Ensemble der Victoria-Versicherung in Köln (1990–96) haben die Architekten T. van den Valentyn und A. Tillmann dagegen einen breiten Zwischenraum vorgesehen.
Der Bürokomplex, der am verkehrsreichen Sachsenring liegt, besteht aus drei niedrigen Gebäuden: vorne ein Zwillingsturm, seitlich dazu ein steinverkleideter, sechsgeschossiger, schmaler Bürotrakt und dahinter ein viereckiger Glaskubus mit einem geräumigen Innenhof.
Die Fassade des Hauptgebäudes ist 2.6° nach außen geneigt.
Die außenliegende Verglasung besteht aus 2.7 m breiten und 1.13 m hohen Verbundsicherheits-

accurate sizing of the cavity and accurate design of the ventilation openings in the area of the roof.

In the double-skin façade for the offices of Victoria Insurance in Cologne (1990–96), for example, the architects T. van den Valentyn and A. Tillmann made provision for a wide cavity.
This office complex which is located by a busy road, the Sachsenring, consists of three low buildings: at the front a twin tower, at the side a stone-clad, six-floor, narrow office block, and behind it a rectangular glass cube with a spacious interior courtyard.
The façade of the main building is tilted 2.6° outwards.
The outer glazed skin consists of 2.7 m wide and 1.13 m high laminated glass (6 + 8 mm glass panes) which is affixed to the transoms of the façade frame via pressure caps recessed in the glass.

Die zweischalige Fassade des Hauptgebäudes ist 2.6° nach außen geneigt. Die VSG-Scheiben der Außenverglasung sind horizontal durch im Glas vertiefte Glashalteleisten befestigt.
Ensemble der Victoria Lebensversicherung, Köln, 1990–96, T. van den Valentyn und A. Tillmann.
The double-skin façade of the main building tilts outwards by 2.6°. The laminated panes of the outer skin are fixed horizontally by means of pressure caps recessed into the glass.
Victoria Life Insurance buildings, Cologne, 1990–96, T. van den Valentyn and A. Tillmann.

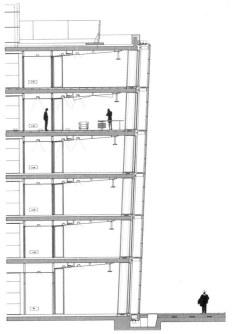

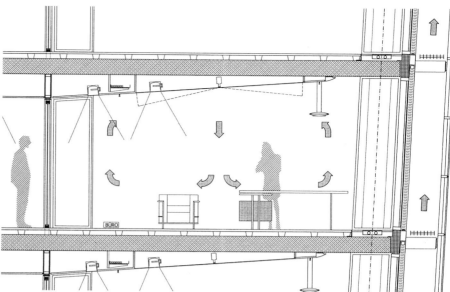

Die Außenluft erreicht den Zwischenraum durch eine Zuluftöffnung am Fuß der Außenverglasung und gelangt durch Lüftungsklappen am Dachrand ins Freie. Im Zwischenraum sind Gitterroststege für Reinigungs- und Wartungsarbeiten eingebaut.
Ensemble der Victoria Lebensversicherung, Köln, 1990–96, T. van den Valentyn und A. Tillmann.

Outside air reaches the cavity through an inlet at the base of the outer skin and escapes at the top through ventilation flaps on the roof edge. Built into the cavity are gantries for cleaning and maintenance access.
Victoria Life Insurance buildings, Cologne, 1990–96, T. van den Valentyn and A. Tillmann.

gläsern (6 + 8 mm VSG), die horizontal durch im Glas vertiefte Glashalteleisten an den Riegeln der Fassadenunterkonstruktion befestigt sind. Die Innenfassade besteht aus vorfabrizierten, geschoßhohen Rahmenelementen aus Aluminium. Sie sind 2.7 m breit, 3.4 m hoch und mit einer Wärmeschutzverglasung mit einem k-Wert von 1.8 W/m²K festverglast.

Im 0.7 m breiten Zwischenraum sind Gitterroststege für Reinigungs- und Wartungsarbeiten eingebaut.

Für den Sonnenschutz sind Rafflamellen aus Aluminium vor der Innenfassade angeordnet.

Die Außenluft erreicht den Fassadenzwischenraum durch eine Zuluftöffnung am Fuß der Außenverglasung. Im Zwischenraum erwämt sie sich und gelangt am Dachrand ins Freie durch Lüftungsklappen, die mit Spindelmotoren gesteuert sind.

Ausschlaggebend bei der Gesamtkonzeption des Gebäudes war die Entscheidung, wegen der Abgase auf eine natürliche Belüftung zu verzichten und die Raumbelüftung über eine Klimaanlage sicherzustellen. Damit dient die zweischalige Fassade hauptsächlich als Lärmschutz.

Das bauphysikalische Verhalten im Winter und im Sommer wurde durch umfangreiche Simulationsuntersuchungen optimiert.

Ein besondere Variante einer zweischaligen Fassadenkonstruktion stellt das Bürohaus am Halensee in Berlin dar, von den Architekten Léon/Wohlhage 1990–96 realisiert:

The inner façade consists of prefabricated, storey-high frame elements of aluminium. These elements are 2.7 m wide, 3.4 m high and glazed with fixed low-E coated glass units with a U-value of 1.8 W/m²K.

In the 0.7 m cavity are gantries for cleaning and maintenance purposes.

For solar control Venetian blinds of aluminium are fitted in front of the inner façade.

The outside air reaches the façade cavity through an intake at the base of the outer glazing. In the cavity it warms and passes out again at the top through air vents controlled by spindle motors.

A key factor in the overall concept for the building was the decision to dispense with natural ventilation because of the vehicle exhaust fumes outside, and instead to use a full air conditioning system.

The double-skin façade thus serves mainly as protection against noise.

The façade's effect on the building in winter and summer was investigated in extensive tests.

A special variant on the theme of a double-skin façade is the office building by the Halensee in Berlin, built by architects Léon/Wohlhage in 1990–96.

It functions like a storey-high solar collector.

The seven-floor office building needs effective protection against noise and fumes, as it is situated right by the city motorway.

The double-skin façade was constructed on the particularly noisy west side.

Es wirkt als geschoßhoher Sonnenkollektor.
Das 7geschossige Gebäude braucht einen wirksamen Schutz gegen Lärm und Abgase, da es unmittelbar an der Berliner Stadtautobahn steht.
Die zweischalige Fassade wurde an der besonders lärmigen Westseite gebaut.
Der Zwischenraum ist an den Geschoßdeckenstirnen durch eine geknickte Betonbrüstung horizontal getrennt.
Die Innenfassade besteht aus raumhohen Schiebetüren mit Wärmeschutzverglasung.
Die Außenverglasung ist vollständig geschlossen, so daß sie einen Schallschutz von 30 dB bewirkt. Sie besteht aus punktförmig gehaltenen, 12 mm starken ESG-Scheiben von 1.2 m Breite und 3.9 m Höhe.
Der Zwischenraum ist 0.85 m tief und für Reinigungsarbeiten begehbar. Er beherbergt die Zu- und Abluftrohre für die mechanische Belüftung. Die Frischluft wird im Dachbereich bezogen.
Für den Sonnenschutz sind helle Stoffstoren unmittelbar hinter der Außenverglasung angeordnet. Bei Kälte bleibt die Innenfassade geschlossen, und

The cavity is separated horizontally at the level of the floors by a bent concrete parapet.
The inner façade consists of storey-high sliding doors with thermally insulating glass.
The outer glazing is completely closed giving a noise protection of 30 dB. It consists of point-fixed 12 mm sheets of toughened glass, 1.2 m wide and 3.9 m high.
The cavity is 0.85 m deep and can be walked in for cleaning.
It contains the inlet and outlet ducts for the mechanical ventilation system. Fresh air is taken in at roof level.
For solar control light-coloured blinds of material are placed directly behind the outer glazing. When the weather is cold the inner façade remains closed and the cavity works like a thermal buffer.
A displacement air system with 1x air change provides for ventilation of the office rooms.
The air inlets are arranged along the corridors. In transition periods the fresh air brought in is warmed by solar radiation; then the users can

Die zweischalige Fassade wurde an der besonders lärmigen Westseite gebaut.
Bürohaus am Halensee, Berlin, 1990–96, Léon/Wohlhage Architekten.
The double-skin façade was built on the west side which is subject to high noise levels from traffic.
Office building at Halensee, Berlin, 1990–96, Léon/Wohlhage Architects.

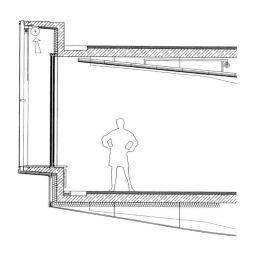

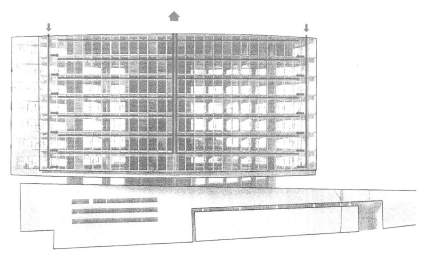

Der geschoßhohe Zwischenraum ist durch eine geknickte Betonbrüstung abgeschlossen. Er beherbergt die Zu- und Abluftrohre für die mechanische Belüftung (oben).

Die Außenverglasung besteht aus punktförmig gehaltenen ESG-Scheiben, die als Schallschutz dienen. Für den Sonnenschutz sind helle Stoffstoren im Zwischenraum angeordnet (unten).

Bürohaus am Halensee, Berlin, 1990–96, Léon/Wohlhage Architekten.

The storey-high cavity is closed off by a projecting concrete parapet. Contained in the cavity are inlet and outlet ducts for mechanical ventilation (top).

The outer glazing is of point-fixed panes of toughened glass which give noise protection. For solar control light-coloured textile blinds are fitted into the cavity (below).

Office building at Halensee, Berlin, 1990–96, Léon/Wohlhage Architects.

der Zwischenraum wirkt als Wärmepuffer. Für die Belüftung der Büroräume ist eine Quellüftung mit einem 1-fachen Luftwechsel eingebaut. Die Auslässe sind entlang des Korridors angeordnet. Während der Übergangszeiten wird die zugeführte Frischluft von der Sonnenstrahlung aufgewärmt; dann können die Benutzer die Schiebetüren der Innenfassade öffnen und durch die einströmende Warmluft das Raumklima individuell steuern. Im Sommer bleibt die Innenfassade geschlossen, und der Zwischenraum wird mechanisch entlüftet.

Um die Kühllasten im Sommer zu reduzieren, wird die Speichermasse des Gebäudes herangezogen. Sie wird während der Nacht durch die mechanische Belüftung mit Frischluft gekühlt.

Zweischalige Konstruktionen werden häufig für Dachverglasungen von Museen eingesetzt, um

open the sliding doors of the inner façade and control the climate in the room individually by admitting warm air. In summer the inner façade remains closed and the cavity is ventilated mechanically.

To reduce the cooling loads in summer the building mass is used as thermal storage. It is cooled during the night through mechanical ventilation with fresh air.

Double-skinned constructions are used often for glazed roofs in museums, to give natural illumination of the art objects and to protect against fluctuations of humidity and temperature.

One such solution was selected by the Renzo Piano Building Workshop for the Fondation Beyeler Museum in Riehen near Basel, built 1992–97. The glass roof is similar in form to a shed roof, overhanging the four long parallel

die Kunstwerke natürlich zu beleuchten und vor Feuchtigkeits- und Temperaturschwankungen zu schützen.

Eine solche Lösung haben die Architekten Renzo Piano Building Workshop für das Museum der «Fondation Beyeler» in Riehen bei Basel, 1992–97, gewählt.
Das Glasdach erinnert formal an ein Sheddach und kragt über die vier langen, parallelen Mauern aus, welche die Nord-Süd-gerichteten Ausstellungsräume definieren. Damit entstehen an den Schmalseiten zwei sonnengeschützte Zonen und an den Längsseiten lange Vordächer, welche aus 22 mm starken VSG-Scheiben mit einem weiß emailbedruckten, rechteckigen Muster bestehen.
Die Ausstellungsräume sind durch raumhohe Verglasungen in Pfosten-Riegel-Konstruktion abgeschlossen. Auf der Westseite bildet eine ähnliche Verglasung eine lange Galerie.
Das zweischalige Glasdach besteht insgesamt aus mehreren Schichten, welche für die Steuerung des Raumklimas und des Tageslichts sorgen. Die Tragstruktur des Daches bildet ein Trägerrost aus Stahlprofilen, der punktuell auf den Mauern aufgelagert ist. Darauf liegt die Dachverglasung, welche die wärmedämmende und wasserdichte Ebene bildet. Sie besteht aus drei flachgeneigten, gebäudelangen Satteldächern, die zwischen die oberhalb der Mauern liegenden Regenrinnen gespannt sind. Die Isoliergläser bestehen aus extra-weißem Glas mit einer 12 mm starken ESG-Scheibe außen, einem Zwischenraum von 16 mm und einer 18 mm starken VSG-Scheibe mit Alarmsicherung innen.

walls which define the north-south exhibition rooms. Along the narrow ends this creates two zones protected against the sun and, along the longitudinal walls, long canopies consisting of 22 mm thick laminated glass panes fritted with a white, rectangular pattern.
The exhibition rooms are finished with storey-high glass walls on a mullion and transom frame. On the west side a similar glazing construction forms a long gallery.
The double-skin glass roof consists of a number of layers which control the air conditioning and daylighting. The support structure for the roof is a grid of steel beams bearing at points on the walls. On this frame is the roof glazing which forms the thermally insulating and waterproof layer. The roof glazing consists of three low-pitch gable roofs along the length of the building – the roofs span between the rain gutters which are located above the walls. The insulating glass

Das Glasdach kragt über die vier langen, parallelen Mauern aus; es bildet an den Schmalseiten zwei sonnengeschützte Zonen, an den Längsseiten lange Vordächer (oben).
Der mechanisch belüftete Pufferraum verhindert Feuchtigkeits- und Temperaturschwankungen (unten).
Museum für die Fondation Beyeler, Riehen bei Basel, Schweiz, 1992–97, Renzo Piano Building Workshop.
The glass roof projects beyond the four long parallel walls; on the narrow sides it forms two zones protected from the sun and on the long sides it forms long canopies (top).
The mechanically ventilated buffer zone reduces variation in humidity and temperature (bottom).
Museum for the Fondation Beyeler, Riehen near Basel, Switzerland, 1992–97,
Renzo Piano Building Workshop.

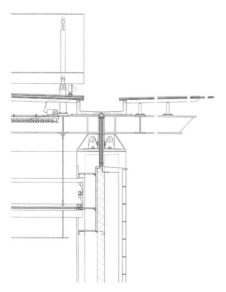

Über der Dachverglasung liegt eine shedähnliche Konstruktion aus schräggestellten Glasscheiben. Diese reduzieren die direkte Sonnenstrahlung, lassen aber das diffuse Nordlicht durch.
Museum für die Fondation Beyeler, Riehen bei Basel, Schweiz, 1992–97,
Renzo Piano Building Workshop.
Above the roof glazing is a shed-like construction of angled glass panes. These reduce direct solar radiation, but admit diffuse northern light.
Museum for the Fondation Beyeler, Riehen near Basel, Switzerland, 1992–97,
Renzo Piano Building Workshop.

Über der Dachverglasung liegt eine shedähnliche Konstruktion aus schräggestellten Glasscheiben, die durch Punkthalter und Stahlgußteile an vertikalen Stützenelementen befestigt sind. Die 12 mm starken ESG-Scheiben sind auf der Rückseite vollflächig weiß emailliert. Sie reduzieren die direkte Sonneneinstrahlung bis auf 5 %, lassen aber das diffuse Nordlicht in die Ausstellungsräume durch.

Unterhalb des Trägerrostes ist eine horizontale Verglasung aus Stahlrahmen mit VSG-Scheiben abgehängt. Sie schließt einen 1.4 m hohen, mechanisch belüfteten Luftraum ab, der als Pufferraum Schwankungen der Feuchtigkeit und der Temperatur verhindert. Der Pufferraum beherbergt bewegliche Lamellen für die feine Regelung des Lichteinfalls und die Leuchten für die Grundbeleuchtung.

Unterhalb dieser Verglasung liegt eine transluzente Decke aus Lochblechen mit einer Vlies-Bespannung, das Velum, das für eine gleichmäßige Lichtstreuung sorgt.

Die zweischalige Dachkonstruktion und die verschiedenen Sonnenschutzmaßnahmen ermöglichen das Ausstellen der empfindlichen Kunstwerke unter hochwertigen Tageslichtbedingungen.

Bei den oben beschriebenen mehrschaligen Fassaden, Abluft- oder Zweite-Haut-Systemen muß eine Klimaanlage ganzjährig für die Belüftung der Räume sorgen. Eine Alternative dazu bieten Zweite-Haut-Fassadensysteme, welche eine natürliche Belüftung der Räume während eines Großteils des Jahres ermöglichen.

is extra-white glass with a 12 mm outer sheet of toughened glass, a 16 mm cavity and an 18 mm inner sheet of laminated alarm glass.

Above the roof glazing is a shed-like construction of angled glass panes which are bolted via point fixings and cast steel fittings to vertical tubular posts. The 12 mm toughened glass panes have a 100 % white frit on the reverse side. They reduce the direct solar radiation down to 5 % but permit diffuse north light to enter the exhibition rooms.

Below the support grid is horizontal glazing of laminated glass on a steel frame. This glazing closes off a 1.4 m high, mechanically ventilated cavity which acts as a buffer zone to prevent variation in humidity and temperature in the exhibition rooms. Contained in the buffer zone are movable louvres for fine adjustment of incoming light and also indirect electric lighting.

Below this glazing is a translucent ceiling of perforated metal sheet covered with a layer of fleece which gives an even spread of light.

The double-skinned roof construction and the various solar control measures mean that sensitive works of art can be displayed in high-quality daylight conditions.

In the multiple-skin façades, ventilation or double-skin systems described above air conditioning has to be used all year for ventilation of the rooms. An alternative to this are double-skin façades which enable natural ventilation of the rooms for most of the year.

Intelligente Glasfassaden

Intelligent Glass Façades

Das Wort «intelligent» verweist auf eine dynamische, gleichsam lebendige Fähigkeit der Fassade, sich den wechselnden Tages- und Jahreszeitverhältnissen anzupassen, um den Verbrauch von Primärenergie eines Gebäudes zu senken.

Als wirklich «intelligent» kann man eine Glasfassade erst dann bezeichnen, wenn sie natürliche, erneuerbare Energiequellen – wie Sonnenenergie, Luftströmungen oder Erdwärme – nutzt, um den Energiebedarf eines Gebäudes für Heizung, Kühlung und Belichtung bereitzustellen. Dabei können verschiedene energiesparende Maßnahmen zum Tragen kommen, wie natürliche Belüftung, nächtliche Kühlung, natürliche Belichtung, Schaffen von Pufferzonen usw.

Dies setzt eine intensive Interaktion zwischen Fassade und Gebäude voraus. Zum Beispiel muß das aero- und thermodynamische Verhalten des jeweiligen Baus erfaßt werden, weil für eine natürliche Belüftung die Luftströmungen im Fassadenzwischenraum und im Gebäude von thermischem Auftrieb und Winddruck abhängig sind.

Zu diesem Zweck werden Computersimulationen, Windkanalversuche mit Gebäudemodellen und Freilandversuche mit originalgroßen Musterfassaden durchgeführt. Für die Simulationen wird häufig die «Computational Fluid Dynamics»-Methode (CFD) angewendet, welche Geschwindigkeit, Temperaturen und Intensität des Ablaufs der Luftströmungen in Schaubildern darstellen kann.

Weitere Untersuchungen finden im Windkanal statt; diese setzen aber die relativ aufwendige Herstellung von genauen, meßbaren Modellen voraus.

Ein effizienter Einsatz energiesparender Maßnahmen setzt allerdings die Entwicklung von Gesamtenergiekonzepten schon während der Entwurfsphase voraus, um eine wirksame Interaktion zwischen Fassade, Umwelt und Gebäudetechnik zu erreichen.

Die zunehmende Komplexität der Entwurfsaufgabe

The word "intelligent" indicates the dynamic, almost living capability of a façade to adapt to changing daily or seasonal conditions in order to achieve a reduction in a building's consumption of primary energy.

A glass façade can only then be properly described as "intelligent" when it makes use of natural, renewable energy sources, such as solar energy, air flows or the ground heat source, to secure a building's requirements in terms of heating, cooling and lighting.

A wide range of energy-saving measures can be implemented, such as natural ventilation, nighttime cooling, natural lighting, the creation of buffer zones etc. This assumes an intensive interaction between the façade and the building. For example the aero- and thermodynamic behaviour of the building in question has to be studied because for natural ventilation the air flows in the façade cavity and in the building are dependent on wind pressure and stack effect. For this purpose computer simulations, wind tunnel tests with building models and field tests with full-size façade models are being carried out. For simulations the computational fluid dynamics (CFD) method is often used; this can visually demonstrate the speed, temperature and intensity of the air flows. Further tests are carried out in wind tunnels; these are dependent on the relatively complicated manufacture of precise, measurable models.

For energy-saving measures to be used efficiently, this means that overall energy concepts need to be developed during the design stage, to achieve an effective interaction between the façade, the environment and the building systems. The increasing complexity of the design task can only be successful if a comprehensive approach is taken in planning, i. e. interdisciplinary cooperation between architects, façade planners and consulting engineers.

Linke Seite: Eine zweischalige Fassade mit einer Außenhaut aus rahmenlosen, drehbaren Glaslamellen dient im Winter als Wärmepuffer und funktioniert im Sommer wie eine einschalige Fassade.
«debis»-Hauptverwaltung, Berlin, 1991–97, Renzo Piano Building Workshop mit Christoph Kohlbecker.
Left page: A double-skin façade with an outer skin of frameless, pivoting glass louvres acts as a thermal buffer in winter and as a single-skin façade in summer.
debis headquarters building, Berlin, 1991–97, Renzo Piano Building Workshop in cooperation with Christoph Kohlbecker.

kann nur durch eine ganzheitliche Planung, d. h. durch eine interdisziplinäre Zusammenarbeit von Architekten, Fassadenplanern und beratenden Fachingenieuren erfolgversprechend angegangen werden.

Das Forschungsprojekt «Green Building» stellt einen der ersten Versuche dar, die künstliche Klimakontrolle zu reduzieren und die Möglichkeiten von natürlichen Maßnahmen auszuloten. Der Entwurf wurde 1990 von Future Systems, Jan Kaplicky und Amanda Levete, zusammen mit den Umweltingenieuren Tom Baker, Andy Sedgwick und Mike Beaven (Ove Arup und Partner, London) erarbeitet.
Die Tragstruktur besteht aus einer dreibeinigen Konstruktion, an der die Geschoßdecken abgehängt werden; im Gebäudekern entsteht ein dreieckiges Atrium. Obwohl die zweischalige Fassade auch Schutz vor Straßenlärm und Abgasen bietet, wurde sie hauptsächlich im Hinblick auf eine natürliche Belüftung entwickelt.
Die eiförmige Gestaltung des Gebäudes wurde aufgrund von Untersuchungen im Windkanal entwickelt, während die Luftströmungen im Fassadenzwischenraum und im Atrium durch die «CFD»-Methode untersucht wurden.
Im Atrium steigt die Luft wegen der Erwärmung durch Abstrahlung der innenliegenden Büros und zieht frische Außenluft durch Öffnungen an der unteren Gebäudeseite nach. Gleichzeitig steigt auch im Fassadenzwischenraum die erwärmte Luft und entweicht durch Öffnungen an der Gebäudespitze. Damit entsteht im Fassadenzwischenraum ein Unterdruck, der beim Öffnen der Bürofenster die Luft aus dem Atrium nachzieht und damit die natürliche Durchlüftung der Büros gewährleistet. Diese Luftströmungen werden zusätzlich von einem Unterdruck an der Gebäudespitze unterstützt.

The "Green Building" research project represents one of the first attempts to reduce artificial air conditioning and to replace it with natural measures. The design was developed in 1990 by Future Systems, Jan Kaplicky and Amanda Levete, together with the environmental engineers Tom Baker, Andy Sedgwick and Mike Beaven (Ove Arup and Partners, London). The support frame consists of a three-legged structure like a tripod, from which the floor slabs are suspended; in the core of the building is a triangular atrium. Although the double-skin façade also offers protection from street noise and vehicle exhaust fumes, it was primarily developed to enable natural ventilation.
The egg-shaped form of the building arose from tests in a wind tunnel, and the air flows in the façade cavity and in the atrium were investigated using the CFD method. Air rises in the atrium as it warms through radiation from the offices, and as it rises fresh air is drawn in through vents on the lower part of the building. At the same time warmed air also rises in the façade cavity and escapes through openings at the top of the building. As a result negative pressure is caused in the façade cavity, and when the office windows are opened the air is drawn in from the atrium thus providing natural ventilation in the offices. These air flows are additionally supported by low pressure at the top of the building. In colder seasons the outside air drawn in at the bottom is preheated

Die Tragstruktur besteht aus einer dreibeinigen Konstruktion, an der die Geschoßdecken abgehängt werden; die Gebäudeform und die zweischalige Fassade wurden im Hinblick auf eine natürliche Durchlüftung der Büros entwickelt.
«Green Building»-Forschungsprojekt, 1990, Future Systems, Jan Kaplicky und Amanda Levete.
The support structure consists of a tripod-like construction, from which the floor slabs are suspended; the building shape and the double-skin façade were designed to optimize the natural ventilation of the office spaces.
"Green Building" research project, 1990, Future Systems, Jan Kaplicky and Amanda Levete.

Im Fassadenzwischenraum steigt die erwärmte
Luft und entweicht an der Gebäudespitze ins Freie.
Damit entsteht ein Unterdruck, welcher Frischluft
aus dem Atrium nachzieht (links); Heizung und Kühlung erfolgen durch separate Wasserkreisläufe
(rechts).
«Green Building»-Forschungsprojekt, 1990,
Future Systems, Jan Kaplicky und Amanda Levete.
*Warmed air rises in the façade cavity and escapes
through vents at the top of the building. This
causes low pressure in the façade cavity, which
draws fresh air in from the atrium (left); heating
and cooling are supplied by separate water return
systems (right).*
"Green Building" research project, 1990,
Future Systems, Jan Kaplicky and Amanda Levete.

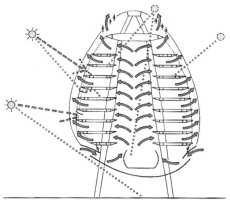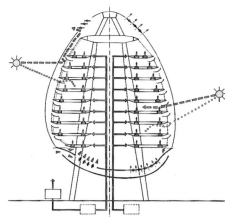

In kälteren Jahreszeiten wird die unten angesaugte
Außenluft mit der aus der Abluft zurückgewonne-
nen Wärmeenergie vorgeheizt.

Verstellbare lichtumlenkende Reflektoren in der
innenliegenden Fassadenebene und speziell
geformte Deckenelemente sorgen für eine natürliche Belichtung bis in die Tiefe der Büroräume.
Weiteres Tageslicht liefert das Atrium im Gebäudeinneren. Sonnen- und Blendschutz werden durch
individuell steuerbare Lamellen geregelt.

Für die Zwischenspeicherung der tagsüber an-
fallenden Wärme sind schwerspeichernde
Geschoßdecken vorgesehen, die nachts die
Wärme wieder an die Luft abgeben.

Obwohl der Entwurf experimentellen Charakter
besitzt und in seiner extrem «organischen» Gestalt
architektonische wie städtebauliche Grundfragen
aufwirft, weist er exemplarisch auf die Tragweite
einer integralen Planung für zukünftige energiesparende Gebäude hin. Dieser Gebäudeentwurf

using the thermal energy reclaimed from the exhaust air. Adjustable light-shelves in the inner
façade and specially shaped ceiling components
ensure natural lighting through into the depths of
the offices. Additional daylight reaches the inside
of the building via the atrium. Solar control and
glare protection can be regulated by means of individually adjustable louvres. Floor slabs which act
as thermal stores are intended to take up excess
heat in the daytime and to be cooled down again
at night through natural ventilation. Although the
design is experimental in character, and its extremely "organic" form raises basic questions in
architecture as well as town planning, it is nevertheless a model of what can be done in integrated
planning of low-energy buildings.

This design was influential in the development of
many interesting solutions with single and multiple-skin façades, with the aim of creating an environmentally-friendly architecture.

Eine natürliche Lichtverteilung in der Raumtiefe er-
folgt durch verstellbare Reflektoren und speziell
geformte Deckenelemente.
«Green Building»-Forschungsprojekt, 1990,
Future Systems, Jan Kaplicky und Amanda Levete.
*Distribution of daylight at the back of the offices is
ensured by adjustable light shelves and specially
designed ceiling elements.*
"Green Building" research project, 1990,
Future Systems, Jan Kaplicky and Amanda Levete.

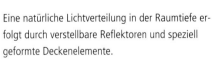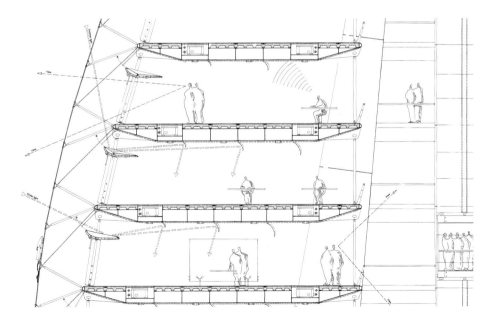

gab wichtige Impulse für die Entwicklung von zahlreichen interessanten Lösungen mit ein- und mehrschaliger Fassade, mit dem Ziel, eine umweltgerechte Architektur zu schaffen.

Einschalige Fassaden

Die zentrale Eingangshalle der «Neuen Messe Leipzig» ist ein Beispiel für ein umweltgerechtes Gebäude mit einschaliger Fassade. Sie wurde 1996 von den Architekten von Gerkan Marg und Partner in Zusammenarbeit mit Ian Ritchie Architects fertiggestellt.

Die gewölbte Glashalle bildet einen temperierten und wettergeschützten Raum, der als Empfang, Informationsstelle und Verteiler zwischen den Messehallen dient. Die 250 m lange, 80 m breite und 30 m hohe Glashalle ist eine filigrane Stahlkonstruktion mit einer raumseitigen, hochtransparenten Verglasung. Die Tragstruktur setzt sich zusammen aus zehn Fachwerkbögen und einer darunterliegenden, gewölbten Gitterschale, die aus runden Stahlrohren in einem quadratischen Modul von 3.125 m besteht. Die Fachwerkbögen stehen als schlanke Dreigurtträger in einem Abstand von 25 m auseinander und dienen als Aussteifung gegen ein Ausbeulen der Gitterschale. Die Verglasung ist 50 cm unterhalb des Gitternetzes an vier Stahlgußarmen – den sogenannten «frogfingers» – mit gelenkigen Punkthaltern aus Edelstahl aufgehängt. Diese Befestigungen verhindern, daß sich durch Windlasten und thermische Ausdehnung hervorgerufene Verformungen von der Tragstruktur auf die Glasscheiben übertragen. Die Verglasung besteht aus 3.105×1.525 m großen Verbundgläsern aus zwei vorgespannten, 8 bzw. 10 mm starken, extra-weißen SGG Optiwhite®-Scheiben. Im Scheitelbereich und auf der Südseite sind die Glasscheiben für den Sonnenschutz mit einer 75prozentigen weißen, reflektierenden Emailbedruckung versehen. Die 20 mm breiten Fugen zwischen den Scheiben sind durch ein aufgeklebtes Silikonprofil geschlossen.

Für das Raumklima strebte die Bauherrschaft Verhältnisse wie in einem temperierten Raum an. Der natürliche Treibhauseffekt kann solche Verhältnisse während fast des ganzen Jahres ohne zusätzliche Maßnahmen sicherstellen. Nur an kalten Wintertagen müssen Bodenheizung und Konvektoren am Fuß des Gewölbes eingeschaltet werden, um die Temperatur auf ein Minimum von +8° C anzuheben.

Die natürliche Belüftung der Halle wird über Klappen am Fuß und im Scheitel des Glasgewölbes

Single-Skin Façades

The main entrance hall of the New Trade Fair Centre in Leipzig is an example of an environmentally-friendly building with a single-skin façade. It was completed in 1996 by the architects von Gerkan Marg and Partners in collaboration with Ian Ritchie Architects. The vaulted glass hall forms a climate-controlled and weather-protected space which serves as a reception area, information centre and distribution point for the trade fair halls. The 250 m long, 80 m wide and 30 m high glass hall is a filigree steel construction with highly transparent glazing on the inside of the frame. The frame consists of ten trussed arches below which a vaulted grid shell of tubular steel, with 3.125 m square grid is suspended. The slim trussed arches, spaced at 25 m, stabilize the shell grid from buckling. The glass is suspended 50 cm below the grid by means of articulated stainless steel point fixings from four cast steel arms – the "frog fingers". These fixing points prevent bending stresses arising through wind loads and thermal expansion being transferred from the support structure to the glass panes. The glazing is of 3.105 × 1.525 m laminated glass composed of two sheets of toughened, extra white glass SGG Optiwhite®, 8 and 10 mm thick. Around the crown and on the south side the glass panes have a 75 % white, reflecting frit for solar control. The 20 mm wide joints between the panes are sealed with silicon gasket profile.

For the inside of the hall, the client wanted a pleasant, moderated climate. The natural greenhouse effect can ensure such conditions almost throughout the year, with no need for additional

Die Tragstruktur der Glashalle ist eine filigrane Stahlkonstruktion aus Fachwerkbogen und einer darunterliegenden Gitterschale, an welcher raumseitig eine hochtransparente Verglasung aufgehängt ist. Neue Messe Leipzig, Leipzig, 1996, von Gerkan Marg und Partner mit Ian Ritchie Architects.
The glass hall is supported by a filigree steel frame of trussed arches and a grid shell to which the highly transparent glazing is suspended on the room side. Neue Messe Leipzig, Leipzig, 1996, by von Gerkan Marg and Partners in cooperation with Ian Ritchie Architects.

Die natürliche Belüftung der Halle wird über Klappen am Fuß und im Scheitel des Glasgewölbes reguliert. Als Sonnenschutz dient eine weiße, reflektierende Emailbeschichtung. Um die Spitzentemperaturen im Sommer zu reduzieren, wird die Verglasung von außen mit Wasser berieselt (oben).

Die VSG-Scheiben sind mit gelenkigen Punkthaltern an Gußarmen aufgehängt. Im Scheitelbereich und auf der Südseite sind die VSG-Scheiben mit einer weißen, reflektierenden Emailbedruckung für den Sonnenschutz versehen (unten).

Neue Messe Leipzig, Leipzig, 1996, von Gerkan Marg und Partner mit Ian Ritchie Architects.

The hall is naturally ventilated by operating vents at the base and at the crown of the glass vault. A white, reflecting frit is used for solar control. Water is trickled down the glass in summer to reduce peak temperatures (top).

The laminated panes are suspended via articulated point fixings to cast arms. Around the crown and on the south side the laminated panes have a white, reflecting frit for solar control (bottom).

Neue Messe Leipzig, Leipzig, 1996, by von Gerkan Marg and Partners in cooperation with Ian Ritchie Architects.

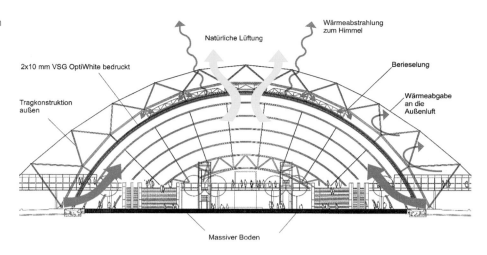

reguliert. Die Luftströmung stellt sich aufgrund der Thermik auch bei Windstille ein. Bei Wind entstehen zusätzlich Sogkräfte bei den Abluftöffnungen. Als Sonnenschutz dient die weiße, reflektierende Emailbedruckung. Um im Sommer die Spitzentemperaturen zu bewältigen, wird die Verglasung von außen mit Wasser berieselt und mit Verdunstung gekühlt. Damit wirkt sie wie eine Kühldecke. Im Sommer werden die Heizschlangen mit Kaltwasserdurchlauf für die Nachtkühlung der Bodenplatte verwendet.

Ein zweites Beispiel für einschalige, «intelligente» Fassaden ist das «Lycée Albert Camus» in Fréjus, Frankreich, das Foster und Partner 1991–93 erbaut haben. Das lineare, zweigeschossige Gebäude ist West-Ost-orientiert. Auf der Südseite

measures. Only on cold winter days is it necessary to switch on the underfloor heating and the convectors at the foot of the glass vault to raise the temperature to a minimum of +8° C. Natural ventilation in the hall is regulated via openings at the low level and at the crown of the glass vault. Because of the natural stack effects in the vault, air flows are created even when there is no wind outside. When the wind does blow outside it creates a suction at the openings which enhances this effect. The white reflecting frit serves as solar control. To cope with peak temperatures in summer, the glass is sprinkled with water from the outside and cooled through the effect of evaporation. Thus it works like a chilled ceiling. In summer cold water is passed through the heating pipes at night to cool the floor slab.

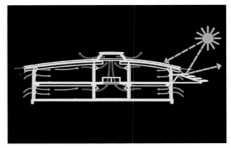

befindet sich ein weit auskragender Sonnenschutz aus breiten Lochblechlamellen. Er ist so ausgelegt, daß die steilen Sonnenstrahlen im Sommer reflektiert werden, die tieferen Strahlen im Winter jedoch in die Klassenzimmer gelangen.

In der Mitte des Gebäudes befindet sich eine zweigeschossige Erschließungszone, die mit einem Oberlicht abgeschlossen ist. Ähnlich wie bei der traditionellen arabischen Architektur erzielt dieser hohe Innenraum eine Kaminwirkung, welche die natürliche Belüftung des Gebäudes unterstützt. Wenn in wärmeren Jahreszeiten die Luft im Innenraum aufsteigt und durch drehbare Lamellen ins Freie gelangt, wird Frischluft von außen ins Gebäude nachgezogen. Kippflügel im Oberlichtbereich der Fassade und in den verglasten Korridor-Trennwänden regeln die Luftströmung. Im Hochsommer ermöglicht das Lüftungskonzept auch die Nachtauskühlung der Gebäudespeichermasse.

Auch das Klimakonzept des Technologiezentrums beim Wissenschaftspark Rheinelbe in Gelsenkirchen, Deutschland, von den Architekten Kiessler + Partnern 1995 fertiggestellt, basiert auf einer natürlichen Belüftung. Das dreigeschossige Hauptgebäude ist durch eine geneigte Verglasung an der Westfassade abgeschlossen, die eine 300 m lange Arkade bildet. Das Bürogebäude dient als Erschließungsachse für neun dreigeschossige Pavillons mit weiteren Büro- und Laborflächen auf der Ostseite. Die 58° geneigte Verglasung ist eine Pfosten-Riegel-Konstruktion, die von einer Stahlkonstruktion aus Vierendeelträgern im Abstand von 7.2 m getragen wird. Die Isoliergläser bestehen außen aus einer 6 mm starken Scheibe, dann aus einem 12 mm breiten Zwischenraum und innen aus einer 2×4 mm starken VSG-Scheibe mit einer Low-E-Beschichtung. Der k-Wert beträgt

A second example for a single-skin, "intelligent" façade is that of the Lycée Albert Camus in Fréjus, France, built by Foster and Partners in 1991–93. The linear, two-storey building stretches west-east. On the south side is a wide solar shade made up of perforated metal louvres. This shade is designed in such a way that steeply angled sunbeams in summer are reflected whereas in winter the lower-angled rays can penetrate into the classrooms. In the middle of the building is a two-storey hallway lit from above. As in traditional Arab architecture this high interior space acts as a solar chimney which supports the natural ventilation of the building. When in the warmer periods of the year the air rises in the interior space and escapes through pivoting louvres, fresh air is drawn in from the outside of the building. Bottom hung windows at the top of the glazed façade and in the glazed partition walls of the corridors regulate the air flows. In high summer this ventilation concept also enables night-time cooling of the building's thermal mass.

Also based on natural ventilation is the climate concept used for the technology centre for the Rheinelbe Science Park in Gelsenkirchen, Germany, which was completed by Kiessler + Partners in 1995. The three-storey main building is closed off on the west façade by tilted glazing, forming a 300 m long arcade. The office building serves as a central communications point for nine three-storey pavilions with further office and laboratory space on the east side. The 58° tilted glazed mullion and transom construction is supported by steel Vierendeel girders spaced at 7.2 m. The insulated glazing consists of an outer sheet of 6 mm glass, a 12 mm cavity and an inner sheet of 2×4 mm laminated glass with low-E coat-

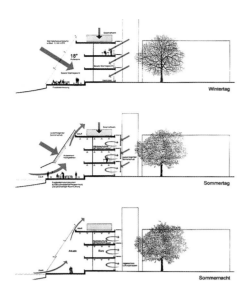

Die geneigte Verglasung an der Westseite bildet eine Arkade. Im Winter wirkt sie als Pufferzone und nutzt die eingestrahlte Sonnenenergie für die Erwärmung der Arkade und der angrenzenden Büros.
Im Sommer werden außenliegende Stoffrollos heruntergelassen und die Hubelemente hochgefahren, so daß Arkade und Büros natürlich durchlüftet werden.
Technologiezentrum im Wissenschaftspark Rheinelbe, Gelsenkirchen, Deutschland, 1989–95, Kiessler + Partner.

The tilted glazing on the west side forms an arcade. In winter it acts as a buffer zone and makes use of the radiated solar energy for warming the arcade and adjacent offices.
In summer the outer textile blinds are let down and the sliding openings raised, to provide natural ventilation in the arcade and offices.
Technology Centre in the Rheinelbe Science Park, Gelsenkirchen, Germany, 1989–95, Kiessler + Partner.

1.3 W/m²K, der g-Wert 0.62. Im unteren Drittel der Verglasung sind die Scheiben als 7×4.5 m große Hubelemente konzipiert. Durch die großflächige Verglasung entsteht eine Pufferzone, welche die eingestrahlte Sonnenenergie für die Erwärmung der Arkade und der Büros nutzt. Bei tiefen Außentemperaturen ist eine Bodenheizung vorgesehen. Im Sommer werden die außenliegenden Stoffrollos heruntergelassen und die Hubelemente hochgefahren. Damit strömt Außenluft in die Arkaden und tritt durch Klappflügel im First wieder ins Freie aus. Während der Nacht ermöglicht die Luftströmung auch die Kühlung der Gebäudespeichermasse. Das Thema «Pufferzone» wird im nächsten Abschnitt eingehend behandelt.

Zweite-Haut-Fassaden
Im Trend liegen heute vor allem sogenannte «Zweite-Haut»-Fassaden. Sie ermöglichen eine natürliche Raumbelüftung und senken damit den Energieverbrauch für mechanische Lüftung und Kühlung gegenüber konventionellen Bürogebäuden. Bei solchen Fassadenkonstruktionen steht der Zwischenraum in Verbindung mit der Außenluft, so daß die Fenster der Innenfassade auch bei hohen, windausgesetzten Gebäuden geöffnet werden können und für die natürliche Belüftung sowie die Nachtauskühlung der Speichermasse im Gebäude sorgen.
Im Zwischenraum ist der Sonnenschutz vor Luftverschmutzung und Witterung geschützt, ist aber trotzdem ebenso wirksam wie ein außenliegender Sonnenschutz. Im Winter bildet der Zwischenraum eine thermische Pufferzone, welche die Wärmeverluste reduziert und passive Gewinne aus der Sonneneinstrahlung ermöglicht.

ing. The U-value is 1.3W/m²K, the g-factor is 0.62. In the lower third of the façade the glazing is designed as 7×4.5 m vertical sliding openings. The extensive glazing gives rise to a buffer zone which utilises the incoming solar energy for heating the arcade and the offices. When temperatures are low outside underfloor heating comes into operation. In summer the exterior textile blinds are let down and the vertical sliding frame raised. This brings outside air into the arcades and out through the openings in the ridge. At night this flow of air cools the building's thermal mass. The concept of "buffer zone" is explained in detail in the next section.

Double-Skin Façades
Double-skin façades are very much in vogue. They enable natural ventilation and thus reduce the energy consumption otherwise needed for mechanical ventilation and cooling in conventional buildings. In such façade constructions the cavity is connected with the outside air so that the windows of the interior façade can be opened, even in the case of tall buildings subject to wind pressures; this enables natural ventilation and nighttime cooling of the building's thermal mass. Solar control measures built into the cavity are protected against air pollution and weathering, but they are just as effective as such devices placed on the exterior. In winter the cavity forms a thermal buffer zone which reduces heat losses and enables passive thermal gain from solar radiation. The concept of the buffer zone can also be implemented in large spaces projects, for example as a winter garden or an atrium, or by bringing together several buildings in a kind of "climate hall".

Das Konzept «Pufferzone» kann auch in sehr großen Dimensionen realisiert werden, beispielsweise als Wintergarten oder Atrium, oder indem man mehrere Gebäude in einer Art «Klimahalle» unterbringt.

Bei starker Sonneneinstrahlung muß der Fassadenzwischenraum gut durchlüftet werden, um eine Überhitzung zu vermeiden. Die ausschlaggebenden Kriterien hierfür sind die Breite des Zwischenraums und die Dimensionierung der Lüftungsöffnungen in der äußeren Hülle.

Der Luftaustausch zwischen Umgebung und Zwischenraum ist abhängig von den Winddruckverhältnissen an der Gebäudehülle, vom thermischen Auftrieb der Warmluft und vom Strömungswiderstand der Lüftungsöffnungen. Diese können entweder immer offen stehen (passive Systeme) oder nach Bedarf durch manuell oder motorisch bewegliche Klappen geregelt werden (aktive Systeme).

Aktive Systeme sind sowohl bei der Konstruktion als auch bei der Wartung sehr aufwendig und damit teuer. Weitere Kriterien für die Gestaltung einer zweischaligen Fassade sind die Anforderungen an den Brand- und Schallschutz.

Ausgehend von diesen Rahmenbedingungen sind verschiedene Lösungen für zweischalige Fassaden entwickelt worden.

Geschoßhohe Zweite-Haut-Fassaden
Wenn die Zu- und Abluftöffnungen pro Geschoß angeordnet sind, ist die geringste Lufterwärmung und damit die optimale Wirkungsweise bei natürlicher Raumlüftung zu erwarten. Deshalb ist der Fassadenzwischenraum meistens horizontal in geschoßhohe Abschnitte unterteilt. Seltener gibt es aber auch Beispiele mit gebäudehohem Zwischenraum oder mit einer Kombination beider Systeme.

Die 1995 von Architectures Jean Nouvel fertiggestellten «Galeries Lafayette» in Berlin weisen eine Zweite-Haut-Fassade mit geschoßhohem Zwischenraum auf.

Die Architekten haben das geschlossene, nach innen gerichtete Volumen des Kaufhauses mit kegelförmigen Atrien versehen und rundherum mit Büroflächen umgeben. Die Zweite-Haut-Fassade soll durch ihre besondere Gestaltung als Informationsträgerin und optische Attraktion dienen. Dafür sind die Deckenstirnen mit 55 cm hohen Leuchtschriftbändern ausgestattet, die mit

When solar radiation is high, the façade cavity has to be well ventilated, to prevent overheating. The key criteria here are the width of the cavity and the size of the ventilation openings in the outer skin. The air exchange between the environment and the cavity is dependent on the wind pressure conditions on the building's skin, the stack effect and the discharge coefficient of the openings. These vents can either be left open all the time (passive systems), or opened by hand or by machine (active systems). Active systems are very complicated and therefore expensive in terms of construction and maintenance. Further criteria in designing a double-skin façade are regulations concerning fire and noise protection. Using these factors as a basis, various solutions have been developed for double-skin façades.

Storey-High Double-Skin Façades
When inlet and outlet vents are placed at each floor, the lowest degree of air heating and therefore the most effective level of natural ventilation is to be expected. The façade cavity is therefore generally divided horizontally into storey-high sections. There are, however, some examples of buildings with a façade cavity stretching the whole high of the building or using a combination of both systems.

The Galeries Lafayette in Berlin built by Architectures Jean Nouvel in 1995 has a double-skin façade with a storey-high cavity. The architects designed the closed, inward-looking volume of the department store with cone-shaped atria and surrounded it with offices. The unusually designed double-skin

Die Zweite-Haut-Fassade soll als Informationsträgerin und optische Attraktion dienen.
«Galeries Lafayette» Berlin, 1991 – 95, Architectures Jean Nouvel.
The double-skin façade is intended to serve as an information carrier and as an optical attraction. Galeries Lafayette, Berlin, 1991 – 95, Architectures Jean Nouvel.

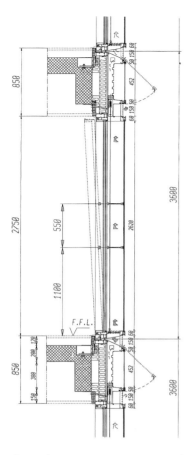

Die Außenverglasung ist mit einer grauen Emailbedruckung versehen, welche die Konturen der
innenliegenden, kegelförmigen Atrien durch eine
zunehmende Bedruckung betont.
Die Lüftungskästen sind mit Leuchtschriftbändern
ausgestattet. Darüber bzw. darunter befinden sich
die Lüftungsschlitze für die Belüftung des Zwischenraums.
«Galeries Lafayette» Berlin, 1991–95,
Architectures Jean Nouvel.

The outer glazing is printed with a grey frit, increas-
ing in density to emphasise the contours of the inte-
rior, cone-shaped atria.
The ventilation units are fitted with illuminated dis-
plays. Above and below these are the openings for
ventilation of the cavity.
Galeries Lafayette, Berlin, 1991–95,
Architectures Jean Nouvel.

Schriftzügen und Logos versehen werden können.
Darüber bzw. darunter befinden sich durchgehende, 15 cm hohe Lüftungsschlitze für die Be-
und Entlüftung des Zwischenraums. Die Öffnungen
bleiben permanent offen und sind mit Vogel-
schutz-Drähten versehen. Die zweischalige Fassade
ist wie ein gebäudehohes Schaufenster gestaltet,
welches den Passanten einen gewissen Einblick in
den Ablauf des Büroalltags gewährt. Eine weitere
optische Raffinesse stellt die außenliegende Verglasung dar. Sie ist mit einer 20 prozentigen Emailbedruckung aus grauen Punkten versehen, wobei
einige Flächen ausgespart sind, um die Projektion
der kegelförmigen Atrien auf die Fassade nachzu-
zeichnen. Die Konturen der Atrien sind zusätzlich
durch eine von 20 % auf 100 % zunehmende Bedruckung betont.
Die Verglasung besteht aus 1.35 × 2.65 m großen,
12 mm starken ESG-Scheiben, die oben und unten
an den Lüftungskästen und in der Mitte durch vier

façade is intended to serve as an information carrier and act as an optical attraction. For this reason
the ends of the floor slab are fitted with 55 cm high
illuminated display screens which can carry either
text or logos on them. Above and below these
strips are 15 cm high slits for ventilation of the cavity. The openings remain permanently open and
are fitted with wires to keep birds out. The double-
skin façade is designed like a shop window stretching the whole high of the building. Passers-by are
permitted a look into the day-to-day business in the
offices. Another optical refinement is the external
glazing. It has a 20 % frit of grey dots, with some
areas not covered in order to project the outline of
the cone-shaped atria onto the façade. The contours of the atria are additionally emphasised by a
fritted pattern increasing in density from 20 % to
100 %. The glazing consists of 1.35 × 2.65 m,
12 mm thick toughened glass fixed top and bottom
to the ventilation units and in the middle by four

symmetrisch angeordnete Punkthalterungen befestigt sind. Die Außenverglasung ist bei den vom Grundriß vorgegebenen Rundungen gebogen, während die Innenfassade der Rundung polygonal folgt. Sie besteht aus 1.35 × 2.75 m großen Rahmenelementen, die alternierend als Festverglasung und als
Dreh-Kippflügel ausgeführt sind. Das 29 mm starke Isolierglas, außen eine 8 mm und innen eine 6 mm starke Scheibe mit einer Low-E-Beschichtung, ist mit Argon gefüllt. Als Sonnenschutz werden perforierte Lamellenstoren aus Edelstahl in den 20 cm breiten Zwischenraum integriert.

Diese zweischalige Fassade dient hauptsächlich als Schutz vor Verkehrslärm. Sie ermöglicht eine natürliche Belüftung der Büros während eines Großteils des Jahres. Bei zu tiefen und zu hohen Außentemperaturen wird eine mechanische Belüftungsanlage eingeschaltet.

Ein weiteres Beispiel für eine Zweite-Haut-Fassade mit geschoßhohem Zwischenraum ist das 31-geschossige, zylinderförmige Hochhaus für die Hauptverwaltung der RWE AG, Essen, das die Architekten Ingenhoven Overdiek und Partner 1991–97 erstellt haben. Im kreisförmigen Grundriß sind die Büros an der Peripherie entlang der Fassade angeordnet, die Nebenräume liegen im Zentrum; der Aufzugsturm bildet einen separaten Baukörper. Die runde Form wurde aus energetischen Überlegungen gewählt, da sie eine minimale Oberfläche bei einem maximalen inneren Volumen bietet. Dazu sind optimale Verhältnisse für Windströmungen und Tageslichteinfall gegeben.

Die Zweite-Haut-Fassade ist aus vorgefertigten,

symmetrically arranged point fixings. The exterior glazing is curved, in line with the curvature of the ground plan, while the interior façade traces a polygonal line around the curvature. It consists of 1.35 × 2.75 m modules with alternate fixed glazings and side/bottom hung windows. The 29 mm thick insulating glass, with an 8 mm sheet on the outside and a 6 mm low-E coated sheet on the inside, has a cavity filled with argon. Perforated louvre blinds of stainless steel are fitted as solar control in the 20 cm wide cavity.

This double-skin façade serves mainly as protection against traffic noise. It enables natural ventilation of the offices for most of the year. If the outside temperature is too low or too high a mechanical ventilation system is switched on.

Another example of a double-skin façade with storey-high cavity is the 31-floor, cylindrical-

Im zylinderförmigen Hochhaus sind die Büros entlang der Fassade, die Nebenräume im Zentrum organisiert. Der Aufzugsturm bildet einen separaten Baukörper.
Hauptverwaltung der RWE, Essen, 1991–97, Ingenhoven Overdiek und Partner.
The offices in this cylindrical high-rise are along the façade, and the ancillary areas in the centre. The lift tower forms a separate volume. RWE headquarters, Essen, 1991–97, Ingenhoven Overdiek and Partners.

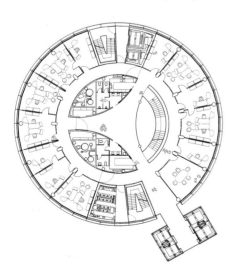

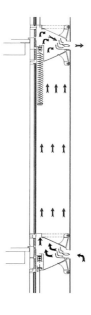

Für die Durchlüftung des Zwischenraums sind Lüftungskästen vor jeder Geschoßdecke angeordnet (oben).
Die Innenfassade ist mit raumhohen Horizontal-Schiebetüren ausgestattet (unten).
Hauptverwaltung der RWE, Essen, 1991–97, Ingenhoven Overdiek und Partner.
For ventilating the cavity, ventilation units are fitted in front of each floor slab (top).
The inner façade has room-high horizontal sliding doors (bottom).
RWE headquarters, Essen, 1991–97, Ingenhoven Overdiek and Partners.

geschoßhohen Elementen von 1.97 m Breite und 3.59 m Höhe gefertigt. Die Außenhaut besteht aus 10 mm starken ESG-Scheiben mit acht punktförmigen, versenkten Befestigungen. Die Innenfassade ist mit raumhohen Horizontal-Schiebetüren ausgestattet, die mit einem Wärmeschutzglas verglast sind. Die Schiebetüren können in der Regel aus Sicherheitsgründen maximal 13.5 cm geöffnet werden, für Reinigungs- und Wartungsarbeiten jedoch vollständig. Im 50 cm tiefen Luftzwischenraum sind Aluminium-Raffstoren für den Sonnenschutz integriert.
Die Durchlüftung des Zwischenraums erfolgt über Lüftungskästen, die jeder Geschoßdecke vorgelagert sind. Die abgerundete Form des Kastens – von den Architekten «Fischmaul» genannt – bildet einen 15 cm hohen Lüftungsschlitz. Um zu verhindern, daß verbrauchte und stark erwärmte Abluft aus einem Zwischenraum in den nächsten einströmt, wurden jeweils zwei nebeneinanderliegende Fassadenzwischenräume zu einem Abschnitt zusammengebaut. Der Lufteinlaß ist bei einem Feld unten, der Abzug beim anderen Feld oben angeordnet, so daß die Luft den Zwischenraum diagonal durchströmt.
Zur Unterstützung der natürlichen Belüftung im Winter und im Sommer sind die Innenräume mit einer Quellüftung ausgestattet. Die Betondecken sind mit perforierten Blechpaneelen verkleidet und wirken so als Speichermasse. Zur Raumkühlung sind zusätzlich Kühlrippen eingebaut. Für eine optimale Tageslichtnutzung wählten die Architekten für die Außenhaut ein extra-weißes Glas.

shaped high-rise of the headquarters of RWE AG in Essen, built by the architects Ingenhoven Overdiek and Partners in 1991–97. The offices are arranged along the façade, around the outer rim of the circular ground plan, and the ancillary spaces are in the centre; the lift tower is a separate unit.
The round shape was chosen for energy-conservation reasons, as it offers minimum surface area for maximum inner volume. It also gives optimum conditions for wind flows and natural lighting.
The double-skin façade is made of prefabricated, storey-high modules 1.97 m in width and 3.59 m high. The outer skin consists of 10 mm thick toughened glass with eight countersunk bolts. The inner façade is fitted with room-high horizontal sliding doors glazed with thermally insulating glass. The sliding doors can in general be opened to a maximum of 13.5 cm, for safety reasons, but for cleaning and maintenance they will open fully. Integrated into the 50 cm wide air cavity are aluminium Venetian blinds for solar control.
The cavity is ventilated via ventilation units fitted in front of each floor slab. The tapered form of the unit – given the nickname "fish's mouth" by the architects – forms a 15 cm high ventilation slit. To prevent the used, warmed air from one cavity being drawn into the next cavity, each two adjacent façade cavities are built as one section. In each section the air inlet is in one façade module at the bottom and the outlet is at the other module at the top, thus producing a diagonal air flow through the cavity.
To support natural ventilation in winter and summer the interiors are fitted with a displace-

Ein drittes Beispiel einer Zweite-Haut-Fassade mit geschoßhohem Zwischenraum ist das Hochhaus «Düsseldorfer Stadttor», von den Architekten Petzinka Pink und Partner 1991–97 erstellt. Das 70 m hohe rhomboide Gebäude steht über dem Südportal des Rheinufertunnels in Düsseldorf. Es besteht aus zwei parallelen, 16geschossigen Türmen, die durch drei durchgehende Attikageschosse miteinander verbunden sind. Auf diese Weise entsteht in der Mitte ein 56 m hohes Atrium. Das Hochhaus ist von einer durchgehenden Glashaut umhüllt, welche die Innenräume gegen Windwirkungen und Verkehrslärm schützt. Bei den außenliegenden, verkehrsausgesetzten Büros ist die Fassade zweischalig ausgeführt. Die Innenfassade besteht aus 1.5 × 2.85 m großen Rahmenelementen aus Brettschichtholz, die mit Low-E-beschichteten Isoliergläsern verglast sind. In jeder

ment ventilation system. The concrete floors are clad with panels of perforated metal sheet, and as a result they act as a thermal store. For cooling the rooms additional cooling ribs are integrated. For maximum daylighting the architects chose an extra-white glass for the outer skin.

A third example of a double-skin façade with storey-high cavity is the "Düsseldorfer Stadttor" high-rise, built by the architects Petzinka Pink and Partners in 1991–97. The 70 m high, rhomboid-shaped building stands at the southern entrance to the Rhine tunnel in Düsseldorf. It consists of two parallel office towers with 16 storeys, connected by three continuous attic storeys; this arrangement gives rise to a 56 m high atrium in the centre. The entire building is enclosed in a glass skin which reduces wind pressure and traf-

Das rhomboide Gebäude ist mit einer durchgehenden Glashaut gegen Winddruck und Verkehrslärm abgeschirmt.
«Düsseldorfer Stadttor», Düsseldorf, 1991–97, Petzinka Pink und Partner.
The rhomboid-shaped building is protected against wind pressure and traffic noise by a continuous glass skin.
"Düsseldorfer Stadttor", Düsseldorf, 1991–97, Petzinka Pink and Partners.

Die natürliche Belüftung erfolgt über Lüftungskästen, die mit innenliegenden, mechanisch verschließbaren Klappen versehen sind (oben).
In jeder zweiten Achse ist die Innenfassade mit geschoßhohen Wendeflügeln ausgestattet. Der begehbare Zwischenraum ist mit einem Sicherheitsgeländer versehen (unten).
«Düsseldorfer Stadttor», Düsseldorf, 1991–97, Petzinka Pink und Partner.
Natural ventilation is via ventilation units fitted on the inside with mechanically operating louvres (top).
The interior façade consists of storey-high modules, which are center rotating doors at alternate bays.
The walk-in cavity has a safety railing (bottom).
"Düsseldorfer Stadttor", Düsseldorf, 1991–97, Petzinka Pink and Partners.

zweiten Achse sind sie als Wendeflügel ausgeführt, die für die natürliche Be- und Entlüftung der Büros geöffnet werden können und als Zugang zum Zwischenraum dienen. Der geschoßhohe Fassadenzwischenraum ist je nach Geometrie des Grundrisses 0.9 m oder 1.4 m breit und vertikal mit Glasschotten unterteilt. Da er begehbar ist, wurde er mit einem Sicherheitsgeländer versehen. Die natürliche Belüftung des Zwischenraums erfolgt über Lüftungskästen, die den Geschoßdeckenstirnen vorgesetzt sind. Sie sind mit innenliegenden, mechanisch verschließbaren Klappen versehen, welche die Intensität der Luftströmung im Winter und im Sommer regulieren. Die Kästen sind alternierend als Zu- und Abluftkasten ausgebildet, um Kurzschlußströme zwischen frischer Zuluft und erwärmter Abluft von Geschoß zu Geschoß zu vermeiden. Zur Optimierung der aerodynamischen Gestaltung der Lüftungskästen wurden umfangreiche Strömungssimulationen durchgeführt. Die außenliegende Verglasung besteht aus 1.49×2.85 m großen, 12 bzw. 15 mm starken ESG-Scheiben, die oben und unten in den Lüftungskästen linear, auf Geländerhöhe punktuell befestigt sind. Im Zwischenraum sind unmittelbar hinter der Außenverglasung hochreflektierende Lamellenraffstoren aus Aluminium angeordnet, die einen g-Wert von 0.10 sicherstellen. Mit geschlossenen Lüftungsklappen erreicht die Gesamtkonstruktion einen k-Wert von 1.1 W/m²K.
Diese zweischalige Konstruktion ermöglicht eine natürliche Raumlüftung auch in 50 m Höhe während 60 % des Jahres. Bei extremen Außen-

fic noise in the office. The façade of the outer offices subject to more traffic noise is designed as a double-skin façade.
The interior façade consists of 1.5×2.85 modules of laminated wood frame, glazed with low-E coated insulating glass. At alternate bays the modules are center rotating to provide natural ventilation of the offices and to give access to the cavity. The storey-high cavity is either 0.9 m or 1.4 m wide, depending on the geometry of the ground plan, and is divided vertically with glass division screens. A safety railing is attached because the cavity can be accessed for cleaning and maintenance. The cavity is ventilated naturally via ventilation units fitted to the front of the floor slabs. They are fitted on the inside with mechanically operating louvres which regulate the air flow of air in winter and summer. The units are designed at alternate bays as an outlet or inlet unit to avoid short-circuit flows between fresh air and warmed air from floor to floor. Extensive air-flow simulations were carried out to optimise the aerodynamic design of the ventilation units. The outer glazing consists of 1.49×2.85 m toughened glass, either 12 or 15 mm thick; these sheets are fixed in a linear plane top and bottom to the ventilation units, and point fixed at the level of the railings. In the cavity, directly behind the outer glazing are highly reflecting louvre blinds of aluminium, which give a g-factor of 0.10. When the air louvres are closed the entire construction gives a U-value of 1.1 W/m²K. This double-skin construction enables natural ventilation of the in-

141

temperaturen oder zu hohem Winddruck wird eine mechanische Lüftung eingeschaltet. Zur Aufnahme der Kühllast sind Kühldecken eingebaut.

Beim Hauptsitz der Commerzbank, 1991–97, Frankfurt am Main, haben die Architekten Foster und Partner das Prinzip «Pufferzone» gleich in zwei Varianten zur natürlichen Belüftung der Büros eingesetzt: als Zweite-Haut-Fassade und als Wintergarten.

Das 60stöckige Hochhaus ist in viergeschossige Einheiten unterteilt, die spiralförmig gegeneinander versetzt sind. In jeder Einheit nehmen die Büroflächen zwei Seiten, der Wintergarten die dritte Seite des leicht abgerundeten Grundrisses ein. Tragstruktur, Erschließung und Nebenräume sind in den Ecken angeordnet. Im Zentrum des Gebäudes befindet sich ein gebäudehohes Atrium, das in zwölfgeschossige Abschnitte unterteilt ist und jeweils drei Wintergärten räumlich miteinander verbindet.

Beim Wettbewerb wurde eine zweischalige Fassade für die natürliche Belüftung der außenliegenden Bürobereiche vorgeschlagen. Sie bestand aus einer dreigeschossigen, geschlossenen Außenhaut, einem durchgehenden Zwischenraum und einer Innenfassade mit Fenstern zum Öffnen. Um den Zwischenraum abzuschließen, waren Lüftungsklappen am unteren und oberen Ende der jeweiligen Abschnitte vorgesehen. Die Wintergärten waren durch ein gebäudehohes Atrium verbunden, um die natürliche Belüftung des Gebäudes zu ermöglichen.

In der Weiterbearbeitung der Zweite-Haut-Fassade wurde die Höhe des Zwischenraumes auf die Fensterhöhe beschränkt, weil der Brüstungsbereich durch die Vierendeel-Tragkonstruktion 1.5 m

terior even at 50 m above ground level, for 60 % of the year. When outside temperatures are extreme, or under high wind conditions, mechanical ventilation systems are switched on. Chilled ceilings are used to take up cooling loads.

For the headquarters of the Commerzbank in Frankfurt am Main, built 1991–97 by Foster and Partners, two variations on the principle of the "buffer zone" for natural ventilation of the offices were used: as a double-skin façade and as a winter garden. The 60-storey high-rise is divided into units comprising four floors, offset spirally against each other. In each unit the office space occupies two sides of the gently curved floor plan, the winter garden occupies the third side. The support structure, circulation areas and service rooms are located in the corners. In the centre of the building is a full-high atrium, divided into twelve-storey sections and linking three winter gardens spatially with each other. In the competition a double-skin façade was suggested for the natural ventilation of the outer office areas. It consisted of a three-storey, sealed outer skin, a continuous cavity and an inner façade with opening windows. To close off the cavity, air louvres were provided at the lower

Das Hochhaus ist in viergeschossige Einheiten unterteilt, die spiralförmig gegeneinander versetzt sind. In jeder Einheit nehmen die Büroflächen zwei Seiten und der Wintergarten die dritte des leicht abgerundeten Grundrisses ein.
Commerzbank, Frankfurt a. M., 1991–97, Foster und Partner.
The high-rise is divided into four-storey units, offset against each other in a spiral pattern. In each unit the offices occupy two sides and the winter garden the third side in a slightly rounded ground plan.
Commerzbank, Frankfurt a. M., 1991–97, Foster and Partners.

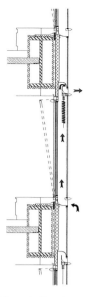

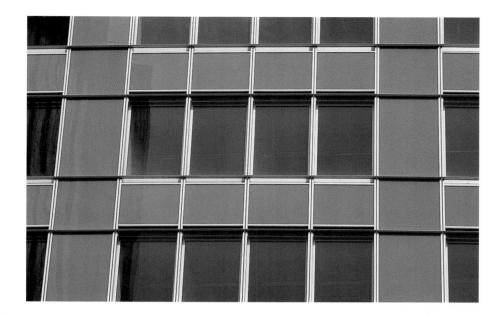

Die Zweite-Haut-Fassade übernimmt die Höhe zwischen den Vierendelträgern. Die Zu- und Abluftöffnungen sind ohne schließbare Klappen ausgeführt. Das gebäudehohe Atrium ist in 12geschossige Abschnitte unterteilt und verbindet jeweils drei Wintergärten miteinander.
Commerzbank, Frankfurt a. M., 1991–97, Foster und Partner.
The double-skin façade spans the distance between the Vierendeel girders. The inlet and outlet openings are not closable.
The full-height atrium is divided into 12-floor sections each linking together three winter gardens.
Commerzbank, Frankfurt a. M., 1991–97, Foster and Partners.

hoch wurde. Die Außenhaut besteht jetzt aus 1.4 × 2.25 m großen, 8 mm starken ESG-Scheiben. Sie liegt 20 cm vor der Innenfassade aus 1.38 × 2.12 m großen Dreh-Kipp-Flügeln mit Low-E-beschichtetem Isolierglas.

Die 12 cm hohen Zu- und Abluftöffnungen befinden sich ober- und unterhalb der mit grau emaillierten Glasscheiben verkleideten Brüstung und sind ohne schließbare Klappen ausgeführt.

Für den Sonnen- und Blendschutz sind Aluminiumlamellen mit elektrischem Antrieb in den Zwischenraum eingebaut.

In der Weiterbearbeitung der Wintergärten sind jeweils drei Wintergärten über ein zwölfgeschossiges Atrium in der Gebäudemitte räumlich miteinander verbunden. Sie sind mit einer 14 m hohen, 3° nach außen geneigten Verglasung mit Low-E-beschichtetem Isolierglas abgeschlossen. Für die natürliche Belüftung sind 3 × 3.6 m große Schwingflügel im oberen Bereich eingebaut.

In kalten Jahreszeiten bleibt die Gartenverglasung geschlossen, so daß sich die Wintergärten dank der Sonnenstrahlung natürlich erwärmen und als Klimapuffer wirken können.

Wenn die Gartenverglasung an wärmeren Tagen geöffnet wird, strömt die Außenluft hinein und steigt oder sinkt im mehrgeschossigen Atrium – je nach herrschenden Temperaturen und Druckverhältnissen – und tritt beim nächsten Wintergarten wieder aus.

Dank diesem Frischluftstrom können die Benutzer der innenliegenden Bürobereiche ihre Räume durch Öffnen der Fenster natürlich belüften.

and upper ends of the cavity. The winter gardens were linked by an atrium extending the height of the building, to enable the natural ventilation of the building.

Further work on the double-skin façade resulted in a reduction in the height of the cavity, down to the height of a window, because the Vierendeel load bearing structure forms a parapet of 1.5 m in height. The outer skin now consists of 1.4 × 2.25 m sheets of 8 mm toughened glass. It is 20 cm in front of the inner façade which consists of 1.38 × 2.12 m side/bottom hung windows with low-E coated insulating glass. The 12 cm high air inlets and outlets are located above and below the grey fritted glass cladding on the parapets; these vents are not closable. For solar control and protection against glare electrically operated aluminium louvres are built into the cavity.

Further work on the winter gardens produced a design which spatially links three winter gardens within the twelve-storey atrium, which is in the centre of the building. Each winter garden is enclosed in a 14 m high, 3° outwardly tilting glazing of insulating glass with low-E coating. For natural ventilation 3 × 3.6 m centre pivoting windows are integrated into the upper part. In colder periods of the year the glazing of the winter garden remains closed, so that air in the winter garden can warm up, as in a greenhouse, and act as a climate buffer zone. When the windows in the winter garden are opened on warmer days the outer air flows in and rises or falls in the multi-storey atrium, depending on the tempera-

Für das 21geschossige Hochhaus der debis-Hauptverwaltung am Potsdamerplatz in Berlin, 1991–97, haben die Architekten Renzo Piano Building Workshop und Christoph Kohlbecker einen anderen Lösungsansatz verfolgt: Mit der finanziellen Unterstützung des «Joule II»-Programms der Europäischen Union haben sie eine zweischalige Fassade mit einer Außenhaut aus rahmenlosen, drehbaren Glaslamellen entwickelt, die im Winter als Wärmepuffer dient und im Sommer wie eine einschalige Fassade mit außenliegendem Sonnenschutz funktioniert. Die 85 m hohe Zweite-Haut-Fassade ist auf das Gebäuderaster von 8.1 m ausgelegt, welches jeweils in sechs Fassadenfelder unterteilt ist. Innenliegend sind 1.35 × 3.75 m große Fassadenelemente montiert, die in der Mitte mit einem Dreh-Kipp-Flügel und oben mit einem Kippflügel mit elektrischem Antrieb ausgestattet sind. Im Brüstungsbereich ist ein Sandwich-Paneel mit einer außenliegenden, grau emaillierten Glasscheibe eingebaut, teilweise mit Elementen aus Terrakotta verkleidet.
Die Außenhaut ist pro Geschoß feldweise in acht drehbare, 1.33 × 0.52 m große Glaslamellen aus 2 × 6 mm starken VSG-Scheiben unterteilt. Diese sind beidseitig von Gußkonsolen aus Aluminium gehalten und durch zwei Senkschrauben gesichert.
Jeweils sieben Glaslamellen werden über Schub-

ture and pressure conditions at the time, and exits at the next winter garden. Thanks to this flow of fresh air the people working in the inner zones can naturally ventilate their office space by opening the windows.

For the 21-storey high-rise headquarters of debis at Potsdamerplatz in Berlin, built 1991–97 by the Renzo Piano Building Workshop and Christoph Kohlbecker, a different kind of solution was studied: With financial support from the "Joule II" programme of the European Union the architects developed a double-skin façade with an outer skin of frameless, pivoting glass louvres which in winter acts as a thermal buffer and in summer like a single-skin façade with an external solar protection.
The 85 m high double-skin façade is designed to a building grid of 8.1 m, divided into six façade modules.
The interior façade consists of 1.35 × 3.75 m modules which have a side/bottom hung window in the centre and an electrically operated bottom hung window above.
At parapet level is a sandwich panel with an outer, grey fritted glass sheet, part-clad with terracotta.
Each floor of the outer skin is divided into eight pivoting, 1.33 × 0.52 glass louvres made of

Für das 21geschossige Hochhaus wurde eine zweischalige Fassade mit einer Außenhaut aus rahmenlosen, drehbaren Glaslamellen entwickelt.
Im Winter dient sie als Wärmepuffer (a), im Sommer funktioniert sie wie eine einschalige Fassade mit außenliegendem Sonnenschutz (b).
«debis»-Hauptverwaltung, Berlin, 1991–97, Renzo Piano Building Workshop mit Christoph Kohlbecker.
For the 21-storey high-rise a double-skin façade was developed with an outer skin of frameless, pivoting glass louvres.
In winter it acts a thermal buffer (a), in summer as a single-skin façade with exterior solar protection (b).
debis headquarters, Berlin, 1991–97, Renzo Piano Building Workshop in cooperation with Christoph Kohlbecker.

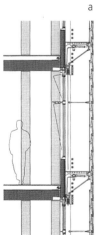
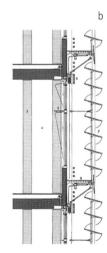

a   b

Die Außenhaut ist geschoßweise in acht drehbare Glaslamelllen unterteilt, welche beidseitig von Guß-konsolen getragen sind. Der Zwischenraum ist durch einen Gitterrost unterteilt und mit einer Glasscheibe gegen Rauchausbreitung abgedeckt.
«debis»-Hauptverwaltung, Berlin, 1991–97,
Renzo Piano Building Workshop
mit Christoph Kohlbecker.

The outer skin is divided into storey-high moduls with eight pivoting glass louvres, supported on both sides by cast brackets. The cavity is divided into sections by gantries covered with a glass pane to prevent smoke spreading.
debis headquarters, Berlin, 1991–97,
Renzo Piano Building Workshop in cooperation with Christoph Kohlbecker.

stangen und Spindelantriebe bis zu einem Winkel von 70° gedreht; die achte kann nur zu Reinigungszwecken geöffnet werden.
Der 70 cm breite Fassadenzwischenraum ist durch einen Gitterrost unterteilt, der mit einer 10 mm starken ESG-Scheibe gegen die Rauchausbreitung im Brandfall abgedeckt ist.
Vor der Innenfassade sind die Aluminium-Raffstoren für den Sonnenschutz angeordnet, die in einer Tonziegelfarbe einbrennlackiert sind.
Bei niedrigen Temperaturen im Winter bleiben die Glaslamellen geschlossen, so daß im Fassadenzwischenraum ein ruhendes Luftpolster entsteht.
Im geschlossenen Zustand stellen die umlaufenden, 10 mm breiten Spalten um die Glaslamellen den minimalen Luftaustausch sicher.
An wärmeren Tagen können die Benutzer die Fenster öffnen und die im Zwischenraum von der Sonnenstrahlung erwärmte Luft in ihre Räume einströmen lassen.
Bei höheren Außentemperaturen werden die Lamellen ausgeschwenkt, so daß die Außenluft den Zwischenraum durchströmen kann.
Damit können die Büros während 60 % des Jahres natürlich belüftet werden.
Für Temperaturen unter 5 °C und über 20 °C ist eine mechanische Belüftung eingebaut.
Zur Nachtauskühlung der Gebäudespeichermasse werden die Kippflügel und die Glaslamellen automatisch geöffnet.

2 × 6 mm laminated glass. These are held on both sides by cast aluminium brackets and two countersunk bolts. Sets of seven glass louvres can be pivoted via bars and spindle motors to an angle of 70°; the eighth louvre can only be opened for cleaning. The 70 cm wide façade cavity is divided by gantries covered with a 10 mm sheet of toughened glass, which prevents smoke spreading in the event of fire.
Arranged in front of the inner façade are aluminium Venetian blinds for solar control; the blinds are powder coated in a brick colour.
In low temperatures in winter the louvres remain closed, so that an air buffer is created in the façade cavity.
When closed the 10 mm wide gaps around the glass louvres ensure a minimal air exchange.
On warmer days the users can open the windows and admit the air from the cavity which has been warmed by the sun's rays.
When temperatures are higher outside, the louvres can be tilted to let the outside air to flow through the cavity. This enables the offices to be naturally ventilated for 60 % of the year.
For temperatures below – 5° C and above 20° C a mechanical ventilation system is used.
For night-time cooling of the building's thermal mass the tilting windows and the glass louvres are automatically opened.

Beim Wettbewerbsentwurf für die Hauptverwaltung der IG Metall in Frankfurt am Main, 1996, haben die Architekten Foster und Partner eine zweischalige Fassade mit außenliegenden, großformatigen Glaslamellen vorgeschlagen.

Foster und Partner haben den Wettbewerb zwar nicht gewonnen, aber dennoch einen Prototypen der Fassade erstellt, der als geschoßhohes, raumtiefes Modell an der Constructec '96 in Hannover ausgestellt war.

Im Entwurf bestand das 72 m hohe Gebäude aus zwei leicht gegeneinander verschobenen Bürotürmen, verbunden durch ein vollverglastes, gebäudehohes Atrium mit der vertikalen Erschließung. Für die natürliche Belüftung der Büros wurde eine Zweite-Haut-Fassade entwickelt.

For the competition for the headquarters of IG Metall in Frankfurt am Main, in 1996, Foster and Partners designed a double-skin façade with exterior, large-size glass louvres.

Foster and Partners did not win the competition, but nevertheless built a prototype of the façade, which they exhibited as a storey-high, room-deep model at Constructec '96 in Hanover.

In the design the 72 m high building consisted of two office towers shifted together slightly, and linked by a fully glazed, building-high atrium with service cores.

For natural ventilation of the offices a double-skin façade was developed.

The outer façade is divided per floor into three large-sized, axis-wide glass louvres which are

Die zwei gegeneinander leicht verschobenen Bürotürme sind durch ein vollverglastes, gebäudehohes Atrium mit der vertikalen Erschließung verbunden.
IG Metall, Wettbewerb, Frankfurt a. M., 1996, Foster und Partner.
The two office towers are slightly shifted together and are linked by a fully glazed, building-high atrium with vertical service core.
IG Metall, Competition, Frankfurt a. M., 1996, Foster and Partners.

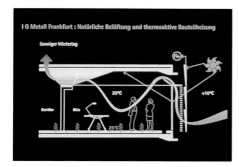

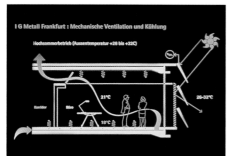

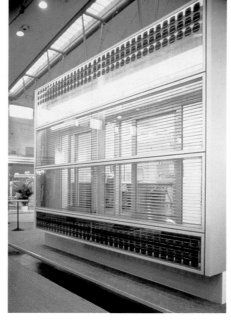

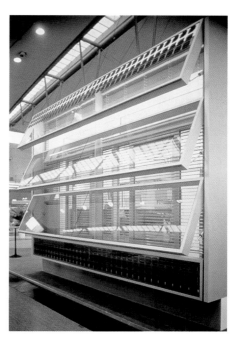

Die Außenfassade wurde geschoßweise in drei groß-formatige, achsenbreite Glaslamellen unterteilt. Für die natürliche Belüftung der Büros können die Benutzer die Schiebetüren und die Lüftungsflügel der Innenfassade von Hand öffnen.
IG Metall, Wettbewerb, Frankfurt a. M., 1996, Foster und Partner.

The outer façade is divided each floor into three, large-sized, axis-wide glass louvres. For natural ventilation of the offices the occupants can open the sliding doors and the bottom hung windows on the interior façade by hand.
IG Metall, Competition, Frankfurt a. M., 1996, Foster and Partners.

Die Außenfassade ist pro Geschoß in drei großformatige, achsenbreite Glaslamellen unterteilt, die als elektrisch betriebene Klappflügel aus einem umlaufenden Aluminiumrahmen und einer Einfachverglasung ausgeführt sind. Die obersten Lamellen sind zu einem Drittel mit PV-Zellen belegt, die den Strom für die Motoren der Fassadentechnik liefern.

Im begehbaren Zwischenraum ist die tragende Stahlstruktur des Gebäudes untergebracht.

Die Innenfassade ist mit breiten Horizontal-Schiebetüren und Kippflügeln im Oberlichtbereich ausgestattet. Sie sind mit Isoliergläsern versehen und dienen für die Be- und Entlüftung der Büros sowie als Zugang zum Zwischenraum.

Für den Sonnenschutz sind breite Metallamellen hinter der Außenfassade vorgesehen.

Die Benutzer können die Schiebetüren und Lüftungsflügel von Hand öffnen und so ihre Räume natürlich belüften.

Eine Querlüftung der Büros ist durch das Öffnen von weiteren Lüftungsflügeln im Flurbereich möglich. Auf diese Weise wird das verglaste, gebäudehohe Atrium als Abluftkamin aktiviert.

Das gleiche Lüftungskonzept kann während der Nacht eingesetzt werden, um die Speichermasse des Gebäudes zu kühlen.

Für die Jahreszeiten mit zu hohen oder zu niedrigen Außenlufttemperaturen ist eine Quellüftung vorgesehen sowie ein in den Betondecken eingelegtes Rohrsystem für Heizung oder Kühlung.

designed as electrically operated top hung glass panels in an aluminium frame. One third of the area of the uppermost louvres are fitted with photovoltaic cells which provide the power for the motors in the façade system.

The building's steel frame is integrated into the walk-in façade cavity.

The inner façade is fitted with wide horizontal glass sliding doors and bottom hung window panes in the upper zone. They are made of insulating glass and provide both ventilation for the offices as well as access to the cavity.

For solar control wide metal louvres are provided behind the outer façade.

The users can open the sliding doors and the bottom hung windows by hand and thus ventilate their office space naturally.

Cross-ventilation of the offices is possible by opening windows along the corridor. In this way the glazed, building-high atrium acts as a chimney.

The same ventilation concept can be used during the night, to cool the building's thermal mass.

For seasons when the outside air temperature is too high or too low a displacement ventilation system is provided as well as a heating and cooling pipe system built into the concrete floors.

Eine Zweite-Haut-Fassade mit Glaslamellen findet sich auch beim Bürohochhaus und beim Wohnbau an der Ecke Bent Street und Macquarie Street in Sydney, welche der Renzo Piano Building Workshop 1996–2000 für die Immobiliengesellschaft Lend Lease realisierte.

Der linsenförmige Grundriß des 44geschossigen Hochhauses ist Nord-Süd gerichtet. Die Büros liegen entlang der West- und der Ostfassade, dazwischen befinden sich die Nebenräume.

Die gebogenen West- und Ostfassaden sind über das Bauvolumen fortgesetzt; sie bilden im Grundriß die «Flossen», im Aufriß die «Segel». Damit entsteht ein riesiger Witterungsschutzschild, der an eine Muschel erinnert.

Die West- und Ostfassaden sind aus geschoßhohen «structural glazing»-Elementen gebaut. Im Durchsichtsbereich wurden 1.35 × 2.4 m große Isolierscheiben aus weißem Glas mit einer weißen Randbedruckung verwendet. Außen liegt eine VSG-Scheibe, die aus einer 6 mm starken Float-Scheibe

A double-skin façade with glass louvres will be used in the office high-rise and apartment building on the corner of Bent Street and Macquarie Street in Sydney, built between 1996 and 2000 by the Renzo Piano Building Workshop for the developer Lend Lease.

The lens-shaped ground plan of the 44-storey high-rise runs north-south, with the offices along the west and east façades and service space in between. The curved west and east façades are continued throughout the building volume; in ground plan they form the "fins", and in elevation the "sails", thus producing a giant weather shield, reminiscent of a shell.

The west and east façades are of storey-high structural glazing units. The glass in the view out area is of 1.35 × 2.4 m insulating extra-white glass with an edge frit. On the outside is a laminated glass consisting of a 6 mm thick sheet with a continuous white-fritted dot pattern on the edge and a sheet of 6 mm low-E coated float-

Die leicht gebogenen West- und Ostfassaden bilden einen riesigen Witterungsschutzschild, der an eine Muschel erinnert.
Bürohochhaus und Wohnbau, Sydney, 1996–2000, Renzo Piano Building Workshop.
The slightly curved west and east façades form a giant weather protection shield reminiscent of a shell.
Office high-rise and apartment building, Sydney, 1996–2000, Renzo Piano Building Workshop.

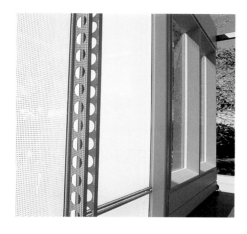

Im Durchsichtsbereich sind Isolierscheiben aus
weißem Glas mit einer Randbedruckung eingesetzt.
Die geschlossenen Bereiche sind durch eine Verglasung aus weißem Glas mit weißem Punktraster verkleidet (oben).
Die Außenverglasung der Wintergärten ist in Glaslamellen unterteilt, die beidseitig von Edelstahlkonsolen
und doppelten Glasposten gehalten werden (unten).
Bürohochhaus und Wohnbau, Sydney, 1996 – 2000,
Renzo Piano Building Workshop.

In the view out area windows of extra-white insulat-
ing glass with a printed edge are used. The closed
areas are clad with extra-white glazing printed with
a white dot grid (top).
The outer glazing of the winter garden is divided
into louvres, attached on both sides to stainless steel
brackets and double glass mullions (bottom).
Office and apartment building, Sydney, 1996 – 2000,
Renzo Piano Buiding Workshop.

mit einem verlaufenden, weiß emaillierten Punktraster im Randbereich und aus einer 6 mm starken
Scheibe mit Low-E-Beschichtung besteht. Innen
liegt ebenfalls eine 6 mm starke Float-Scheibe mit
Low-E-Beschichtung. Die Kombination von weißem
Glas und neutralen Beschichtungen läßt Tageslicht
mit hoher Farbechtheit durch, trotz des tiefen
τ-Werts von 0.34. Für den Sonnen- und Blendschutz sind innenliegende Stoffstoren vorgesehen.
Die geschlossenen Bereiche vor der Brüstung und
den Stützen sind mit weißem 2 × 6 mm VSG-Glas
verkleidet, welches mit einem weißen Punktraster
von 60prozentigem Deckungsgrad emailliert ist
und vor weiß einbrennlackierten Blechpaneelen
liegt. Diese emaillierte Verglasung ist bei den
«Flossen» und den «Segeln» mit verlaufendem
Muster weitergeführt.
An der schmalen Nord- und Südseite schaffen die
«Flossen» je eine windgeschützte Zone, die durch
eine zweischalige Fassade mit einem breiten Zwischenraum, einer Art «Wintergarten», charakterisiert ist.
Da der «Wintergarten» natürlich belüftet ist und
einen einmaligen Blick auf das Opernhaus von
Jørn Utzon und den Hafen bietet, wird er für Be-
sprechungen, Pausen oder Entspannung genutzt.
Die Außenverglasung besteht aus 12 mm starken
ESG-Scheiben aus weißem Glas. Sie ist pro
Geschoß in sechs 1.20 × 0.46 m große Glaslamellen unterteilt, die beidseitig von Edelstahlkonsolen gehalten werden. Die oberen vier Lamellen sind bis zu einem Winkel von 45° drehbar. Die
unteren zwei sind fest und dienen als Brüstung.
Für den Sonnenschutz sind außenliegende Stoff-
rollos, bei der sonnenexponierten Nordfassade zusätzlich auskragende Lamellendächer vorgesehen.
Entsprechend der Nutzung ist die Innenfassade mit
Türen, Festverglasungen und Klappflügeln für die
Raumbelüftung gestaltet.

glass. Inside is a 6 mm sheet of low-E coated
float-glass. The combination of extra-white glass
and neutral coat admits daylight with a very natural colour, despite the low τ-value of 0.34. Interior, textile blinds are provided for solar control and glare protection.
The opaque areas in front of the parapet and the
columns are clad with 2 × 6 mm laminated extra-
white glass fritted with a white dot pattern giving
60 % cover; behind this glass cladding are white
powder-coated metal sheets. This fritted glazing
is continued with a decreasing dot pattern on the
"fins" and the "sails".
On the narrow north and south sides the "fins"
create a wind-protected zone characterised by a
double-skin façade with a wide cavity, like a winter garden. As this "winter garden" zone is naturally ventilated and has a spectacular view of Jørn
Utzon's Opera House and of the harbour, it is
used for meeting, break or relax. The outer
glazing consists of laminated 12 mm toughened
extra-white glass. Each floor is divided into six
1.20 × 0.46 m glass louvres which are fixed on
both sides by stainless steel brackets. The upper
four louvres can be rotated through 45°. The
lower two are fixed and serve as parapets. For
solar control there are exterior textile blinds, and
on the north façade which is exposed to the sun,
there are in addition horizontal metal sunscreens.
In accordance with floor plan requirements, the
inner façade is fitted with doors, fixed glazing
units and bottom hung windows for ventilation.

A similar glass construction will be used for
the 16-floor apartment block.
Here the "winter gardens" serve as an extension
of the living area. The glass louvres will be fixed
on double glass mullions and can be rotated
through 90°.

149

Eine ähnliche Glaskonstruktion ist auch beim 16geschossigen Wohnhaus realisiert. Hier dienen die «Wintergärten» als Erweiterung des Wohnraumes. Die Glaslamellen werden an doppelten Glaspfosten befestigt und sind bis zu einem Winkel von 90°drehbar.

Gebäudehohe Zweite-Haut-Fassaden

Bei einer Zweite-Haut-Fassade mit einem gebäudehohen Fassadenzwischenraum ist zu vermeiden, daß die mit steigener Höhe stark erwärmte Luft in den oberen Stockwerken durch offene Fenster wieder in die Innenräume einströmt. Deshalb wird der gebäudehohe Zwischenraum als großer Schacht für die Abluft oder die Zuluft verwendet.

Sauerbruch Hutton Architekten haben beim Erweiterungsbau für die Hauptverwaltung der GSW (Gemeinnützige Siedlungs- und Wohnbaugenossenschaft mbH) in Berlin, 1995–99, eine Zweite-Haut-Fassade mit gebäudehohem Zwischenraum als Abluftschacht realisiert. Der Gebäudekomplex besteht aus einem dreigeschossigen Flachbau mit ovalem Aufbau und einem schmalen, 19geschossigen Hochhaus mit einem leicht geschwungenen Grundriß von 10 m Breite und 65 m Länge. Die zweischalige Fassadenkonstruktion liegt an der Westseite. Die Innenfassade ist in Elementbauweise mit 1.8×1.9 m großen Fensterflügeln ausgestattet, die mit einem elektrischen Motor nach außen gekippt werden können. Die Außenfassade ist eine Pfosten-Riegel-Konstruktion, welche mit 10 mm starken ESG-Scheiben verglast ist. Am Fuß und

Building-High Double-Skin Façades

In double-skin façades with a full, building-high cavity one problem that has to be overcome is that of the rising air, which has been warmed, re-entering the building through open windows at the upper levels. To prevent this happening the full-high cavity is used as a large shaft either for air inflow or outflow.

Sauerbruch Hutton Architects built a full-high cavity as an air outlet shaft for the headquarters of the GSW (Gemeinnützige Siedlungs- und Wohnbaugenossenschaft mbH) in Berlin. The building complex consists of a three-storey basement with an oval pavilion on the roof and a 19-storey high-rise with a gently curved ground plan 10 m wide and 65 m long.
The double-skin façade is on the west side.
The inner façade consists of prefabricated mod-

Das schmale, 19-geschossige Hochhaus weist einen leicht geschwungenen Grundriß auf. Die Zweite-Haut-Fassade mit gebäudehohem Zwischenraum liegt an der Westseite.
Hauptverwaltung der GSW, Berlin, 1995–99, Sauerbruch Hutton Architekten.
The narrow, 19-storey high-rise building has a slightly rounded ground plan. The double-skin façade with full-height cavity is on the west side.
GSW headquarters, Berlin, 1995–99,
Sauerbruch Hutton Architects.

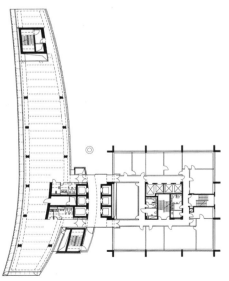

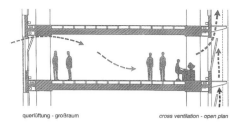

querlüftung - großraum   cross ventilation - open plan

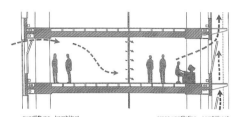

querlüftung - kombi/ost   cross ventilation - combi/east

Die Innenfassade ist mit nach außen kippenden Fensterflügeln ausgestattet. Die Außenfassade ist mit ESG-Scheiben festverglast. Im Zwischenraum sind Laufstege mit Gitterrosten für die Wartung eingebaut (rechts).

Durch den natürlichen Auftrieb erzeugt die steigende Warmluft im Zwischenraum der Westfassade einen Unterdruck, der die Abluft aus den Innenräumen absaugt und frische Außenluft bei der Ostfassade nachzieht (links).

Hauptverwaltung der GSW, Berlin, 1995–99, Sauerbruch Hutton Architekten.

The interior façade is fitted with outwardly bottom hung windows. The outer façade has fixed glazing of toughened glass. Gantries are built into the cavity for maintenance (right).

Through natural stack effect the warm air rising in the cavity on the west façade creates low pressure which draws in fresh outside air from the east façade (left).

GSW headquarters, Berlin, 1995–99, Sauerbruch Hutton Architects.

am Dachrand befinden sich bewegliche Lüftungsklappen.

Ein speziell aerodynamisch entwickeltes Vordach über dem Dachrand schützt den Zwischenraum vor Regeneintritt.

Für die Wartung sind Laufstege mit Gitterrosten im 0.9 m breiten Zwischenraum eingebaut. Vertikale, 0.6 × 2.9 m große Lamellen aus Aluminiumblech dienen als Sonnenschutz. Sie sind drehbar und mit insgesamt neun Rottönen verschiedener Helligkeit einbrennlackiert. Im Ruhezustand werden sie in Dreiergruppen senkrecht zur Fassade zurückgefaltet.

Die Bürogeschosse werden natürlich durchlüftet. Aufgrund des thermischen Auftriebs steigt die Luft im Zwischenraum der Westfassade, und es bildet sich im Bereich der unteren Geschosse ein Unterdruck. Dieser saugt bei geöffneten Flügeln die verbrauchte Luft aus den Innenräumen ab, während frische Außenluft an der Ostfassade nachgezogen wird. Der aerodynamisch geformte Dachabschluß verstärkt den Unterdruck und unterstützt damit den Kamineffekt.

Die Ostfassade wurde ursprünglich als einschalige Konstruktion mit Flügeln zum Öffnen geplant.

Dieses Lüftungskonzept wurde 1992 bei Planungsbeginn erarbeitet, als der Grundriß einbündig ausgelegt war, mit tiefen Büroräumen zur Westfassade und einem Korridor entlang der Ostfassade. In der Weiterentwicklung des Projekts wurde es jedoch notwendig, auch einen zweibündigen Grundriß zu ermöglichen. Somit wurde eine Zuluftzone zwischen den Büros an der Ostseite freigelassen, um die Außenluftzufuhr zu den Büros

ules with 1.8 × 1.9 m bottom hung windows which can be tilted outwards by means of an electric motor. The outer façade is a mullion and transom construction glazed with 10 mm toughened glass. At the base and at the roof edges are openable louvres.

A specially designed, aerodynamic canopy above the roof edge prevents rainwater entering the cavity. For maintenance gantries are built into the 0.9 m wide cavity.

Vertical, 0.6 × 2.9 m louvres of aluminium sheet serve as solar control. They are pivoting and powder coated in a total of nine shades of red of varying brightness. In the rest position they are folded back vertically to the façade in groups of three.

The office floors are naturally ventilated.

The buoyancy causes the air to rise in the cavity of the west façade and low pressure is created at the level of the lower floors. When the windows are opened, used air is drawn from the office space and fresh air flows in from the east façade.

The aerodynamic design of the roof edge causes an increased low pressure and this supports the stack effect. The east façade was originally designed as a single glazing with opening windows.

This ventilation concept was worked out in 1992 at the beginning of the design, when the idea was to have a single row of deep offices along the west side and a corridor along the east side.

In further development it became necessary to have a double row of offices. So an air inlet zone

151

auf der Westseite sicherzustellen. Deshalb wurde auch die Ostfassade als zweischalige Konstruktion mit innenliegenden Lüftungsflügeln gebaut.

Der 1998 preisgekrönte Wettbewerbsentwurf für die Deutsche Post in Bonn der Architekten Murphy/Jahn kann als Weiterentwicklung der Verbindung von «Wintergarten» und Zweite-Haut-Fassade betrachtet werden. Der gebäudehohe Fassadenzwischenraum wird hier für die Zuluft verwendet.
Das 240 m hohe Gebäude ist in vier 10geschossige Abschnitte unterteilt. Diese bestehen im Grundriß aus einem zentralen Wintergarten, der von zwei gegeneinander leicht verschobenen, nach außen abgerundeten Bürotürmen mit eigenen Nebenräumen flankiert ist.

was left free in between the offices on the east side to admit outside air to flow to the offices on the west side. Therefore the east façade, too, was built as a double-skin construction, with openable panels on the inside.

The prize-winning design in 1998 by the architects Murphy/Jahn for the competition for the Deutsche Post in Bonn can be regarded as a further development of the combination of "winter garden" and double-skin façade. The full-height façade cavity is used here for air inflow.
The 240 m high building is divided into four 10-storey sections. In plan, these consist of a central winter garden, flanked by two office towers, with their own service spaces; these towers are shifted slightly towards each other and are curved on the outside.

Das Hochhaus ist in vier 10geschossige Abschnitte unterteilt. Diese bestehen im Grundriß aus einem zentralen Wintergarten, der von zwei gegeneinander leicht verschoben, nach außen abgerundeten Bürotürmen mit eigenen Nebenräumen flankiert ist.
Deutsche Post, Bonn, 1998 –, Murphy/Jahn Architekten.
The high-rise is divided into 10-storey sections. In plan these consist of a central winter garden flanked by two office towers with ancillary areas; the towers are shifted slightly towards each other and are gently curved on the outside.
Deutsche Post, Bonn, 1998 –, Murphy/Jahn Architects.

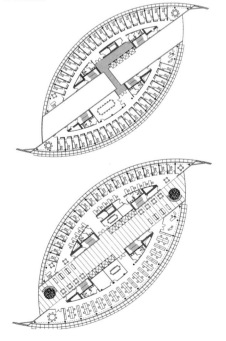

Bei der Südfassade sind die geschoßhohen Glasscheiben der Außenhaut leicht schräg nach außen geneigt, und der Spalt ist mit einer Lüftungsklappe verschlossen. Im Zwischenraum sind breite Sonnenschutzlamellen eingebaut.
Deutsche Post, Bonn, 1998 –, Murphy/Jahn Architekten.

On the south façade the storey-high glass panes of the outer skin are tilted slightly outward and the gap is finished with a louvre. Wide solar control louvres are built into the cavity.
Deutsche Post, Bonn, 1998–, Murphy/Jahn Architects.

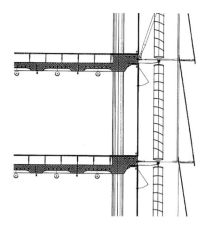

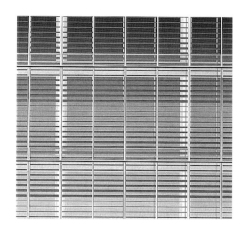

Die außenliegenden, abgerundeten Bürofassaden sind als zweischalige Konstruktion geplant. Die Außenhaut besteht aus geschoßhohen, achsbreiten Glasscheiben, die mit Punkthalterungen befestigt sind. Bei der Südfassade sind sie leicht schräg nach außen geneigt, und der Spalt ist mit einer Lüftungsklappe verschlossen. Im Zwischenraum sind breite Sonnenschutzlamellen eingebaut. Die Innenfassade ist mit Lüftungsflügeln ausgestattet und raumhoch verglast, um das Tageslicht maximal auszunutzen. Im Winter bleiben die Lüftungsklappen der Außenfassade geschlossen, so daß der Zwischenraum als thermischer Puffer wirkt. Während der Übergangszeiten und im Sommer stehen die Klappen offen, und der Zwischenraum wird mit frischer Außenluft durchströmt. Damit können die Büros durch Öffnen der Fensterflügel während eines Großteils des Jahres natürlich belüftet werden. Die entstehende Abluft wird dem Wintergarten zugeführt.

Die Nordfassade funktioniert wie die Südfassade. Die geschoßhohen Glasscheiben bilden hier aber eine glatte Außenhaut. Die vorgesehenen Lüftungsflügel sind bündig eingebaut.

Wenn die Außentemperaturen zu hoch oder zu tief für eine natürliche Belüftung sind, wird eine Quellüftung eingeschaltet.

Die 10geschossigen Wintergärten bilden eine natürlich temperierte Übergangszone zwischen innen und außen und dienen als zentraler Ort der Begegnung für die Angestellten. Im Winter werden sie durch die Wärmestrahlung und die Abluft aus den Büros beheizt. Während der Übergangszeiten und im Sommer wird die Raumtemperatur durch das Öffnen von Lüftungsflügeln in den gegenüberliegenden Verglasungen natürlich reguliert. Zur Reduktion der Spitzentemperaturen im Sommer wird die thermische Speichermasse des Gebäudes während der Nacht durch natürliche

The outer, curved office façades are designed as a double-skin construction. The outer skin consists of storey-high, axis-wide glass sheets which are point fixed. In the case of the south façade they are tilted slightly towards the outside and the gap is finished with a louvre.

Wide solar control louvres are built into the cavity. The inner façade is fitted with openable windows and fully glazed to give maximum daylighting.

In winter the louvres in the outer façade remain closed to enable the cavity to act as a buffer zone. During transition periods and in summer the louvres are open and fresh outside air flows through the cavity. Thus the offices can be naturally ventilated for a large part of the year, by opening the windows. The exhaust air flows out through the winter gardens.

The north façade works like the south façade. However, the storey-high glass panes here form a smooth outer skin. The air louvres are built flush with the façade.

When temperatures outside are too high or low for natural ventilation a displacement ventilation system is switched on.

The 10-storey winter gardens form a natural temperate buffer zone between the inside and the outside and serve as a meeting place for the employees in the building.

In winter the winter gardens are heated through thermal radiation and exhaust air from the offices. During transition periods and in summer the air temperature is controlled naturally by opening the glass louvres in the opposite glazings.

To reduce peak temperatures in summer the building's thermal mass is cooled at night through natural ventilation and during the day by a cooling pipe system.

Lüftung, am Tag durch Bauteilkühlung mit Grundwasser gekühlt.

Schachtfassaden

Eine Schachtfassade ist die Kombination einer zweischaligen Fassade mit gebäudehohem Zwischenraum und einer solchen mit horizontalen Unterteilungen.

Der gebäudehohe Zwischenraum bildet einen Abluftkanal, an den beidseitig die geschoßhohen Zwischenräume durch Überströmungsöffnungen angeschlossen sind. Die aufgewärmte und verbrauchte Abluft strömt von den geschoßhohen Zwischenräumen in den gemeinsamen Abluftkanal. Von da aus steigt sie weiter, bis sie ins Freie gelangt. Die Kaminwirkung des Schachtes unterstützt im Bereich der unteren Geschosse diese Strömung, indem die eingeschlossene Luft aufgrund der Aufwärmung Auftrieb erfährt.

Die thermische Auftriebskraft in den Schächten stellt die natürliche Belüftung auch bei Windstille sicher. Ab einer gewissen Höhe entsteht jedoch ein Überdruck im Abluftschacht, so daß die stark erwärmte Abluft in den Zwischenraum zurückströmt. Deshalb muß die Höhe des Schachtes begrenzt werden. Diese Begrenzung ist von verschiedenen Faktoren – wie Gebäudehöhe, vorherrschenden Windlagen usw. – abhängig und muß von Fall zu Fall neu errechnet werden.

Ein Beispiel für eine Schachtfassade ist das Photonikzentrum in Berlin-Adlershof, 1995 – 98, erbaut von Sauerbruch Hutton Architekten. Das Forschungszentrum besteht aus zwei amöbenför-

Shaft Façades

A shaft façade is a combination of a double-skin façade with a building-high cavity and a double-skin façade with a cavity divided horizontally. The full-height cavity forms a chimney for exhaust air; on both sides of this vertical shaft and connected to it via overflow openings are storey-high cavities. The warmed, exhaust air flows from the storey-high cavity into the central vertical shaft. There it rises, due to the stack effect and escapes into the open at the top. The buoyancy in the shaft supports this flow at the level of the lower floors in that as the trapped air is warmed it is drawn upwards.

Even when there is little air flow outside natural ventilation of the building is ensured by the buoyancy in the shaft.

However, at a certain height the pressure situation reverses and warmed air might return in the storey-high cavities. For this reason it is necessary to limit the height of the shaft. This limitation is influenced by various factors, such as overall building height, prevailing wind etc., and it has to be calculated individually for each building.

One example of a shaft façade is the Photonics Centre in Berlin-Adlershof, built 1995 – 98 by Sauerbruch Hutton Architects.

The research centre consists of two amoeba-shaped buildings separated by a curved passage. The higher, three-storey building contains offices, laboratories and workshops. The lower, single-storey volume serves as a testing hall.

Das Forschungszentrum besteht aus zwei amöbenförmigen Baukörpern.
Das dreigeschossige Gebäude ist mit einer Schachtfassade versehen. Die farbig gestalteten Doppelstützen bilden die Abluftschächte, an welche jeweils links und rechts geschoßhohe Fassadenzwischenräume grenzen.
Photonikzentrum, Berlin-Adlershof, 1995 – 98, Sauerbruch Hutton Architekten.

The research centre consists of two amoeba-shaped buildings.
The three-storey building has a shaft façade. The coloured double columns form the ventilation shafts, which border right and left on storey-high façade cavities.
Photonics Centre, Berlin-Adlershof, 1995 – 98, Sauerbruch Hutton Architects.

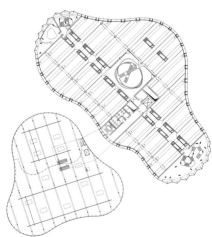

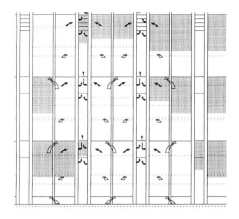

Die frische Außenluft strömt durch Lüftungsöffnungen auf Fußbodenhöhe ein. Die Abluft gelangt durch Überströmungsöffnungen in die Abluftschächte und entweicht durch Glaslamellen am Dachrand ins Freie. Photonikzentrum, Berlin-Adlershof, 1995 – 98, Sauerbruch Hutton Architekten.

Fresh outside air flows in through the slit at floor level. Exhaust air passes through overflow openings into the ventilation shafts and escapes to the outside through glass louvres on the roof edge.
Photonics Centre, Berlin-Adlershof, 1995 – 98, Sauerbruch Hutton Architects.

migen Baukörpern, die durch eine geschwungene Gasse getrennt sind. Das höhere, dreigeschossige Gebäude beherbergt Büros, Labors und Werkstätten. Das niedrigere, eingeschossige dient als Versuchshalle.

Der dreigeschossige Bau ist mit einer Schachtfassade versehen. Vorfabrizierte, farbig gestaltete Doppelstützen aus Beton bestimmen die Tragstruktur des Gebäudes und bilden die 0.75 m breiten Abluftschächte. An die Abluftschächte grenzen jeweils links und rechts geschoßhohe, 1.5 m breite Fassadenbereiche, die durch Überströmungsöffnungen mit dem Schacht verbunden sind.

Die Außenhaut ist eine Pfosten-Riegel-Konstruktion mit einer Einfachverglasung.

Die Innenfassade besteht aus geschoßhohen Rahmenelementen mit vertikalen Schiebeflügeln mit Low-E-beschichtetem Isolierglas. Im 0.70 m breiten Zwischenraum sind unmittelbar hinter der Außenverglasung farbige Rafflamellen aus Aluminium angeordnet.

Die frische Außenluft strömt durch offene Lüftungsschlitze auf Fußbodenhöhe in die geschoßhohen Zwischenräume. Für die Be- und Entlüftung der Innenräume können die Benutzer die vertikalen Schiebeflügel von Hand öffnen.

Die erwärmte und verbrauchte Abluft gelangt durch Überströmungsöffnungen in die 0.75 m breiten Abluftschächte. Hier steigt sie bis zum Dachrand auf und entweicht durch Glaslamellen ins Freie. Das Lüftungskonzept ermöglicht auch eine Nachtauskühlung der Speichermasse des Gebäudes.

The three-storey building has a shaft façade. The building's frame is designed as prefabricated double columns of painted concrete, which constitute the 0.75 m wide chimneys for the exhaust air. To the left and right of the shafts are storey-high 1.5 m wide façade cavities which are connected to the cavitiy shafts via overflow openings.

The outer skin is a mullion and transom construction with single glazing. The inner façade consists of storey-high frame units with vertical sliding windows of low-E coated insulating glass. Immediately behind the outer glazing in the 0.70 m cavity are coloured Venetian blinds of aluminium.

Fresh air from the outside flows through the ventilation slits at floor level into the storey-high cavities. For ventilation of the inner areas the users can open the vertical sliding windows by hand. The warmed, used air exits through overflow openings into the 0.75 m wide ventilation shafts. Here it rises to roof level and escapes through glass louvres into the open air.

The ventilation concept also permits night-time cooling of the building's thermal mass.

One example for the use of a double-skin façade with shaft on a high-rise is the headquarters of ARAG-Versicherung in Düsseldorf, which is currently being built by the architects RKW Rhode Kellermann Wawrowsky and Partners in cooperation with Foster and Partners.

Ein Beispiel für die Verwendung einer Zweite-Haut-Fassade mit Schachtprinzip bei einem Hochhaus ist die Hauptverwaltung der ARAG-Versicherung in Düsseldorf, die zur Zeit von den Architekten RKW Rhode Kellermann Wawrowsky und Partnern in Zusammenarbeit mit Foster und Partnern gebaut wird. In den unteren Geschossen dient die zweischalige Fassade dazu, den Schallschutz gegen Verkehrslärm zu verbessern, in den oberen soll sie eine natürliche Raumbelüftung ermöglichen. Das 130 m hohe Gebäude hat einen geschwungenen Grundriß mit vertikalen Erschließungskernen an beiden Endpunkten. Das Hochhaus ist in siebengeschossige Abschnitte unterteilt, die als unabhängige Einheiten mit eigener

In the lower floors the double-skin façade gives added protection against traffic noise, and in the upper it enables natural ventilation.
The 130 m high building has a curved ground plan with vertical service cores at both ends. The high-rise is divided into seven-storey sections, designed as independent units each fitted with separate plant floor. The units themselves consist of six storeys with offices and a double storey with garden and building services. By dividing the shaft façade in this way seven-storey ventilation shafts are created which are connected via overflow openings to the façade units with storey-high cavities on both sides. 40 cm high ventilation units serve as inlet open-

Das Hochhaus ist in 7geschossige Abschnitte unterteilt, die als unabhängige Einheiten mit eigener Technik ausgestattet sind.
ARAG Versicherung, Düsseldorf, 1994–1999, Architekten RKW Rhode Kellermann Wawrowsky und Partner in Zusammenarbeit mit Foster und Partnern.
The high-rise is divided into 7-storey sections, each fitted with independently building services.
ARAG Versicherung, Düsseldorf, 1994–1999, Architekten RKW Rhode Kellermann Wawrowsky and Partners in cooperation with Foster and Partners.

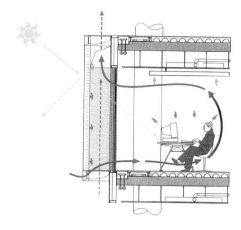
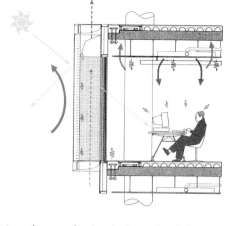

Die Schachtfassade besteht aus 7-geschossigen Abluftschächten, an welche beidseitig die Fassadenelemente mit geschoßhohem Zwischenraum über Überströmungsöffnungen angeschlossen sind. Als Zuluftöffnungen dienen Lüftungskästen, die vor der Deckenstirne der Geschosse angeordnet sind. Die Innenfassade besteht aus geschoßhohen Horizontal-Schiebetüren, die Außenverglasung aus punktgehaltenen ESG-Scheiben.

ARAG Versicherung, Düsseldorf, 1994–1999, Architekten RKW Rhode Kellermann Wawrowsky and Partners in Zusammenarbeit mit Foster und Partnern.

The shaft façade consists of 7-storey ventilation shafts, to which are connected on both sides the façade units with storey-high cavity and overflow openings. Ventilation units fitted to the floor slabs act as air inlets. The inner skin consists of storey-high horizontal sliding doors, and the outer skin is of point-fixed toughened glass.

ARAG Versicherung, Düsseldorf, 1994–1999, Architekten RKW Rhode Kellermann Wawrowsky and Partners in cooperation with Foster and Partners.

Technik ausgestattet sind. Die Einheiten selber bestehen aus sechs Geschossen mit Büroflächen und einem Doppelgeschoß mit Garten zur Unterbringung der Gebäudetechnik. Indem die Schachtfassade diese Unterteilung übernimmt, ergeben sich siebengeschossige Abluftschächte, an welche beidseits die Fassadenelemente mit geschoßhohem Zwischenraum über Überströmungsöffnungen angeschlossen sind. Als Zuluftöffnungen dienen 40 cm hohe Lüftungskästen, die vor der Deckenstirne der Geschosse angeordnet sind. Die frische Außenluft strömt durch einen Lamellenrost in Fußbodenhöhe in den 55 cm breiten Zwischenraum ein und kann über geöffnete Fenster für die natürliche Raumbelüftung herangezogen werden. Infolge der Erwärmung steigt die verbrauchte Luft und strömt durch die Überströmungsöffnungen in den siebengeschossigen, verglasten Abluftkamin. Darin gelangt sie bis zum Technikgeschoß und entweicht durch Glaslamellen ins Freie. Die große Höhe des Abluftkamins stellt die Absaugwirkung auch bei Windstille sicher. Die Innenfassade besteht aus geschoßhohen

ings; these are fitted to the front of each floor slab. Fresh air from the outside flows through a grille at floor level, into the 55 cm wide cavity, and can then be drawn into the offices for natural ventilation by opening the windows. Warming causes the air to rise and to exit through the overflow openings into the seven-storey glazed chimney. There it rises to the floor with the building services and escapes through glass louvres to the outside. The great height of this shaft ensures a suction effect even when there is no wind outside.

The inner façade consists of storey-high horizontal sliding doors with aluminium frames, which the users can open individually to ventilate the offices.

The outer façade is a mullion and transom construction with point-fixed single glazing.

Venetian blinds of aluminium, fitted behind the outer glazing, give solar control.

Underfloor convectors are to be fitted in front of the inner façade for heating purposes.

Chilled ceilings are planned for cooling.

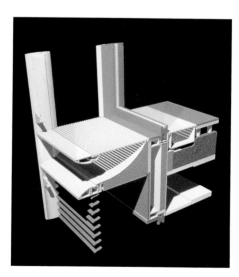

Horizontal-Schiebetüren mit Aluminiumrahmen, welche die Benutzer für die Belüftung der Büros individuell öffnen können. Die Außenfassade ist eine Pfosten-Riegel-Konstruktion mit punktgehaltener Einfachverglasung. Als Sonnenschutz sind Rafflamellen aus Aluminium unmittelbar hinter der Außenverglasung vorgesehen.

Für die Heizung sollen Unterflurkonvektoren vor der Innenfassade angebracht werden, für die Kühlung sind Kühldecken geplant.

Klimahallen

Zweischalige Fassaden werden meist als Lösung für windausgesetzte Hochhäuser in Betracht gezogen. Doch auch bei niedrigen Gebäuden kann das Prinzip «Pufferzone» eine energiesparende Wirkung entfalten. Wintergärten, Atrien und Klimahallen können als erhebliche Vergrößerung eines Fassadenzwischenraums interpretiert werden. Sie schaffen eine temperierte Pufferzone, die Wärmeverluste reduziert und passiv Wärmegewinne aus der Sonnenstrahlung erzielt, und sie können für die natürliche Belüftung des Gebäudes eingesetzt werden.

Ein Beispiel für einen gebäudehohen Wintergarten ist die Nordfassade des Bürogebäudes der Werbeagentur Thompson, in Frankfurt a. M., 1992 – 95. Dem Entwurf legten die Architekten Schneider + Schumacher das Konzept eines «Büroregals» zugrunde. Die «Tablare» sind die Geschosse, denen der gebäudehohe Wintergarten wie ein kastenartiges Schaufenster vorgelagert ist.

Der Wintergarten beherbergt die vertikale Haupterschließung und dient als Schallschutz gegen Ver-

Climate Halls

Double-skin façades are regarded mostly as a solution for high-rises subject to high wind pressure. Yet the buffer zone principle can also have an energy-saving effect in low-rise buildings. Winter gardens, atria and climate halls can be interpreted as a much-enlarged façade cavity. They create a moderated buffer zone, which reduces heat loss and achieves passive heat gain from solar radiation.

They can also play a role in the natural ventilation of a building.

One example of a winter garden extending the full height of a building is the north façade of the offices of Thompson Advertising Agency in Frankfurt am Main, built in 1992 – 95.

The design is based on the "set of shelves" concept devised by the architects Schneider + Schumacher. The individual "shelves" are the floors and in front of them is the full-height winter garden, like a giant shop window.

The winter garden contains the main vertical communication zones and serves as noise protection against the traffic noise, as well as acting as a thermal buffer in the colder seasons. As it faces north, the danger of overheating in summer is low.

The 66 m long, 21 m high and 2.8 m deep "glass box" is suspended from the roof storey from a cantilevered steel construction.

This support structure consists of paired forked columns spaced at 7.2 m, which are tied back to the roof floor slab. They feed the vertical

Der gebäudehohe Wintergarten dient als Schallschutz gegen Verkehrslärm und als Wärmepuffer in den kalten Jahreszeiten.
Werbeagentur Thompson, Frankfurt a. M., 1992 – 95, Schneider + Schumacher.
The full-height winter garden serves as protection against the traffic noise and as a thermal buffer in the colder periods of the year.
Thompson Advertising Company, Frankfurt a. M., 1992 – 95, Schneider + Schumacher.

Die Verglasung ist im Dachgeschoß von einer aus-kragenden Stahlkonstruktion abgehängt. Die Trag-konstruktion besteht jeweils aus zwei Gabelstützen, die mit Zugstäben an der Dachgeschoßplatte zurück-gebunden sind (oben).
Die Isoliergläser sind an den vier Ecken durch Punkt-halterung an eine Verbindungsspinne geschraubt, die durch Klemmhalter an den vom Erd- bis zum Dachgeschoß gespannten Edelstahlseilen befestigt ist (unten).
Werbeagentur Thompson, Frankfurt a. M., 1992 – 95, Schneider + Schumacher.
The glazing is suspended from a cantilevered steel construction in the roof storey. The support structure consists of paired forked columns which are tied back to the roof floor slab (top).
The insulating glass is point-fixed at the four corners with countersunk bolts to a connection "spider". These "spiders" are clamped to the stainless steel cables stretching from ground floor to roof level (bottom).
Thompson Advertising Agency, Frankfurt a. M., 1992 – 95, Schneider + Schumacher.

kehrslärm sowie als Wärmepuffer in den kalten Jahreszeiten. Da er sich nach Norden ausrichtet, ist die Gefahr einer Überhitzung im Sommer gering.

Der 66 m lange, 21 m hohe und 2.8 m tiefe «Glas-kasten» ist im Dachgeschoß von einer auskragen-den Stahlkonstruktion abgehängt. Die Tragkon-struktion besteht aus zwei Gabelstützen in 7.2 m Achsabstand, die mit Zugstäben an der Dachge-schoßplatte zurückgebunden sind. Damit entste-hen Befestigungspunkte, an welchen die Glasfas-sade aufgehängt ist. Diese Tragkonstruktion dient dazu, die Vertikallasten aus der hängenden Vergla-sung in die Dachgeschoßplatte umzuleiten. Die Horizontallasten werden durch Druckstäbe in die Geschoßdecken geleitet.

Die Verglasung besteht aus 1.8 × 3.4 m großen Isoliergläsern, die aus einer 15 mm starken ESG-Scheibe außen, einem Zwischenraum von 20 mm und einer 6 mm starken ESG-Scheibe innen zusammengesetzt sind. Sie sind an den vier Ecken durch Punkthalterung mit Senkschrauben an einer Verbindungsspinne aus Edelstahl befestigt. Die Verbindungsspinnen sind durch Klemmhalter an den abgehängten Edelstahlseilen von 12 mm Durchmesser festgemacht, die im Abstand von 1.8 m vom Erd- bis zum Dachgeschoß gespannt sind.

Um den Wintergarten in das gesamte Energiekon-zept optimal einzubeziehen, wurden umfangreiche bauklimatische Untersuchungen durchgeführt. Als beste Lösung erwies sich die Variante mit einer Isolierverglasung außen und einer Einfachvergla-sung innen. In der kalten Jahreszeit bildet der

loads from the suspended glazing into the roof floor slab.

The horizontal loads are fed into the floor slabs of the various storeys through compression struts.

The glazing is of 1.8 × 3.4 m insulating glass, with a 15 mm outer sheet of toughened glass, a 20 mm cavity and an inner sheet of 6 mm toughened glass. The panes are point-fixed at the four corners with countersunk bolts to a stainless steel connection "spider".

These "spiders" are clamped to the suspended 12 mm cables of stainless steel, stretching from ground floor to roof level at 1.8 m inter-vals.

Extensive analysis was carried out, to ensure the best possible integration of the winter gar-den into the overall energy concept.

The best solution turned out to be a combina-tion of insulating glass on the outside and single glazing on the inside. When the weather is colder the winter garden forms a buffer zone, into which flows the used air from the offices which thus warms the space. In summer a nat-ural air flow is created by opening the vents in the floor and at roof level.

As part of the Potsdamer Platz project in Berlin the architects Richard Rogers Partnership built the two office buildings B4 and B6 in 1993 – 98 for Daimler Benz.

In both buildings the aim was to make the most extensive possible use of natural forms of en-ergy in this dense inner-city context.

Wintergarten eine Pufferzone, die aus der Abluft der Büros belüftet und damit beheizt wird. Im Sommer dagegen stellt sich durch das Öffnen von Lüftungsklappen im Fußboden und Dachgeschoß ein natürlicher Luftstrom ein.

Im Rahmen des Potsdamerplatz-Projekts in Berlin haben die Architekten Richard Rogers Partnership 1993–98 für Daimler Benz die zwei Bürogebäude «B4» und «B6» realisiert, die eine weitgehende Nutzung von natürlichen Energieformen im dichten städtebaulichen Kontext anstreben. Die Gebäude sind an eine verglaste, zweigeschossige Ladenstraße angebaut. Darüber befinden sich fünf Geschosse mit zweibündiger Büronutzung, nach dem Muster der typischen Berliner Blockbauweise, sowie zwei Dachgeschosse. Um die Sonnenenergie passiv zu nutzen, ist der Innenhof mit einem leicht gewölbten Glasdach abgeschlossen und der Blockbau nach Süden abgetreppt und großflächig verglast. Die Pufferwirkung des Atriums reduziert die Wärmeverluste. Durch die Verglasungen gelangt viel Tageslicht zu den innenliegenden Büros, und die Sonnenstrahlung kann die frische Außenluft, die für die natürliche Belüftung der Büros herangezogen wird, aufwärmen. Die Durchlüftung des Innenhofs stellt sich aufgrund des Auftriebs der steigenden Warmluft ein. Die Außenluft strömt in Fußbodenhöhe durch mehrere Zuluftkanäle ein und entweicht durch Lüftungsflügel im Dachbereich wieder ins Freie. Die wirksame Durchlüftung und der niedrige g-Wert der Verglasung verhindern eine Überhitzung im Sommer. Das Glasdach mit einer Stichhöhe

The buildings are built along a glazed, two-storey shopping-hall, therfore the lower two floors of B 4 and B 6 are also intended for shops. Above are five floors of offices, leading off both sides of a central corridor, according to the traditional Berlin block-plan with an inner courtyard. On top are two attic storeys.
To make passive use of solar energy the inner courtyard is fitted with a slightly domed glass roof, and the building's volume is stepped down towards the south and extensively glazed. The buffer effect of the atrium reduces heat losses.
A great deal of daylight enters the offices inside through the glazing, and the solar radiation can heat the fresh air from the outside which is used for natural ventilation of the offices.
The inner courtyard is ventilated through the natural buoyancy. Air from the outside flows in through several inlets at floor level and escapes through glass louvres at roof level.
The effective ventilation and the low g-factor of the glazing prevents overheating in summer.
A glass roof reaching only 3.2 m at the rise covers the 28×28 m inner courtyard.
The support frame is a grid shell with triangular geometry designed on a 1.8×1.8 m grid. The triangular panes of insulating glass are composed of an outer sheet of 10 mm toughened glass with low-E coating, a 16 mm cavity and an inner sheet of 12 mm laminated glass. This achieves a U-value of 1.6 W/m²K, a τ-value of 0.63 and a g-factor of 0.32.

Daylight factors at 14.4m above atrium floor

Daylight factors at entrance and circulation levels

Um die Sonnenenergie passiv zu nutzen, ist der Innenhof mit einem leicht gewölbten Glasdach abgeschlossen und der Blockbau nach Süden abgetreppt und großflächig verglast.
Bürogebäude «B4» und «B6», Berlin, 1993–98, Richard Rogers Partnership.

For passive use of solar energy the interior courtyard is topped with a gently curving glass dome and the traditional Berlin block-plan with an inner courtyard is stepped down towards the south and extensively glazed.
B4 and B6 office buildings, Berlin, 1993–98, Richard Rogers Partnership.

Die Fassaden wurden als Baukastensystem entwickelt. Ihre Grundkonstruktion kann entsprechend der Lage mit unterschiedlichen Füllungselementen versehen werden. Bei der Südost-Fassade sind Isoliergläser mit tiefer Transmission und mit integrierten Sonnenschutzlamellen eingebaut (oben).
Die Konstruktion des Glasdaches ist eine Gitterschale mit dreieckiger Geometrie, die auf einem quadratischen Raster aufgebaut ist (unten).
Bürogebäude «B4» und «B6», Berlin, 1993–98, Richard Rogers Partnership.

The façades modules were designed as a kit of parts. The infills can be varied according to the exact position and requirements. On the south-east façade the insulating glass used has low transmission levels and integrated louvres for solar control (top).
The support frame for the glass dome is a grid shell with triangular geometry built up on a square grid (bottom).
B4 and B6 office buildings, Berlin, 1993–98, Richard Rogers Partnership.

von nur 3.2 m überspannt den 28 × 28 m großen Innenhof. Die Tragkonstruktion ist eine Gitterschale mit dreieckiger Geometrie, die auf einem 1.8 × 1.8 m großen Raster aufgebaut ist. Die dreieckigen Isoliergläser sind aus einer 10 mm starken ESG-Scheibe mit Low-E-Beschichtung außen, einem Zwischenraum von 16 mm und einer 12 mm starken VSG-Scheibe innen aufgebaut. Sie erreichen einen k-Wert von 1.6 W/m²K, einen τ-Wert von 0.63 und einen g-Wert von 0.32. Ähnliche energiesparende Ziele liegen auch der Gestaltung der Fassaden zugrunde. Die 2.7 × 2.75 m großen Fassadenfelder wurden als Baukastensystem entwickelt. Ihre identische Grundkonstruktion kann der Lage entsprechend mit unterschiedlichen Füllungselementen versehen werden. Es kommen zum Beispiel zwei Typen von Isoliergläsern im Durchsichtsbereich zur Anwendung: In der Regel sind es Isoliergläser mit einer 10 mm starken Außenscheibe, einem Zwischenraum von 22 mm und einer 6 mm starken Innenscheibe, die eine hohe Transmission aufweisen ($\tau = 0.75$; $g = 0.57$); bei sonnen- und lichtexponierten Situationen wurden aber Isoliergläser mit tieferer Transmission ($\tau = 0.63$; $g = 0.32$) verwendet. Im Oberlicht- und Brüstungsbereich sind feste Elemente oder Senk-Klapp-Flügel für die natürliche Belüftung eingebaut. Je nach Situation sind Sandwichpaneele, Isoliergläser mit hoher Transmission oder Isoliergläser mit integrierten Lamellen Oka-Solar® eingesetzt. Als zusätzliche Sonnenschutzmaßnahme für die Südfassaden sind

Similar energy-saving aims influenced the design of the façades. The 2.7 × 2.75 m façade modules were designed as a kit of parts. Their identical basic construction can be varied, by using different infills, according to the orientation and performance requirement. For example two types of insulating glass are used in the central panels in the view out area: in general this is insulating glass with a 10 mm outer sheet, a 22 mm cavity and a 6 mm inner sheet, giving a high degree of transmission ($\tau = 0.75$; $g = 0.57$); for situations with high exposure to sun and daylight, insulating glass with lower transmission was used ($\tau = 0.63$; $g = 0.32$). Fixed or top hung elements are infilled into the upper and lower panels for natural ventilation. Depending on the requirement sandwich panels, insulating glass with high transmission or insulating glass with integrated Oka-Solar® louvres are used.
Exterior textile blinds are added to the south façade for extra solar control.
Interior blinds help protect against glare.

In the competition for the Microelectronics Park in Duisburg, won by Foster and Partners, two large, glazed climate halls were proposed, in which nine multi-storey buildings with offices, workshops and laboratories were to be housed.
In the first phase of construction, completed in 1997, the enclosing climate halls were reduced

außenliegende Stoffrollos montiert. Für den Blendschutz sind innenliegende Rollos vorgesehen.

Beim 1988 gewonnenen Wettbewerb für den Mikroelektronik-Park in Duisburg hatten Foster und Partner zwei große, verglaste Klimahallen vorgesehen, worin neun mehrgeschossige Gebäude für Büros, Werkstätten und Labors untergebracht werden sollten. Beim 1997 fertiggestellten ersten Bauabschnitt sind die umschließenden Klimahallen auf zwei verglaste Atrien reduziert, welche sich zwischen drei fünfgeschossigen, kammartig organisierten Gebäuden befinden. Die Atrien bilden einen wettergeschützten Raum für Ausstellungen und Vorträge oder «Straßencafés». Sie schaffen einen thermischen Pufferraum und erlauben eine natürliche Belüftung und Belichtung der an die Atrien angrenzenden Arbeitsräume. Über die Bürotrakte und die Atrien ist ein bogenförmiges Dach gespannt, welches über den Atrien verglast ist. Die Dachverglasung liegt auf einer Tragkonstruktion aus gebogenen Stahlträgern und runden Stahlstützen. Sie besteht aus Isoliergläsern mit einer 8 mm starken ESG-Scheibe außen, einem Zwischenraum von 12 mm und einer 10 mm starken VSG-Scheibe innen. Der k-Wert beträgt 1.3 W/m²K, der g-Wert 0.34. Auf dieser Dachverglasung liegt eine Konstruktion mit gerillten Aluminiumrohren für den Sonnenschutz. Für die Be- und Entlüftung der Atrien sind bei der Schrägverglasung im Erdgeschoß und beim Aufzugsturm im Obergeschoß Lüftungsflügel eingebaut. Die Atriumsfassade der Büros besteht aus geschoßhohen Rahmenelementen aus Stahlprofilen. Sie sind in drei horizontale Bänder unterteilt, oben festverglast, in der Mitte

to two glazed atria, which are located between three five-storey "building fingers".
The atria form a weather-protected space for exhibitions and lectures or even "street cafés". They create a thermal buffer zone and enable natural ventilation and lighting of the working zones next to the atria. An arched roof spans the office sections and the atria; above the atria the roof is glazed. The roof glazing lies on a support frame of curved steel beams and tubular steel columns. The glass itself is insulating glass with an outer sheet of 8 mm toughened glass, a 12 mm cavity and an inner sheet of 10 mm laminated glass. The U-value is 1.3 W/m²K, the g-factor 0.34.
On this roof glazing is a grid of ribbed aluminium tubes for solar control.
For ventilating the atria, buttum hung windows are built into the outside tilted glazing at ground floor level and into the glazing near the lift tower in the upper storey.
The atrium façade of the offices consists of storey-high modules of steel profiles. They are divided into three horizontal bands, with fixed glazing at the top, top hung windows in the middle and, at parapet level, perforated wooden panels to reduce reverberation.
The offices inside can be naturally ventilated by opening the windows, when fresh air flows from the outside into the atria. This air-flow also enables night-time cooling of the building's thermal mass in the summer. However, fresh air can also be drawn in through a ventilation duct laid into the ground, where in winter it can be pre-warmed, and in summer pre-cooled.

Unter einem bogenförmigen Dach befinden sich zwei verglaste Atrien zwischen drei fünfgeschossigen, kammartig organisierten Gebäuden.
Mikroelektronic-Park, Duisburg, 1989 – 97, Foster und Partner.
Located under a curved roof are two glazed atria between three five-storey "building fingers". Microelectronics Park, Duisburg, 1989 – 97, Foster and Partners.

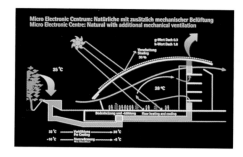

Die Dachverglasung liegt auf einer Stahlkonstruktion. Für die Belüftung der Atrien sind bei der Schrägverglasung im Erdgeschoß und beim Aufzugsturm im Obergeschoß Lüftungsflügel eingebaut. Die Frischluft kann – vorgewärmt bzw. vorgekühlt – durch einen im Erdreich eingelegten Zuluftkanal angesaugt werden.
Mikroelektronic-Park, Duisburg, 1989 – 97, Foster und Partner.

The roof glazing rests on a steel frame. For ventilating the atria, openings are built into the sloping glazing in the ground floor and into the glazing near the lift tower in the upper storey. Fresh air, either pre-warmed or pre-cooled, can be drawn in through a ventilation duct in the ground.
Microelectronics Park, Duisburg, 1989 – 97, Foster and Partners.

mit Klappflügeln und im Brüstungsbereich mit perforierten Holzpaneelen für die Nachhall-Dämpfung versehen. Die innenliegenden Büros können natürlich belüftet werden, wenn durch Öffnen der Lüftungsflügel frische Außenluft in die Atrien einströmt. Diese Durchlüftung ermöglicht auch die Nachtauskühlung der thermischen Speichermasse im Sommer. Die Frischluft kann aber auch über einen im Erdreich eingelegten Zuluftkanal angesaugt werden, wo sie im Winter vorgewärmt bzw. im Sommer vorgekühlt wird. Um den Energieverbrauch niedrig zu halten, werden Erdwärme und -kälte sowie die thermische Speichermasse des Gebäudes genutzt. Alle Büros können aber je nach Bedarf mit einer mechanischen Belüftung nachgerüstet werden. Die außenliegende Fassade ist eine Pfosten-Riegel-Konstruktion, die ebenfalls in drei horizontale Bänder unterteilt ist. Oben sind sie festverglast, in der Mitte mit Dreh-Kipp-Flügeln und bei der Brüstung mit emaillierten Glaspaneelen versehen. Für den Sonnenschutz sind der Süd-

To keep energy consumption low, use is made of the ground heat source and of the thermal storage mass of the building.
All the offices can also be equipped with mechanical ventilation systems if required. The outer façade is a mullion and transom construction which is also divided into three bands. At the top they have fixed glazing, in the middle side/bottom hung windows and at parapet level fritted glass panels. For solar control the south-west façade has large, tiltable aluminium louvres.

In 1990 Francis Soler won the first prize in the competition for the International Conference Centre in Paris. His design consisted in three fully glazed pavilions: large climate halls accommodating various types of functions.
The central pavilion comprises the entrance hall and the diplomats' offices; the pavilion on the left contains the press centre and the one on the

west-Fassade drehbare Großlamellen aus Aluminium vorgesetzt.

1990 gewann der Architekt Francis Soler den ersten Preis des Wettbewerbs für das «Internationale Konferenzzentrum» in Paris. Sein Entwurf sah drei vollverglaste Pavillons vor; diese bilden große Klimahallen, in denen je nach Nutzung unterschiedliche Baukörper untergebracht sind. Der zentrale Pavillon umfaßt die Empfangshalle und die Räumlichkeiten für die Diplomaten, der linke das Pressezentrum und der rechte die Konferenzzimmer. Im Untergeschoß des rechten Pavillons befinden sich ein Pressesaal und ein großes Auditorium. Die drei Klimahallen weisen dieselbe umschließende Tragstruktur und eine außenliegende Glashülle als Wetterschutz auf, die von Nicholas Green, YRM Antony Hunt Associates, Paris, entwickelt wurde. Die 25 m hohe, 47 m breite und 97 m lange räumliche Tragkonstruktion besteht aus Vierendeelträgern, die auf einem Rastermaß von 12.5 m Achsabstand und 3.30 m Höhe aufgebaut sind, so daß ein filigranes Erscheinungsbild ohne diagonale Aussteifungen entsteht. Die außenliegende Einfachverglasung besteht aus vorgespannten 3.3 m hohen, 1.56 m breiten und 15 mm starken Scheiben aus weißem Glas, welche an jeder Ecke mit einem speziell entwickelten Befestigungsteil aus Edelstahl gehalten werden. Für den Sonnenschutz sind Aluminiumlamellen vorge-

right, the conference rooms. In the basement of the right-hand pavilion is a press hall and a large auditorium.

The three halls have the same support structure and are enclosed in an external glass weatherskin, developed by Nicholas Green, YRM Antony Hunt Associates, Paris.

The 25 m high, 47 m wide and 97 m long space frame consists of Vierendeel girders on a grid spacing of 12.5 m horizontally and 3.30 m vertically. Diagonal bracing is not required which gives rise to a filigree appearance.

The external glazing consists of 3.3 m high, 1.56 m wide and 15 mm thick sheets of white glass, held at the corners by specially designed stainless steel fixing bolts.

Aluminium louvre blinds afford solar shading. On the inside of the atria are different kinds of thermal insulation solutions, depending on the requirements of the particular function.

In the central pavilion there is a second layer of glazing on the inside of the space frame, providing a double-skinned façade at this point. Cold or warm air is blown into the cavity to keep a constant temperature in the entrance hall.

In the press pavilion no second skin is necessary because the building itself has its own insulated façade with opening windows.

In the third pavilion the high standard of comfort requirements in the conference rooms

Die drei vollverglasten Pavillons sind Klimahallen, die verschiedene Funktionen erfüllen.
Wettbewerb «Internationales Konferenzzentrum», Paris, 1990 – 94, Francis Soler.
The three fully glazed pavilions are climate halls, within which various types of functions are accommodated.
International Conference Centre Competition, Paris, 1990 – 94, Francis Soler.

Der zentrale Pavillon beherbergt die Empfangshalle
und die Räumlichkeiten für die Diplomaten (oben);
die drei Klimahallen weisen dieselbe umschließende
räumliche Tragstruktur und eine außenliegende Glashülle als Wetterschutz auf (links unten); beim zentralen Pavillon ist eine zweite Einfachverglasung auf der
Innenseite vorgesehen (unten rechts).
Wettbewerb «Internationales Konferenzzentrum»,
Paris, 1990–94, Francis Soler.

*The central pavilion comprises the entrance hall and
the diplomats' offices (top); the three halls have the
same space frame support structure and are
enclosed in an external glass weather-skin (bottom
left); in the central pavilion a second layer of glazing
is placed on the inside of the space frame (bottom
right).*
*International Conference Centre Competition, Paris,
1990–94, Francis Soler.*

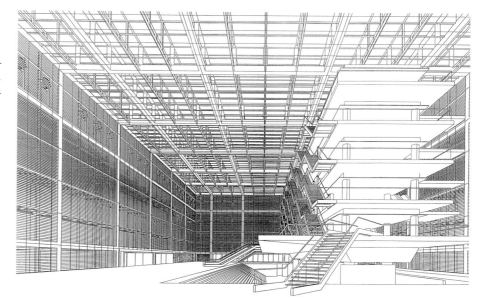

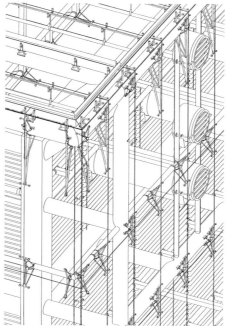
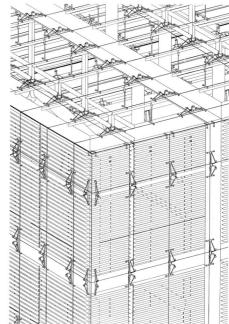

sehen. Was den innenliegenden, wärmedämmenden Raumabschluß betrifft, sind die Glashallen je
nach Klimaanforderung verschieden gestaltet. Für
den zentralen Pavillon ist auf der Innenseite
der räumlichen Tragstruktur eine zweite
Einfachverglasung vorgesehen, damit die Klimahalle eine doppelte Glashülle erhält. In den
Zwischenraum wird kalte oder warme Luft
eingeblasen, so daß die Temperatur in der
Empfangshalle konstant bleibt. Beim Pressepa-
villon ist keine zweite Hülle notwendig, weil der
Baukörper mit einer eigenen wärmedämmenden
Fassade mit Fenstern zum Öffnen ausgestattet ist.

made it necessary to use both insulating glass
and also to provide an artificial air conditioning
system.
In 1994, after four years of planning, the project
was shelved for political reasons.

The project for the Training Center of the Ministry of the Interior of North Rhine-Westphalia,
in Herne-Sodingen, built 1992–99, uses the
concept of a fully glazed climate hall.
The design by the architectural partnership of
Jourda & Perraudin and Hegger Hegger Schleiff
Planer + Architekten proposes a 72×168 m

Dagegen sind die klimatechnischen Anforderungen bei den Konferenzzimmern im dritten Pavillon sehr hoch, so daß sowohl eine Isolierverglasung als auch eine Klimaanlage vorgesehen sind. Nach vier Jahren Planung wurde das Projekt 1994 aus politischen Gründen sistiert.

Auch das Projekt für die Fortbildungsakademie des Innenministeriums von Nordrhein-Westfalen in Herne-Sodingen, 1992–99, verfolgt das Konzept einer vollverglasten Klimahalle. Der Entwurf der Architektengemeinschaft Jourda & Perraudin Architectes und Hegger Hegger Schleiff Planer + Architekten sieht eine 72×168 m große Glashalle vor, in der zwei langgezogene Gebäudegruppen mit insgesamt neun Einzelbauten leicht schräggestellt zu einem gemeinsamen begrünten Freiraum angeordnet sind.

Das Projekt wurde im Rahmen eines Forschungsprojekts für die Europäische Union hinsichtlich des bauklimatischen Verhaltens eingehend untersucht. Die «mikroklimatische Hülle» – wie sie die Architekten bezeichnen – schafft einen halböffentlichen, witterungsgeschützten Raum, der mit Pflanzen, Wasserbecken, Wegen und Terrassen gestaltet ist. Hier können sich die Besucher treffen und auf den eingerichteten Terrassen sogar ganzjährig «draußen» essen. Im Winter reduziert die Glashalle die Wärmeverluste der umhüllten Gebäude und ermöglicht die passive Nutzung der Sonnenenergie. Um eine Überhitzung im Sommer zu vermeiden und gleichzeitig aktiv Energie zu gewinnen, sind PV-Module in der Dachverglasung und teilweise auch in der Westfassade eingebaut. Die Spitzenleistung beträgt 1 Megawatt.

large glazed hall in which are arranged two linear groups of buildings, each with nine individual buildings slightly angled towards a shared green space.

The expected climatic effects of this proposal were extensively studied as part of a research project for the European Union. The "microclimatic skin", as the architects called it, creates a semi-public, weather-protected space landscaped with plants, pools, paths and terraces. Here visitors can meet and even eat "outside" all year round on the terraces.

In winter the glazed hall reduces heat loss from the enclosed buildings and enables passive utilisation of solar energy.

To avoid overheating in summer and to gain active energy photovoltaic modules are built into the roof glazing and partly also in the west façade. Together these modules can produce 1 megawatt at peak output.

For natural ventilation and for night-time cooling skylights can be opened in the roof and glass louvres in the façade. Some of the interior rooms are mechanically ventilated; fresh air from the outside is drawn in via ventilation tunnels and thus pre-heated or pre-cooled.

The support frame of the 72×168 m hall is a timber construction with cast steel connection junctions. This timber frame has four rows of round timber columns which in the cross direction carry the 2.2 m high trussed beams of the primary structure, and in the longitudinal direction the trusses carry the secondary beams. On these lie the rainwater gutters of paired wooden beams and the shed-like aluminium frame elements of the roof glazing, which are

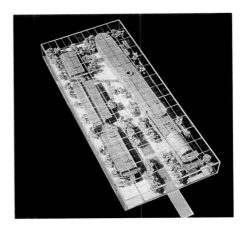

Die verglaste Halle beherbergt zwei langgezogene Gebäudegruppen mit insgesamt neun Einzelbauten, die um einen gemeinsamen begrünten Freiraum angeordnet sind (oben).

Die Fassaden bestehen aus einer tragenden Holzkonstruktion, an welche vorfabrizierte «structural-glazing»-Elemente eingehängt sind (unten).

Fortbildungsakademie des Innenministeriums Nordrhein-Westfalens, Herne-Sodingen, Deutschland, 1992–99, Jourda & Perraudin Architectes in Zusammenarbeit mit HHS Planer + Architekten.

The glazed hall contains two linear groups of buildings with a total of nine different volumes arranged around a shared open green space (top).

The façade consists of a wooden support frame, from which the prefabricated structural glazing units are suspended (bottom).

Training Centre of the Ministry of the Interior of North Rhine-Westphalia, Herne-Sodingen, Germany, 1992–99, Jourda & Perraudin Architectes in cooperation with HHS Planer + Architekten.

Die Dachverglasung ist mit monokristallinen PV-Zellen verglast, um die Überhitzung im Sommer zu vermeiden und gleichzeitig aktiv Energie zu gewinnen. Die PV-Module sind mit unterschiedlicher Belegung erstellt und wolkenartig verteilt.
Fortbildungsakademie des Innenministeriums Nordrhein-Westfalens, Herne-Sodingen, Deutschland, 1992–99, Jourda & Perraudin Architectes in Zusammenarbeit mit HHS Planer + Architekten.
The roof glazing is fitted with monocrystalline photovoltaic cells which prevent overheating in summer and at the same time enable active recovery of energy. The photovoltaic modules give various coverage and are distributed in a cloude-like pattern.
Training Centre of the Ministry of the Interior of North Rhine-Westphalia, Herne-Sodingen, Germany, 1992–99, Jourda & Perraudin Architectes in cooperation with HHS Planer + Architekten.

Für die natürliche Be- und Entlüftung oder für die Nachtauskühlung können im Dach Lüftungsflügel, in der Fassade Lamellenflügel geöffnet werden. Einige Innenräume sind mechanisch belüftet; die frische Außenluft wird über Lüftungskanäle angesaugt und vorgewärmt beziehungsweise vorgekühlt.
Die Tragstruktur der 72 × 168 m großen Halle ist eine Holzkonstruktion mit Verbindungsknoten aus Gußstahl. Sie besteht aus vier Reihen Rundholzstützen, die in der Querrichtung die 2.2 m hohen Fachwerkträger der Primärstruktur, in der Längsrichtung die unterspannten Träger der Sekundärstruktur tragen. Darauf liegen die Regenrinnen aus doppelten Holzträgern und die shedähnlichen Aluminium-Rahmenelemente der Dachverglasung, die mit 1.2 – 2.70 m großen VSG-Scheiben mit monokristallinen PV-Zellen bestückt sind. Die PV-Module sind mit 63 %, 73 % und 86 % Belegung erstellt und wolkenartig verteilt, um die Tageslichtverhältnisse für die Innenhäuser zum optimieren.
Die tragende Holzkonstruktion der Fassade besteht aus 15 m langen Fachwerkträgern in 6 m Achsabstand, die sich vom Boden bis zum Dachrand spannen. Zusammen mit horizontalen und vertikalen Trägern bilden sie eine tragende Unterkonstruktion, an welche vorfabrizierte «structural glazing»-Elemente eingehängt sind, die aus einer 8 mm starken ESG-Scheibe auf einem umlaufenden, mit Silikon verklebten Aluminium-Rahmen bestehen.

filled with 1.2 × 2.70 m laminated glass panes with monocrystalline photovoltaic cells. The photovoltaic modules give 63 %, 73 % and 86 % coverage and are distributed in a cloud-like pattern, to optimise the daylight conditions for the buildings inside.
The wooden support frame for the façade consists of 15 m long trussed mullions at 6 m spacing; these mullions span from the floor up to the roof edge. Together with horizontal transoms they form a support frame, from which the prefabricated structural glazing units are suspended; each of these units consists of an 8 mm sheet of toughened glass bonded with silicon into an aluminium frame.

Zusammenfassung und Ausblick

Summary and Outlook

Die Idee einer hochentwickelten «polyvalenten Glashaut», die je nach Jahreszeit und Bedarf als Wärme- oder Sonnenschutz dient, war der Leitgedanke in Mike Davies' Artikel von 1981.

Dieser Text steckte als Zusammenfassung einer Studie für die Firma Pilkington Glass Limited aus dem Jahre 1978 die Zukunftsziele der Glasindustrie nach der Energiekrise ab.

Solche Zielvorstellungen haben zur Entwicklung von zahlreichen neuen Glasprodukten geführt.

Heute sind Glasscheiben mit einer reineren Zusammensetzung und mit hochwertigen selektiven Beschichtungen sowie Verbundgläser, Isolier- und Mehrfachisoliergläser mit verschiedenen Einlagen und Füllungen auf dem Markt erhältlich, die differenziertere Eigenschaften für den Wärme- und Sonnenschutz aufweisen.

Trotz vieler technologischer Fortschritte konnte die Glasindustrie aber bis anhin die Vorstellung von Davies' «polyvalenter Wand» noch nicht vollständig umsetzen.

Gläser mit veränderbaren Eigenschaften, mit thermochromen und thermotropen Schichten oder mit elektrochromen Materialien wurden bisher nur als Prototypen entwickelt. Produkte mit Flüssigkristallen sind zur Zeit nur begrenzt für die Außenanwendung einsetzbar. So müssen neuere Wärme- und Sonnenschutzgläser weiterhin mit traditionellen Maßnahmen ergänzt werden.

Da aber die ökologische Zielvorstellung darin liegt, den gesamten Bedarf an Primärenergie eines Gebäudes auf ein Minimum, im Idealfall auf Null, zu senken, muß auch der Energieverbrauch für Lüftung, Beleuchtung und Kühlung reduziert werden.

Dies kann durch «intelligente Fassaden» geschehen, die sich dynamisch den wechselnden Klimaverhältnissen anpassen.

Als wirklich «intelligent» kann man eine Fassade dann bezeichnen, wenn sie natürliche, erneuerbare Energiequellen – wie Sonnenstrahlung,

The idea of an advanced "polyvalent glass skin" which can serve either as thermal or solar protection, according to requirements and time of year, was the main idea in Mike Davies' article of 1981.

This article, a summary of a study carried out in 1978 for Pilkington Glass Limited, set out the future goals of the glass industry in the wake of the energy crisis.

These declared aims led to the development of countless new glass products.

Today a range of different glass panes are available, including glass with a purer base mix, high quality selective coatings, as well as laminated glass, insulating glass and multiple-layer insulating units with various interlayers and fillings which have different thermal and solar insulation properties.

Despite the many technological advances, however, the glass industry has not yet been able to fully realise Davies' idea of a "polyvalent wall".

Glass with variable properties, with thermochromic and thermotropic layers or with electrochromic materials has so far only be developed as prototypes.

Products using liquid crystals have at present only limited application on the outside of a building. Thus new types of thermal and solar control glass still have to be supplemented with traditional methods.

However, as the ecological goal is to reduce the total primary energy needs of a building to a minimum, ideally down to zero, energy consumption for heating, cooling and lighting must also be taken into consideration.

This can happen with "intelligent façades" which adapt dynamically to the changing climate conditions.

A façade can only be described as truly "intelligent" when it makes use of natural, renewable

Luftströmungen und Erdwärme – nutzt, um den Energiebedarf für Heizung, Kühlung, Belüftung und Beleuchtung eines Gebäudes sicherzustellen.

Der Vorteil von Glasfassaden ist das Potential an Energiegewinn aus der Sonnenstrahlung in Form von Wärme und Tageslicht.

Im Winter können die Wärmegewinne sogar einen Großteil der Wärmeverluste wettmachen. Im Sommer sind sie aber unerwünscht und können durch geeignete Sonnenschutzmaßnahmen, natürliche Belüftung und Nachtauskühlung der thermischen Speichermasse vermindert werden.

Dem Entwurf von «intelligenten Glasfassaden» müssen fortschrittliche Gesamtenergiekonzepte zugrundeliegen, welche die Interaktion zwischen Fassade, Gebäudetechnik und Umwelt ermöglichen. Das führt zu einer zunehmenden Komplexität der Entwurfsaufgabe, die nur durch eine ganzheitliche Planung – d. h. durch eine interdisziplinäre Zusammenarbeit von Architekten, Fassadenplanern und beratenden Fachingenieuren – erfolgversprechend angegangen werden kann.

Eine «intelligente Fassade» steht architektonisch und technisch im Einklang mit den vorgegebenen Bedingungen von Standort und Klima. Beispiele für eine gelungene Interaktion zwischen Fassade, Gebäude und Umwelt lassen sich in zahlreichen traditionellen Bau-Kulturen finden.

Stets haben innovative Architekten teils sehr alte Ideen aufgegriffen und in eine neue Form gegossen, wie die folgenden Beispiele zeigen.

Bei der berühmten Villa Rotonda außerhalb Vicenzas, 1566 – 67, hat der italienische Architekt Andrea Palladio die natürlichen Luftströmungen und die thermische Speichermasse des Gebäudes genutzt, um die sommerlichen Temperaturen zu mildern.

In der zentralen Kuppelhalle steigt die Warmluft und entweicht ins Freie durch Öffnungen im Scheitel. Damit zieht sie frische Luft nach, die zuerst zur Kühlung durch die Kellerräume geführt wird.

Dieses Prinzip war Palladio von den Costozza-Villen bei Vicenza bekannt, wo natürliche Höhlen als Erdkanäle für die Zuluft genutzt werden.

Ein ähnliches Konzept für die natürliche Belüftung mit vorgewärmter oder -gekühlter Zuluft kommt beim umgebauten Plenarsaal des Reichstags in

energy sources, such as solar radiation, air flows and ground heat, to secure a building's needs in terms of heating, cooling, ventilation and lighting.

The advantage of glass façades is the potential for energy gain from the solar radiation in the form of heat and daylight.

In winter the heat gains can even compensate for a large part of the heat losses.

In summer, however, such heat gains are undesirable and can be reduced through the use of appropriate solar control measures, natural ventilation and night-time cooling of the building's thermal mass.

The design of "intelligent façades" must be based on advanced integrated energy concepts which enable an interaction between the façades, the building services and the environment.

This leads to an increasing complexity of the design task which can only be tackled with any degree of success by means of an integrated approach to planning, i. e. interdisciplinary cooperation between architects, façade planners and consulting engineers.

An "intelligent façade" is in tune both architecturally and technically with the physical and climate conditions existing at its particular location.

Examples of a successful interaction between façade, building and environment can be found in the architectural history of many cultures.

Innovative architects have always drawn on old ideas and taken some of them up in new form, as the following examples show.

In the case of the famous Villa Rotonda outside Vicenza, built 1566 – 67, the Italian architect Andrea Palladio used the natural ventilation and the thermal mass of the building to reduce summer temperatures. Warm air rises in the central domed hall and escapes through openings at the apex, thus drawing in fresh air from below which first flows through the cellars to cool it.

This principle was known to Palladio from the Costozza Villas near Vicenza where natural caves were used as ventilation ducts in the ground for bringing in fresh air.

A similar concept for natural ventilation with prewarmed or precooled incoming air was used by Foster and Partners in redesigning the

Um die sommerlichen Temperaturen zu mildern, hat der Architekt Andrea Palladio die natürlichen Luftströmungen und die thermische Speichermasse des Gebäudes genutzt (a).
Dieses Prinzip war Palladio von den Costozza-Villen bei Vicenza bekannt (b).
Villa Rotonda bei Vicenza, 1566 – 67, Andrea Palladio.
The Italian architect Andrea Palladio used the natural ventilation and the thermal mass of the building to reduce summer temperatures (a).
This principle was known to Palladio from the Costozza Villas near Vicenza (b).
Villa Rotonda near Vicenza, 1566 – 67, Andrea Palladio.

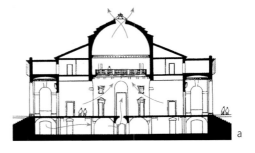

a

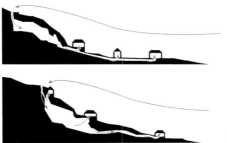

b

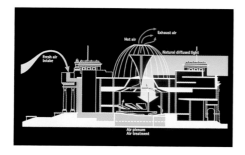

Für die natürliche Belüftung mit vorgewärmter oder -gekühlter Zuluft wird die Frischluft über den Ecktürmen auf der Westseite angesaugt und durch Lüftungsschächte ins Kellergeschoß geführt.
Umbau des Reichstags, Berlin, 1992–99, Foster und Partner.
For natural ventilation with prewarmed or precooled air the fresh air is drawn in via the corner towers on the west side and fed through ventilation shafts in the cellar.
Reichstag (new German Parliament), Berlin, 1992–99, Foster and Partners.

Ein Klimakonzept kann auf der Kombination einfacher, traditioneller Maßnahmen und raffinierter Technologie basieren.
Britischer Pavillon für die Expo '92, Sevilla, 1992, Nicholas Grimshaw und Partner.
The climate concept can be based on a combination of simple, traditional techniques and advanced technology.
British Pavilion at Expo '92, Seville, 1992, Nicholas Grimshaw and Partners.

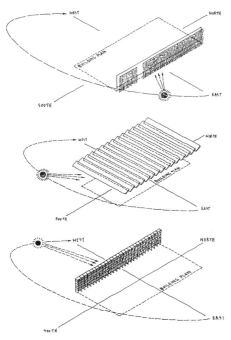

Berlin, von Foster und Partnern, 1992–99, zum Tragen. Die Frischluft wird über den Ecktürmen auf der Westseite angesaugt und durch Lüftungsschächte ins Kellergeschoß geführt. Indem sie durch massive Lüftungskanäle strömt, wird sie im Winter vorgewärmt, im Sommer vorgekühlt. Interessant ist, daß für die Zuluftführung Schächte genutzt werden, die der Architekt P. Wallot in Zusammenarbeit mit dem Ingenieur D. Grove bereits 1894 für das ursprüngliche Lüftungskonzept des Gebäudes eingerichtet hatte.

Das Klimakonzept des Britischen Pavillons für die Expo '92 in Sevilla, von Nicholas Grimshaw und Partnern realisiert, basierte auf der Kombination einfacher, traditioneller Maßnahmen und raffinierter Technologie. Für die Kühlung der hohen Verglasung der Ostfassade wurde ein Wasserschleier eingesetzt. Den Strom für die Umwälzpumpe lieferten segelförmige PV-Zellen auf dem Dach, die gleichzeitig die Beschattung sicherstellten. An der Westfassade wurden sandgefüllte Blechbehälter aufgestellt, die als thermische Speichermasse wirkten.

Beim Projekt für das «Museum of London», 1996, haben Ian Ritchie Architects die gezielte Tageslichtnutzung thematisiert. Der zylindrische, vollverglaste Bau soll als Schaufenster des Museums dienen. Die Raumverglasungen können je nach Bedarf opak oder transparent gestaltet werden. Für den Sonnenschutz wird ein gebogener Schild aus Lochblech um das runde Glasgebäude herumgefahren (s. Seite 168).

Plenary Hall in the Reichstag in Berlin, in 1992–99. Fresh air is drawn in via the corner towers on the west side and fed through ventilation shafts in the cellar. The thick ventilation ducts prewarm the air passing through them in winter, and precool it in summer.
An interesting feature is that for the incoming air the same shafts are used which the architect P. Wallot, and the engineer D. Grove, had installed back in 1894 as part of the original ventilation concept for the building.

The climate concept for the British Pavilion at Expo '92 in Seville, built by Nicholas Grimshaw and Partners, was based on a combination of simple, traditional techniques and advanced technology.
For cooling the high glass façade on the east side, a veil of water was used. Energy for the water circulation pumps came from sail-shaped photovoltaic cells on the roof, which also served a shading function. On the west façade sand-filled metal containers were set up to act as a thermal store.

In the project for the Museum of London, in 1996, Ian Ritchie Architects made full use of natural daylight. The cylindrical, fully glazed structure is intended to be a kind of shop window of the museum. The room glazing can be made opaque or transparent as required. For solar control a curved shield of perforated metal-sheets is tracked around the circular glass building (see page 168).

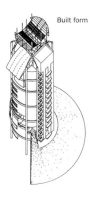

Built form

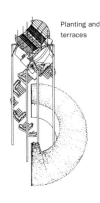

Planting and terraces

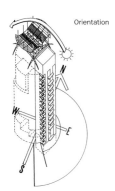

Orientation

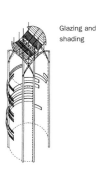

Glazing and shading

Die Orientierung und die Form der Gebäude richten sich nach den Sonnen- und Windeinflüssen.
Menara Mesiniaga, Selangor, Malaysia, 1989–92, T. R. Hamzah & K. Yeang Architects and Planners.
The orientation and the form of the buildings are determined by sun and wind.
Menara Mesiniaga, Selangor, Malaysia, 1989–92, T. R. Hamzah & K. Yeang Architects and Planners.

Weitere Ansätze eines umweltbewußten Bauens zeigen die Projekte des Architekten Ken Yeang in Malaysia. Die Orientierung und die Form der Gebäude richten sich nach den Sonnen- und Windeinflüssen. Auch wenn die Entwürfe nur einer bestimmten Klimazone entsprechen, illustrieren sie den Willen, von den Alten zu lernen und Bewährtes, Althergebrachtes mit neuesten Technologien und Materialien zu verbinden.

Wie diese Beispiele zeigen, wird die «Intelligenz» einer Fassade nicht unbedingt durch eine komplexe Steuerungstechnik oder eine aufwendige Materialkombination definiert, sondern auch dadurch, daß sich die Fassade nach den klimatischen Gegebenheiten richtet und natürliche Energiequellen nutzt – und dies mit einem Minimum an technischem Aufwand.
Die meisten der bisher realisierten Bauten zeigen aber, daß Planung, Konstruktion und Steuerungstechnik einer «intelligenten Fassade» sehr aufwendig und somit teuer sind.
Dank energiesparender Konzepte können die jährlichen Gesamtkosten der Gebäudetechnik zwar reduziert werden, doch die Mehrinvestitionen für den Bau übertreffen beim derzeitigen Entwicklungsstand noch die Einsparungen.
Trotz der höheren Investitionskosten liegen «intelligente Fassaden» im Trend. Der Begriff «Nachhaltigkeit» – d. h. ein sorgfältiger Umgang mit unseren beschränkten Ressourcen – spricht eine wachsende Zahl von Bauherren und Investoren an. Das ehrgeizige Ziel, optimale Lösungen für umweltgerechte Gebäude mit minimalem Energieverbrauch und Kapitaleinsatz zu erarbeiten, wird die Architektur, die Technik und nicht zuletzt die Industrie weiterhin herausfordern.

Further ideas for environmentaly-friendly architecture are in the projects of the architect Ken Yeang in Malaysia. The orientation and form of his buildings are determined by the sun and the wind. Even if these designs are made only for a particular climate zone they demonstrate the desire to learn from old techniques and improve the good ideas from the past with modern technology and materials.

As these examples show, the "intelligence" of a façade is not necessarily determined only by the complexity of its control mechanisms or material combinations used, but also by the ability of the façade to take account of climatic conditions and use natural energy sources – and to do this with a minimum of technical equipment.
Most of the buildings completed so far show, however, that the design, construction and operation of an "intelligent façade" is a very complicated and therefore costly process.
Thanks to energy-saving concepts the annual cost of running building systems can be reduced, but at the current level of development, the extra investment needed to implement these concepts is not yet covered by the savings.
Yet, despite the higher investment costs "intelligent façades" are in fashion. The term "sustainability", i. e. careful use of our limited resources, is becoming attractive to more and more clients and investors. The ambitious goal of designing optimum solutions for environmentally-compatible buildings which do not demand high capital investment and which consume minimal amounts of energy will continue to be a challenge to architecture, technology and not least to industry.

Dank   Acknowledgement

An dieser Stelle möchte ich allen, die zur Entstehung der vierten Auflage dieses Buchs beigetragen haben, meinen verbindlichen Dank aussprechen. Herr Robert Steiger vom Birkhäuser Verlag hat mich im Frühjahr 1994 zu dieser Darstellung ermutigt und seitdem den Fortgang der Arbeit – von der ersten bis zur vierten Auflage – mit viel Engagement und Geduld begleitet. Frau Franziska Forter hat mir auch diesmal den Vorgang des Verfassens durch ihre intensive redaktionelle Mitarbeit entscheidend erleichtert. Frau Ingrid Taylor, English Experts, hat wiederum die fachkundige Übersetzung ins Englische geleistet. Für diese vierte Auflage besorgte Frau Diana Eggenschwiler die sorgfältige Schlußkorrektur, und Frau Christine Bäckman und die Firma Jung Satzcentrum haben das reiche Material durch ein klares Layout aussagekräftig gestaltet. Mein besonderer Dank gilt allen Architekten und anderen Fachleuten sowie den Spezialfirmen, die mir mit großzügiger Hilfsbereitschaft Informationen und Dokumentationsmaterial zur Verfügung gestellt haben, insbesondere:

I should like to record my gratitude to all those who have helped in the creation of this fourth edition of the book, in particular to Robert Steiger of Birkhäuser Verlag who encouraged me to undertake this task in Spring 1994 and who since then has accompanied its progress, through four editions, with great diligence and patience. Thanks once again to Franziska Forter whose assiduous editorial work was a great help and to Ingrid Taylor of English Experts who again provided the specialist translation into English.
I am indebted also to Diana Eggenschwiler for the meticulous final proofreading, and to Christine Bäckmann and the Jung company for the clear layout and presentation of the extensive material.
My special thanks is extended to all those architects, individual experts and specialist companies who so generously supplied information and documentary material, in particular to:

Arup Associates:
   H. Allen
Ove Arup & Partners:
   A. McDowell, A. Sedgwick
Asahi Glass Europe:
   H. Yamamoto
BASF Schweiz AG:
   W. Alig, A. Albertin
Baubibliothek der ETH-Zürich:
   A. Alig, U. Häberlin, K. E. Lehmann, E. Meyer
Benthem Crouwel Architekten:
   J. Benthem, A. Roosjen
Bivetti + Keiser Architekten:
   C. Bivetti, R. Keiser

BGT Bischoff Glastechnik:
   G. Bischoff, T. Korn, K. Wittmann
Brigitte Bruder Architektin
J. Brunet + E. Saunier Architectes:
   J. Brunet, E. Saunier
Jean Pierre Buffi & Associés:
   J. P. Buffi, M. Buffi, B. Hassina
James Carpenter Design Associates Inc.:
   J. Carpenter, R. Kress, L. Lowings, R. Uss
Jo Coenen:
   J. Coenen, N. Johnson, T. Kemme
DETAIL Zeitschrift für Architektur + Baudetail:
   C. Schittich

Dewhurst Macfarlane and Partners:
 T. Macfarlane, P. Trench
Di Blasi Associati:
 O. di Blasi
Dornier Deutsche Aerospace GmbH:
 R. Braun, T. Meisel
Eckelt Glas:
 W. Dirisamer
EMPA-Dübendorf:
 H. Manz
EWI Ingenieure und Berater:
 T. Kählin
Fabrimex AG:
 W. Maag
Figla Corporation:
 M. Moribayashi
Fondation Beyeler:
 M. Brüderlin
Foster and Partners:
 Sir Norman Foster, S. Behling, M. Bowmann,
M. Braun
 B. Haw, K. Harris, D. Nelson, H. Turner
Fraunhofer-Institut für Solare Energiesysteme:
 H. R. Wilson
Future Systems:
 J. Kaplicky, A. Levete
Joseph Gartner & Co:
 F. Gartner, W. Heusler, A. Fauland,
R. Soükup, W. Schulz
Andreas Gerber Architekt
Gesellschaft für Aerophysik mbH:
 B. Bauhofer, L. Ilg
Gesellschaft für Licht und Bautechnik mbH:
 H. Müller, M. Kramer
Glas Trösch:
 U. Moor, P. Beck
Götz GmbH:
 T. Lödel
Nicholas Grimshaw and Partners:
 N. Grimshaw, D. Hutchinson, D. Kirkland,
 G. Stowell, S. Templeton
von Gerkan Marg und Partner:
 M. von Gerkan, V. Marg, B. Pastuschka
T. R. Hamzah & Yeang:
 K. Yeang
Herzog + Partner:
 T. Herzog, V. Herzog-Loibl
Hegger Hegger Schleiff, HHS Planer +
Architekten:
 M. Hegger, G. Schleiff, R. Metz
HL-Technik AG:
 K. Daniels, J. Stoll
Michael Hopkins and Partners:

M. Hopkins, B. Dunster, C. Endicott,
 J. Pringle
Richard Horden Associates:
 R. Horden, S. Forbes-Waller, S. Kirby
Hunter Douglas Europe:
 N. Pulskens, W. Reichmut
J.-M. Ibos & M. Vitart:
 J.-M. Ibos
Ingenhoven Overdiek Kahlen und Partner:
 C. Ingenhoven, A. Nagel, M. Reiss, E.
Schmitz-Riol
Kaiser Bautechnik Ingenieurgesellschaft mbH:
 N. Kaiser, P. T. Benedik
Ulrich Knaack Architekt
Kiessler + Partner Architekten:
 S. Auerbach Jean Lelay Architekt
Mecanoo Architekten:
 A. Fransen, H. Hollander
Murphy/Jahn Architects:
 H. Jahn, S. Cook
Nippon Sheet Glass NSG Europe:
 T. Furutami, K. Maeda
Architectures Jean Nouvel:
 J. Nouvel, W. Keuthage, C. Kruk, J. Simon
Okalux Kapillarglas GmbH:
 R. Kümpers
Permasteelisa/Scheldebouw:
 M. Colomban, B. van de Linde
Petzinka, Pink und Partner:
 K. Petzinka, T. Pink, M. Stamminger
Renzo Piano Building Workshop:
 R. Piano, S. Canta, M. Carrol, J. Lelay,
 O. de Nooyer, B. Plattner, M. Varratta
Pilkington Glass Limited:
 D. Button, R. Jennings
Pilkington Solar International GmbH:
 W. Böhmer
Ian Ritchie Architects:
 I. Ritchie, J. van den Bossche,
 S. Conolly, H. Rambow, A. Summers,
 G. Talbot
RFR:
 H. Bardsley, J. F. Blassel, H. Dutton
Richard Rogers Partnership:
 Sir Richard Rogers, M. Davies, R. Paul
Sabiac SA, Saint-Gobain:
 A. Büchi, B. Giger, A. Minne
Sauerbruch Hutton Architekten:
 L. Hutton, R. Mühlich
Schneider + Schumacher Architekten:
 T. Schneider, M. Schumacher
Schott Glaswerke GmbH:
 R. Langfeld, F. G. K. Baucke

Seele:

H. Trischberger

Siemens-Albis AG:

H. M. Berger, W. Engler, R. Müller

Siemens Architekturabteilung:

G. R. Standke, B. Engel

Francis Soler:

F. Soler, C. Westerburg

Transolar:

M. Schuler

Tuchschmid AG:

B. Flury, W. Luessi, W. Kirchmeier

Universität Stuttgart, Institut für
Baukonstruktion 2:

S. Behling, J. Achenbach, J. Hieber,
J. Marquart, P. Seger

Universität Stuttgart, Institut für Leichte
Tragwerke IL:

W. Sobek, M. Kutterer

University of California, Lawrence Berkely
Laboratory:

C. M. Lampert

Universität Stuttgart, Labor für Bildschirm-
technik:

T. Kallfass

University of Uppsala, School of Engineering,
Department of Technology:

C. G. Granquist

YRM Antony Hunt Associates:

A. Hunt, N. Green

R.-J. van Santen bureau d'études façades

VEGLA Vereinigte Glaswerke GmbH:

K. Wertz, U. Hermens

Michael Wigginton Architect

Pieter Zaanen Architect and Associates:

P. Zaanen, M. Snijders

Ausgewählte Bibliographie

Selected Bibliography

Allgemeines / General

Balkow, D., von Bock, K., Krewinkel, H. W., Rinkens, R.; Glas am Bau; Deutsche Verlags-Anstalt DVA, Stuttgart, 1990

Bauen mit Glas: 13 Standpunkte; Glasbau Atlas; in: Detail 3/1998, S. 300–330

Beinhauer, Benemann, Gutjahr, Müller, Hrsg.; Fassaden der Zukunft: mit der Sonne Leben; ILB-Fachhochschule Köln, 1992

Button, D., Colvin, J., Cunliffe, J., Inmann, C., Jakson, K., Lightfoot, G., Owens, P., Pye, B., Waldron, B.; Glass in Building; Butterworth Architecture, Oxford, 1993

Glas Trösch; Glas und Praxis: Kompetentes Bauen und Konstruieren mit Glas; Bützberg, 1994

Interpane-Gruppe; Gestalten mit Glas; 1990

Krewinkel, H. W.; Glasarchitektur: Material, Konstruktion und Detail; Birkhäuser Verlag, Basel, Berlin, Boston, 1998

Oswald, P., Hrsg., unter Mitarbeit von Rexroth, S.; Wohltemperierte Architektur, C. F. Müller, Heidelberg, 1994

Petzold, A., Marusch, H., Schramm, B.; Der Baustoff Glas; 3. Auflage, K. Hofmann, Schorndorf, Verlag für Bauwesen, Berlin, 1990

Pfaender, H. G., Überarb. u. erg. von Schröder, H.; Schott-Glaslexikon; 4. Aufl., mvg-Moderne Verlagsgesellschaft, München, 1989

Pilkington Glass Ltd./Flachglas AG; Das Glas-Handbuch; 1997

Ritchie, I; (Well) Connected Architecture; Academy Edition, London, 1994; Architektur mit (guten) Verbindungen; Ernst & Sohn, London, Berlin, 1994

Schaal, R.; Glas als Baumaterial; Lehrstuhl für Architektur und Konstruktion, Schriftenreihe Nr. 7, ETH Zürich, 1989

Schittich, C., Staib, G., Balkow, D., Schuler, M., Sobek, W.; Glasbau Atlas; Institut für internationale Architektur-Dokumentation GmbH, München, 1998

Vegla; Glas am Bau: technisches Handbuch; 1995–96

Wiggington, M.; Glass in Architecture; Phaidon, London, 1996

Wörner, J.-D., Hrsg.; Glas im Bauwesen: Architektur und Konstruktion; Darmstädter Statik-Seminar 1998, TU Darmstadt

Einführung / Introduction

Intelligentes Bauen mit Dynamischen Gebäudehüllen; in: Arch+ 99, Juli 1989, S. 71–74

Banham, R.; The Architecture of the Well-Tempered Environment; Architectural Press, London, 1969

Davies, M.; A Wall for all Seasons; in: RIBA Journal, February 1981, S. 55–57

Davies, M.; Eine Wand für alle Jahreszeiten; in: Arch+ 104, Juli 1990, S. 46–51

Davies, M.; Das Ende des mechanischen Zeitalters; in: Arch+ 113, Sept. 1992, S. 48–56

Scheerbart, P.; Glasarchitektur; Verlag der Sturm, Berlin, 1914

Der Werkstoff Glas / Glass, the Material

Compagno, A.; Tragende Transparenz; in: Fassade 2–3, 1998

Dutton, H.; Structural Glass Design from La Villette, Paris and after; in: Symposium Proceedings, Technische Universität Delft, 1992, S. 4–0 bis 4–36

Hestnes, A. G.; Grundlagen passiver Solarenergienutzung; in: Thermische Solarenergienutzung an Gebäuden, Comett-Projekt SUNRISE, Fraunhofer-Institut für Solare Energiesysteme, Freiburg, 1994, S. 27–40

Knaack, U.; Konstruktiver Glasbau; Verlagsgesellschaft Rudolf Müller, Köln, 1998

Rice, P., Dutton, H.; Le verre structurel; Editions du Moniteur, Paris, 1990

Rice, P., Dutton, H.; Transparente Architektur: Glasfassaden mit Structural Glazing; Birkhäuser Verlag, Basel, Berlin, Boston, 1995

Ritchie, I.; Art of Glas Architecture; in: Beinhauer u. a., Hrsg.; Fassaden der Zukunft: mit der Sonne Leben; S. 17–38

Schulz, C., Seger, P.; Großflächige Verglasungen; in: Detail Nr. 1, 1991, S. 13–22

Wiggington, M.; Glass today – Report and Proceedings of the Glass in the Environment Conference; Crafts Council, London, 1986

Wiggington, M.; Daring Glass Applications in Recent Architecture; op. cit., S. 5–0 bis 5–14

Die Glasscheibe / The Glass Pane

Fenestration 2000; Review of Advanced Glazing Technology and Study of Benefit for the UK; Phase II, ETSU S 1342, Halcrow Gilbert Associates Ltd., 1992

BGT-Bischoff Glastechnik, Hrsg.; Konstruieren und Gestalten mit Glas; Bretten, 1/1993

Button, D. A., Dunning, R.; Fenestration 2000: an Investigation into the long-term Requirements for Glass; Phase I, Pilkington Glass Ltd. and the UK Department of Energy, St Helens, July 1989

Dolden, M.; James Carpenter Profile; in: Progressive Architecture, 3/1988, S. 113–117

Forter, F.; Die Kraft des Unsichtbaren: James Carpenter Design Associates; in: Fassade 2/1998

Glas Trösch, Hrsg.; Modernes Sonnenschutzglas mit zeitloser Ästhetik; Bützberg, 1994

Glas Trösch, Hrsg.; Silverstar®: Technologievorsprung auf Glas; Bützberg, 1994

Lampert, C. M., Yan-ping Ma; Advanced Glazing Material Study; Phase III, ETSU S 1215, Pilkington Glass plc, St Helens, 1992

Ortmanns, G.; Die Bedeutung von Schichten für das moderne Funktionsisolierglas; in: Glasforum, Nr. 6, 1990, S. 38–42

Ortmanns, G.; Hochwärmedämmendes Isolierglas; in: Glasforum, Nr. 1, 1992, S. 42–47

Ortmanns, G.; Klimasteuerung durch Glasbeschichtungen; in: Oswald, P., Hrsg.; Wohltemperierte Architektur, S. 112–115

Pepchinski, M.; Verwandlung des Raumes durch Licht und Glas: Arbeiten von James Carpenter; in: Glasforum, Nr. 5, 1990, S. 18–23

Das Verbundglas / Laminated Glass

Glas und Sonnenschutz; in: Arch+ 100/101, Oktober 1989, S. 109–113

Baucke, F. G. K.; Electrochromic Applications; in: Materials, Science and Engineering, B10, 1991, S. 285–292

Benson, D., Tracy, E.; Wanted: Smart Windows that Save Energy; in: NREL In Review, June 1992, S. 12–14

Benson, D. K., Tracy, C. E., Ruth, M. R.; Solid-state Electrochromic Switchable Window Glazing FY 1984 Progress Report; Solar Research Institute, Colorado, USA, April 1986

Burg, M., Müller, H., Wüller, D.; Eine «Intelligente» Solarfassade; in: HLH, Nr. 10, 1993, S. 592–595

Dietrich, U.; Partly Transparent Shading Systems Based on Holografic-Optical Elements; in: Solar Energy in Architecture and Urban Planning, 3. European Conference CEC, H. S. Stephens and Associates, May 1993, S. 246–249

Eicker, U., Pfisterer, F.; Semi-Transparente Photovoltaikfassaden; in: Beinhauer u. a., Hrsg.; Fassaden der Zukunft: S. 315–320

Granqvist, C. G.; Electrochromic Coatings for Smart Windows: a Status Report; in: Renewable Energy; 2nd World Renewable Energy Congress, Vol. 1, Pergamon Press, Oxford, 1992, S. 115–123

Granqvist, C. G.; Electrochromic Oxides: a Band-structure Approach; in: Solar Energy Materials and Solar Cells 32, Amsterdam, 1994, S. 369–382

Granqvist, C. G.; Electrochromic Tungsten-Oxide-Based Thin Films; Physics, Chemistry and Technology; in: Academic Press Inc., 1993, S. 301–370

Granqvist, C. G.; Handbook of Inorganic Electrochromic Materials; Elsevier Science B. V., Amsterdam, 1995

Gutjahr, J.; Die Anwendung holographisch-optischer Elemente in Gebäudefassaden; in: Beinhauer u. a., Hrsg.; Fassaden der Zukunft: S. 167–168

Häberlin, H.; Photovoltaik; AT Verlag, 1991

Hegger-Luhnen, D., Hegger, M.; Multifunktionale Glashaut mit lichtlenkenden Hologrammen und Solarzellen; in: Beinhauer u. a., Hrsg.; Fassaden der Zukunft: S. 187–200

Meisel, T.; Elektrochrome Schichten: Anwendung und Technik; Dornier GmbH, Friedrichshafen, 1993

Meisel, T., Braun, R.; Large Scale Electrochromic Devices for Smart Windows and Absorbers; in: SPIE 1728, 1992

Müller, H., Gutjahr, J.; Tageslichtbeleuchtung in Büroräumen; in: Deutsche Bauzeitschrift, DBZ, Nr. 2, 1992

Müller, H. F. O.; Tageslichtbeleuchtung an Arbeitsplätzen; in: Licht 7–8/1994

Müller, H. F. O.; Fassaden mit Lichtlenkenden Hologrammen; in: Glas 2/1996

Müller, H. F. O.; Holographische Farb- und Lichtspiele; in: Glas 3/1997

Nagai, J.; Recent Development in Electrochromic Glazings; in: SPIE 1728, 1992

Raicu, A., Wilson, H. R.; Enhanced Energy Savings in Buildings with Thermotropic Protection against Overheating; Conf. Proc., EuroSun '96, Freiburg, 1996

Susemihl, I., Chehab, O.; Die Energieaktive Fassade: Fassadenelemente mit integrierten Solarzellen; in: Beinhauer u. a., Hrsg.; Fassaden der Zukunft: S. 299–314

Wilson, H. R., Raicu, A., Rommel, M., Nitz, P.; Überhitzungsschutz mit thermotropen Schichten; 9. Internationales Sonnenforum '94 in Stuttgart, Tagungsband DGS

Wilson, H. R.; Potential of thermotropic layers to prevent overheating; SPIE 2255, 1994

Wilson, H. R., Raicu, A., Nitz, P., Russ, C.; Thermotropic Materials and Systems; Conf. Proc., EuroSun '96, Freiburg, 1996

Das Isolierglas / Insulating Glass

Braun, P. O.; Transparente Wärmedämmung von Gebäudefenstern; in: Thermische Solarenergienutzung an Gebäuden, op. cit., S. 121–143

Grimme, F. W.; Wärmeschutz; in: Thermische Solarenergienutzung an Gebäuden, op. cit., S. 87–115

Herzog, T., Schrade, H. J.; Lichtdach in Linz; in: Beinhauer u. a., Hrsg.; Fassaden der Zukunft, S. 201–206

Platzer, W.; Fenster und Verglasungen; in: Thermische Solarenergienutzung an Gebäuden, op. cit., S. 45–80

Platzer, W. J.; Licht und Wärme; Entwicklungslinie bei TWD Materialien; in: Sonnenenergie, Nr. 2, April 1992, S. 3–8

Platzer, W.; TWD: Grundlagen und Materialien: Solarenergienutzung durch transparente Wärmedämmung; in: Fassade 3/96

Sick, F.; Tageslichtnutzung; in: Thermische Solarenergienutzung an Gebäuden, op. cit., S. 149–182

Svendsen, S., Jensen, K. I.; Development of Evacuated Windows Based on Monolithic Silika Aerogel Spacers; in: Herzog, T., Hrsg.; Solar Energy in Architecture and Urban Planning; Prestel, München, New York, 1996, S. 165–167

Die Fassade / Façades

Achstetter, G.; Sonnenschutz; in: Oswald, P., Hrsg.; Wohltemperierte Architektur, op. cit., S. 104–111

Compagno, A.; Sonnenschutzmaßnahmen; in: Fassade 4/1995 und 1/1996

Daniels, K.; Gebäudetechnik: Ein Leitfaden für Architekten und Ingenieure; R. Oldenbourg Verlag, München, Verlag der Fachvereine an den schweiz. Hochschulen und Techniken, Zürich, 1992

Hopkins, M., and Partners; Engineering Research and Prototype Development for Low-Energy Buildings; Commission of the European Communities, CEC DGXII, Joule-II Programme, Interim Report, March 1994

Müller, H.; Fenster und Fassaden; in: Deutsche Bauzeitschrift, DBZ, Nr. 2, 1991, S. 261–264

Müller, H., Balkowski, M.; Abluftfenster in Bürogebäuden; in: HLH 34/10, S. 412–417

Schaal, R.; Klimafassaden; Auszug vom 2. Bauphysik-Kongreß, VDI Berichte Nr. 316, Düsseldorf, 1978

Intelligente Glasfassaden/ Intelligent Glass Façades

Behling, S. und S.; Sol Power: the Evolution of Solar Architecture; Prestel, München, New York, 1996

Compagno, A.; Intelligente Glasfassaden; in: Der Architekt 5/1998

Daniels, K.; Skin Technology; Werkbericht 10, HL-Technik AG, München/Zürich, März 1992

Daniels, K., Stoll, J., Pültz, G., Schneider J.; Hochhäuser natürlich belüftet? Werkbericht 11, HL-Technik AG, München/Zürich, Juli 1992

Daniels, K.; Gebäudetechnik für die Zukunft – «weniger ist mehr»; Werkbericht 12, HL-Technik AG, München/Zürich, 1994

Daniels, K.; Integrale Planungskonzepte: Ein Muß für die Zukunft? Werkbericht 13, HL-Technik AG, München/Zürich, 1994

Daniels, K.; Technologie des ökologischen Bauens: Grundlagen und Maßnahmen, Beispiele und Ideen; Birkhäuser Verlag, Basel, Boston, Berlin, 1995

Daniels, K.; Low-Tech, Light-Tech, High-Tech: Bauen in der Informationsgesellschaft; Birkhäuser Verlag, Basel, Boston, Berlin, 1998

Herzog, T., Hrsg.; Solar Energy in Architecture and Urban Planning op. cit.

Heusler, W., Schwab, A., Ernst, J. ; Zweite-Haut-Fassaden; in: Fassade 4/1995

Heusler, W., Compagno, A.; Mehrschalige Fassaden; in: Fassade 1−2/1998

Meyer, K. H.; Energiesparende Lüftung und Kühlung; in: Oswald, P.; Hrsg.; Wohltemperierte Architektur, op. cit., S. 78−83

Oswald, P.; Die Architektur intelligenter Gebäude; in: Oswald, P., Hrsg.; Wohltemperierte Architektur, op. cit., S. 94−99

Schwab, A., Heusler, W., Ernst, J.; Zweite-Haut-Fassaden im Wohnungs- und Verwaltungsbau; in: Fassade, Nr. 6, 1993, S. 36−45

Schöning, W., Oswald, P.; Zweischalige Klimafassaden; in: Oswald, P.; Hrsg.; Wohltemperierte Architektur, op. cit., S. 128−143

Stoll, J.; Großflächige Verglasungen: Sonnenschutz und Lüftung; in: Beinhauer u. a., Hrsg.; Fassaden der Zukunft: op. cit., S. 67−89

Stoll, J. ; Glas als energetische Hülle; in: Wörner, J.-D., Hrsg.; Glas im Bauwesen, Kap. IV.

Yeang, K.; Bioclimatic Skyscrapers; Artemis, London, 1994

Bildnachweis   Illustration Credits

o = oben/top; m = mitte/middle;
u = unten/bottom; l = links/left; r = rechts/right

Umschlag/Cover:

	Renzo Piano BW, Genua
8	Mike Davies, Richard Rogers Partnership, London
10	Tim Macfarlane, London
12 o	Umzeichnung aus: Button, D., Pye, B.; *Glass in building*, Butterworth Architecture, Oxford, 1993, S. 40
12 m	Umzeichnung aus: Balkow, D., von Bock, K., Krewinkel, H.W., Rinkens, R.; *Glas am Bau*; DVA-Stuttgart, 1990, S. 49
12 u	Umzeichnung aus: *Glass in building*, op. cit., S. 163
15, 16 ol	Hermann Forster AG, Arbon
16 or	Hueck Swiss, Münchenstein
17 u	aus: *Glasbau Atlas*, Edition Detail, München, 1998
18 mr	Foster and Partners, London
19 ml, ul, 20 mr	RFR, Paris
23 o	Benthem Crouwel Architekten, Amsterdam
23 u	J. M. Monthiers, Paris
24 o	Georges Fessy, Paris
26 o	Ulrich Knaack, Düsseldorf
26 u	Ottavio di Blasi Associati, Mailand
27	Kenji Kobayashi, Tokyo
28 o	S. Gose und P. Teuffel, Stuttgart
28 u	Institut für Leichte Flächentragwerke, IL, Universität Stuttgart
29 o	Seele, Gersthofen
31	Umzeichnung aus; *Werkbericht Nr.10*, März 1992, HL-Technik, München, S. 16
32	Umzeichnung aus: *Glass in building*, op. cit., S. 163
33 o	Umzeichnung aus: *Glass in building*, op. cit., S. 6
33 u	Umzeichnung aus: *Glass in building*, op. cit., S. 162
35 o	Nicholas Grimshaw and Partners, London
36 l	Joceline van den Bossche, London
36 r	Ian Ritchie Architects, London
37, 38 l	Jo Reid and John Peck, London
38 r	Nicholas Grimshaw and Partners, London
39 l	P & G Morisson, Den Haag, Niederlande
40	James Carpenter, New York, USA
41	Umzeichnung aus: Lampert, C.M., Yan-ping Ma: *Fenestration 2000; Advanced glazing material study; Phase III*, ETSU S 1215, Pilkington Glass plc, 1992, S. 41
42	Umzeichnung aus: *Glass in building*, op. cit., S. 168
43	Glas Trösch, Bützberg, Schweiz
44	Umzeichnung aus: *Glass in building*, op. cit., S. 133
45	James Carpenter Design Associates, New York, USA
46	Balthazar Korab, New York, USA
47 ol	Mikio Sekita, New York, USA
47 ur	David Sundberg, New York, USA
48 ol, or	James Carpenter Design Associates, New York, USA
49 ol	Glas Trösch, Bützberg, Schweiz
49 ur	RFR, Paris
52	Robert Keiser, Langenthal, Schweiz
54	Bruno Flury, Tuchschmid AG, Frauenfeld, Schweiz
56 l	Shunji Ishida, Genua

56 r	Renzo Piano BW, Genua	97 l	Nicholas Grimshaw und
57	Nippon Sheet Glass NSG Europe,		Partner
	Themse, Belgien	99 l	RFR, Paris
58, 59 ol	Institut für Licht- und Bautech-	100	Seele, Gersthofen
	nik ILB, Fachhochschule, Köln	101 ur	GLB Gesellschaft für Licht- und
59 u, 60 ml	Hegger Hegger Schleiff		Bautechnik mbH, Köln
	HHS Planer + Architekten,	102 r	Josef Gartner & Co., Gundelfin-
	Kassel		gen
61 ur, ul	Photo Helke Rodemeier, Köln	103	Dieter Leistner, Mainz
62	Michael Kramer, Köln	107 ol	Dominique Perrault, Paris
63	Willi Maag, Fabrimex, Schwer-	108 l	Gianni Berengo Gardin, Mailand
	zenbach, Schweiz	108 r	Renzo Piano BW, Genua
64 o	Fraunhofer Institut für Solare	109 r, l	Gianni Berengo Gardin, Mailand
	Energiesysteme, Fraunhofer-ISE,	110 l	Jean Pierre Buffi & Associés,
	Freiburg i. B.		Paris
64 u	Umzeichnung aus: *Fenestration*	112 ur	Prof. Dr.-Ing. Rolf Schaal, Pfaff-
	2000; op. cit., S. 43		hausen, Schweiz
66	Vegla Vereinigte Glaswerke	113 l	Josef Gartner & Co., Gundelfin-
	GmbH, Aachen		gen
67	Prof. Claes G. Grandqvist, Upp-	114, 115	Michael Hopkins und Partner,
	sala		London
68	Dornier, Deutsche Aerospace,	116 o, 117 ol	Mecanoo Architekten, Delft
	Friedrichshafen	116 u, 117 or	Christian Richters Fotograf,
69	Asahi Glass Europe B.V., Amster-		Münster
	dam	119 ul	Arup Associates, London
70	Georges Fessy, Paris	121	Foster and Partners, London
74 mr	Foster and Partners, London	122, 123 ol	Josef Gartner & Co., Gundelfin-
77 r	Richard Davies, London		gen
79	Georges Fessy, Paris	122 ur,123 or	T. van den Valentyn Architekt,
80 u	A. Weindel, Fraunhofer Institut		Köln
	für Solare Energiesysteme,	124, 125 ur	Brigitte Bruder Architektin,
	Fraunhofer-ISE, Freiburg		Berlin
81 u	Okalux Kapillarglas GmbH,	125 ol, or	Léon/Wohlhage Architekten,
	Marktheidenfeld-Alfeld		Berlin
83	BASF Schweiz, Wädenswil	125 ul	Josef Gartner & Co., Gundelfin-
85	Isolar®Glas, Rickenbach,		gen
	Schweiz	126 o	Fondation Beyeler/Thomas Dix,
86 o	Hunter Douglas Europe,		Basel
	Rotterdam	126 ur	aus: *Detail*, Nr. 3/98 Zeitschrift
86 u	INGLAS GmbH, Friedrichshafen,		für Architektur + Baudetail,
	Deutschland		München
87 o	Peter Bartenbach, München	128	Michel Denancé, Paris
87 u	Peter Bonfig, München	130 – 131	Future Systems, Jan Kaplicky
88	Siemens AG, München-		Amanda Levete, London
	Zürich	133 o	HL-Technik AG, München
89 o	Figla Co Ltd, Tokyo/Pine Brooks	134 or	Foster and Partners, London
	NY, USA	134 ol	Paul Raftery, London
89 u	aus: *Glasbau Atlas*, Edition	135 l	Kiessler + Partner Architekten,
	Detail, München, 1998		München
90	Okalux Kapillarglas GmbH,	135 r	Ralph Richter/architekturphoto,
	Marktheidenfeld-Alfeld		Düsseldorf
94 u	Jan Lambot, London	137 or	Permasteelisa, San Vendemiano,
95	Peter Cook VIEW, London		Italien